MW01256871

Ancient Sichuan
and the Unification of China

SUNY Series in Chinese Local Studies
Harry Lamley, Editor

Ancient Sichuan
and the Unification of China

Steven F. Sage

State University of New York Press

Published by
State University of New York Press, Albany

© 1992 State University of New York

For information, address State University of New York Press,
State University Plaza, Albany, N.Y., 12246

Production by M. R. Mulholland
Marketing by Theresa A. Swierzowski

Library of Congress Cataloging-in-Publication Data

Sage, Steven F., 1947–
    Ancient Sichuan and the unification of China / Steven F. Sage.
        p.   cm.—(SUNY series in Chinese local studies)
    Includes bibliographical references and index.
    ISBN 0-7914-1037-4 (CH: alk. paper).—ISBN 0-7914-1038-2 (pbk.:
    alk. paper)
    1. Szechwan Province (China)—History.   2. China—History—To 221
B.C.   3. China—History—Ch in dynasty, 221–207 B.C.   I. Title.
II. Series.
DS793.S8S34   1992
951'.38—dc20
                                                                                      91-23124
                                                                                      CIP
10   9   8   7   6   5   4   3   2   1

Contents

Maps

Figures

Acknowledgments

Recovering and reconstructing Sichuan's ancient history has been a quest, demanding stoic efforts by a small army of Chinese archaeologists, epigraphers, and historians. During the 1980s the pace of their discoveries picked up and the volume of publication multiplied vastly. It is to these scholars, first and foremost, that a debt of gratitude must be rightfully acknowledged. For their quest became my own, and it is the fruit of their copious labors which this book interprets for a wider public outside China.

Particular individuals who lent their time and enthusiasm were Professors Tong Enzheng of the Sichuan University History Department and Xu Guangji of the Institute of Archaeology, Chinese Academy of Social Sciences. In the early 1980s they advised regarding what to look for and where to find it, and provided informative tips on the personalities and politics of Chinese archaeological study. Tong Enzheng subsequently read a late draft of the manuscript and offered encouragement. Many others helped in ways great and small: Wang Jiayou of the Sichuan Provincial Museum; Yuan Zhiyong, an assistant at that unit who lent me his bicycle and served as informal tour guide to some out of the way archaeological sites; and even an anonymous junior staffer at the Chongqing Municipal Museum who unselfishly extended me the courtesy of keeping the building open well past the posted hours, while I viewed and photographed artifacts. Xu Xiaoguang of Beijing University wrote the calligraphy title. To all, *xie xie!*

Professor Harry Lamley of the University of Hawaii is concurrently editor of the SUNY series in which this monograph appears. Lamley combined a Socratic teaching manner with the patience of Job. As a specialist in Chinese local history, he is a master at revealing the threads of interconnected meaning that stitch together seemingly incoherent data. Early on he stressed that a history must embody some clear theme, not simply recount disparate bits of information. I hope that this work, with its threads and its theme, is truly worthy of his tutelage. Another pillar of the University of Hawaii, Wilhelm Solheim, gave of his expertise in East and Southeast Asian archaeology, and read my first (dissertation) draft with painstaking thoroughness. Quite a few mistakes in matters of detail might have gone unnoticed but for him. Robert W. Bagley of Princeton University graciously offered photographs of the Sanxingdui site. Barry Blakeley of Seton Hall University read the nearly completed manuscript in draft and called attention to some items regarding Chu.

At Middle Tennessee State University, the late chairman of our History Department Bart McCash showed me his customary generosity and solicitude in many ways, great and small. Departmental secretary Jennifer Vecchio, formerly of the United Nations High Commission on Refugees, also deserves a specially hearty *obrigado*. Without her devoted support this book might still be in refugee status. Lee Post and David Moore, student workers, assisted with some of the graphics. In Washington, at the Library of Congress, Robert Dunn and Cathy Stachniak helped me by retrieving uncatalogued materials that otherwise would have been inaccessibly frozen in that institution's cataloguing glacier. And in Washington as well a true friend and true scholar, Igor Birman, inspired me by the example of his own unswerving perseverence despite having suffered much for committing the one unforgiveable intellectual transgression, that is, being prematurely right.

Historians in the People's Republic of China, aided by the handmaiden discipline of archaeology, have lately come to realize that their country's ancient civilization issued not from one source but rather represented a coalescence, drawing together diverse regions into an interactive whole. Sichuan was one of these regions, an important one. This multicentric view of Chinese antiquity may be unsettling to academicians indoctrinated with previous notions. Some traditionalists may also find abhorrent anything connected with Qin, the state that brought about Chinese imperial unity only to be reviled by orthodox Confucians for over two millennia.

The present work was not intended to incite the ire of old-fashioned scholars; it does not pursue controversy for controversy's sake. Rather, it aims first to present a picture of pre-Qin Sichuan, and then to gauge how great a role Sichuan played in cementing the unity of China. For the fact cannot be denied that Qin united China and did so with considerable reliance on the Sichuan lands it had earlier annexed. My motives in emphasizing this fact are of purely disinterested scholarly detachment. Beyond a passion for extra-spicy *ma po dou fu*, I have no Sichuanese connections, personal or familial.

Which brings to mind family. Without the encouragement of my dear ones, mother, brother, and especially my wife, Rachel, this study would have been impossible. Another deserving of honorable mention is my erstwhile rich uncle, Sam. He provided me with funding via a fellowship, a grant, and a job. It put enough *ma po dou fu* on the table to keep body and soul together while burning out my innards. Play it again, Sam.

A Note on Transliteration

This work follows the *pinyin* system of phonetic transliteration for Chinese terms. Although hardly ideal for rendering Chinese sounds pronounceable to English speakers, *pinyin* orthography is standard in contemporary China. Hobson's choice. Here is an informal guide to the perplexed, those readers neither trained in the Chinese language nor familiar with *pinyin*.

Sichuan of course is *pinyin* for what used to be written *Szechwan*, home of the spicy food and pandas. It is a two syllable word, *si* and *chuan*. The *si* is not the Spanish for "yes," but rather more like Colonel Sanders of Kentucky might address a gentleman, emphatically, "Sir!", only dropping the final *r*. That vocal emphasis approximates the proper falling tone in Mandarin. Then the syllable *chuan* should be sung out in a high C-note, the Mandarin level tone.

The state of Qin annexed Sichuan, in 316 B.C. Qin was located in what is now Shaanxi ("West of the Passes") province, different from neighboring Shanxi ("West of the Mountains") province. As for the name Qin, no, in *pinyin* there should not be a letter *u* between the *Q* and the *i*. And never mind what the linguistics majors tell you; English speakers are best off just regarding the *Q* here as equivalent to a *ch*. Thus *Qin* comes out sounding like what you call the mandibular protuberance below your oral cavity. To get the Mandarin rising tone approximately correct, say it with some interrogative doubt in your voice, as if phrasing a one word question: "Chin?"

To annex Sichuan, Qin had to maneuver against the state of Chu. *Chu* is like what you do with your mandible in a Sichuanese restaurant, or like the pandas, what is left of them, do with stalks of bamboo. The state of Chu was located on the Yangtze River. Chinese do not use the term *Yangtze* much for this major waterway; they prefer *chang jiang*, which means "The Long River." However, as that name is not nearly as familiar in English as Yangtze, herein Yangtze it shall be.

Ancient Sichuan was divided into two regions, Shu and Ba. Pronounce *Shu* as if referring to an item of footwear. *Ba* is like what Ebenezer Scrooge said, before *humbug*, only in a high-C note. But do not worry too much about the tones. In Sichuan, although Mandarin is spoken, the tones are different anyway from those of standard broadcasters' Mandarin. For that matter, all the Chinese pronunciations of today are rather removed from what they were in the periods of antiquity covered by this book.

MAP 1

Major provinces of modern China

Introduction

The road to Shu is as difficult as ascending to heaven.

> —Tang dynasty poet Li Bo, 701–762 A.D.

I came back by bus from the war areas, and remember of the long journey south only how wonderful it was to cross the range of the Ch'in-ling Mountains, which separates North China from Szechwan. One crosses through the pass, and in half an hour, one has left behind the eroded hills that face the arid country of the north to find oneself in the warm moist air of Szechwan, where bamboo begins to grow on the south face of the range.

> —journalist Theodore White, reminiscing about 1943 A.D.[1]

Traveling the same road twelve centuries apart, Li Bo and Theodore White expressed a pair of proverbial feelings: Shu, that is, Sichuan, may be hard to reach, but worth the effort. A standard relief map shows Sichuan distinctly. It appears as a large dark green blotch, for a lush, natural lowland basin, encircled by yellow and brown hues signifying rugged higher ground. Only the narrow blue band of a river, the Yangtze, connects the green to other lowlands far downstream. Terrain sets Sichuan apart. One might reasonably expect an international frontier demarcating the basin from China but there is only a provincial line, for Sichuan lies well within the Chinese embrace. One hundred ten million people inhabit this land; it is the country's most populous province.

The classical ancients a thousand years and more before Li Bo's time regarded Sichuan as somewhat offcenter in their conception of the world. And so it is, far removed from the Yellow River and the loess soil lands and central plains, that hallowed northern Chinese core of literate East Asian civilization. Sichuan is mentioned but scantily in ancient literature, and ambiguity shrouds its relevance to the core zone. There are indeed some mythical allusions to culture heroes, gossamer threads that purportedly connect Sichuan to the Yellow River area. But truly historical references are rare prior to the annexation of Sichuan by the state of Qin in 316 B.C., and before then the annals treat Sichuan as quite foreign, contradicting the myths.

The problem is a practical one for some scholar toiling to compile a historical atlas, and the Chinese, to be sure, are meticulous historians and cartographers. The mapmaker ponders: When, at what date, should Sichuan be included within the limits of China? A historian may ask a follow-on question: Given its geographic position and its virtually self-sufficient economic potential, what force has kept Sichuan in China?

When Li Bo made his trip, Sichuan already was the richest and most heavily populated part of China. Yet notwithstanding its importance through imperial times down to modern China, the Sichuan of preimperial antiquity until recently belonged to a dark age. The wealth of documentation covering China's classical heartland shed but dim light on this peripheral region. Odd bits of data did not mesh well, long daunting a serious appraisal of ancient Sichuan.

That did not begin to change substantially until about the mid-1970s. Since then progress has been steady. Archaeologists and historians now have more information, much more, than Li Bo about early Sichuan. We now know that Sichuan was not some unenlightened, semisavage outback prior to its political incorporation into China. In Sichuan modern Chinese scientists have lately uncovered an ancient country well along the road to true civilization, with its own cities, fine artisanship, and a form of literacy.[2] This book assembles the recent findings from Sichuan and places them in a historical context.

The name *Sichuan* means "four streams," but was not used for the region until the Song and Yuan dynasties in the thirteenth century A.D.[3] Prior to then the Sichuan basin usually had been divided into two or more administrative entities. To apply the medieval term *Sichuan* when speaking of more remote ancient times, strictly speaking, is an anachronism, but a convenient one, like referring to *China* before its unification under the eponymous Qin dynasty. There are simply no other convenient, commonly used expressions, so *Sichuan* will have to do.

Ancient Chinese themselves spoke of Sichuan by joining two names of subregions within the basin, Ba and Shu, as *Ba-Shu*. Ba was that portion lying along the Yangtze and some tributary streams in eastern Sichuan. Shu included the present provincial capital of Chengdu, its surrounding plain and adjacent territories in western

Sichuan. The present unit of study is set by the modern frontier of Sichuan province and includes as well some adjacent zones. Most noteworthy among these border areas is the Han River valley of southern Shaanxi province. Both Li Bo and Theodore White traversed the Han on their way into Sichuan from the north. It figures greatly in the history of Sichuan and China.

After ascending and descending the Qinling Mountains, crossing the Han valley, and climbing once again up and down over the Daba mountains, one at last arrives in Shu. A broad lowland plain then stretches south, dotted by great cities like Chengdu, district towns, and innumerable tiny hamlets. One of these small places, called Sanxingdui, provides the setting for a great archaeological mystery story, an Indiana Jones tale come true. Excavated from 1981 to 1986, Sanxingdui is the site of a genuine lost and found proto-civilization. Its treasure pits had lain undisturbed since archaic times beneath a rural village.

Chapter 2 presents the findings on Sanxingdui and related remains from early Shu, as well as the evidence of mythology, inscriptions, and history. Along with other peoples, the Shu people helped to vanquish the Shang and establish its long lived successor, the Zhou dynasty. This episode briefly projected Shu power as far away as the central plains. Thereafter, however, the Shu receded into near oblivion in western Sichuan. Little material on them is available, although recent studies on the typology of Shu bronzes have supplemented the sparse and uncertain textual data.

Eastern Sichuan was occupied by an ethnic melange collectively called *Ba*. Chapter 3 reviews what is known of these peoples' origins, material culture, the enigmatic Ba script, and the Ba role in history. History for the Ba meant war. They were renowned for their war chants and their war drums, many of which were excavated and studied during the 1970s and 1980s. More often than not the principal Ba adversary in war was Chu, a more powerful country on the middle Yangtze and Han Rivers. As Chu pushed upstream into Sichuan, Ba relocated closer to Shu in western Sichuan.

Ba and Shu never merged into one political unit although much sharing and borrowing resulted from their contact, leading to the Ba-Shu culture. It took shape while the late Spring and Autumn and Warring States periods unfolded in the northern lands around the Yellow River.[4] During this time Shu surfaced from obscurity. Bronzes, weaponry, and other artifacts all attest to renewed interchange with the outside but the Ba-Shu culture also exhibited unique features, including an independent form of writing. The description of Sichuan's Ba-Shu culture was one of the major accomplishments of Chinese archaeology in the 1980s.

Chu greatly influenced this Ba-Shu culture, as is well attested by recent artifact finds. The Han and Yangtze Rivers gave Chu relatively easy access and the possibility of attaching Sichuan to a southern superpower stretching downstream to the Pacific. During the fourth century B.C. a process was well underway toward bringing that about. Sichuan's other neighbor, the state of Qin, lay beyond the Qinling mountain barrier, seemingly irrelevant in Sichuanese matters. But human beings, when making history, sometimes defy geography.

Chapter 4 shows how Qin greatly strengthened itself by a drastic internal reform, surpassed the strength of its enemies, and at length turned its attention southward to Sichuan. Qin engineers built an alpine road to Shu, traces of which were discovered and surveyed in the 1980s. Qin statesmen adroitly availed of the political schism between Ba and Shu. Their role in Sichuan was overtaking that of Chu. In 316 B.C. a Qin army crossed over and seized Shu, Ba, and the Han River valley. There would be no Chu empire of the south.

Hitherto the warring states of the central plains had mutually sparred for advantage, even predominance, but their goals fell short of attempting universal conquest. Around the time Sichuan fell into Qin hands, that changed. Sichuanese resources were harnessed to the protracted Qin war effort on all fronts. The native Shu nobility was first coopted, then suppressed. Shu towns became fortified Qin bastions. Shu was sinified, culturally made part of Qin, while Qin enlisted the peoples of Ba as auxiliaries. The sinification of Sichuan under Qin lasted a full century. It was a bumpy and often painful process during which the procedures of assimilating conquered territories evolved.

Chapter 5 cites newly discovered documents including a land reform plan for Sichuan and details regarding the migration of northern settlers in Shu. Major public works projects were conceived and implemented. Other texts and archaeology fill in the picture of how Qin remade Ba and Shu by separate means appropriate to each. Dividing, and ruling, Qin perpetuated a dipolarity in Sichuan that still persists. With Sichuan consolidated, Qin straddled both the Yellow River and Yangtze worlds to create a synthesis of north and south that proved irresistible.

In 221 B.C. the Qin juggernaut crushed all its foes and founded the Qin empire; that is, China. The First Emperor brutally and incautiously tried to remake everything at once. But all men are mortal, even first emperors. Qin disintegrated just over a decade after winning Chinese unity, although the resulting turmoil left Qin institutions intact in Sichuan. Continuity was maintained there. The reunification of China by the succeeding regime owed much to a sound support base in Sichuan and the Han area, from which the new dynasty drew its name. Chapter 6 details how Han Sichuan prospered, expanded, and became fully assimilated into Han China.

Sichuan was but one of the distinct regions that Qin combined to establish China. The northern steppe, the northeast, and the coastal states constituted other regions, as did Chu in the south and the Qin homeland itself on the western fringe. The core states of the loess soil zone and the Yellow River floodplain, together, were yet another region. This central plains area has long possessed a certain historiographic and sentimental primacy. In archaic times its cities arose before urbanization elsewhere in China. The written Chinese language developed there, followed later on by classical philosophy. Chinese historians traditionally have viewed the central plains as a beacon from which emanated all the illuminating rays of civilization.

That picture is being adjusted. As truth is sought from facts, enshrined doctrine means less in evaluating each region's role in the making of China. Every region devised, contributed, received, and adapted elements, an interactive process lasting many centuries. Qin forged the achievement of Chinese unity itself. A mature, dispassionate Chinese historiography of late has devoted serious attention to Qin, overcoming both orthodox complacency and Maoist mania to do so. Archaeologists are uncovering more of the Qin past, in the original Qin homeland and in Qin's Sichuan colony.

The newly gained understanding of Sichuan before Qin rule enhances an appreciation of just how crucial was the later Qin annexation of Ba and Shu. In particular, the ruins of Sanxingdui give some notion of the region's power, manifest and latent. When ancient sources comment on the indispensibility of Sichuan to Qin, it is now evident what they mean. Adding Sichuan more than doubled the extent of Qin. Immense Sichuan reserves of grain, metals, and capable manpower strengthened the Qin armies. Flotillas bearing Qin troops debouched from Sichuan and down the Han and Yangtze Rivers to destroy Chu, the main stumbling block to total Qin dominance. With Chu neutralized, Qin devoted its full attention northward to the central plains and inexorably triumphed.

In Sichuan north and south, the worlds of the Yellow and Yangtze Rivers, were first brought under one banner. In Sichuan the Qin and then the Han regimes tested the social mechanisms of Chinese power. In Sichuan those techniques were sustained, even when hobbled or eradicated elsewhere. The sheltered Sichuan basin might be thought of as the chrysalis out of which issued imperial China.

This book is based in very large part on Sichuan archaeological findings as published through 1990. The work of Chinese scientists and historians has scored significant gains and yet it is not beyond criticism. All too few habitation sites have been explored in sustained digging lasting more than a season. Most finds come from tombs, yielding many objects while raising unanswered questions concerning how these were used in a living context. Only more extensive probing can answer such questions, but the Sichuan basin today teems with people and economic activity. Wider operations to retrieve the past will inevitably disrupt the lives of modern Sichuanese and progress thereby is slow.

A treasure hunt attitude prevails among many ordinary folk, and so Chinese scholars must expend too much effort in salvage operations. Reacting to the chance discovery of yet another ancient Shu graveyard absorbs the time and energies of trained personnel, assets that might be more profitably directed toward uncovering the remains of cities and towns. And no surveys of potential, unexcavated sites are available, although such data would be tremendously useful to historians.

Most published work is evidently conscientious. Art historians and epigraphers have described and analyzed sufficient material to make discernible the outlines of early Sichuan history. Chinese journal articles over the years have run a wide gamut from overly adventurous to judiciously sober. Less of the former style is seen lately. Cool professionalism marks the site reports from Sanxingdui and subsequent critiques.

In previous years some researchers appeared to start with an unsubstantiated premise and then selectively present data to fit it, not unlike the manner of nineteenth century romantics like Heinrich Schliemann. Fashions of interpretation have come and gone. For example, during the early 1980s various approaches aimed at portraying the Shu people as a branch of the northern Qiang barbarians. After 1985 proponents of this view ceased being published in accessible journals, and subsequent migration hypotheses have been phrased more circumspectly.

A preoccupation of several theorists continues to be the ethnic identification of ancient peoples and the relation of their supposed remains to textual leads. Artifacts are frequently discussed in the context of some bit of literary evidence with a view to proving the passage's veracity. This methodology is understandable in the Chinese context, but it means that those outside the confines of Sichuan archaeology must exercise care in using the data. On the other hand, if Chinese scholars refrained from all interpretation in the light of texts, their site reports would be reduced to dull inventories of recovered goods and so hold less interest as grist for historians.

In relying on Chinese scholarship some allowance must be made for the tendency by a few writers to anachronistically cast Ba and Shu as frontier "minority peoples" in a role too neatly analogous to today's non-Han minorities vis-à-vis the controlling ethnic majority. A deep-seated conceit on the part of many in China still assumes every single technological or cultural advance to have radiated outward from the Yellow River heartland. And there has been a stubborn reluctance, now waning a bit, to acknowledge that any area now within China's borders may have received salutory influences from some foreign quarter.

Provincialism and localism, too, occasionally infuse Chinese site reports and are detrimental in their own ways. As for the constraints of Marxism-Leninism, these are mercifully relaxed in most post-Cultural Revolution work. Ba and Shu have not been seriously mutilated on procrustean beds of primitive society, slavery, feudalism, and so forth. The once obligatory quotations from Marx, Engels, and the omniscient political authorities are now either innocuously pro forma or have been dropped altogether. Yet not much in the way of theory has emerged to fill the void. Chinese scholars say all too little about how they suppose ancient Sichuan society actually functioned.

Academic autocracy, entrenched bureaucratic stubbornness, and factionalism survive to impede Sichuan archaeology as elsewhere in China and the world at large. But experience abroad and contact with overseas specialists have nurtured a new breed of professionals. Their expertise is progressing markedly, the repertoire of techniques expanding. During the 1980s ancient Sichuan became a high-priority locale of excavation activity. Historians may now avail themselves of new archaeologically provided materials, abundant in some aspects although still modest in others. It is hoped that this book may make these finds and their meaning accessible to both China hands and nonsinologists, for as with every region on the Chinese rim, Sichuan's history is part of world history.

Recognizing some of China's technical inadequacies in the face of an immense archaeological task, during March 1991 the national Cultural Relics Bureau announced a relaxation of its strict policy under which all foreign specialists had been forbidden from participating at Chinese digs. Some joint excavations may henceforth be planned. Initially these will be limited to paleolithic and early neo-lithic prehistory, and so it is unlikely that non-Chinese scholars can uncover Ba or Shu remains soon. But the revised policy nevertheless should help by augmenting scarce resources, by bringing overall Chinese standards closer to the state of the art elsewhere, and by further breaking down xenophobic barriers.

Much additional scholarly work remains to be done. Critical peer review within China (1990) has faulted shortcomings in the first (1987) Sanxingdui report, a reexamination that itself is a measure of that site's portentous significance. Sanxingdui was probably the rul-ing center of Shu, followed in turn by Chengdu, although other Shu towns existed as well and must be surveyed. In Ba the locations of ancient cities are mentioned by texts but no site yet compares with Sanxingdui.

Studies on the origins of the Shu and the Ba peoples still have not fully sorted fact from fable. This research should continue with-out preconceived bias. The standards of Chinese archaeology are ris-ing, commensurate to the challenge. Earnest students seek training in the latest techniques. Shu and Ba towns and tombs await excavation, like time capsules, containing artifacts to appraise and documents to be read. The scripts of Ba and of the Ba-Shu culture persist in thwart-ing decipherment, but as with hieroglyphics and cuneiform, these writings too will someday be demystified.

Sichuan's hidden past is emerging from the earth after more than two millennia. The ramifications of Sichuan in antiquity extend over all China, and have lasted to this day.

2

Shu

Shu has both a geographic and an ethnic connotation.[1] Shu
lands centered on the Chengdu plain in western Sichuan and included the valley of the Min River, a major Yangtze tributary that in
ancient times was considered the headwaters of the Yangtze itself.
Shu also occupied the upper Han River valley. As an ethnic term, *Shu*
refers to the distinct people who inhabited these lands in and around
western Sichuan. Ancient Shu is known from various data: myths,
etymology, inscriptions, some stray historical references—and from
startling archaeological finds at Sanxingdui, the first Shu capital.

Archaic Shu in Chinese Myths

Preimperial Chinese history, that is, the Xia, Shang, and Zhou
dynasties, took place upon the loess plateau and north central plains
straddling the Yellow River. Most mythological stories of China's
foundation also are centered in this region. As the civilization arising
there spread outward, it interacted with surrounding cultures.[2]
Chinese historiography usually treats Sichuan only among those
peripheral regions receiving stimuli from the distant central plains.
Yet a few strands of myth contradict orthodoxy by relocating incidents offcenter, in Sichuan. As related here, these tales do honor
Sichuan by association but seemingly out of context. They were probably conceived for expedient reasons at various times and then selectively cited whenever convenient. Thus repeated and perpetuated,
the myths became a variant quasi-history indiscriminately interspersed with conventional records, inconsistencies notwithstanding.

Literary evidence for China's mythological heritage in any event
is widely scattered among a variety of disparate texts, hard to reconcile, and without any single cohesive or internally consistent system.
Compared to the colorful, rich resources of myth found in some other
ancient civilizations, the Chinese texts relate material in a laconic and

unelaborated style, sometimes offering little detail beyond genealogy. However, a succession of patriarchal founder figures can be reconstructed from the accounts that have come down.

First in order were the primeval Celestial, Earthly, and Human Emperors (respectively Tian Huang, Di Huang, and Ren Huang). After them come a series of culture heroes, who taught mankind those skills setting human beings apart from beasts, such as fire making, farming, animal husbandry, writing, and governing. Of the inventive heroes, Youchao is linked with shelter, Suiren with fire, Paoxi (sometimes called Fuxi) with herding, and Shennong with agriculture. The Yellow Emperor, a political unifier, then begins a line of Five Emperors (*wu di*) followed in turn by two noted sage rulers, Yao and Shun. In the reign of Yao there was a major inundation of the land, so Yao commissioned an official, Gun, to control the waters. Gun failed but his son Yu assumed authority and finished the job during the reign of Shun. Shun rewarded Yu by handing over the kingdom to him.

Yu traveled far and wide to dredge the rivers and so eventually contain the floods. The extensive flood control efforts required coordination, and in bringing this about Yu managed to unify the territories drained by the Yellow; Han, Huai, and upper Yangtze Rivers. His Xia dynasty beginning 2205 B.C. fits chronologically into a protohistoric twilight zone between myth and ascertainable history. Subsequent to the Xia, the historicity of the succeeding Shang and Zhou dynasties is proven and well augmented by archaeology.

Textual accounts of the pre-Xia founder figures endow them with superhuman longevity, attributes, and accomplishments. When their stories are set in a geographic locus, it usually is somewhere on the loess plateau and alluvial plains along the Yellow River, well removed from Sichuan. Distant Shu would seem geographically incongruous in these tales.[3] However, scattered among various classical works of philosophy, history, and fable are putative deeds of the patriarchs set in or near Sichuan. These occasional references are too sparse and diffuse to form a consistent or coherent Shu-based alternative mythology. However, they do show a heterodox belief that had gained adherents by Han times, to the effect that during idealized bygone days the venerable fathers of Chinese civilization had sojourned, married, sired sons, and performed feats in western Sichuan.[4]

References to this area in connection with the mythical patriarchs go back as far as Ren Huang, the Human Emperor. The source is *Hua yang guo zhi*, a compilation of material about Sichuan edited in the fourth century A.D. by Chang Ju.[5] It starts with the Human Emperor, one of nine brothers, dividing all known territory into nine partitions (*jiu you*) on his succeeding the Earthly Emperor. The arrangement was like that of a pound sign (#, or tic-tac-toe grid) on which he took the central partition as his seat. *Hua yang guo zhi* relates: "Shu, as a country, began with the Human Emperor, along with Ba in the same territorial partition."[6] Sichuan, in this context also known alternatively as Huayang or as the land of Liang and Min, formed one of eight outer partitions.[7]

By commencing a history of Shu with the Human Emperor, Chang Ju may have merely been following a stylistic convention. Such antiquarian yarn spinning amounted to a form of provincial boosterism. *Hua yang guo zhi* could possibly also reflect biased publicity from the third century A.D. Three Kingdoms period, when the rump Han dynasty, ousted from its capital and driven to refuge in Sichuan, needed to assert a legitimizing appeal.[8] Whatever the particular circumstances and motivations underlying them, these stories tying Sichuan to China via the Human Emperor offer precedent for the theme of imperial unity, with Sichuan portrayed as an integral part of the larger Chinese body politic. Further myths of semisacred figures following the Human Emperor reinforce this line.[9]

The next mythical patriarch connected with Shu was the twenty-seventh century B.C. Yellow Emperor, according to Han dynasty court historian Sima Qian.[10] He quote a scholar as claiming, "The kings of Shu (*shu wang*) are descendants of the Yellow Emperor."[11] Because Sima Qian's genealogies for the Xia, Shang, and Zhou monarchies also trace their antecedents to the Yellow Emperor, the Shu rulers were thereby bonded to the Chinese nation with an acceptable, semidivine pedigree.

Other texts tell of the Yellow Emperor's progeny in Shu. One of his two legitimate sons, Shaohao, succeeded him as reignant. The other legitimate son, Changyi, is said to have dwelt at the Ruo River and wed one Shushanshi. Some texts write the character *shu* of this name identically to the Shu of Sichuan.[12] A river formerly called the Ruo indeed flows in Sichuan, lending the story a superficial credibility.[13] The union of Changyi and Shushanshi produced a son, Zhuanxu, who inherited the throne after his uncle Shaohao and ruled from 2514–2437 B.C. by traditional reckoning. Several generations later Zhuanxu's descendants are said to have included the sage emperor Shun, the flood controller Yu who founded the Xia dynasty, and ultimately the Qin state's ruling clan nearly two millennia afterward.

Although some of Zhuanxu's descendants became dynasts in their own right, his own sons did not directly succeed him as emperor. That honor went to Ku, a grandnephew of Zhuanxu.[14] Ku, or Emperor Ku (Di Ku, traditional dates 2436–2367 B.C.) as he is usually known, also had a link to Shu. According to *Hua yang guo zhi*, "Emperor Ku enfeoffed his progeny in Shu, to become noble through the generations." Imagination thus amply peopled Shu with a brood of aristocratic cousins, related to the Yellow Emperor's northern mainline stock. Eventually, over a millennium later, an unnamed king of Shu was said to have sprung from among their number.[15] The interim between Ku and the first Shu king included Yu, sometimes Yu the Great (Da Yu), whom texts also link to northwestern Sichuan.

The mythological function of Zhuanxu and Ku was little more than to plug genealogical gaps, but with Yu the stories assume more significance. The dates of his reign as the first Xia dynasty ruler are 2205–2197 B.C., moving the record closer to history not only chronologically but in the body of lore widely held credible, or at least plausible. Some fantastic elements still adhere to Yu, yet his crowning achievement of flood control is archtypically Chinese and down to earth, a metaphorical if not precisely literal truth. Whereas the preceding mythical kings receive only pro forma veneration, Yu is respected as would befit a mortal hero. He does not amount to a verifiable historical character, but a real man's shadow might conceivably lurk behind the surrounding pious haze.

Given Yu's cultural importance, the recorded facts of his birth, life, and career profoundly affect history as it is perpetuated and believed, more so than with his misty mythical antecedents. An ascription of Yu's origins to a particular locality transcends issues of narrow provincial pride, bearing directly on larger Chinese notions of roots and self-identity. It is on just this crucial question, the birthplace of Yu the Great, that the classical texts offer divergent leads.

Older writings bring Yu into the world at Mt. Song, close by the Yellow River within the present Henan province in the loess soil zone. Yu later made his capital in the same vicinity.[16] This area and a radius of about 300 kilometers around it constitute the very heart of nascent Chinese civilization, within which archaeologists currently seek remains of the Xia and where the Shang dynasty's capital cities have been found. The weight of Chinese opinion accepts this version for the birthplace of Yu, which has nothing to do with Sichuan.

But in an apparent discrepancy, no less than Sima Qian reported Yu as "arising from among the western Qiang." The Qiang were pastoralists whose name was recorded as early as Shang period inscriptions. In Han dynasty times, when Sima Qian wrote, the western Qiang ranged over Gansu and parts of northwestern Sichuan.[17] It is impossible to reconcile the origin of Yu near the central plains with this and other literary clues indicating an alternative far western location. Some texts adhering to the more westerly tradition of Yu variously pinpoint his actual birthplace as Shiniu or Kuaerping, both situated along the upper Min River on a plateau northnorthwest of Chengdu in Sichuan.[18]

Wherever Yu's origins may be found, ancient geographers agreed that his achievements of alleviating floods and setting boundaries took place in Sichuan as well as along the Yellow River. Yu was said to have restored the nonary division of empire first set down by the Human Emperor, the nine partitions once again including northwestern Sichuan, together with the Han valley, as Liang province (*liang zhou*). Liang province and the other eight are described in some detail by the *Yu gong*, China's earliest geographical text, probably composed sometime after 500 B.C. although imputed to Yu.[19]

Yu gong names readily recognizable rivers, mountains, and marshes all over northern China, but devotes slightly more attention, proportionately, to those in Yu's Liang province and the adjoining northwestern Yong province.[20] That has buttressed a partisan interpretation claiming a major role for Sichuan at the inception of Chinese dynastic history. Creatively reading the sources on Yu, some have taken the Min River in northern Shu as the central locus of his flood management efforts. Local conceit even stretched interpretation to assert the Min River area as the Xia people's homeland.[21] Notwithstanding its dubious historical validity, this claim again squelched notions of Sichuanese uniqueness while stressing the Sichuan bond to China proper.

A final incident, near the end of Yu's reign and life, concludes the Sichuanese counterclaim on him. Just before he died, Yu convened a broad-based assembly of nobles at a mountain called Kuaiji in modern Zhejiang province, far from Sichuan. The assembly amounted to a founding convention, its delegates representing all regions within the Xia polity. Those absent must be considered foreign, too peripheral for inclusion in Yu's nation-building efforts. The oldest sources on the Mt. Kuaiji assembly make no mention of Shu, or "Liang," or Sichuan under any other name. Not to be left out, *Hua yang guo zhi* (347 A.D.) crashes the party ex post facto by about two millennia, counting the "lords of Shu" among some 10,000 aristocrats who swore fealty to Yu at Mt. Kuaiji.[22] Here the text goes beyond placing Yu in Shu, to put Shu in China.

From Yu's birth through his great deeds to his end, local sources construed Sichuan to have been an important place in his life. As suggested, later political considerations could have abetted this myth making. One might more innocently suppose that some Yu legends were transferred to a Sichuan milieu along with the many north Chinese migrants whom Qin authorities resettled in Shu during the third century B.C.[23] There they toiled on large-scale hydraulic projects that recalled the legendary labors of Yu. But whether naive folklore or the product of deliberate textual tampering, the Sichuan version of Yu represented only an undercurrent. It never caught on as Chinese scholarly orthodoxy although it did serve a purpose consistent with imperial Chinese state-building goals.

One last mythical patriarch figure with an ascribed Sichuan connection is Peng Zu, a Methusaleh-like symbol of longevity said to have been a Shang dynasty palace archivist. Sichuanese lore later on maintained that Peng Zu was born in Shu and returned there to retire and eventually die after serving the Shang court. A county and a mountain bear the name Peng, and a temple marks his alleged burial mound.[24]

These tales and genealogies surely reveal more about propagandistic classical historiography than about preclassical, archaic China. Various strands of legend found their way into the texts at different times and under diverse circumstances, but they share a common element. Such stories are a projection backward by men of the Warring States period, the Han, and later times, for whom Sichuan had become indispensible to the unity of China as a whole. Mainstream Chinese legends recast against a Shu backdrop not only satisfied, but also exceeded, the shallow requirements of provincial vanity. They flattered Sichuanese pride by providing a local tradition of respectable antiquity and lineage, thereby binding Shu to China since the dawn of time.

Pre- and Protohistoric Shu

During the upper pleistocene, long before classical Chinese myths and mythmakers, human beings already inhabited Sichuan. The milder, wetter climate then prevailing offered a hospitable environment to paleolithic hunters, one of whose remains has been found. In 1951, a fossilized skull and upper jaw were dug up by a road crew near Ziyang, some eighty kilometers southeast of Chengdu. Workers dutifully turned over these relics of "Ziyang Man" to authorities but the exact discovery site could not be pinpointed again.

MAP 2

Early cultures of China

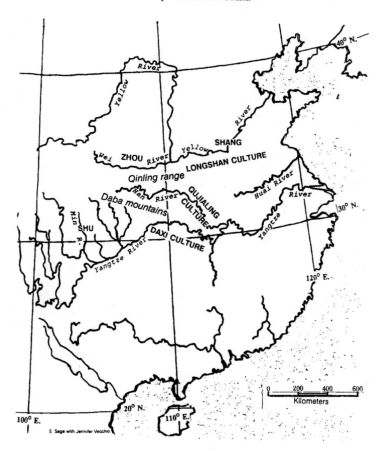

Chinese physical anthropologists classified the limited fossil fragments as racially proto-Mongoloid.[25]

The quest for further traces of Ziyang Man led to finds of quartzite pebble tools at nearby Liyuqiao, but this Liyuqiao culture, from around 25,000 ago, actually predates the Ziyang fossil itself by a considerable margin. Later on came the Fulin culture, known from a paleolithic assemblage on high ground about 170 kilometers southwest of Chengdu. Fulin retouched cores and leaf-shaped flake blades were smaller than Liyuqiao implements and show improvements in striking and finishing techniques.[26]

Many millennia divide these paleolithic artifacts from neolithic times in northwestern Sichuan, without any continuous strata sequences. As in many other places a tendency to adopt smaller, microlithic tools characterized the lead-up to settled neolithic life. In the upper Han valley in southern Shaanxi, that is, on the northern approaches to Sichuan, are remains of successive neolithic cultures, beginning with the Lijiacun culture. Its pottery was a simple unpainted, hand-cast, cord-marked slipware (*ni dun tao*), with a black exterior and brown or red interior. There also was a rope-marked, sandy-textured (*jia sha tao*) ware. Later Han valley neolithic sites are classified within the northern Yangshao and widespread Longshan cultures.[27]

Within western Sichuan itself the locale of Sanxingdui has been closely studied.[28] Sequential strata there show the transition from a neolithic technology to the adoption of bronze. Sanxingdui lies in Guanghan county some forty kilometers north of Chengdu. It was apparently the main center for a culture also identified in other Chengdu plain locations. The site includes ceramic ware even at its earliest habitation level; there is no known prepottery neolithic in Sichuan. This lowest level at Sanxingdui and at the adjacent Yueliangwan dig is the least well documented, and its cultural affinities elsewhere are uncertain.

Calibrated carbon-14 dates show the entire Sanxingdui culture lasted from about 4170–2875 B.P.[29] In historical terms the complete Sanxingdui sequence spanned the pre-Shang, Shang, and early western Zhou periods. At least three successive cultural stages were initially identified among five or more layers although the periodization of Sanxingdui strata later became a controversial, unresolved topic.[30]

Pottery remains certifiably belonging to the bottom, earliest layer are sparse. The date of occupation is estimated at around 2100 B.C., plus or minus seventy-five years. According to the 1987 site report, above the first stage came a stratum devoid of cultural remains

MAP 3

Sites of early Shu culture

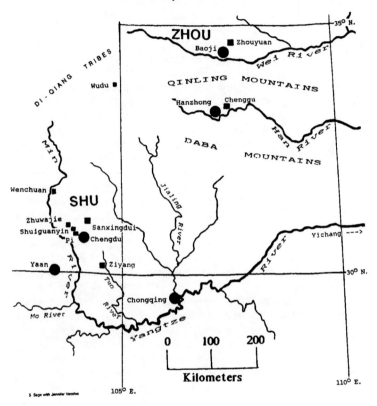

before the beginning of the second habitation stage. Left unanswered was the identity of the first stage inhabitants and whether they should be thought of as pre-Shu or as proto-Shu.[31]

Sanxingdui's second stage is regarded as contemporary with the early to middle Shang. Sandy-textured brown pottery became the most abundant ceramic, followed by a brown slipware. Characteristic types include horn-shaped wide-mouthed jars, tall necked goblets (*gao bing dou*), narrow-necked *hu* flasks, small flat bottomed jars, and vessel covers. A kind of bird-shaped ladle with a beak for the handle makes its initial appearance. Pottery decoration at the second stage was more varied than in the first, with a repertoire of cord-marked, rope-marked, comb-marked, incised, and stamped adornment including water chestnut, heart, and shell patterns.

Rectangular structures were characteristic of the second stage in contrast with the round or square huts reported for the preceding stratum. Post holes remain from the wooden columns that supported thatched roofs. Walls consisted of lightly baked mud. Only a score of such dwellings were identified, all roughly about 15.3 square meters, each one circumvented by a ditch. The data are not yet sufficient to draw firm inferences from the dwellings' spatial relationships to one another. If such a modest concentration of wooden houses constituted the totality of Sanxingdui, the place could hardly have been consequential.

But this was surely no mean village. Surrounding the settlement stood an irregular three-sided, tamped-earth wall, the extant remnants of which are reported to measure from five to thirty meters thick. Each stratum of the compressed earth is between twelve and twenty-five centimeters. The rampart stretches a full kilometer on the east by 600 meters on its western side and 180 meters on the south. Apparently no barrier was needed on the north where the inhabitants relied on a stream for natural defense.[32] Only a portion of the ground within this considerable enclosure has been excavated so far. As for buildings, if the Sanxingdui denizens modeled their town after contemporary urban settlements on the central plains then an architecture in stone masonry is unlikely to be found.[33]

Protohistoric texts lend support to a notion that Sanxingdui was peopled by Shu migrants from the Min mountains north of the Chengdu plain.[34] Pronounced northern affinities show in pottery from the so-called second and third stages, such as the three legged *he* vessels. Harder to account for are the bird-beak–shaped ladle handles, of which like examples outside Sichuan are known only from near Yichang, in Hubei, to the east.

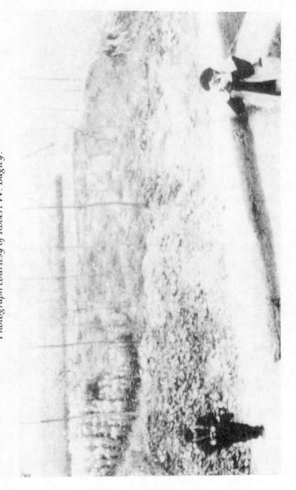

FIGURE 1

Excavation near the Sanxingdui city wall.
Photograph courtesy of Robert W. Bagley.

FIGURE 2

A test square excavation at Sanxingdui.
Photograph courtesy of Robert W. Bagley.

FIGURE 3

Bird beak shaped ladle handles from Sanxingdui (1–4), from near Yichang (5, 6), and from Chengdu (7). (*Wen wu*, no. 5, 1989, p. 39)

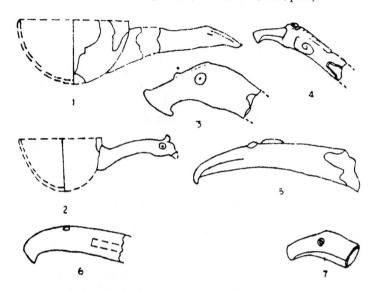

According to the Sanxingdui site report, general continuity marked the transition from the second to the third stage. The ground reveals considerable ash residue and a greater abundance of pottery shards, strongly indicative of increased population or at least of more intensified activity. More stone tools of diverse types are found as well, reflecting broader economic pursuits. Practical polished stone implements include axes, adzes, awls, pestles, and stone spindle whorls, but present as well is a kind of stone amulet (*bi*) that may have been used ritually or as a standardized unit of weight.

Ceramic goods at the third stage clearly show an ongoing northern influence, readily visible in the tall cooking vessels with three hollow legs (*he*). On the other hand, the bird beak ladles, tall goblets, and small flat-bottomed bowls are identifying marks of the Sanxingdui culture. These are known from elsewhere in the Shu part of Sichuan at Chengdu and Hanyuan, as well as at Langzhong in the north and Yaan in southern Sichuan. Alongside the common rope-marked decoration at Sanxingdui, the north Chinese angular mean-

FIGURE 4

Chengdu plain examples of the *he* vessel, a ceramic type derived from the
Yellow River culture zone. (*Wen wu*, no. 5, 1989, p. 41)

der whorl or "thundercloud" (*yun lei*), the rice grain (*mi li*), and other
patterns make an appearance. Brown sandy-textured pottery and a
brown slipware are most common, but some other wares previously
present in small quantities no longer are seen.

A few bones of pigs and deer are found among the settlement
debris, likely evidence of a mixed economy combining hunting and
maybe some animal husbandry along with agriculture. Rice would
seem a likely candidate for the staple grain but no early rice remains
have actually yet been identified here or anywhere else in Sichuan,
despite their prevalence in regions to the south and east.[35] Kitchen
garbage anyway is hardly memorable; neither are pottery shards,
neolithic tools, crude structures, nor tamped-earth walls. What grabs
the imagination at Sanxingdui is its buried treasure.

Associated with the late stage are two substantial underground
caches discovered and excavated in 1986. To all appearances, these
had lain undetected since their original burial. The first pit, about a
meter and a half below the surface, measured 3.4 by 4.6 meters and
contained over 300 artifacts wrought in gold, bronze, jade, stone,
bone, ceramic, and ivory, plus fragments of seashell and charred
bone. Most of the goods were concentrated in the rectangle's southwest and southeast corners. Their positions were carefully noted in
situ before removal. Shortly thereafter, a second rectangular pit was
located thirty meters to the southeast. Pit no. 2 lay just over half a
meter below the surface, its 5.3 by 2.2 meters virtually crammed with
objects. There were also many ivory elephant tusks, but its bronzes
have attracted the most scholarly attention.

Pit no. 2 yielded 439 bronze artifacts. The largest is a robed, male
human figure with a prominent nose, the head topped by a crownlike

headdress. Its eyes are large, slanted, and almond shaped; the ears are flared and with pierced lobes. Decoration on the robe broadly conforms to the later well-known dragon robes worn by Chinese emperors, in its conceptual scheme. However, the garment fastens on the left, recalling a line in *Shu wang ben ji* so describing Shu attire.[36] This sartorial fashion sets frontier peoples apart from ethnic Chinese (i.e., the Hua-xia, and later the Han people), who traditionally have fastened their robes on the right. Standing 181.2 cm. above an attached pedestal, the statuette is a regal figure that may indeed represent a Shu king, whose arms and hands are arranged in a manner to grasp some object such as a scepter. The 78.8 cm. pedestal supporting this figure bears a symmetrical *tao tie* (demon mask) relief in angular meander whorl on each of the four sides of its upper tier.[37]

Other bronze human figures from both pits portray human heads, perhaps representations of courtiers wearing stylized headdresses that could have denoted rank. Four types have been recognized. Thirty-six examples of Type A have a braided queue of hair; the single Type B specimen wears a cylindrical hat; three Type C heads have a kind of turban, and the one Type D head a cap with a bowlike device in the back. There also were fifteen bronze masks in Pit no. 2, and one in Pit no. 1. Three of the masks have pluglike cylinders protruding from the eyes. A partial inventory of the major remaining items in the pits includes a crouching bronze tigerlike beast and another in gold, plus a bronze dragon and a bronze tree.

On stylistic grounds the Chinese excavators assume these bronze effigies and masks to have been of indigenous manufacture. They bear many features in common with pieces from the central plains nuclear area, but in other aspects the bronzes are clearly the product of a distinct subtradition. The actual smelting works have not yet been reported, nor have the results of any metallurgical analysis been released as concerns casting technique, alloy ratios, and so on.

Jade items include scepters, ceremonial halberd heads, and amulets in quantity, besides some in stone. Among the many scepters, one in particular has aroused comment because it bears an incised motif. Four etched rows of human figures stand abreast on it, hands clasped in front, the rows divided by tiers of angular whorl relief alternating with tiers of wavy lines depicting what could be stylized mountains. A small bronze kneeling figure, also from Pit no. 2, illustrates how the scepters were grasped by outstretched arms. Sanxingdui scepters exhibit some features in common with Yellow River nuclear area examples, yet betray unique details; for example, one type has a toothed blade.[38]

FIGURE 5

Front and rear views of a bronze statue from Shang times, excavated at Pit #2, Sanxingdui, Sichuan. (*Wen wu*, no. 5, 1989, p. 4)

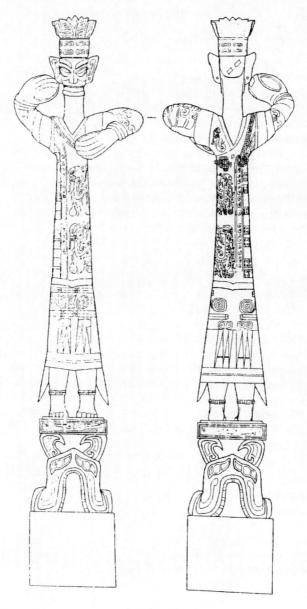

A consensus among Sichuan archaeologists interprets the pits as surrogate sacrifices; that is, offerings to supernatural forces with goods and images substituted for human victims. Apart from the regal standing figure, the human effigies were either decapitated or consisted only of heads. Many other goods were broken and traces of scorching were present as well. The aspect of the pits, and their contents, have suggested to one scholar that they represent traces of a religious sacrifice to the cosmos (*tian*), earth, and to West Mountain (*xi shan*, a.k.a. *yu lei shan*), on the edge of the Chengdu plain.[39]

Sanxingdui was evidently the capital, or principal center, of a fairly powerful entity. The Sanxingdui culture occupied the Chengdu plain and may have extended to Yaan in southern Sichuan, where similar ceramics have been found.[40] Northward, the upper Han River valley was likely also part of this culture area, and its zone of contact with societies based along the Yellow River.[41] Moreover, far to the east along the Yangtze at Yichang in Hubei there are likenesses noted between a local Shang period neolithic pottery and that of Sanxingdui, in particular the presence there of the bird's head–shaped ladle handles. These Yichang items have given rise to speculation about a possible eastern origin of the people who settled at Sanxingdui, but a few shared features constitute insufficient grounds on which to postulate migration paths.[42] Suffice to say that the Sanxingdui people held sway and kept in touch over a rather wide expanse.

Outside influences may help account for several new pottery types that make an appearance and mark the last, or so-called fourth, Sangxingdui stage. This crockery consists of cups and bowls having pointed bases. They are rare in the Sanxingdui upper stratum, and most specimens are known from Chengdu and from Shuiguanyin on the Chengdu plain.[43] The fate of Sanxingdui becomes hazy following its third stage, but over generations Chengdu assumed more and more importance as an economic and political pivot of Shu.[44]

Chengdu city, the political heart of Shu in historical times and still the modern capital of Sichuan, includes several sites of the Sanxingdui culture. A massive edifice there attests to the location's pivotal function. It was a large earthen mound at Yangzishan, on the present northern outskirts of Chengdu city. On the basis of ceramic remains, the mound is believed to postdate the Sanxingdui third stage, but it may have been piled up gradually over many years. Built for ritual purposes and perhaps influenced by central plains models, its form consisted of a huge square having three supermounted layers.[45] Pierced stone *bi* amulets from Yangzishan resemble those found at the Sanxingdui and Yueliangwan sites and testify to a continuity in

FIGURE 6

Front, profile, and rear views of bronze busts from Pit #2, Sanxingdui, from top to bottom types A, B, C, and D. (*Wen wu*, no. 5, 1989, pp. 5–9)

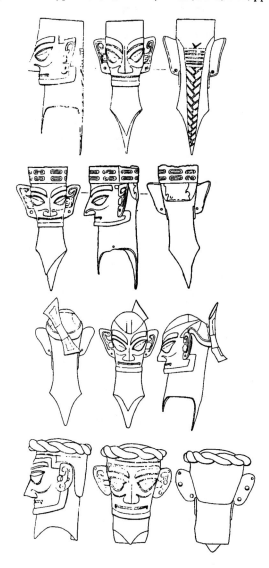

Shu ceremonial paraphernalia. The mound had impressive dimensions, 10 meters high by 103.6 meters at the base, with the middle and upper tiers measuring respectively 67.7 and 31.6 meters on a side. Considerable labor must have gone into constructing this huge altar, indicating the ruling class of Shu commanded a manpower resource and the agricultural surplus for its maintenance.

Another Chengdu dig is in the neighborhood of No. 12 Bridge Street (shi er qiao jie) just north of the municipal Culture Park. Salvage efforts covering an area of about 5,000 square meters proceeded from late 1985 to the spring of 1987, after the remnants of an ancient wooden structure were located while scooping out earth for a building foundation.[46] Congested urban conditions have placed practical limits on this and follow-up excavations, so it may be a long time before a complete picture emerges of the origins and early life of Chengdu.

From the configuration of wood and bamboo remains at the No. 12 Bridge Street Chengdu site it was possible to theoretically reconstruct one large, long-collapsed building. The house, or hall, is believed to have featured a raised platform floor consisting of planks set atop a log framework anchored into the ground by stakes. Above this, log columns with lashed crossbeams supported a pitched roof. The lattice walls and roof were of smaller branches laid horizontally and vertically in rows. Flat planks finished the roof, and the wall covering was of thatch. Overall length may have been 35 meters, width 16 meters, and height 18 meters from floor to roofbeam.

An early, middle, and late stage are distinguished at No. 12 Bridge Street. The wood and bamboo frame building belongs to the early stage.[47] Subsequent stages at the site include ceramics dated with reference to those at Sanxingdui. They conform in general type to Sanxingdui wares and include the latest known bird-beak–shaped ladle handle. A spindle made of ceramic from the middle stage is marked with a single emblem resembling writing from the central plains. Apart from the ceramics are stone axes, awls, and hoe blades, bone needles, a bone arrowhead, two bronze arrowheads, and a bit of cracked tortoise shell that may have been used for oracle purposes.[48]

The people of Sanxingdui and then at Chengdu and related sites occupied the area historically known as Shu. They apparently maintained substantial contacts with the Shang of the central plains, with whom they shared art motives, technology, and customs, while pursuing a local culture of their own. To call Sanxingdui the first seat of a lost Shu civilization would be to exaggerate, but not by much. These are sensational finds, of a hitherto unknown cousin of the leading force in early East Asian civilization, the Shang.

Lost civilizations, a la Indiana Jones, are supposed to include ruins of impressive architecture. But there are none here, nor indeed among the Shang either. Compared to the grand masonry of western Asia, the Mediterranean world, or ancient Peru, the wooden structure at Chengdu is little more than a pathetic shed. But each lost civilization must be reckoned on its own terms. Among the Shang, what defined the might of their king was less buildings so much as urbanism itself, the power over a hierarchy capable of concentrating many people in one place to serve the ruling family. The city, demarcated by a tamped-earth wall, was the administrative, ceremonial, and defensive locus of the politically prominent lineages and their wealth. Ritual, art, and writing were the paths to authority, access to which came via control over a few key resources; namely, bronze and the command over bronze metallurgists.[49]

Except for writing, all these components are amply evident in the related proto-civilization at Sanxingdui. Eventually in Sichuan there would appear a unique system of writing, still undeciphered as befits a lost civilization. But because a readable written record is not present for this Sichuan era, it is hard to determine whether the ritual, art, and urban components fit together in quite the same way as with the Shang. Inferences about Sanxingdui life must be guarded if based on understanding gained from studying the distant Shang. And whereas Sanxingdui's third stage was contemporary with late Shang, the Sanxingdui culture proved stronger and more durable, outlasting the Shang dynasty. Continuity is apparent between the upper strata at Sanxingdui proper, the following stage at Yueliangwan, the Chengdu sites of Yangzishan and No. 12 Bridge Street, and other Chengdu plain sites from immediately subsequent periods.

With Yueliangwan and the Yangzishan remains in Sichuan, the temporal juncture between the Shang and Zhou dynasties has been reached. This is when *Shu* is mentioned for the first time in a traditional central plains text, *Shang shu*.[50] Inferentially, one might now conclude that these Sichuanese of the Sanxingdui culture were identical to the Shu known from written history. However, some knotty problems must be examined in the course of making that identification. The difficulties arise in the course of connecting the word *shu*, in texts and inscriptions, to western Sichuan and its inhabitants of the late second millennium B.C.

The Name *Shu*

The character *shu* has resisted several attempts at etymological analysis. Before it referred to Sichuan and the Sichuanese, it may have had other meanings. Dictionaries classify *shu* under the ideographic radical for "insect"; in this form, the first example is on a bone inscription from around the eleventh century B.C. Even earlier there is a character essentially alike in other particulars, except that it lacks the "insect" radical.[51] At the top of the character is another stylized element signifying an eye. One etymological suggestion makes much of the supposed eye, downplaying the insect. But as Shu has primarily an ethnic and geographic connotation, these pictographic elements seem incongruous and are difficult to account for logically.

Alternative explanations ignore the curious pictographic form of *shu*, concentrating instead on phonetic relationships to arrive at some very divergent notions. Lexicography in China begins with a text called *Er ya*, a compendium of terms and their meanings reflecting first millennium B.C. usage. *Er ya* defines *shu* as an isolated, solitary mountain peak.[52] By extension, *shu* also was taken to mean sole, or single, according to a Han period linguistic work on dialects, *Fang yan*.[53] Both these ancient etymologies depend on the sound of the character but ignore its written composition and the nagging question of why it includes the element for "insect."

The *Shuo wen* dictionary (c. 100 A.D.) did proceed from the pictographic element for an insect grub, or larva, and classical commentary appended to the definition relates *shu* to the character *can*, meaning "silkworm."[54] Because *can* figures in the name of an ancient Shu king, Cancong, that explanation seems to accord neatly with history. Certain historians have seized on this to mean that a silkworm was the mythical progenitor of the Shu people, and silkworms their subsequent totem. Slim evidence for this has been discerned in a silkwormlike image on the ornamentation of a bronze blade unearthed at Chengdu. It was supposed to be the Shu totemic emblem, but accepting that notion requires a leap of faith.[55]

Rather strong contrary evidence casts doubt on the *can* hypothesis as an interpretation of *shu*. For one thing, the earliest rendition of the character found in Shang dynasty inscriptions lacks the insect element.[56] The Shang furthermore already employed a separate character for *can*, whereas *shu* appears in contexts indicating a place or a tribe of people, but in no examples as an allusion to silkworms.[57] Some later classical passages nevertheless do make a clear distinction between the silkworm, *can*, and another type of poisonous caterpillar called a *shu*.[58] This leaves ambiguous the basic relationship between the character *shu*, silkworms, and other arthropods, but the word could have taken on insect connotations through phonetic borrowing.[59]

An alternative etymology for *shu* concentrates not on the insect

FIGURE 7

Left, a character sometimes read as "shu" as it appears in oracle bone inscriptions from the Shang capital at Anyang, Henan province. Right, a similar character from later oracles found at Zhouyuan, Shaanxi. (after *Kao gu yu wen wu*, no. 6, 1985, p. 72)

element, but rather the prominent stylized "eye" at the top of the character. Conjecture relates this eye to a legendary version of Shu origins mentioning a "vertical-eyed man" (*zong mu zhi ren*), figuratively perhaps meaning a "man of vision."[60] The ocular peculiarity is ascribed yet again to Cancong, the earliest Shu king, in *Hua yang guo zhi*, ch. 3, *shu zhi*, the history of Shu, thereby connecting the character *shu* directly to the Shu people via a protohistoric person.[61]

Cancong and the Shu were believed to have originally occupied stone dwellings in the Min Mountains, part of the plateau along the frontier between modern Sichuan and Gansu provinces.[62] That region also is associated with the pastoral Qiang people. *Hua yang guo zhi* adds that after he died, Cancong's body was placed in a stone coffin entombed within a stone vault, which then supposedly set a pattern for Shu burials.[63] Some old stone coffin burials have indeed been found in northwestern Sichuan and folklore as well as a few toponyms there are said to preserve allusions to Cancong. This mixed evidence has been favored by scholars trying to prove a northern origin of the Shu.[64]

However, on closer examination, the stone coffin graves actually excavated all belong to a time much later than the Shu progenitor Cancong, and moreover no stone coffin inhumations have been discovered at Sanxingdui or any other locations on the Chengdu plain, the heartland of Shu.[65] The pottery found in the extant stone coffin graves also is very different from that at Sanxingdui and related sites.[66] So satisfying archaeological confirmation of the Cancong story in *Hua yang guo zhi* has not been forthcoming. Any connection of the eye element in the *shu* character to Cancong must stand on its own merits as philological speculation.

To summarize the divergent and likely confusing etymological views on *shu*, the ideograph includes a stylized element for an eye along with the sign for an insect. Classical dictionaries variously define *shu* as a mountain peak having no apparent tie to Sichuan or as a kind of insect. Relating the "insect" and the "eye" to the people known as the Shu has involved tortuous reasoning. Both approaches make the connection via the legendary Shu chieftain Cancong, but despite their convergence on Cancong, neither attempt has won full acceptance. In addition to the inconclusive lexicography, there has also been study of a character identified as *shu* in the Shang oracle bones.

Shu in Oracle Bone Inscriptions

Shang civilization dominated the Yellow River plains during the second half of the second millennium B.C., a time contemporary with the settlements of Sanxingdui and early Chengdu in Sichuan. Masters of bronze metallurgy, the Shang are best known for their weapons and ornate ceremonial vessels cast in this medium. Despite its distinctive regional characteristics, the bronze work at Sanxingdui clearly belongs with that of the Shang in a common larger tradition. Evidence of Shang contacts with Sichuan also may derive from surviving Shang writings, which consisted of pictographic signs ancestral to modern Chinese characters. At the Shang capital city, Anyang, thousands of inscriptions were recorded on pieces of animal bone and sometimes on tortoise shells. They are the remains of a ritual prognostication procedure performed by specialists of the Shang royal court.

The oracle worked as follows. Scribes would incise a message onto the surface of a piece of bone or shell, seeking guidance regarding a particular vital question. Topics might include harvests, the royal hunt, or matters of public policy such as relations with surrounding peoples. It was frequently asked whether conditions were propitious for embarking on a campaign against one or another neighboring group. After writing down the plea, the bone was then subjected to heat until it cracked. A prognosis was esoterically derived by examining the resulting fissure. Most of what is known about Shang foreign affairs comes from studying these so-called oracle bones.[67]

Because the oracles covered a wide range of subjects, just a relative few concern Shu either directly or tangentially. The characters *shu*, *sou*, and *qiang* are of interest in this context. A character looking like an antecedent rendition of *shu* occurs in over forty oracles, where it refers either to a group of people or a place. All but two of the inscriptions including *shu* were found around the ruins of Anyang, in modern Henan province. The two exceptions are from a site called Zhouyuan, in Shaanxi province.

A majority of oracle bone specialists concur that this *shu* character in both the Anyang and Zhouyuan inscriptions signifies the Shu people, and further accepts that these Shu inhabited the upper Han valley of Shaanxi and the Chengdu plain of western Sichuan. That would confirm the equation of *shu* in oracle bones with the Sanxingdui culture.[68] Nonetheless, certain nagging doubts expressed by a persistent minority of scholars deserve attention. There are problems regarding the character *shu* itself and other questions arising from its meaning in the context of some inscriptions that can be read and understood.

The first problem is that of the graphic identification of *shu;* that is, whether the oracle bone ideograph is truly the same character known later from texts. At a glance the character strongly resembles *shu* although in the Anyang version it lacks the set of calligraphic strokes that form the classifying radical for "insect." This omission of the insect radical occasioned hesitation by some scholars in endorsing the character as really equivalent to the familiar *shu*.[69] Some progress toward dispelling that doubt came after a trove of later oracle inscriptions on tortoise shell was found in 1977 at Zhouyuan. The collection included two inscriptions featuring the character, by then unmistakably *shu* and incorporating the insect radical. During the interim between the Anyang and Zhouyuan divination archives, the stylistic convention on writing this character had apparently changed, with the extra strokes appended.[70]

The second problem concerned equating the *shu* of inscriptions with the faraway Shu lands of Sichuan and the Han river in southern Shaanxi. Those who maintain a prima facie identity of *shu* to Sichuan are bolstered by the mention of *shu* at Zhouyuan, situated much closer to Sichuan than Anyang, and so more likely to have seen contact with the Sanxingdui people. Then, so the reasoning goes, if *shu* at Zhouyuan meant the Shu of Sichuan, so too should the very similar character *shu* in inscriptions from Anyang.[71] Opponents to this line concede *shu* in oracle bones to have been an antecedent form for Shu, but hold that the bone writings meant another Shu, much closer to the Shang center at Anyang. To resolve the matter, reference is made to what the inscriptions actually say.

Although some of the bone messages can be read, the task of interpreting them confidently is daunting due to their laconic, fragmentary, and disjointed nature. Oracle archives at both Anyang and Zhouyuan amount to ingenuous primary sources, never intended to be read as ageless history or literature. Rather, they are day-to-day internal working documents, drawn up to aid royal decision making according to the ritualistic procedures of their time. What information they offer is spare but all the more precious for its unimpeachable bona fides. Most of the oracle bones found at Anyang derive from the reign of the Shang king Wu Ding, traditionally dated 1324–1265 B.C. The forty or so inscriptions on Shang-Shu relations during this period refer to random events, but cannot be assembled in any firm chronological sequence.

Some of the inscriptions are too short or incomplete to be understood. Of those readable examples including the character *shu*, most concern developments in war or diplomacy. On one occasion, the Shang king sought advice on whether to send envoys (*shi*) to Shu.[72] Another inscription alludes to "300 Shu bowmen," from which it may be inferred that archery already had become a Shu military skill. A Shu driver (or drivers), as of a cart or chariot, are mentioned as well on a bone fragment.[73]

So the Shang court recorded some substantive dealings with a district called Shu and its people, although not specifying just where Shu was located. But at least four nearly identical passages on separate oracle bones mention the Shang king treating with representatives from Shu together with those of a place called Fou. If Fou can be found, this should shed light on the location of Shu, presumably nearby. And Fou has been tentatively fixed in southern Shanxi province, in fair proximity to Anyang yet at a great remove from Sichuan.[74] Other Shang oracles comment on the harvest in Shu, information that would be more easily available, and more worthy of comment, if Shu were assumed to be a nearby district rather than a distant entity in Sichuan.[75]

As for the Zhouyuan oracles, these were recorded between one and two centuries after those of the Shang at Anyang. They reflect the separate vantage point of southwestern Shaanxi, at a time of heightened tension between the ruling Shang dynasty and its restive Zhou cousins.[76] Two inscriptions mention the Shu, in one of which only the character *shu* itself is still legible. The other inscription, reading *fa shu*, indicates a military foray against the Shu.[77] However, as the actual compass direction of this expedition is not specified, it could just as easily mean south to Sichuan or east to Shanxi.

If *shu* in the oracle bones did not refer to the Shu in Sichuan, but the Shu in Sichuan after all were in contact with the Shang, then by what name was the Sanxingdui culture known in Shang writings? One suggestion is that Shu was originally called *Sou*, and that the character *shu* was only later substituted for *sou*. Ancient commentaries to the well-known historical texts *Shang shu* and *Hou han shu* make the equation between *shu* and *sou*, a case of phonetic borrowing dating to Han dynasty times.[78] But searching back for examples of *sou* in Shang and Zhou inscriptions runs into further ambiguity. The character accepted as *sou* by some specialists has been given at least three other readings by others.[79] And even if *sou* in fact were an allusion to the Shu entity centered on Sanxingdui, the inscriptions it appears in provide very little historical information.

Certain Chinese researchers have proposed that the Sou, in turn, belonged to the Qiang group of peoples, a rationale resting on mentions of Sou in association with the Di branch of the Qiang in post-Han dynasty commentaries.[80] That is very late testimony. The already tenuous connecting strands here are further stretched in trying to link the Shu with the Qiang during the late second millennium B.C.[81] Notwithstanding its drawbacks, this theory exerts a certain attraction because oracle bone inscriptions mentioning the Qiang are relatively abundant and offer possibilities as historical sources. At least one extant Shang example includes the *qiang* and *shu* characters in a single context, suggesting two proximate peoples.[82] The Qiang theory traces Shu origins, as migrants to Sichuan from the north, and dovetails with some of the legendary sources and philological reasoning recounted earlier. However, it lacks hard, incontrovertible proof.[83]

These reservations about *shu* (or *sou*) for the present effectively must restrain any fully confident use of the oracle inscriptions as historical raw material. The uncertainties are disappointing, but they are more than balanced by the very tangible certainty of Sanxingdui and the spectacular bronze age culture that flourished there. Called by whatever name, the power that made its headquarters at Sanxingdui was one to be reckoned with by its neighbors. Convenience and a fair measure of confidence dictate that this power should properly be known as Shu.

The Shu Enter History

Toward the end of the second millennium B.C. friction steadily increased between the Zhou power at Zhouyuan and the Shang kings farther east. Oracle bone archives from both places preserve their mutual communication and also mention many other regional groups, both friendly and hostile.[84] The Zhou controlled the valley of the Wei River and other waters tributary to the Yellow River. By the twelfth or eleventh century B.C. they had achieved preeminence among the peoples in Shaanxi and were emboldened to challenge Shang claims on universal authority. To unseat the Shang would require allies. It is in this context that the first traditional textual reference to Shu appears. The Shu are numbered among eight nations, or peoples, assembled together in a Zhou coalition to throw off the Shang yoke. In order as listed in the *Shang shu*, the eight were the Yong, Shu, Qiang, Mao, Wei, Lu, Peng, and Pu.[85]

Among these the Qiang harbored grievances against the Shang, a predatory enemy that had marched against them, taken captives, and likely slain many Qiang in ritual sacrifices. Shang oracles show that the Qiang were an ongoing foreign policy concern along the western marches.[86] The Shu as well may have had cause to oppose the Shang. Even discounting the problematic oracle bone references to *shu*, there is still an annal entry as well as a poetic allusion in *Shi jing* to a long range Shang military expedition that reached the Han valley, on the outer approaches of Shu.[87] In addition to the Shu, some of the other groups like the Peng and Pu are encountered later on in historical sources, in Sichuan or nearby around its circumference. So here, at last, is a sufficiently credible textual reference to Sichuan.

King Wu, martial king of the Zhou, marched his motley league eastward to the Shang capital's outskirts. At a place called Muye, or "Shepherd's Field," he delivered a why-we-fight harangue on the reason for revolt. The king deplored various substantive and ritual transgressions committed by the Shang, claiming justification for his war to overthrow them. He proclaimed a new order to be at hand. King Wu then had the multitude present arms (halberds and spears), enjoined a cautious battle plan suiting an ad hoc host of disparate allies, and bid them prepare for war.

What followed was quite likely the largest East Asian military engagement ever fought to that date. The historicity of the Muye battle is beyond dispute, confirmed by the discovery in 1976 of a bronze vessel cast just a week after the Zhou victory and inscribed to dedicate it.[88] Judged in terms of consequences Muye ranks among the decisive battles of history, for it ended Shang power and established the classical Zhou dynasty that would last more than 700 years. Muye set a pattern. At the conclusion of those seven Zhou centuries, first one king and then another was to set out from the old Zhou base on the Wei River in Shaanxi, unite Sichuanese power behind him, and make a successful bid for supreme rule.

In its own time the Muye campaign performed an integrative function, bringing together distant peoples in a common cause. Some pageantry commemorated the event. When the allied peoples later mustered in review, several of them brought along resplendently plumed birds such as peacocks and the like. The Qiang had a kind of game fowl and the Shu a type of pheasant.[89] One can only guess at the symbolic purpose of these birds. They might have been token tributes of allegiance to the Zhou king or totemic battle standards.[90]

The various peoples, including the Shu, thereby cemented a bond of identity with the Zhou, while gaining firsthand experience in a military endeavor involving large masses of warriors. Organization and discipline were required, as well as bronze halberds, the standard weaponry of their day. Muye, although fought hundreds of kilometers from Sichuan, thus also was a milestone event in the history of Shu and Sichuan. Following Muye the Shu brought more of Shang and Zhou material culture to the Chengdu plain. The post-Muye Shu culture can be traced there by a trail of improved pottery, jades, bronze vessels, and bronze swords, spears, and halberd blades, the very panoply of Zhou power.

Archaeologically, in Sichuan, significant finds of bronzes subsequent to the Sanxingdui pit contents are known from Shuiguanyin in Xinfan county and Zhuwajie in Peng county, both north of Chengdu city. In southern Shaanxi is the Chenggu site along the Han River. Artifacts recovered at these places along with the weaponry testify to the strong influence of northern culture in both ritual and the techniques of warfare.

Some bronzes adhere to the Shu subtradition of bronze casting. For example, at Wenchuan, on the high plateau northwest of Chengdu, was found a distinctively Shu *lei* bronze vessel bearing *kui long* dragon decoration, and equipped with two looped handles. These handles are in the form of birds' heads, very much like the bird-beak ladle handles from Sanxingdui, Chengdu, and elsewhere.[91] On the other hand, certain bronzes are outright imports, as indicated by the inscription on a Shang bronze vessel found in conjunction with bronze weapons at Zhuwajie. The vessel bore three characters indicating ownership by an elder of the Tan clan. Another bronze piece from an early western Zhou period grave uncovered at Baoji, Shaanxi province, has a nearly identical inscription.[92]

The locale near Sanxingdui continued to be an important Sichuan center of the Shu in Sichuan during early Zhou. Just a few score meters from the Shang period remains at Sanxingdui is the related site known as Yueliangwan on the former Zhongxing commune, which includes material later than that of Sanxingdui proper. Technical progress is evident. Whereas the lower level pottery at Yueliangwan is hand-modeled slipware, overlying strata contemporary with the late Shang or early Zhou period have yielded mainly wheel thrown examples made of a coarse-textured clay. The upper level pieces bear more of the typically northern decorative motifs, such as the angular meander whorl, cicada, square, and cowrie patterns. The pottery shapes conform to their predecessors at adjacent Sanxingdui.[93]

Yueliangwan contains as well a hoard of precious jades. These several hundred jade ritual objects are classified according to a specialized terminology. They include a cylindrical *cong*, best known from the Shang capital at Anyang but only rarely noted in subsequent Zhou contexts. Three *chuan* amulets could be of either Shang or Western Zhou date. Jade *zong* could signify landholding rights, and a stone *bi* was likely a sanctioned standard weight unit. Several *fu* jade ceremonial axes and *zhang* scepters from the Sanxingdui complex fit a description of Zhou military command regalia included in the later ritual handbook *Zhou li*.[94]

However, there is no guarantee that the jades were used here for the very same ritual functions as those of the Zhou. Furthermore, the Han dynasty text *Shu wang ben ji* centuries later made the point that the Shu were "ignorant of proper ritual." The Shu may have accorded different significance to the objects than those prescribed in *Zhou li*, and likely followed rites unfamiliar to the authors of whatever sources later were used to compile *Shu wang ben ji*. But the jades, like the Sanxingdui bronzes, confirm that Sichuanese participated in historical East Asian civilization around the time of a crucial episode, the Zhou overthrow of Shang power.

Ceramics provide a dating sequence covering the Sichuan periods contemporary with the late Shang into Western Zhou times. Following the Sanxingdui and Yueliangwan strata noted previously, there are the periods represented by the upper level stratum recovered from the Yangzishan altar mound, two lower levels at Chengdu's No. 12 Bridge St., and then an early and middle sequence at Shuiguanyin on the Chengdu plain. An upper level from No. 12 Bridge Street is contemporary with the late Shuiguanyin stratum.[95]

Shuiguanyin in Xinfan county and Zhuwajie in Peng county are respectively about twenty-five and forty kilometers north northwest of Chengdu. Lower level strata at Shuiguanyin date to sometime earlier in the Shang, with tools of chipped and polished stone such as axes, choppers, awls, and grinders, but no metal weapons.[96] As at Sanxingdui, the next upper stratum features numerous pottery pieces strongly reminiscent of north Chinese wares, including high-necked *dou* goblets, *hu* flasks, and a three-legged *gui* cooker similar to the Sanxingdui *he* examples. Mundane utensils were all of stone, bone, or ceramic, but associated inhumations of late Shang or early Zhou date featured bronze arrowheads, spears, battle axes, and halberd blades.

The use of bronze among the Shu appears to have been limited initially to ceremonial objects and thence to equipment for waging war. After Sanxingdui there are no more known sacrificial pits containing ritual bronzes in the Sanxingdui style. Virtually all the metallic remains from the early Zhou period in Shu are specimens of weaponry. Bronze weapons from various Shu sites show the Sichuanese becoming more self-contained during the Western Zhou period. Halberd blades in particular have been meticulously studied. The armaments were wrought in adherence to Shang and early Zhou models, in patterns that later fell out of vogue on the central plains but persisted for several more centuries among the Shu. In Sichuan, these became a markedly local tradition as Shu metallurgists continued to draw inspiration from the increasingly outdated northern models they had on hand.[97]

Shang period examples are found at Chenggu in the upper Han valley and at Baoji on the upper Wei River, both in Shaanxi.[98] The blades from Shuiguanyin all conform to the same range of shapes, subdivided into four types collectively known as the Shu style. Shu style halberd blades are isosceles triangular; that is, symmetrical in shape and relatively narrow from the top to the bottom edge. Eight halberd blades found cached at Zhuwajie also are of the derivative Shu style. All the various Shu style subtypes were superseded by other forms outside Sichuan.[99]

Within Sichuan, the Shu style of halberd evolved on its own course through. the tenth, ninth, and early eighth centuries B.C., the time known as the Western Zhou period. Blades remained triangular but became rather wider, like large arrowheads. This shape diverged noticeably from contemporary evolution on the central plains. There, the lower edges of halberd heads came to deviate from the triangular, developing into a long curved taper (called a *hu*), resembling the cutting blade of a scyth. This development north of Sichuan probably owed something to the ample combat experience of endemic central plains warfare. But in the Sichuan basin by the end of the western Zhou period the Shu had apparently fallen out of touch. A few hundred years after Muye they still disposed a panoply of blades a bit wider but still very similar to weapons in use at the time of that decisive battle and lacking the scythlike curve.[100] Contact had become rarer, if not actually ceasing altogether.

The evolution of workmanship on swords and spear points recapitulates that of halberds in tracing a Shu technological debt to the north followed by relative stagnation in Sichuan itself. Specifically, a northwestern bronze short sword variety featuring a typical "willow leaf" (*liu ye*)–shaped blade was precursor to Shu swords. Spear points from the Zhuwajie cache are derivative of middle and late Shang types such as those found at Chenggu, Shaanxi; in their turn the Zhuwajie points may be placed in a stylistic progression leading to subsequent Shu spear point examples elsewhere on the Chengdu plain.[101] Another has been found on the high plateau area northwest of Chengdu.[102] As with the halberd blades, these weapons exhibit peculiarities identifying them as Shu manufactures.

Although much of central plains high culture had close parallels among the Shu, the latter people remained culturally distinct. *Shu wang ben ji*, albeit a late source, described them, as noted, "wearing their hair in a knotted style, fastening their garments on the left, and ignorant of proper ritual." So the Shu were different. Their foreignness is evident too in that they were said by another classical source not to possess surnames. That is, the Shu aristocracy were considered somehow outside the family, despite their putative descent from the mythical Yellow Emperor.[103]

Among other dissimilarities was an apparent absence of chariots. Shu bronze weaponry may have been inspired by Shang and early Zhou prototypes, but the central plains manner of chariot warfare does not seem to have been pursued south of the Qinling and Daba Mountains in Sichuan. At least, no chariot burials have been reported, although they are known in the north. Charioteering was a notable feature of Shang and Zhou high culture. It could be that these battle wagons were unsuited to the alternately hilly and soggy terrain of Sichuan, but if they lacked chariots, the Shu lords must have seemed pedestrian to their northern counterparts.

Even more critical than the absence of chariots, for the purposes of history, is the lack of writing. Bronze and other objects of native Shu manufacture do not feature readable inscriptions in the language of the central plains. This means that following the Muye battle, the Shu again recede into blurry protohistory. The only sources focusing particularly on them are much later works, *Shu wang ben ji* and *Hua yang guo zhi*. What history these texts offer must be gleaned from a matrix of legendary lore. For early Shu the record offers little beyond naming a few royal persons. After the first Shu king, Cancong, the texts give the names of two successors, Baihuo and Yufu, who settled near a Mt. Jian, roughly sixty kilometers northwest of Chengdu. Nothing more is said about either Baihuo or Yufu other than that the Shu worshipped them as deities following their deaths.[104]

Apart from the meager pickings in *Shu wang ben ji* and *Hua yang guo zhi*, only a few questionable references to a *shu* appear elsewhere in early Zhou texts, but these do not indisputably mean the Shu of Sichuan. Three problematical instances should be examined, for their possible historical significance as relates to Shu during the Western Zhou centuries. They consist of two spare mentions among classical writings and a Zhou bronze inscription.

One occurrence of *shu*, in *Yi zhou shu*, recounts a Zhou follow-up expedition in the wake of the Muye battle, against "Mo, Xuanfang, and Shu."[105] A substantial prisoner haul was taken after a campaign lasting just five days. Given the brevity of the episode, commentators assumed this particular *shu* was not that in Sichuan, but rather fairly close to Muye. It has been identified with a small locality, Shuting, in Taian county, Shandong province, a place known independently from the *Zuo zhuan*, a later Zhou text.[106]

A similar problem of identifying and locating "Shu" also comes up in an inscription of 182 characters on a bronze vessel called the Ban *gui*. The Ban *gui* was cast sometime during the eleventh–tenth century B.C. Western Zhou reigns of either King Cheng, King Mu, or King Zhao.[107] Its inscription offers an authentic glimpse into a period for which source materials are not abundant and for Shu are rarer still. According to this inscription, the king (i.e., either Cheng, Mu, or Zhao) commended Ban, the earl of Mao, to assume duties formerly performed by an earlier duke and to serve devotedly as a model ruler for the "four quarters" (*si fang*) of the realm.

Four characters follow: *bing, fan, shu*, and *chao*. After these four characters, the remaining Ban *gui* text records the earl's fulfillment of a royal order to pacify territories east of the Zhou capital. The Ban *gui*'s possible relevance to Shu lies in how the four characters *bing, fan, shu*, and *chao* are interpreted. All four may be read as place names, specifying respective points of the four quarters. In this version, *shu* is identified with Shu of the Chengdu plain and upper Han valley, whereas Bing, Fan, and Chao are also taken to lie at remote extremities of the Zhou world.[108]

An alternative reading takes issue, however, considering the four characters as a clause with the earl of Mao as its subject and *bing* not as a place name, but a verb meaning "to govern" or "to hold." In this view Fan, Shu, and Chao do not specify points of the four quarters and need not be placed too remotely from Zhou. Rather, all three may be locations on the north China plain that the king is giving in fief to the earl.[109]

The interpretation is crucial for Sichuan history, because it relates to the status of Shu vis-à-vis the Western Zhou court during the centuries following Muye. If Shu was one of the far "four quarters" in the Zhou world-view, this implies a close continuing relationship, despite the great distances involved. On the other hand, if the Ban gui's shu signifies merely a small locality, perhaps in Shandong or Shanxi, then the bronze inscription is irrelevant to Sichuan. The dilemma remains unresolved in the absence of new evidence.

One other text, the annalistic Zhu shu ji nian, makes mention of a "Shu." In its chronology of events during the Zhou, envoys from this Shu and a place called Lu are recorded as having presented jade offerings at the Yellow River in the second year of Zhou King Yi; that is, 893 B.C.[110] Again the problem revolves around which Shu is meant. If Sichuan, then Shu may be considered a member of the Zhou polity, dutifully trekking from afar to offer obeisance in terms of established protocol . But the text's reason for listing Shu in association with Lu is not clear unless the two were separately and coincidentally carrying out the same ritual. This Lu was located in southern Henan, much closer to the Shandong Shu of Zuo zhuan than to Sichuan.[111] If a direct connection between Shu and Lu is implied, then the Zhu shu ji nian annal entry does not likely mean Sichuan.

For the Western Zhou years, the Yi zhou shu, Ban gui bronze inscription, and Zhu shu ji nian references to a "Shu" may well have no bearing at all on Sichuan. The possible existence of one or more other places called Shu, apart from Sichuan, inhibits the use of these texts and inscriptions without cautious reserve.[112]

If in the present context these three questionable references are set aside, the picture that remains is one of a Shu slipping out of contact with the central plains during the Western Zhou years. By the Spring and Autumn period in the north, Shu was virtually absent from northern chronicles and played no role in the alliance systems among Zhou vassals.[113] It would be overstating the case to say Shu was totally, utterly cut off from the north, but the lack of unequivocal textual references, and the narrow stylization in bronze workmanship, together point to a diminution of contacts across the Qinling Mountains.

Notwithstanding the disappearance of Shu from surviving Zhou

period texts, Shu itself did not disappear. For reasons unknown Sanxingdui declined in significance, and was perhaps even abandoned.
But the society that had made Sanxingdui a cult center and no doubt
also a political center could not simply vanish. It endured as an entity
in western Sichuan, the Shu people practicing agriculture over a wide
area. Shu smiths perpetuated their own bronze subtradition despite
their isolation from central plains stimuli. Western Sichuan metallurgy may have been inspired originally by Shang or Zhou examples and
even derivative. But the Shu were not, in the end, dependent on their
erstwhile northern neighbors for the continuance of metal working in
Sichuan. And Shu ceramics in the post-Sanxingdui period show a
clear continuity with those of the final Sanxingdui stages, albeit with
modifications, a greater proportion of wheel-thrown pieces, and the
appearance of some entirely new vessel types undocumented at
Sanxingdui.[114] What followed during the ensuing Sichuan centuries
was clearly an outgrowth of the society now best known from Sanxingdui.

Shu in Transition

In the absence of other accounts, the semilegendary texts *Shu
wang ben ji* and *Hua yang guo zhi*, ch. 3, remain the principal written
information on Shu after the Western Zhou period. Both texts give
the name Duyu as successor to Cancong, Baihuo, and Yufu, the rulers of Shu. This Duyu was said to have seized control at some juncture during the first half of the first millennium B.C., although just
when is not precisely dated. The name Duyu thereafter may refer to a
subsequent line of kings.[115] Like his predecessors, Duyu ruled as
"king" (*wang*) but also took on an additional title, Wang Di, signifying
both sovereignty and exalted, even semidivine pretentions. It thus
would seem that the Shu under Duyu owed no fealty to the faraway
Zhou monarch. Mythical elements still cling to accounts of Shu
rulers; Duyu's consort, Li, supposedly issued forth from a well at a
place called Zhuti, on the upper Yangtze.[116]

Duyu adopted an itinerant style of rule, governing lands around
Mt. Min near the upper Min River but also ruling from Jushang, the
location of which is not ascertainable (perhaps this was Sanxingdui),
and from a town at Pi, near Chengdu. There was "much shifting back
and forth" by the Shu among these sites, a phrase that could imply
a transitional mixed economy combining upland pastoral trans-
humance with some farming on the Chengdu plain. Alternatively,
the shifting might mean an occasional move of the king's mobile

court. The economic trend tended toward more cultivation, though, and Duyu is credited with "teaching the people agriculture."[117]

Duyu controlled an expanse comprising, from north to south, the upper Min River area, the Bao and Xie defiles through the Qinling range, the Chengdu plain, Xionger (modern Qingshen, between Chengdu and Emei), Mt. Emei, and the upper Yangtze with some local tributary streams. *Hua yang guo zhi* even says Duyu considered the southern lands his "garden," implying not only considerable territorial breadth but some degree of economic integration throughout the Shu lands.[118] Beyond those limits of control or political sway, Shu played a role in transmitting aspects of northern culture, such as weaponry, to peoples still farther south.

Artifact finds attest to this Shu function in transferring technology. At Huili, in southwesternmost Sichuan close to Yunnan province, a stone mold for making trianguar Shu-style bronze halberd blades has been found. Actual blades from Yunnan include triangular examples but these bear decoration of a distinctive southern variety, that of the Dian culture. Still other Shu-style halberd blades are known from Guizhou province. In Yunnan and Guizhou, the northern cultural elements that had filtered through Shu melded with those of a very different, southeast Asian world.[119] However, it is on the Chengdu plain that Shu life was concentrated in terms of both population and political authority.

Shu at the end of Duyu dynastic rule, that is, into the Spring and Autumn period, was a sprawling land, large when compared to Yellow River states nominally vassal to the Zhou. It possessed an agricultural base exploiting fertile lands and some urban settlements or ritual centers, but there is no evidence yet of a specie economy. Writing probably did not come into active use until sometime later. A paucity of data inhibits comment on the internal bonds holding Shu together beyond acknowledging the obviously compelling authority of those leaders on whose behalf the treasure pits of Sanxingdui were furnished. The social dynamics and political life of Shu may become more apparent when Sanxingdui, Chengdu, and the other towns yield up more of their buried secrets.

What is clear is that the Shu were a distinct people, not full participants in the Zhou polity although they had early on adopted some material culture from countries on the loess plateau and central plains. They could not readily bask in the steady light of Zhou civilization, because the height of the Qinling Mountains blocked most of its rays. The Shu of about 1100–770 B.C. sheltered rather in the Zhou penumbra.

So the Muye campaign had represented a high point in Shu contact with the outside. Ties between the Zhou and Shu subsequently attenuated, diminishing to near insignificance by the eighth century B.C. In 770 B.C., an event occurred to place Zhou itself yet farther away from Shu, geographically. Pressure by frontier raiders in that year compelled the Zhou monarch to abandon his ancestral Shaanxi homeland and relocate eastward to a new capital, at Luoyang in present Henan province on the central plains near the Yellow River. Meanwhile a new power, the semibarbarous but loyal state of Qin, covered the royal retreat and then replaced Zhou as master of the former Zhou lands in Shaanxi.

Whatever dealings Qin may have had with Shu, they left little or no trace in the archaeological record, and no Qin relations with Shu are recorded for the whole Spring and Autumn period.[120] The upstart Qin dukes' rise to prominence did not lend them sufficient prestige to exact Shu allegience. At this time Qin owed nothing to Shu, nor Shu to Qin. As for any continued Shu contacts with the displaced Zhou, these would have had to traverse Qin territory after 770 B.C.[121] No such contacts are attested in the textual sources. The poverty of material remains also bears out a rupture between western Sichuan and the central plains.

In the eighth century B.C., higher East Asian culture still remained the property of royal or ducal courts. Cities amounted to administrative and ceremonial support centers built around palaces. Literacy was an esoteric skill all but limited to some few court annalists. There existed as yet neither a cash economy nor entrepreneurship such as later emerged. Costly crafts involving specialized techniques, like bronze casting, depended on royal or noble patronage. Relations between aristocratic courts were conducted on a formal, strictly hierarchical basis, an arrangement evident in Zhou ritual texts. When the obtrusive dukes of Qin interposed their court between Shu and the Zhou to disrupt an already weakening bond, the redrawn political geography only spelled deeper isolation for Shu.

Shu isolation is archaeologically attested in the localized, rather stagnant style of its bronze working, as seen in the continued manufacture of halberd blades that were obsolete by central plains standards. Textual evidence is negative, the complete absence of references in Spring and Autumn period texts all but confirming Shu exclusion from northern political consciousness. Neither the *Chun qiu, Zuo zhuan*, nor *Guo yu* chronicles contain a single allusion to Shu in Sichuan for the entire two and one-half century span from 722 to 481 B.C. These are the major sources for the time, offering a year-by-year account of aristocratic intrigues and geopolitical trends. Their omission of Shu is conspicuous but understandable. When Zhou power ebbed eastward and Qin arose, Shu was cut off from the north.

With Shu lapsed into obscurity and absent from the pages of history, the only textual information on the place is that provided by fable. One tale records a dynastic transition, telling of how Bieling, a man from Chu, became king of Shu.[122] This happened sometime around 666 B.C.[123] Chu lay along the middle course of the Yangtze, in Hubei and Hunan, downriver from Sichuan. From its location Chu straddled two worlds, that of Zhou civilization in the north and a native, southern cultural sphere. Like Qin, Chu exemplified the rising strength of states peripheral to the Yellow River and central plains geopolitical core zone.

Nothing is known of Bieling's life or status in Chu. The texts provide only a concise, matter-of-fact account saying that he perished but the corpse then could not be located. It floated, however implausibly upstream against the current, to Shu. Eventually reaching Pi, a town in Shu, the cadaver came to life again face to face with King Duyu. As it happened, Duyu was at that time struggling with an uncontrollable flood. Duyu deputized this now resurrected Bieling to cope with the waters, and when he succeeded, Duyu commended the country over to him and departed.[124] Bieling became progenitor of the Kaiming dynasty, lasting twelve generations as Shu sovereigns.

The Bieling tale in Shu is an obvious parallel to the northern myth in which Kings Yao and Shun entrusted flood control to Gun, father of Yu the Great. When Yu took over from Gun and successfully channeled the rampaging waters, Shun endowed him with the kingdom. It is an idealized parable of riteous and orderly succession in government, transplanted to Sichuan with the names changed.[125] A later source offers an alternative version, stating that the Kaiming kings first occupied the far south of Shu before ascending the Min River toward the Chengdu plain and there taking over from Duyu.[126]

Although not strictly historical, this account may be taken as a metaphor marking the start of a new era in Shu, during which influences from downstream Yangtze areas began to play a role. The name *Kaiming* literally means "the opening of brightness" and thus pointedly marks a new beginning. It is evident archaeologically that Shu under the Kaimings did indeed take on many elements of southern culture, from Ba in eastern Sichuan and from Chu still farther east.

After Bieling came the Kaiming monarchs Cong Di and Lu Di. Under Lu Di, Shu is said to have attacked Qin to the north, reaching

Qin's then capital of Yong on the Wei River in Shaanxi. The Kaimings also probed west along the inner Asian frontier of Sichuan, expanding into the Qingyi area.[127] Ba influences grew more apparent in Shu, resulting in an invigorated hybrid Ba-Shu culture. Stimulated by these contacts with Ba, Shu experienced too the indirect impact of accelerating historical trends on the central plains.

Something of a ripple effect occurred. During the late Spring and Autumn period and the following Warring States period Shu adjoined Ba, which in turn felt a heavy influence from the central Yangtze state of Chu. Chu was a major player in Zhou dynasty interstate politics. Thus Sichuanese history coalesced again with that of the Zhou community of states. Meanwhile the background of Ba, as one-half of the Ba-Shu culture, requires telling in its own right.

Ba and the Ba-Shu Culture

Ba comprised several confederated peoples living along the Han River and by the Jialing and Yangtze Rivers in eastern Sichuan. Remembered for their legendary ferocity in battle, the Ba are tangibly known from their bronze weapons and war drums. When they enter into historical chronicles the record is of armed confrontation with Chu, a mighty state straddling the middle Han and Yangtze. Valor notwithstanding, the Ba were forced westward by Chu deeper into Sichuan, toward Shu. A shared Ba-Shu culture then evolved from their contact. Among its other accomplishments the mixed Ba-Shu society practiced an incipient form of literacy unique to Sichuan. This script remains undeciphered, but archaeology, etymology, and classical texts have all offered clues on the Ba peoples and the Ba-Shu culture.

Eastern Sichuan in Prehistory

The upper Yangtze has been a home to humans at least since late paleolithic times. At Tongliang, forty kilometers from Chongqing, a fossil humerus was found in 1975 along with ten stone scraping implements. This sole reported paleolithic discovery in eastern Sichuan hardly constitutes a significant sample from which to draw sweeping conclusions, yet it is worth noting that the Tongliang tools are different in workmanship from those collected farther west at Liyuqiao, near Ziyang.[1]

Daxi, a point on the south bank of the Yangtze some sixty kilometers west of the Sichuan-Hubei provincial line, is the type site for a neolithic culture straddling the Yangtze gorges. The Daxi culture has been documented at nearly twenty locations in eastern Sichuan and western Hubei. All Daxi culture sites are situated either on the Yangtze's banks or close by. The culture lasted from the sixth millennium through most of the fourth millennium B.C., during which time there

MAP 4

Sites of Ba and the Ba-Shu culture

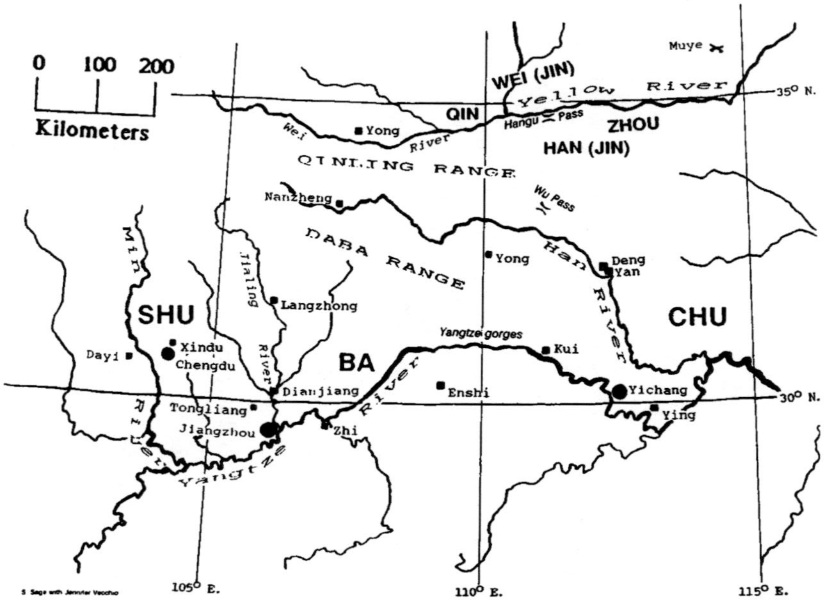

were at least five successive stages.[2] Even at the earlier stages Daxi people were consuming and probably cultivating rice, a surmise based on the grain husks commonly found as temper in their pottery clay.[3]

The predominantly red, hand-modeled pottery from the early and middle Daxi stages betrays some lower Yangtze cultural influences. As time went on, the Daxi people gradually switched to fashioning more wheel-thrown black pottery, some examples of which resemble wares of the Qujialing culture on the lower and middle Han valley. Ceramic likenesses are evident in vessel shapes, color, and decoration, indicating significant Daxi contacts eastward. Paralleling the changes in pottery over time, a refinement in Daxi polished stone tools also is apparent. As elsewhere, these tended toward smaller size and more refined workmanship in the middle and later stages.

Within Sichuan, the Daxi culture exerted an influence on local neolithic cultures along the Jialing River.[4] Outside Sichuan and Hubei, certain features recalling Daxi practices are noted as well. For instance, some Daxi burial styles were duplicated in later inhumations from north central China, and Daxi-like motifs can be seen on ceramic decoration as far north as the Yellow River–based Yangshao culture.[5] Despite such evidence of cross-cultural fertilization, nothing definite can be stated of the Daxi people's ethnic identity or why, after over 2,000 years in eastern Sichuan, the Daxi culture ceased to exist about 3300 B.C. Crockery is no substitute for historical texts, and of the latter, the Daxi people left none.

Following the Daxi culture's final stage, ongoing contacts between eastern Sichuan and downstream regions went on as before, facilitated by the nearby riverine access. A certain continuity is noted by some between Daxi and the Qujialing culture along the middle course of the Han River in central and northwestern Hubei.[6] It has also been suggested that the Ba people were descended from those of the Qujialing culture, but without ceramic sequences to back up the contention.[7]

However, much less is known about who immediately replaced the Daxi folk within Sichuan in areas along the Yangtze. A neolithic culture noted in the region around Wanxian was apparently not connected with Daxi. And northeastern Sichuan artifacts may be related to those of the Longshan culture in its Shaanxi version, but are distinguished from Daxi, particularly as regards pottery.[8]

Certain pottery remains in eastern Sichuan suggest relations with the Chengdu plain during the heyday of activity at the Sanxingdui, Yangzishan, and Shuiguanyin sites there; that is, contemporary with the protohistoric Xia and then the historical Shang and Zhou periods farther north.[9] At some time in this long twilight between prehistory and the recorded historical past, legends record that a group called the Ba arrived in eastern Sichuan.

Ba Origins

Sources for Ba origins, like those about the Shu, include a share of obviously contrived myths as well as certain legends that may convey bits of historical information. The mythical genealogies can be disposed of first. These tie the Ba to Chinese tradition via patriarchal figures, in this case Fuxi and the Yellow Emperor. *Shan hai jing*, a repository of dubious geographic lore, refers to Fuxi by his dynastic title Tai Hao. "In the southwest there is the country of Ba. Tai Hao begat Xianniao, Xianniao begat Chengli, Chengli begat Houzhao; and Houzhou was the first man of Ba."[10] Fuxi is honored elsewhere as the first domesticator of animals, but no other extant sources make any mention of Houzhou or a Ba descent from Fuxi. It would appear that *Shan hai jing* offers just a genealogical fiction not unlike those locating Shu antecedents on branches of the same Chinese family tree. Another seemingly invented genealogy, in *Hua yang guo zhi*, traces Ba along with Shu to the Yellow Emperor and Gaoyang, also known as Zhuanxu, thereby making them cousins of people in Shu.[11]

A separate Ba origin story meriting more serious attention was preserved in the geographic text *Shui jing zhu* and in a chapter of the Latter Han dynasty history, *Hou han shu*, with certain details appearing in other sources.[12] According to this account, at some unspecified time, five clans (*shi*) dwelt at a place called Wuluozhongli Mountain. These were the Ba, Fan, Tan, Xiang, and Zheng. The mountain contained two caves, colored black and red. Members of four clans were born in the black cave, but Ba clansmen were delivered in the red cave. A word pronounced *ba* in some eastern Sichuan dialects supposedly means "cave," which could account for the Ba name according to scholarly conjecture.[13] Wuluozhongli may be Mt. Hen, in southwestern Hubei province. Polished stone tools have been found in habitable caves there, but any connection with the Ba must on present evidence remain a matter of faith.[14]

As the story continues, at the outset the five Wuluozhongli clans had no overall leader so they selected one via a series of two contests. The first contest had competitors toss a sword at a hole in a rock, but a Ba clansman named Wuxiang scored the only bull's eye. In a second competition the object was to build a floatable earthen boat. Again only Wuxiang's boat proved worthy, so he earned chieftainship and thereafter was known by the title Linjun.[15] His paramouncy among the five clans then extended the Ba name to cover all of them.

Linjun navigated his earthen boat up the Yishui, an old name for the Qing River of southwestern Hubei.[16] At a place called Yanyang he encountered a goddess. She called attention to the broad lands around, rich in fish and salt, and invited Linjun to settle and share this wealth. But Linjun coveted it all, so he declined her proposal to merely share. Aggressively defending her property, the goddess transformed herself into an insect and bid a swarm of such creatures fly forth and blot out the sun's rays. Darkness descended. For many days Linjun waited and observed, at length seizing a chance to shoot her with an arrow whereupon the light returned.

Linjun then established the town of Yicheng where the Ba and their four subject clans settled down. After his death, Linjun's soul returned in the incarnation of a white tiger. Ba ritual accordingly entailed giving tigers human blood to drink, says the account given in *Hou han shu*. Yicheng has been identified with the site of present-day Enshi in Hubei, just south of the Sichuan frontier.[17] From there an easy passage leads to eastern Sichuan via the Peiling River (now called the Wu River), which flows into the Yangtze at the present town of Peiling (a.k.a. Fuling).

Peiling, known as Zhi in *Hua yang guo zhi*, became the first Ba center within Sichuan and the reputed burial site of the earliest Ba kings to rule there.[18] Situated at the confluence of the Peiling and Yangtze Rivers, Peiling was an ideal point from which the Ba could begin advancing along water routes to other districts of eastern Sichuan. Their expansion subsumed some of the peoples encountered, including the Pu, Zong, Zu, Gong, Nu Rang, Yi, and Dan tribes.[19] So *Ba* really refers to a confederation of different groups.

Although this migration tale neatly deposits the Ba in eastern Sichuan where they are known from historical material, its principal weakness is the lack of a time frame. Ba artifacts were abundant in western Hubei by eastern Zhou times, that is, the Spring and Autumn period, but their incidence does not confirm the legendary version of a Ba origin in that area.[20] Moreover, the Linjun tale is difficult to mesh with other clues indicating a Ba homeland on the Han River north of the Yangtze, rather than in Hubei south of the Yangtze.[21]

As in the case of Shu origins, the picture is complicated by evidence from Shang oracle bone inscriptions. Among the thirteenth century B.C. writings on bone from the Shang capital at Anyang is a character that some authorities read as *ba*, occurring in the compound *ba fang*, or "Ba country."[22] This would indicate a place inhabited by an independent people on the periphery of the Shang realm. The two readable *ba fang* inscriptions tell of a contemplated expedition against the Ba. It seems Wu Ding, king of the Shang, sought guidance via the oracle regarding whether the royal consort should have a general named Xi invade the Ba country from a place called Chi. The attack was to be part of a coordinated campaign with the king himself commanding another wing of the Shang army. For this reading to be credible the putative *ba* must be within striking distance of the Shang base. Southwestern Hubei and southern Sichuan, the setting for the Linjun story, would seem too far out of reach.

One explanation gets around the discrepancy by suggesting that *ba fang* was situated in the upper Han River valley in the Shang period and that only subsequently, during the Spring and Autumn period, did the Ba follow the Han River downstream toward Wuluozhongli, presumed to have been in Hubei.[23] A bronze cache of late Shang or early Zhou date from Chenggu, on the upper Han, is identified by some archaeologists as having belonged to the Ba.[24] The pieces, goblets and shallow vessels, are in a markedly Shang style with *tao tie* demon mask relief decoration in angular volute.

But typically Ba artifacts are documented along the upper Han for later times as well, particularly the fifth and fourth centuries B.C. The name Fan, one of the five clans at Wuluozhongli, even appears on a Ba bronze signature seal of Han dynasty date unearthed at present-day Feng county in the Han valley, southern Shaanxi province; that is, far from Hubei.[25] Interpreting all this to fit migration theories becomes complicated; either a retrograde movement occurred back to the upper Han River area, or some Ba never left. Therefore, any hypothetical Ba peregrinations in the protohistoric era remain little better than conjecture.

The speculation is in some measure spurred on by an urge for historiographic tidiness. Situating the supposed "Ba country" of oracle bones in the upper Han valley lends support to a tradition whereby the Ba, like the Shu, participated in the Zhou campaign to overthrow Shang power. The *Shang shu* source on this campaign fails to mention Ba among the eight allies of Zhou who fought in the culminating battle of Muye. However, a people called the Pu were there, and these Pu are sometimes considered a constituent or subordinate of the Ba.[26]

Subsequent accounts do place braves of the Ba per se at the scene of this milestone event. Muye represented the inception of

Zhou rule and later was looked upon as a key politically legitimizing episode. Its significance as such lasted for many centuries, gathering an accretion of sentiment that eventually outweighed whatever may have actually transpired long before on the field of combat.[27]

Therefore, it is not surprising to have later texts arranging a place for Ba on the winning side at Muye. *Ba zhi*, the history of Ba in *Hua yang guo zhi*, states that Ba braves performed war chants and dances before the battle to intimidate the Yin (i.e., Shang) troops, resuming the celebration with more singing and dancing after their victory. *Yi zhou shu* mentions the Ba along with other peoples such as the Qiang and the Shu who presented exotic birds to the Zhou king some time after Muye.[28]

The chronicle *Zuo zhuan* does offer some indirect evidence for an early Ba association with the Zhou, perhaps as far back as Muye. Centuries thereafter, the Zhou still recalled that, following the Muye campaign, Ba became one of the southern lands loyal to Zhou King Wu.[29] Subsequent Ba relations with the Zhou house indeed seem to have been even more cordial than those between the Shu and the Zhou. The Zhou dynasty bestowed its royal surname, Ji, upon some of the Ba aristocracy and took Ba women as wives.[30] This made the Ba in-laws and country cousins to the Zhou, giving them a reason to keep in touch even as the Shu receded into obscurity at the western side of the Sichuan basin.

As observed, the population under Ba control was far from homogenous, with several sources mentioning various constituent groups. There were the five separate clans at Wuluozhongli and then yet another set of peoples absorbed by the Ba in Sichuan. Searching for a single Ba origin therefore may be futile. If some of the Ba really did enter Sichuan with Linjun from Hubei, another segment can just as plausibly be linked to the Han valley, closer to the Zhou and the Shang. Some Han valley groups who came under Ba domination may have earlier been related to the Shu.[31] Yet diversity notwithstanding, a basic Ba cultural identity did manifest itself, and can be identified archaeologically in eastern Sichuan and surrounding areas.

Ba Culture

Ba territory "extended east to Yufu and west to Bodao, touching Hanzhong on the north, and reaching Qianpei to the south."[32] That ancient description takes in eastern Sichuan and some adjacent lands of the present Shaanxi, Hubei, and Guizhou provinces. The Yangtze served as a fluid corridor flowing through Ba and connecting it to

Chu, the growing power downriver. In addition to the Yangtze was the Han River. A Ba presence along the Han permitted Ba a marginal role in the Zhou community of statelets during the Spring and Autumn period. In particular, Ba touched on both Chu and Qin in the Han valley, with the results not always friendly. This Han valley zone between Sichuan and the Zhou civilization later would figure significantly in history.

Within Sichuan, the principal Ba settlements named in *Hua yang guo zhi* arose around the confluence of major streams. First among these was Peiling, where the Ba rulers were said to have been entombed.[33] Another junction was at Jiangzhou, later to be called Baxian (Ba county), close to the present site of Chongqing.[34] Located near where the northward-flowing Qian and southward-flowing Jialing Rivers converge with the Yangtze, it was a natural and inevitable hub of communication and control.

The Jialing enters Sichuan from Shaanxi province and then nearly bisects the Sichuan basin flowing southward before meeting the Yangtze. Occupation of its length meant Ba command over eastern Sichuan just as the Shu position along the Min River guaranteed authority over the western Sichuan basin. Significant Ba sites eventually developed along the Jialing, at Dianjiang (modern Hechuan) where the waters of two important tributaries join with the Jialing, and further north at Langzhong. Langzhong was particularly well situated for contact with Shu and with the state of Qin.[35]

The impression of the Ba conveyed by textual sources is that of a bellicose folk who adopted the tiger as a totem, recalling the beast's mythical association with the Ba hero and founder Linjun. Their war chants and dances were widely famous.[36] In addition to fighting well these people seem to have lived well. Paddy rice culture was developed but the Ba also pursued a mixed economy, planting a variety of grains, raising several types of domestic beasts, feeding silkworms on mulberry trees, and cultivating hemp, the lac tree for lacquer, and tea. They reportedly fished and hunted wildfowl, turtles, and rhinoceros. Other alleged Ba products included bronze, iron, and salt as well as certain valued medicinal herbs.[37]

Grave goods have been recovered at sites near Chongqing and Peiling, giving some notion of Ba cultural life, albeit in Warring States times and a bit later. Tombs of nearby peoples also revealed certain features of Ba influence. Nearly all the tangible evidence is from inhumations since no settlements to compare with Sanxingdui in Shu have yet been excavated, nor is any well-described sequence of ceramic wares available for study.[38] The odd specimens of pottery that can be examined are mainly hand-shaped with only very few wheel-thrown, unpainted pieces. Apart from pottery, the other mundane but informative debris of an ordinary village are still unavailable. What material evidence does exist on the Ba within the frontiers of Sichuan usually is of a later date than Ba remains in western Hubei along the middle Han and Yangtze Rivers.[39]

Without any documented settlement sequences, a holistic view of Ba society is not yet obtainable, but impressions of the Ba can be derived from their distinctive bronzes and other objects. Several characteristic Ba bronze items reveal something of Ba values and beliefs. Warfare seemingly assumed the paramount place among those values. Objects include the unique Ba bronze war drums and the bronze swords, pikes, battleaxes, and halberd blades that made up Ba weaponry.

Ba bronze war drums, known as *chun yu*, are found in eastern Sichuan and the adjacent provinces of Guizhou, Yunnan, Hunan, and Hubei with rarer examples coming from as far afield as Anhui.[40] Although some slight stylistic variations have been described, the drums all conform to a standard gourdlike shape with a narrow base bulging to a wider diameter near the top. Top and bottom surfaces are flat. Smaller *chun yu* are about twenty-seven centimeters in height, ten centimeters base diameter, and thirteen centimeters top diameter; larger drums might double those dimensions. A bronze figurine of a crouching tiger, the Ba totem beast, usually surmounts the drum. The smaller drums are sufficiently portable to accompany troops on expeditions, which would account for their widespread incidence.[41]

The drums are attested in historical sources from the Spring and Autumn period and their function as a military signaling device is well established. In the field they were used together with a kind of resonant gong (*zheng*) to create contrasting sounds for communicating at a distance even amidst the din of battle.[42] Along with the Ba war chants and dances, an intimidating effect on the enemy would also be likely. Ba *chun yu* may be an adaptation into bronze from a kind of drum earlier produced in ceramic on the central plains.[43] However, the *chun yu* also appear related to the widespread bronze drums (*tong gu*) of the southwestern Yunnan, Guangxi, and Guizhou provinces, drums that also often are topped with crouching animal figurines. These latter are typically southern, arising out of a bronze-working tradition distinct from that of the northern, central plains culture area.[44]

Just as the *chun yu* drums constituted an identifying Ba cultural artifact, so did their armory feature a particular type of edged bronze

FIGURE 8

A Ba *chun yu* drum. (Chongqing Municipal Museum)

weapon. These blades range in length from about thirty to nearly sixty centimeters and are perforated at the haft to facilitate mounting to a grip, but they lack pommels and guards. Their derivation from central plains styles is apparent, but a tiger motif engraved on many pieces clearly distinguishes them as belonging to the Ba. The distribution of these blade finds in eastern Sichuan and adjacent lands conforms to the extent of Ba territory according to textual data. Such Ba-style swords are differentiated from a southeast Asian type of bronze sword found in Yunnan, more ornately decorated, mounted, and having a differently shaped blade ridge.[45] Some time later, in the Warring States period, the Ba blades evolved into a type suitable for mounting on a long shaft in the manner of a pike, or pole arm.[46]

During the Warring States period Ba bronzesmiths developed a varied repertoire of pieces in addition to the drums and blades; most were also military accoutrements. One such item, a decorated helmet, was found in a tomb together with a blade weapon at the Jutang gorge on the Yangtze near the Ba frontier with Chu.[47] From farther down the Yangtze at Jingmen in Hubei comes a *qi* battleaxe blade bearing a four character inscription and an engraved figure in relief, performing what seems to be a war dance. The dancer appears to be wearing a scaly tunic, perhaps a suit of armor, and clutching a fish and a lizard in either hand. Because the battleaxe was found with one of the sword-pike blades, and in view of its dancing motif, the piece has been identified as of Ba provenance.[48]

Ba metal workers cast bronze using copper, tin, antimony, and aluminum in proportions virtually identical to those employed by craftsmen on the central plains.[49] The similarity in metallurgical technique is not surprising, in view of the river communications route ensuring continuous contact. By boating along the Yangtze the Ba could proceed to Chu, and beyond, with much greater ease than the people of Shu experienced in dealing with the community of Zhou states over the Qinling Mountains. Consequently, Ba kept more in touch with ongoing central plains trends than did Shu.

Intermittent fighting with downstream enemies encouraged the importation of arms into Sichuan, and the replication there of imported styles. Another weapon type, the halberd blade (*ge*), marks this process in Ba as it did in Shu. Ba halberds kept abreast of central plains style changes during Spring and Autumn and then Warring States times. Whereas Shu halberd blades continued to be cast for the most part in a triangular shape (*wu hu*), Ba blades were given the curved, scythlike cutting edge (*hu*). Tiger insignia on the halberds often identify them as Ba equipment.[50]

The Ba also developed another cultural feature, one of infinitely greater potential than the marginal advantage of a differently shaped halberd. This was writing. The presence of four engraved characters on a supposed Ba battleaxe from Hubei was noted earlier. A few dozen objects found in Sichuan also carry markings, but they still are not decipherable. These written signs are clearly distinguished from oracle bone, bronze scripts, or any other script on the central plains. Although the markings undoubtedly were intended to impart some meaning, there are no lengthy inscriptions of more than a few signs, no stelae, no monuments, no books. The basis of a literate civilization existed in Sichuan, but just the basis. Ba literacy should be considered an aspect of what might have been, of promise not quite actualized.

The writing is currently known from examples on halberds, spears, and other weapons, as well as from impression seals. Several

FIGURE 9

Undeciphered pictographs from Ba bronze inscriptions. (*Wen wu*, no. 10, 1987, p. 31)

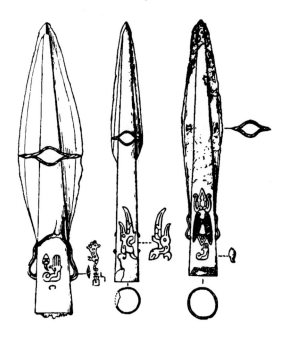

chun yu drums bear signs as do some bells (*zhong*).[51] Systematic efforts at a translation are stymied by the lack of any bilingual texts like the Persian Behistun inscriptions or the Egyptian Rosetta Stone to offer initial clues. Perhaps the idea of writing on the central plains inspired a parallel effort in Ba, but the great majority of Ba characters do not appear derivative from any other script. No complete catalog of all the inscriptions has yet been published, nor can most of them be dated with any degree of precision.[52]

Ba characters are largely but not exclusively, pictographic. They portray birds, panthers, turtles, tigers, fish, plants, human faces and standing human figures, and boats with masts and oars. One pictograph present on both a *chun yu* and a spear shows a human hand and forearm in conjunction with a flower bud. More abstruse signs include something that might be a basket, and a series of three connected circles resembling a constellation of stars.[53] All are distinct from writing in Chu or among the Zhou-affiliated countries of the central plains and loess plateau.

These Ba pictographs consistently adhere to set conventional forms. Recurrently combined symbols such as the hand and flower bud further suggest that the signs are indeed a form of writing, not mere ornamentation. This interpretation is reinforced by the presence of abstract or geometric designs along with the obvious pictographs. Inscriptions usually consist of just one sign with some of two, three, or four signs. Only one example is longer, a lacquer tray found at Changsha, Hunan, with eleven signs. Some of these are also familiar from Ba examples in Sichuan, so the tray is considered to be of Ba origin. Apart from the specimens on impression seals, some magical or mystical significance has been suggested for the script.[54]

Whatever its ultimate potential may have been, the use of script never progressed far enough to grant the Ba a compelling regional advantage in the fields of commerce or political organization. Ba writing betrays a rudimentary quality. Nothing seems to have been set down systematically in the way of record keeping, either for business, legal, or administrative purposes. Perhaps the script had not evolved to a degree capable of accommodating the sophisticated demands of statecraft. The Ba pictographs, so far as can be determined, remained mostly limited to marking weaponry with what might have been nothing more than good luck charms or the names of warriors.

Without a more intensive use of writing, it is legitimate to question how far Ba political institutions advanced toward a true state structure, a level of organization that might have imposed enduring central direction over the various peoples of eastern Sichuan. The written word surely has a unifying capacity provided that a script comes into widespread and systematic use. But the region called Ba remained a political mosaic, a composite of groups and doubtless of languages as well. This ethnic diversity may likely have been a factor retarding the readier acceptance of the script and its deeper development as a tool in government and commerce.[55]

Because the Ba consisted of not one but several lineage and ethnic entities, the sources of Ba culture are varied. Ba writing could be an independent innovation or a result of stimulus diffusion, from the central plains or perhaps another indeterminate direction or directions. Some Ba customs, such as their war chants and dances, were distinctive and famous enough to warrant repeated comment in historical texts over the centuries. Ba war drums appear to betray a distinctly southern cast. Other categories of bronze work, such as several types of Ba weaponry, can be more confidently related to central plains models. This is not surprising as the Ba engaged in armed conflict with states on approaches to the plains. When not at war, Ba maintained political links with those states, with the Zhou royal court, and with countries such as Yelang in the mountains south of Sichuan.

The sophisticated culture of the central plains exerted a strong attraction for these southern Yelang mountaineers, who added to it their own ingredients. On the Han River and in Sichuan, along the banks of the Yangtze, the Ba thereby furthered a process of north-south fusion and adaptation. Without such adaptation central plains culture could never have spread to permeate the broader east Asian civilization. The Ba played an early precursor role anticipating China's march to the tropics.

But the Ba peoples were not alone in creatively adapting the high culture of the north to rest upon a southern firmament. The state of Chu was arising just east, along the lower Han and the Yangtze in Hubei. Chu also merged a southern paddy-rice agricultural base, southern traditions and southern temperament with the stately northern legacy of the Xia, Shang, and Zhou. Chu, itself a cultural hybrid of north and south, would emerge as both the principal Ba mentor and antagonist.

Chu in Sichuan

Chu was expanding. That much is very evident from the chronicle known as the Spring and Autumn Annals, with its interleaved Zuo commentary (*Chun qiu* and *Zuo zhuan*). Chu expansion brought the state into contact with Ba, which in turn brings Ba into the pages of history.[56] Whereas the several episodes involving Ba in *Zuo zhuan* hardly amount to an overflowing fount of information, they stand in contrast to the bare slate on Shu contacts with the outside at the same time. Shu was in virtual eclipse, historically.

Once a Zhou ally, Shu had become only an outlier to Qin, a state long relegated to the Zhou civilization's fringe. But Ba remained, via Chu, at least a bit player in affairs of the Zhou family of states. The events set down in *Zuo zhuan* offer glimpses of how Chu pressured Ba, put an end to Ba power east of the Yangtze River gorges, and eventually breached the gates of Sichuan.

Chu occupied parts of the central plains at its northern limits and extended southward to cover virtually all of Hubei and much of Hunan provinces on the present-day map. Geographically, then, Chu had one foot within, and one outside, the Zhou political community. From the earliest recorded times Chu had been known to the states on the central plains. The name *chu* even appears in oracle bones.[57] Blessed with rich agricultural resources and a wide open southern frontier beckoning expansion, Chu rulers could defy the Zhou kings. By the Spring and Autumn period the Chu noble house had begun to exalt itself, adopting the title *wang*, or king, on a near par with the Zhou sovereign. Chu in fact exerted an almost regal preeminence over its southern neighbors, including Ba.[58]

The emergence of Ba from protohistory into the pages of history proper begins with an incident involving Chu. A vignette from spring, 703 B.C., recounts how a viscount of Ba (*ba zi*) dispatched an emissary named Han Fu to obtain the good offices of Chu in establishing Ba relations with a small but strategically placed statelet, Deng. Located at the present crossroads town of Xiangfan in Hubei province, Deng controlled the juncture of a north-south route and the Han River. A Ba interest in neighborly ties with Deng suggests that the Ba viscount sought to open lines of communication with the central plains farther north. Ba contact with the Zhou capital, set at Luoyang since 770 B.C., would be facilitated by passage through Deng. Significantly, though, Ba made this demarche to Deng only after first clearing it with Chu, the regional power broker.[59]

Chu sent an official to accompany Ba's Han Fu to Deng but their mission met with disaster. On reaching a place called Yu on the southern outskirts of Deng, the two emissaries were robbed and killed by local people. Chu followed up that summer by ordering a combined expeditionary force of Chu and Ba troops to beseige Yu in reprisal. The allied army was placed under the command of a Chu general, Dou Lian. The Deng state meanwhile chose to support Yu. Marching to the relief of Yu, Deng forces attacked the Ba troops. Three times the Ba contingent fell back before Deng assaults, but although they retreated the Ba troops were not subdued. Dou Lian came up to support the Ba force and in combat with the Deng men ordered his Chu troops to feign defeat and retire. The Deng army pursued the Chu soldiers whereupon the Ba troops turned to hit the enemy from behind. Pressed on two sides, the Deng army was routed. The men of Yu then dispersed.

The manner of their achieving joint victory again points out the junior status of Ba in relation to Chu. An allied Ba-Chu army operated under a Chu general, although the Ba portion maintained its own unit integrity. The enemy perceived Ba as the weaker opponent, at least in this tactical context, and attacked the Ba troops first. Yet weakness notwithstanding, the Ba troops preserved discipline and effectively carried out their part of a victorious battle plan. Victory, however, came at the cost of continued Ba ingratiation to Chu. For Ba the Chu factor simply could not be circumvented.

Twenty-eight years later, in 675 B.C., Ba fell out with Chu after a combined operation in western Hubei.[60] Ba forces had helped Chu quell an internal revolt. The scene was Shen, near the Han River in the region between modern Wuhan and Yichang. In the course of this campaign the Ba troops felt sufficiently intimidated by their Chu allies that they too rebelled. The Ba army occupied the nearby town of Nachu and then mauled Chu forces outside Ying, the Chu capital on the Yangtze. Next spring the Chu army sallied forth from the capital to once more confront Ba, but suffered another reverse at Jin, also on the Yangtze.

Although the incident points up Ba prowess and even rashness in war, Chu was too large and powerful even in the seventh century B.C. to be conquered outright by Ba. The aggressive Ba seem to have merely taken advantage of local Chu difficulties in gaining maneuvering room against that potent regional giant. Ba had rankled under the might of Chu, pressed to supply armed Ba contingents to meet Chu needs but watchful for opportunities to wriggle out of the obligation. Cooperation between Ba and Chu seems at best intermittently cordial, at times grudgingly given, and prone to betrayal.

The Chu setback proved only temporary. By 634 B.C. Chu was back in action along the upper Yangtze at Kui, a statelet straddling the river's gorges near the modern Sichuan-Hubei frontier. Kui rulers traced their descent to an offshoot line of the Chu royal house and in times past venerated the same ancestral spirits as Chu. However, these observances had been discontinued. Their cessation by the Kui viscount sacrilegiously challenged Chu authority. Chu punished the impudent lapse by annihilating Kui and carrying off the viscount to Chu.[61] This removed a buffer between Chu and eastern Sichuan.

Then in 611 B.C. Chu suffered a year of hunger that emboldened some peoples in western Hubei to seize the moment and attack the weakened state.[62] Chu launched a riposte through lands of the Pu, a group associated with the Ba. The campaign went well due to the absence of internal cohesion among the Pu, whose towns and villages could not coordinate a proper defense. Chu replenished its food stocks from Pu granaries and advanced up the Han valley toward Yong, another statelet that had turned against Chu during the famine. Both Pu and Yong had a history going back centuries and were among the eight allies helping the Zhou to overthrow Shang power. But the era of smaller states was passing.

Now Chu aimed to eradicate Yong and set Chu power firmly in the Han valley near the present Sichuan-Hubei-Shaanxi provincial junction. Seeking cobelligerents against Yong, Chu found them in the Qin and Ba, as well as some loosely knit southern entities. Bringing together Chu, Qin, and Ba in a common endeavor to eliminate a buffer statelet had portentious significance. Three centuries later these very contenders would be locked in mutual confrontation on the same ground. The conquest of Yong ensured Chu an even more dominant position overlooking Ba and brought Chu into closer proximity with Qin, in Shaanxi. Chu had built a position in eastern Sichuan and along the middle stretch of the Han River.

Ba for its part was also established in the Han valley of Shaanxi and was paying tribute to Qin in the mid-seventh century B.C.[63] Ba swords and halberds, identifiable by their characteristic design, have been recovered at several places in southern Shaanxi, materially attesting to the Ba presence there a bit later in the Warring States period.[64] Ba is relatively well documented during the seventh century, at least insofar as its actions brought it into conflict or cooperation with Chu. That is also when the Kaiming dynasty replaced King Duyu's line in Shu, and the founder of the Kaimings was said to have come to Shu from Chu.[65]

However, the following sixth century is an historical blank for both Ba and Shu, and the fifth century nearly so. One solitary entry for 475 B.C. notes Ba besieging Yu on the Han River near where Chu and Ba had marched together in 703 B.C. By this time Yu had come under the Chu rulers, whose army relieved the town and beat back the Ba force.[66] Information becomes scarcer in the generations after this event, but what is available shows Chu gradually encroaching into Ba territory. Ba insolence toward Chu, shown by its readiness to attack during moments of Chu weakness, provided Chu with reason enough to push into Sichuan and suppress or uproot the source of trouble.

Economic factors may have added a lure of their own. Eastern Sichuan was well provided with salt from fossil brine deposits and the Yangtze afforded a means for transporting this commodity in bulk.[67] The Chu need for metallic ores, mainly copper, tin, and gold, also spurred movement and trade southward and westward toward lands in present Hunan and Guizhou provinces as well as Sichuan.[68] An exchange of goods, at least among elites, can be inferred from the incidence of Chu manufactures in Ba graves.[69] Dynastic diplomacy was an instrument in Chu expansion. During the Warring States period the Ba and Chu houses intermarried, although the sources do not specifically name the princes or princesses involved.[70]

Ba factionalism virtually enticed Chu penetration. One story reports a Ba general, Manzi, appealing to Chu for aid to him during a time of internecine turmoil in Ba. Manzi promised to cede three towns to Chu in return. The king of Chu obliged, and after order was restored sent an envoy to Ba demanding Manzi fulfill his part of the bargain. Manzi apologetically reneged and informed the Chu representative that he would offer his head instead, but no Ba towns. Thereupon he committed suicide. When the decapitated head was brought to the Chu king he remarked that if only he had officials of such caliber he would not require any towns. Manzi's head was buried with honors in Chu, and the torso was interred and venerated in Ba.[71] Even if overdrawn, the tale illustrates the ambiguities in Ba-Chu relations.

Through various means, probably combining force, blandishment, economic pressure, treachery, and noble intermarriage, Chu pushed into eastern Sichuan, and toward Ba lands in the Han valley. Details are lacking on just when each key point passed into Chu hands, but by the middle fourth century B.C. the Ba court had successively abandoned Zhi (Peiling), Jiangzhou (near Chongqing), Dianjiang (Hechuan), and Pingdu (in modern Fengdu county).[72]

Retreating far up the Jialing river, Ba established its final capital at Langzhong, not far from Shu territory and nearer to Qin as well. The towns of Chengdu, Guangdu, and Xindu remained in Shu hands as did a Kaiming period town at Lushan county, in hills west of the Chengdu plain. But much of eastern Sichuan experienced Chu control or influence.[73] Under Chu suzerainty some Ba people and manufactures from eastern Sichuan dispersed into adjoining portions of western Hubei and Hunan, where Ba styles are evident in grave goods.[74] The Xia-li district in Chu's capital city of Ying was settled by Ba expatriates who seem to have practiced their distinctive customs within a kind of reserved residential quarter.[75]

Chu expansion up the Han and Yangtze Rivers into Ba lands is confirmed by odd references in several texts offering data on the Warring States. One instance tells of an attack on Chu by a contingent from Wu, fighting far from its home on the lower Yangtze. The Wu expedition reached Ba and Shu at the western extreme of its march, a very distant point but an appropriate one from which to harass Chu. Elsewhere, Chu is described as having made the Yangtze and Han Rivers its "pond" (*chi*) and encompassing, or enveloping (*bao*), Ba and Shu on the west.[76] A third source says Chu extended along its western reaches from the central Han valley, while holding Ba and Qianzhong (around the Sichuan-Guizhou-Hunan tri-province frontier point) to the south.[77]

The incursion of Chu into eastern Sichuan did not obliterate Ba as an entity but did bring about a decline of Ba power relative to surrounding states and peoples. Relocated at Langzhong, away from the Yangtze in north central Sichuan, the new Ba capital came within the expanding sphere of Qin influence. A change also took place in the ethnic character of Ba, which in any case never had been homogenous. At Langzhong, the Ba court found itself amidst a local people called the Zong, renowned for bravery in battle.[78]

Yet although Chu culture and Chu power penetrated Sichuan the extent to which Chu really exploited Sichuanese territory is uncertain. Economic integration with Chu proper cannot have been complete, because no Chu coinage has been reported from any Sichuan sites. Examples of the Chu script are also lacking. And there exists neither archaeological evidence of any Chu garrisons in Sichuan nor any account of direct clashes between Chu and Qin soldiers when Qin later annexed Shu and Ba in 316 b.c. An offhand remark by a Qin official, purportedly uttered at that time, described the people of Ba and Shu as "following the customs of the Rong and Di."[79] Accurate or not, those were northern tribes, far from Chu. If Chu customs had been widely adopted by the ordinary Sichuanese such a remark would have been unlikely.

Although not amounting to a complete takeover of the Sichuan basin, Chu pressure bore upon Shu directly and indirectly. The Ba retreat westward toward the Chengdu plain had further catalyzed Shu in its reemergence from centuries-long obscurity. Shu ceremonial at the palace of the self-styled Kaiming kings was influenced by Chu royal court music. Given the importance of ritual in arbiting the relationship of man to the cosmos, this is a telling measure of Chu's prestige in Sichuan.[80] Toward the pinnacle levels of Shu society, among those titled few who practiced rites and who could afford to be buried with bronze objects, Chu culture largely represented high culture itself.

Even so, the Kaimings did not limit their foreign contacts only to Chu. Prudence dictated otherwise. In 474 b.c., Shu emissaries presented gifts at the Qin court, the first recorded contact between these neighbors on opposite sides of the Qinling range.[81] Renewed Shu dealings with the north and with Chu thereafter continued on a more sustained basis. The sources reveal no motives for why the Kaiming kings of Shu chose to contact Qin, although a desire to counterbalance both Ba and Chu perhaps served to motivate.

Qin was for some time to come only marginally interested, so Chu still remained the paramount outside force in Sichuan. It was principally Chu that brought the peoples of the Sichuan basin onto a wider tableau. From virtual irrelevance to central plains affairs during the Spring and Autumn era, Shu had begun reintegrating, at a remove, in the geopolitics of the Zhou family of states. Ba acted as the main cultural tutor to Shu in this process although their political dichotomy persisted.

The Ba-Shu Culture

The Chu advance into Sichuan and the Ba retreat westward were but reverberations inside Sichuan of Warring States period developments on the central plains. During this violent era the kind of chronologically precise information available for the preceding Spring and Autumn period ending in 481 B.C. is simply not available. With the paucity of exactly dated documentation, a greater burden rests on whatever can be inferred from excavated material remains. Fortunately, these are present in modest quantity around the Chengdu area, the heart of Shu. Artifacts recovered there confirm the opening of Shu to styles and innovations from Ba and Chu. In Sichuan a period that may be called that of the Ba-Shu culture began sometime in the fifth century B.C. and continued through most of the following fourth century.

The label *Ba-Shu culture* derives from archaeology and refers to the incidence of Ba objects and styles found among those of Shu. Elements from Chu are evident as well in what was a culturally receptive environment. Western Sichuan had been receiving influences from downstream Yangtze areas at least since the Kaiming dynasty in Shu replaced the preceding Duyu kings, but Ba influence becomes more plainly evident only during the fifth and fourth centuries.

Even then, Ba and Shu did not actually amalgamate. Neither was every aspect of Ba culture adopted in Shu. Largely lacking from Ba-Shu assemblages in Shu, for example, are the Ba *chun yu* drums. That is understandable because these drums were originally part of a military signaling system peculiar to the Ba army, or so it would seem from their overall distribution. A rare *chun yu* present among the opulent late Shu bronzes found on the grounds of a Chengdu technical school campus lacks the surmounted tiger figurine ordinarily associated with Ba drums.[82] Although Ba and Shu interacted more closely than in the past, the two entities remained politically separate, as historical accounts make clear. Ba never controlled the Chengdu plain, the economic heartland and power center of Shu.

In addition to Ba and Shu, occasional references in the sources mention other, smaller countries in southern Sichuan. These included the land of the Bo around Yibin, where the Min River meets the Yangtze, and that of the Qiong or Qiongdu near present Xichang. There were also the Za, on the hilly margins of the Sichuan basin west of the Chengdu plain. From the little information available, the various ethnic polities seem to have been semiautonomous but under the influence of the Kaiming kings.[83] A typology of bronze axe heads from southern Sichuan, Yunnan, and Guizhou provinces supports the notion of Shu, or Ba, interchange with peoples of these areas during the period of Ba-Shu culture.[84]

Much of what may be known about the Ba-Shu high culture derives from tombs in western, central, and northeastern Sichuan. All those opened so far are the burials of well-to-do persons, perhaps including some royalty. With the displacment of the Ba westward, a characteristic style of inhumation came into vogue in areas where the Ba settled near or influenced the Shu people.[85] This practice was the boat burial, so-called from the boat-shaped coffins into which were usually placed a set of grave goods along with the deceased. Several examples of boat burial are known from the fourth century B.C. although the practice continued for at least two hundred years beyond then. A metaphorical allusion in the text *Huai nan zi* to "ships of Shu, which without water will not float" may in some vague manner recall this burial form, but its specific ritual significance is not explained by any extant text.[86]

Ba-Shu period boat burials have been discovered at Pi, Peng, and Mianzhu counties, although the oldest examples excavated so far are from four cemeteries in Dayi county, some twenty kilometers west of Chengdu.[87] At Dayi, ceramic vessels placed in the tombs are of unmistakeable Shu origin, like those at previous Shu sites dating back before the Ba influx. But the wooden boat-shaped coffins were new to western Sichuan. They vary somewhat as to length and width, sometimes with several coffins laid parallel inside the same tomb. A few lacquerware pieces, some beads of various materials, tiny bronze bells (perhaps part of belt buckle adornment), and a jade amulet were present, but the ritual or ideological significance of this bric-a-brac is unknown. All boat coffins include weapons among their goods, strongly suggesting that the rite of crossing the Ba Styx was reserved for deceased fighting men. The Dayi and Mianzhu panoplies consists of bronze battle axes, spears, blades, and halberds. Many of the pieces bear Ba pictorial script markings.

These boat burials remained unique to Sichuan and were widely although not universally practiced among the elite. Interments of the dead tangibly preserve traces of religious credo, as all cults must deal with questions of human mortality and the hereafter. New cults tend to arise in times of change; they are a product of that change, and this was a time of change in Sichuan. However, besides the actual boat coffins, little exists among the associated grave goods to differentiate boat burials from other types of entombment in Sichuan.[88] On the strength of present evidence it is impossible to state whether boat burial was the outward manifestation of a fully developed doctrine about the afterlife or merely an occasional mortuary fashion.

Near-contemporary interments in more conventional wooden coffins have been excavated at Xindu, twenty kilometers north of Chengdu, at Yangzishan, Baihuatan, Jingchuan Hotel, and Qingyang in Chengdu city, near Emei and at Yingjing south of Chengdu, and at Yihan in northeastern Sichuan. Although the burial containers in these tombs differ from the boat coffins, the sets of accompanying grave goods are very similar.[89]

The Xindu burial, from about 400 B.C., is believed by some excavators to be that of the ninth, tenth, or eleventh king in the Kaiming line at Shu, or at least an important noble. His burial chamber and sarcophagus closely resemble Chu examples constructed to symbolize the dead noble's palace with its living quarters and ancestral temple. Shu adoption of this pattern shows that Chu belief systems had gained some currency in western Sichuan beyond the zone of actual Chu suzerainty.

Utilitarian pottery items in the Xindu grave are derivative of centuries-old Shu types, such as those at Sanxingdui and Shuiguanyin. There was thus a cultural continuity in Shu, at least in the mundane aspects of life. However, the more sumptuous bronze furnishings placed in these tombs include vessels cast in Chu or adhering closely to Chu models. One vessel even bears the inscribed name of a prominent Chu family.

Lacquerware luxury objects in red and black, resembling Chu pieces from Hubei and Hunan, also were buried to accompany the occupants of the Xindu and Yingjing tombs.[90] The cadaver at Xindu was well equipped for combat in the hereafter, with a cache of bronze blades, arrows, and halberds. Some weapons in the tomb are of older Shu types, whereas others reflect Ba, Chu, or central plains workmanship. The Xindu, Mianzhu, and Emei goods included bronze belt hooks and elaborately decorated spoons, a mark of developing gentility.

Other Ba-Shu period tombs uncovered within Chengdu city and surrounding areas have provided many artifacts supplementing the Xindu material. All were apparently of prominent individuals. The

Mianzhu and Emei burials were lavishly outfitted with bronze vessels and weapons, apparently the property of Shu military leaders.[91] Grave no. 172 at Yangzishan, grave no. 10 on the campus of Baihuatan Middle School, and another burial opened on the grounds of a modern academy each contained halberds, spears, arrows, and ritual bronzes.[92] There were also bronze belt hooks, ladles, spoons, and mirrors, including one mirror believed manufactured in the state of Han (Jin) on the central plains. The Yangzishan grave also had several sets of bronze bits and related pieces, for bridling a horse and hitching it to a carriage or chariot. These equestrian accoutrements are the earliest known from anywhere in Sichuan.

In a previous time the only bronze goods known in Sichuan had been weapons and ritual items, including vessels, masks, and statuettes. But as these fourth century b.c. entombments show, Shu noblemen of the Ba-Shu period used a wider variety of bronze goods than their antecedents of previous centuries. Several of the Yangzishan tomb cast bronzes have markings in a native Ba-Shu script, strongly suggesting local manufacture. Finely worked jade was present, too.

Weapons still constitute the largest category of grave goods in Ba-Shu tombs. On spears, swords, and halberds, the Ba tiger appears among incised decorative motifs of the Shu such as birds, fish, tortoises, and insects.[93] Halberd blades, the best-documented category of weapon, underwent change whereby the scyth-shaped version finally supplanted the old fashioned, triangular Shu blades based on ancient Shang and early Zhou types. The improved shape gave the blade a longer cutting edge and permitted it to be joined to a staff at several points, securing it firmly so it could be wielded vigorously in battle.[94]

Several examples of scyth-shaped blades in western Sichuan are marked with cast tiger heads, a totemic device hinting Ba ownership. The advent of scythlike halberds in Shu could have owed something to the Ba, but with Shu lines of contact also opening northward other sources were possible as well.[95] Examples of the more effective halberd blades were present in the Xindu, Baihuatan, Mianzhu, and Dayi graves and at other sites of the Ba-Shu culture. However, the scyth-shaped blades did not completely supplant the earlier triangular Shu halberds. Some of the antiquated Shu halberd blades remained in armories well into the Ba-Shu period, and they have been recovered from the Xindu, Yangzishan, Mianzhu, and Baihuatan tombs together with the later scythlike version.

Swords as well as halberds featured in the Sichuan panoply. These are ultimately based on Western Zhou prototypes, and have

FIGURE 10

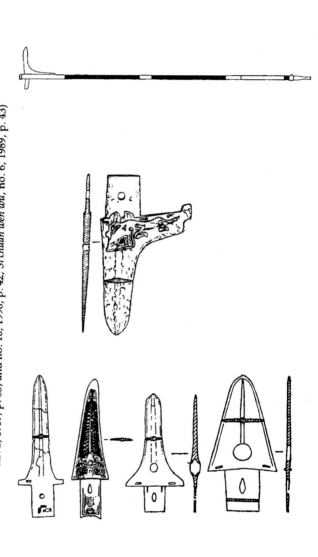

Left, Shu style bronze halberd blades derived from Shang and early Zhou prototypes, and center, a Ba-Shu halberd blade with tiger markings. The blades were hafted to a shaft, as shown. (*Wen wu*, no. 10, 1987, pp. 28, 31; no. 2, 1989, p. 63; and no. 10, 1990, p. 42; *Si chuan wen wu*, no. 6, 1989, p. 43)

slender, willow-leaf–shaped, double-edged blades. The basic Zhou type continued in use among the Ba, even after central plains societies had developed swords of other styles. By the Ba-Shu period, two Sichuan sword variants had diverged from an earlier Zhou pattern. One relatively longer version from Ba sites is often marked with typically Ba tiger motifs. These are found in northeastern Sichuan.[96] A shorter version is associated primarily with Shu burials on the Chengdu plain, west of the plain at Lushan, and as far south as Emei.[97] The cutting edges of the two sizes also show differences when viewed in cross section, but sufficient similarities remain that the variants are collectively called Ba-Shu style swords.[98]

In the case of five examples excavated from the Xindu tomb and some other contemporary blades, remains of short wooden handles are present. These handles show the blades were wielded conventionally as swords, like their Zhou ancestral forms.[99] However, some Ba-Shu swords of similar design may have been used alternatively for throwing in battle, as a missile weapon.[100] Other swordlike Ba-Shu blades are believed to have been hafted to long shafts and employed as pikes.[101] An increasing tempo of warfare would have stimulated experimentation in weapons and tactics. These modifications could be cases of the Sichuanese adapting existing equipment to meet new military exigencies brought about by the increasing strife with outsiders from Chu, Qin, and elsewhere.

Variations in halberd blades and swords provide useful markers for cultural diffusion and an indication of the importance of warfare during the Ba-Shu period. By this time, though, edged weapons for shock combat were yielding primacy in central plains warfare to missile projectors, particularly the crossbow. Unlike compound bows that require great mastery both to manufacture and to use, the crossbow with its standardized bronze trigger lock could be turned out in large, even mass quantities. The product is fundamentally a plebian weapon, most effective when discharged in volley by ranks of foot soldiers.

Such crossbow-armed infantry levies constituted the military dimension of central plains societal trends during the Warring States period.[102] Crossbows also were present in Sichuan during the Ba-Shu period. Durable bronze crossbow trigger mechanisms and bolts have been recovered from the Xindu tomb, a Dayi burial, and Yangzishan grave no. 172.[103] However, as of 400 B.C. or so crossbows may still have been only a supplementary device among the Sichuanese, because the examples recovered are far outnumbered by blade weapons.

In a development of even greater potential impact, metallurgists were looking beyond bronze and starting experimentation with a utilitarian new material, iron. One inconspicuous item from a Dayi boat grave is a small iron scraper blade. This scraper and an iron tripod from the Chengdu Yangzishan grave no. 172 are the oldest known ferrous objects found in Sichuan.[104] Viewed in context, their discovery conveys some notion of the new metal's still modest importance in this region during the fourth century. By then iron was known to Ba and Shu, although its use remained limited to humble household accessories. Sichuan smithies had not yet adapted iron to weaponry; that would come later, in Han times. Among the respectable sample of known Ba-Shu period blades, spears, and halberds, virtually all are of bronze.

The modest iron objects exhibit no traits that might positively identify them as indigenous manufactures or imports from some quarter outside Sichuan. If any Warring States ironworks functioned in Ba, Shu, or on the margins of Sichuan, their remains are yet to be located. Apart from these limited traces, the incidence of ferrous metals still remained exceptional and anticipatory.[105] At a later date iron smelting based on local ore deposits became a major Sichuan industry but in the Warring States period as yet only the harbingers of an iron age are detectable there.

Iron implements by and by would be employed increasingly for everyday items, replacing the neolithic holdover materials of stone and bone in farm and home utensils. But in Sichuan, as elsewhere in China, iron was hardly noticeable at first. It brought changes to be sure, although via increments rather than by effecting a sudden revolutionary transformation. Expensive prestige objects would continue to be made of bronze for a long time to come.

One reason for that was a steady improvement in the skills of alloying, casting, and plating bronze. For example, an analysis of the alloyed contents in bronze tools and weapons from Emei, near the southern margin of Shu, shows superlative craftsmanship of a distinctive local character.[106] Because the requisite copper, tin, and lead constituting bronze all were available along with human talent, little need was yet felt for switching over to the relatively unfamiliar medium of iron, replete with its own technical problems.

Sichuanese advances in military and metallurgical techniques were matched by gains in other crafts as well. Sericulture in particular is suggested by textual tradition. Silk production could not have been possible without a rather increasingly sophisticated social organization. Wherever practiced, sericulture involves a complicated chain of operations. Growing the mulberry trees, harvesting and distributing the leaves, feeding the silkworms, and unraveling the fibers from cocoons all require much patience. This is followed by collection of the thread and weaving it into cloth. Only a settled people accustomed to painstaking routine are capable of succeeding in this series of chores. Silk production became a characteristic enterprise in Shu, one of the first regions in China to develop the skill. Because bolts of silk were a medium of exchange on the central plains, the development of sericulture may be linked to an expanding Shu commerce with the outside.[107]

By the fourth century B.C. the use of coins had become established along with silk for economic transactions in the central plains states. In time, a Shu trade with the north despite the difficult overland routes could be expected to instigate Sichuanese adoption of metallic currency as well. Some evidence for this exists although it remains inconclusive. Ba-Shu grave goods include a kind of bridge-shaped bronze token, six to seven centimeters in length, interpreted by some Sichuanese historians as coins. These are found in boat coffin interments at Pengxian, Baxian, and Shaohua. There is no standard placing of the tokens in relation to the deceased; some are found at the head, others at the breast or abdomen. The tokens are not inscribed and so no intrinsic factors confirm their use as money, although describing them as mere ornaments begs further questions about what they might have signified. After 316 B.C. the tokens continued to be placed in tombs, sometimes along with Qin coinage. It seems plausible that a diversifying Sichuan economy had taken up using bronze specie prior to that date.[108]

Evidence for economic progress also exists in agriculture and hydraulic engineering. Paddy rice had become a major crop, if not the staple on the Chengdu plain. Its cultivation required carefully managed irrigation works and made desirable the rechanneling of existing waterways. Toward this end the Kaiming rulers are said to have commenced a digging project aimed at diverting part of the Min River's flow eastward into the parallel bed of the Tuo River. The intention was to alleviate flooding along the Min while providing water for farming in the lands between the Min and the Tuo. This endeavor would have required the coordinated efforts of laborers along a considerable distance, and presupposes a degree of political organization equal to the tasks of conceiving and executing the plan.[109]

In addition to the material advances of the Ba-Shu period in western Sichuan, there also took place the adoption of signature seals and written scripts. The seals indicate that some kinds of documents

FIGURE 11

Ba-Shu signature seals. (*Wen wu*, no. 1, 1990, p. 33)

were probably employed although no actual such records have yet surfaced. Ba-Shu seals could be circular or square. Some depict insect-like creatures or weapons along with abstract script elements. One elaborate seal from a Dayi boat grave shows a circle divided into six segments. Another seal found in the Xindu tomb combines graphic renditions of two human figures on either side of a ritual vessel along with abstract representational symbols.[110]

As for scripts, at least three versions were used. One was the apparently pictographic Ba writing also known from eastern Sichuan. Tiger-totem motifs and pictographic signs of this Ba script figure prominently in the adornment of weapons taken from Ba-Shu graves.[111] The second script is possibly phonetic, although its phonetic values are unknown.[112] One design looks very much like the Chinese character *wang*, meaning "king" or "prince." It appeared on a bronze weapon next to an angled volute sign of unknown reading. But that single character is an exception, as most signs in this Ba-Shu script cannot be related to equivalents on the central plains, nor to the Ba pictographs.

A sample of inscriptions in bronze, each bearing more than one character, has been studied with a view to proving the script's phonetic nature. The seven bronzes are from both eastern and western Sichuan. Five are halberd blades, of which four are scyth-shaped and one an example of the Shu style (*wu hu*). Two of the scyth-shaped blades also have tiger totem markings. Another inscription is on a belt buckle, and the remaining one appears on the base of a bronze vessel.

The basis for considering this script phonetic is the resemblance of some signs to the much later writing, definitely phonetic, of a tribal group in Yunnan.[113] A third possibly phonetic Sichuan script is known from but a solitary example on the lid of a bronze *he* vessel taken out of a Ba-Shu period grave at Baihuatan, in Chengdu city. It

FIGURE 12

Undeciphered Ba-Shu inscriptions from bronze weapons. (*Si chuan wen wu*, no. 6, 1989, p. 46)

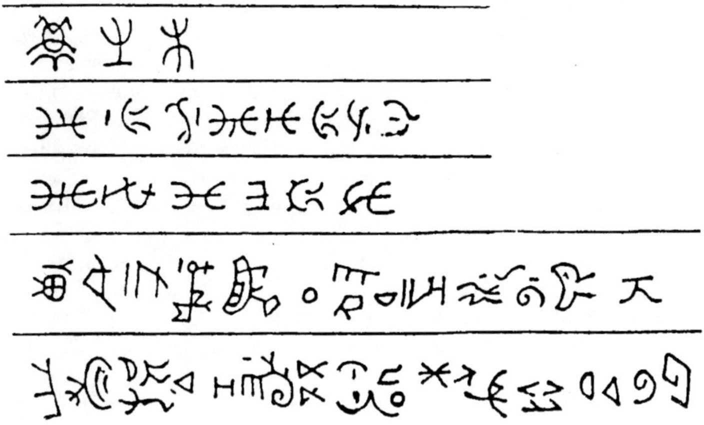

dates to about 476 B.C. The writing consists of lines, curls, and whorls inscribed in a circumference around the lid's outer rim.[114]

Progress toward translating the Ba-Shu script, or scripts, like the Ba pictographs, is impeded by the lack of any bilingual examples with a known control language.[115] It cannot even be ascertained what language the Ba-Shu scripts recorded, whether it was a Ba dialect, the speech of the Shu, or perhaps even some other tongue. Were the script truly phonetic, then its origins must be presumed separate from the ideographic writing of the central plains that eventually evolved into Chinese characters.

The Ba and Ba-Shu scripts continued to be current in Shu for much of the fourth century B.C. when the Ba and Shu peoples lived in proximity and a shared culture began to develop. Yet if either the Ba or the Shu employed the scripts to keep archives or accounts, these still await discovery. There are no historical narratives, apart from the tersely retold material in *Shu wang ben ji* and *Hua yang guo zhi* texts. They offer but fleeting hints and very few chronological signposts. The deepening Chu influence in Sichuan, the subsequent westward drift of the Ba, and their associating with the Shu are developments reconstructed from inventories of these peoples' effects; that is, the

Ba-Shu cultural assemblage. Although broad trends may be identified the detailed course of political events is lost.

Nevertheless something can be deduced about the life of the Sichuanese and the quickening pace of their economic advance. Fortuitously, among the possessions from the Baihuatan grave no. 10 at Chengdu is an expressively decorated bronze illustrating people going about their tasks. The bronze, a jar of the standard *hu* shape, is closely indebted in craftsmanship to central plains models but its excavators nevertheless consider the specimen a native Sichuanese product.[116] If they are correct then the jar's reliefs constitute a glimpse back into the living Ba-Shu culture.

Around the jar are sets of human figures shown in silhouette, engaged in various activities. Altogether there are four pictorial strips, or registers. The top register shows people wearing long gowns, their hair arranged in topknots. They are congregating amidst a grove of trees, probably mulberry. The people have baskets with them and appear to be gathering the leaves. Other figures are armed with short bows. Some stand on a platform under a canopy supported by columns and are shooting the bows or preparing to do so. A man with a long, streaming pennant is passing by. Three persons are crouching near a cauldron, apparently involved in cooking.

The second register offers a lively view of dancing and music making, with warriors striking bells suspended from a roof beam. Still other warriors brandish spears. A group of kneeling archers are shooting straight up at a flight of wild geese or ducks winging above their heads. Birds that were successfully downed are collected nearby. There are more crouching figures and cauldrons. Taken together it conveys the action of a hunting party, but its intensity is even exceeded by the scene below.

Battles on land and water dominate the third register, probably the most explicit artistic representation of actual fighting from Warring States times. Unlike the robed figures above, these soldiers wear a shorter kind of kilt. Some defend a fortification from an upper tier, opposed by enemies attempting to storm the position by ascending a glacis. Men on either side hold short swords and shields, spears, and halberds having scyth-shaped blades. One attacking warrior has been decapitated by a defender and the victim's headless body is caught in the act of tumbling down. The picture of amphibious fighting shows two small craft being poled along. Each has a high prow decorated with an animallike head, balanced by an upturned aft in which the keel is fashioned to mimic a fish tail. One boat is manned by a crew of two, the other by four sailors poling the craft along. Above, as if from

FIGURE 13

Details of illustrated motifs on a Warring States period bronze found in
Sichuan
(*Wen wu*, no. 7, 1979)

a shoreline, a group of braves holding halberds and spears menaces the boatmen. There are no chariots among these battle scenes.

The fourth register below depicts various quadruped fauna. Human figures appear to be pulling two of the beasts with what seems like a harness or leash, but the animals are too impressionistically rendered to determine whether they are meant to be sheep, dogs, deer, or other creatures. Similar animals adorn the top lid covering the jar. These incorporate composite features, such as rabbitlike ears and feline claws with wings, horns, and snouts, like fantastic creatures from some wild bestiary of myth or imagination. Separating the four registers are patterns of abstract volute designs, surmounted by a demon mask between the top and second register.[117]

Because the jar has no written inscriptions it is impossible to ascertain whether its pictorial views illustrate a connected story or are merely occasional scenes of life. Either way, they supplement the artifacts from tombs and the exiguous textual evidence. The views on the jar show that music and dance played a prominent role, as many texts about the Ba have recorded. Scenes of mulberry leaf harvesting support records suggesting that sericulture had become a part of the economy. The panorama of fighting gives a notion of how Warring States weaponry was actually wielded, and the two war canoes, like the boat-shaped coffins, underscore the importance of riverine craft to the Sichuanese at war or peace.

Sichuan on the Eve of Qin Conquest

Grave goods from Ba-Shu tombs showed that the Shu nobles had become well armed with late model weaponry along central plains military lines. And, as the illustrated bronze *hu* so vibrantly portrayed, those war implements were actively used in battle. No doubt the Sichuanese fought in many skirmishes but only one is actually recorded by a historical chronology for the Ba-Shu period. The clash occurred in 387 B.C.[118] Portentiously, it pitted Shu against Qin, at Nanzheng in the Han valley. This point controls the upper Han between the Qinling and Daba ranges that separated Qin and Shu. Formerly a buffer, the Han valley now became the scene of border warfare to decide who would control the northern approaches to Shu. If Qin held the valley, it would be in a better position to check Chu and extend its own writ into Sichuan. Although the dispute of 387 B.C. did not decisively resolve this crucial issue of who would dominate the Han headwaters, it presaged momentous developments to follow later in the century.

Shu contention with Qin for the Han valley showed how ripples of conflict from the Warring States were bound to lap over into Sichuan, affecting Shu as well as Ba. Physical obstacles like mountain ranges no longer could isolate the region from the states of the northern loess plateau and central plains. Northern literary evidence indicates an awareness that Sichuan existed beyond the mountains, as a distant land but not totally unknown. Two texts in particular include descriptions of Sichuan.

The texts in question, *Yu gong* and *Shan hai jing*, offer geographic but not much historical data. *Yu gong* was piously attributed to the archaic Xia dynasty's purported founder, Yu the Great, but scholarly determinations of its true date of composition mainly have favored some time in the late fifth or fourth centuries B.C.[119] It thus would reflect the state of geographic knowledge then current on the central plains. According to this text, Yu divided his realm into nine provinces, including one, Liang province, embracing portions of Sichuan. *Yu gong* recounts terrain features there in some detail.

Commentators on the *Yu gong* agree on placing at least northern Sichuan within the scope of "Liang province." The name *Liang* to designate this area could derive from Mt. Liang, a peak overlooking one access route to Sichuan through the Daba range. Some scholars venture that *Liang* reflects geographic terminology then current either in Qin or on the central plains, perhaps in the state of Wei (Jin). One traveler from Wei (Jin) is recorded elsewhere as having visited Sichuan in 361 B.C.[120] It would seem that by the mid-Warring States period details about Sichuan were circulating more widely.

Yu gong states that Mt. Hua and the Hei River (*hei shui*), or "black water," formed the boundaries of Liang province and that cultivation was begun around Mt. Min. The Hei River has not been located to universal satisfaction but Mt. Min has always meant the hilly area between Gansu and Sichuan.[121] *Yu gong* goes on to mention the Tuo and Qian Rivers, both of which are names of streams in Sichuan. Liang province was said to contain jade, iron, silver, bears, and foxes; all of which can be found in Sichuan. Its soil was rated of poor to middling quality, at grade three of a possible nine on the *Yu gong* scale for measuring agricultural fertility.[122]

Another text, *Shan hai jing*, should not be overlooked for the gleanings it contains on Sichuan. This "Classic of Mountains and Seas" is a flawed work, a repository too often juxtaposing the irrelevant or incoherent alongside bits of plausible data. Because it abounds in fantastic elements such as descriptions of strange beasts and part-animal, part-human creatures, *Shan hai jing* was never accorded canonical status among the surviving works of antiquity. Its genealogical and mythological information often is incongruent with material from Warring States classics composed by central plains authors. However, much of its lore has been assumed to date from the early Warring States period and to reflect a perspective on the world from southern, Yangtze lands, including Sichuan.[123]

Unlike *Yu gong*, *Shan hai jing* actually refers to the lands of Ba and Shu by name. It recounts locations in Sichuan such as Mt. Min and the Min River (in Shu) and Mt. Wu (overlooking the Yangtze gorges) among many others. The Shu dynastic name *Kaiming* appears six times in one section of *Shan hai jing* but not in a clear enough context to provide substantive historical information on Shu.[124] As for Ba, *Shan hai jing* refers to a Ba country (*ba guo*) and the Ba people (*ba ren*), as well as listing Ba among territories of the known world. One passage also mentions the Wu region in eastern Sichuan as the source for an elixer of eternal life. That would be in keeping with the image of a wondrous, storied, but not really familiar land. The historical value of *Shan hai jing* for Sichuan in the early Warring States period is that this text alludes specifically to Ba and Shu, describing the two regions separately. They remained distinct, notwithstanding the impact of Ba culture on Shu.

In the middle fourth century B.C. the Sichuan basin remained politically and ethnically fragmented. The Shu, isolated for a time after the Sanxingdui culture, had come into close contact with Ba during the subsequent Kaiming dynasty. The Ba, an agglomeration of groups, were compelled to relocate nearer to Shu at this time but did not achieve a political coalescence with the Shu entity. Although as a clearly defineable geographic unit the entire Sichuan basin would appear ideally suited for domination by a single strong unifying power, that development had not yet taken place.

Chu art was admired and imitated in Shu, and in eastern Sichuan Chu held a sphere of influence at the expense of Ba. Given time, the mixing of Shu, Ba, and Chu culture begun in the Ba-Shu period might have led to political unity. Had the Chu role in Sichuan continued to grow, Sichuan could have been wholly absorbed into that country, forming a gigantic state stretching along the whole length of the Han and Yangtze Rivers. But Chu stopped short of imposing a unifying protectorate over all Sichuan. In addition to the Shu and the ethnic grouping collectively referred to as Ba, various smaller entities made Sichuan even more of a mosaic. In the highlands west of Chengdu and south toward Yunnan several peoples remained outside the limits of Shu control. Still others inhabited the Sichuan-Guizhou border area.[125]

Is it possible to extrapolate any sense of political dynamic in Ba-Shu Sichuan from these modest tangible remains and fragmentary textual leads? Can Shu and Ba fit comfortably within any social scientific definition of "state" or "chiefdom" derived from other times and places? Certainly Shu of the late Sanxingdui period had been a markedly stratified society where wealth in the form of bronzes and jade treasures represented authority. Some qualitative threshold in level of organization was surpassed between the lower and upper Sanxingdui strata. Bronze statuettes and symbolically severed bronze heads from the sacrificial pits bespeak an awesome, sanctioned power.

Thereafter, the proliferation of bronze weapons in post-Sanxingdui Shu may be consistent with a process whereby coercion supplemented custom in hierarchical relationships. Less can be said about redistributive networks within Sichuan as Sanxingdui is the only systematically excavated settlement, but the presence of richly furnished tombs throughout Shu demonstrates that not all power or wealth was concentrated at the political center. Some kind of regional nobility existed, reminiscent enough of central plains equivalents for later Chinese sources to apply terms like "marquis" (hou) and "viscount" (zi) to the Shu and Ba context.

Just how the proximity of Ba had an impact politically on Shu in the fourth century B.C. cannot yet be ascertained, although the Kaiming Shu king at Chengdu still commanded respect far afield in Sichuan and north to Gansu and the Han valley (see Chapter 4). On the strength of present evidence Shu seems quite extensive for a chiefdom albeit rather rudimentary by central plains standards to be considered a full-fledged state.[126] Ba by then had passed its peak as a political unit.

Evident beginnings of a unique regional variant society did exist in Sichuan, a civilization fusing native features with those borrowed from surrounding lands. The high culture of the Zhou polity around the central plains and loess highlands would inevitably leave some mark. If not absorbed by Chu or by some other power, the Sichuan basin might have developed in political independence while nevertheless mirroring the larger neighboring civilization in its external forms. That is what happened in two other outlying societies, Vietnam and Korea. Those nations were able to adopt liberally from China while holding onto their own languages, political autonomy, and sense of separate identity through much of history.

In Sichuan, though, time gave out before its peoples could coalesce of their own accord. Promising starts had been made toward a native Sichuanese literacy yet the Ba-Shu level of sophistication fell

short of that achieved by central plains states. Nothing survives to
positively attest that Ba or Shu elites kept commercial books, compiled archives, disputed philosophy, or devised a written literature.
As for raw power, the persistent dichotomy between Ba and Shu did
not contribute toward maximizing Sichuan's full potential. Sichuan as
a region launched no initiatives to tilt the political balance among the
contending central plains states, nor was either Ba or Shu recognized
as a fully accredited member of the fractious Zhou community. They
lay beyond the pale.

Nevertheless, the material accomplishments of the Ba-Shu culture, built on the basis set down during the bygone Sanxindui era in
Shu, made Sichuan worthy of attention. It had become an attractive
prize. Sichuan was sufficiently developed to be worth annexing but
not daunting enough to present serious resistance to a determined
invader. Qin duly took note as had Chu already.

In 316 B.C. a Qin official urged his king to grab Sichuan. He
called Shu "a primitive land, following the customs of the Rong and
Di," both being northern barbarians more familiar to Qin than were
peoples living in the south.[127] It was an offhand, dismissive, and
arrogant remark but a measure of Qin confidence. The ethnic impreci-
sion reveals too how Sichuan remained mysterious, and that despite
Chu inroads the Sichuanese were still distinct, something other than
Chu in culture. Chu material influence in Ba and Shu was visible yet
the Chu grip of control had not been consolidated. Nor would it ever
be. Sichuan's future lay with Qin, and so with China.

4

Enter Qin

Seven major vassals of the Zhou vied for primacy in the fourth century B.C. Two of them, Chu and Qin, bordered on Sichuan. The Yangtze and the Han Rivers offered Chu fluid inroads up toward Ba and Shu. If geography alone dictated the pattern of human history, Chu would likely have absorbed the region. But Qin and not Chu annexed Sichuan, defying the natural logic of terrain. First Qin transformed itself internally to become the most aggressive, rigorously controlled state. Then, redirecting the focus of its outward policy away from the central plains and toward the south, Qin built an access route to Shu over the intervening mountains. A Qin invasion followed in 316 B.C. Its consequences rank this date among the most memorable in Asian history.

The Balance of Power, Middle Fourth Century B.C.

While the Ba-Shu culture remade Sichuan with elements drawn from outside, central plains society was itself experiencing technological, economical, and political change. Commerce underwent great expansion.[1] Cities were growing, filled with people no longer engaged in food production but who had to be fed nonetheless. Progress in urbanization, artisanship, and manufacturing, however impressive, actually heightened competition among states for arable land. Land remained the most valuble resource as the various states' economies were still basically agricultural. Competition among the states certainly stimulated progress in many fields but no single innovation, no marginally advantageous military edge enabled any one state to dominate the others.

The persistent and increasing importance of land is evident in several aspects of the changing economy. A notable technical advance of the period occurred in metallurgy. Bronze use was supplemented by a type of cast iron best suited for agricultural implements. Iron plowshares could turn furrows deeper into the soil, which meant that crop yields increased, in turn producing more taxable wealth. But ore extraction and smelting and iron working all required heavy inputs of capital and labor, which under fourth century B.C. conditions could be provided only by the governments of states.

The larger and more centralized a state was, the better it could concentrate the capital and resources needed to promote an evolving iron technology. Because the end product consisted of iron farm tools, the benefits of iron to a state lay in its use on the land. So iron was a factor accelerating the appetite of governments to absorb more territory. Within states this meant central authorities tried to reduce or eliminate the landholdings of semiautonomous nobles and bring them under control. Between states, land hunger exacerbated armed territorial disputes even though very little of the iron itself went into weaponry.[2]

As for weapons, these were still made mostly of bronze although new ways of using bronze for war had been developed. The crossbow trigger was the most important. Military technique kept pace in adapting this device to the battlefield. Just as the iron industry promoted state centralization, so too did the manufacture and use of crossbows. Individually, the crossbow is not a very accurate missile launching device. Its tactical effect comes from the release of missiles in volleys. That requires large numbers of crossbows manufactured to uniform specifications and capabilities, and ammunition bolts of standard design and weight. The sophisticated bronze crossbow triggers must be cast to precision tolerances. Stocks and bows should be of equal size and degree of torsion; if not, then a barrage of bolts will disperse over too wide an area to inflict telling casualties.

But to fashion great quantities of triggers, bows, and bolts in adherence to demanding specifications was a task for large enterprises, and only powerful states could afford to build and staff the requisite workshops. Even then, only large states could afford to train and field the growing plebian armies equipped with these weapons. In this way crossbows as an instrument of war also sped up the political centralization process within states. State centralization, again, came down to concentration of agricultural real estate within the tax base available to governments.

By the fourth century B.C., all viable states maintained contingents of crossbow archers. Crossbows diffused quickly and widely enough that they granted no one state a lead. It was the same with the introduction of siege engines and with the increasing skills in horsemanship and cavalry tactics. There existed no deus ex machina, no technical military secrets, at least none remaining secret very long. Talented commanders themselves might serve first one state and then another in a fashion foreshadowing that of Italian Renaissance *condottieri*. On switching allegiences they took away their knowledge and sometimes their specialist crews.

With armies growing the cost of warfare rose, making it an activity that only extensive, well-organized states could afford to pursue. The goal of a state at war was to capture, hold, exploit, and tax new tracts of land, making war pay for war. Inevitably either the requirements or the application of new techniques came back to the factor of land. Land was still the basis of power, within states and among states. Progressing techniques intensified existing struggles for land, but the chivalrous aristocratic sparring of an earlier era gave way to total war involving whole populations. Energetic states grew by seizing tracts from indigenous fiefs or weaker neighboring statelets, stitching the landed patches together into extensive domains.

Most states sought alliances for defensive and offensive purposes, intriguing to survive and to capture border districts. Yet such bilateral and multilateral leagues, cynically concluded for mere tactical advantage, invariably proved ephemeral. Kaleidoscopic shifts annually altered the alliance pattern but lent no lasting superiority to any one contender. This endemic warfare meanwhile mocked the Zhou dynasty's mandate to preside as sovereign over a family of federated states. Inconclusive feuding destabilized the political order even as it led to strategic impasse.

In the drive to acquire land and commanding advantage the bigger states had two main options. The first course was to direct their energies inward toward hotly contested ground on the central plains and hope to break the stalemate. An alternative was to enlarge the sphere of action beyond the traditional Zhou geographic horizon. Both approaches could be tried concurrently, but at the risk of weakening each through divided effort.

Adopting the latter course favored states on the periphery. They might annex new lands for colonization and so strive to produce an agricultural surplus. More food could support an increased population, which meant more troops, who in turn might eventually be deployed in preponderant numbers to win the central plains by attrition. Chu had already embarked on this strategy, pushing into Sichuan and elsewhere in the south. The modestly sized states along the Yellow River lacked room for expansion on the external marches and could contemplate only insignificance or extinction.

By the mid-fourth century B.C., brutal competition had shaken out a congeries of ministates, leaving seven prosperous, well-armed, and mutually suspicious great powers: Yan, Qi, the three related Jin states Zhao (Jin), Wei (Jin), and Han (Jin), Chu, and Qin. Aside from them, there remained but a few diminished old-style duchies wedged into mere interstices along the big seven's frontiers.[3] The Zhou royal dominions had contracted to a size about equal to one of these smaller, less significant powers. Ba and Shu in Sichuan had both by this time slipped outside this political community, long since ceasing to pay even formal obeisance to Zhou.

The state of Yan, holding parts of present Hebei, Liaoning, and greater Beijing, faced the northern pastures then sparsely inhabited by seminomadic stock-raising tribes. These lands and peoples harbored the potential for exerting an imperial sway and would eventually do so, but not in the fourth century B.C. The primacy of Beijing lay far in the future. South of Yan, Qi occupied the territory of modern Shandong with an outer frontier toward the sea. However, despite superb natural harbors on their indented coastline, Qi's rulers never developed seaborne commerce or militarily significant naval power, nor indeed anything like a nautical orientation. On the landward side, though, Qi projected considerable might.

Another Zhou feudatory, Jin, had in 453 B.C. been split asunder by three powerful subvassal houses. These proceeded to establish successor states: Zhao (Jin), Wei (Jin), and Han (Jin).[4] Devolution in Jin ran counter to the prevailing political tendency toward coalescence. The breakup also reduced the collective power of the three Jin states. Thereafter Zhao (Jin), Wei (Jin), and Han (Jin) still occasionally acted in concert but their mutual jealousies cancelled out any benefits unity might have conferred. Of the three Jin successor states, Zhao alone had a frontier facing outward, toward the northern steppes. This offered chances to obtain cavalry mounts but few other resources appropriate for central plains warfare.

The partition of Jin had fragmented Wei (Jin) territory into virtually discontiguous eastern and western parcels, respectively held in check by Qi and by Qin. Wei (Jin) nevertheless remained formidible and resilient through most of the fifth, fourth, and third centuries B.C. Its confrontation with Qin over disputed loess plateau lands west of the Yellow River became an obsessive issue for both parties.

Han (Jin), the smallest of the three Jin successors, was set right in the cultural heartland on the central plains. The location proved to be strategically constricting, its circumference everywhere beset by potent rivals. Although of only modest size, its central position nevertheless made Han (Jin) a power, for its boundaries virtually en-

MAP 5

The major warring states of the middle fourth century B.C.

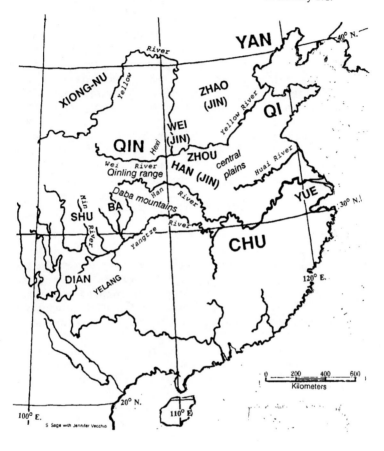

YAN

40° N.

River

XIONG-NU

Yellow

ZHAO
(JIN)

Yellow River

QI

WEI
(JIN)

QIN

Hexi

ZHOU

central
plains

Wei River

Qinling range

HAN (JIN)

Huai River

Daba mountains

Han River

YUE

30° N.

SHU

BA

Min River

Yangtze River

CHU

DIAN

YELANG

120° E.

0   200   400   600
Kilometers

20° N.

100° E.

110° E.

S. Sage with Jennifer Vecchio

veloped the relic Zhou royal house's much reduced enclave near the Yellow River. The Zhou ruler held court there exempt from outright annexation by dint of ritual eminence, the inertia of tradition, and the mutual standoff of the big states.

To the south, Chu sprawled along the middle Yangtze and westward into Sichuan. Steady expansive pressure had brought within Chu a melange of smaller political entities until its territory comprised virtually all of modern Hubei, Hunan, Anhui, and Jiangxi provinces. Ba lands, in eastern Sichuan, figured among the more recent Chu acquisitions. The Yangtze and Han Rivers offered lateral arteries enhancing the state's internal cohesion and beckoning it to extend power further upstream, deeper into Sichuan. In 334 B.C. Chu also would move to annex the fertile southeastern barbarian kingdom of Yue, extending its borders to cover Jiangsu, part of Zhejiang, and the Yangtze River mouth.

Qin, Loyal Vassal of Zhou

Among the big seven powers that left Qin, ensconced off to the west. Rough terrain granted Qin a natural defensive bulwark toward the central plains with access funnelled only through defiles, the most important being the Hangu and Wu passes.[5] Seclusion thus effectively guaranteed Qin safety from overwhelming attack by competing Zhou vassals. To the south across the Qinling Mountains was the Han valley, and still further south beyond the Daba range lay Ba and Shu in Sichuan.

On its northern and western frontiers Qin faced an expanse of arid pasture and suffered occasional nomad forays. Partially isolated from the Zhou center but exposed to the steppe, Qin lagged economically and culturally relative to the Yellow River countries. The state consequently retained an outback image, being considered a semibarbarous kin to its rough neighbors on the open marches.[6] Indeed, Qin could fight on the nomads' own terms, parrying raids to keep them from becoming a mortal threat.

Because Qin faced no dire peril its rulers enjoyed relatively unconstrained policy options. Externally, the Han valley frontier with Ba and Shu might be one field of action, the central plains another. Qin usually had chosen involvement in the latter area. Judged from the historical record, Qin contacts with Sichuan were only sporadic. A Shu embassy to Qin in 474 B.C. is recorded. However, few if any identifiable Qin artifacts have been found in Sichuan from the Ba-Shu period, when Chu influence there was noticeable and growing, long uncontested by Qin. Poor communication through the Qinling and Daba Mountains between Qin and Sichuan were always an inhibiting factor.

Qin policy might have ignored Sichuan completely were it not for developments arising in the Han River valley. Along the upper Han valley the borders of Qin, Chu, Ba, and Shu all touched. Mixed cultural influences are seen in the area's archaeological remains.[7] The Han valley was both buffer and access route, a dual and contradictory role inviting conflict. Chu for centuries had controlled the lower and middle stretches of the Han, having ejected Ba from the area during Spring and Autumn times.[8]

A north-south hill path wending down from Qin forded the upper Han River at Hanzhong (Nanzheng). It permitted limited passage in either direction, and once a Shu force even crossed the Qinling Mountains to approach Qin's principal Wei River town of Yong before halting.[9] Then in 387 B.C., Qin and Shu clashed at Nanzheng.[10] No immediate consequences are recorded but the incident showed how Qin could not completely ignore its southern frontier.

A decade after fighting Qin, in 377 B.C., Shu forces venturing even farther afield ran into those of Chu. The place of this encounter was Zifang, likely situated near the central Han or a tributary valley.[11] Chu then took defensive measures. Some interest in Sichuan was also aroused in the north. An annal entry for 361 B.C. records a journey to Shu by someone from a place called Jiayang, in Wei (Jin).[12] The Sichuanese were being drawn into the vortex of central plains interstate politics.

Ample reasons existed for Qin to pursue a Sichuan policy. Sichuan held rich resources and was developing economically during the Ba-Shu period. There had been frontier problems, and Chu was staking out a sphere of influence in the basin and in the Han valley. If Qin totally disregarded these areas they would be lost by default to Chu. Nevertheless, successive dukes of Qin had not heretofore accorded high priority to relations with Ba and Shu. Their first impulse for maximizing Qin power and prestige was involvement in central plains affairs.

Two reasons account for this Qin *Drang nach Osten*, both deeply rooted in history. One was a very old confrontation with Wei (Jin) over the parcel of land between the Luo and Yellow Rivers, part of present Shaanxi province. Then known as Hexi, literally meaning "west of the (Yellow) river," the district had changed hands repeatedly. In 409 B.C. Qin armies were ejected from Hexi, and thereafter its reconquest had become an avowed matter of honor for the Qin ducal house. As a practical concern, possession of Hexi would support Qin access to the middle and lower reaches of the Yellow River, downstream from its sharp turn eastward (at the southwestern corner of Shanxi province on the modern map).

East of Hexi, a Qin salient at the Hangu pass facilitated entrance to the central plains. Hangu pass was a strategic east-west choke point between hard to traverse loess hills and the Yellow River. In Qin hands this outpost enabled intervention from a forward jump-off point against Wei (Jin) and Han (Jin), states that otherwise beleaguered the small Zhou royal preserve. Were it not for Qin the Zhou king would have been nothing but a sacred hostage of these two Jin powers. Qin was on the central plains for the duration. The conduct of fourth century B.C. positional warfare entailed a system of depots, fortresses, and guarded communication lines, a considerable investment. Disputing Hexi and maintaining Hangu thus had the effect of riveting Qin attention eastward, making any pullout or redirection of effort very difficult.

The other compelling reason for Qin involvement on the central plains traced even farther into the past and had an aura of sanctity about it. This was the special Qin relationship with the Zhou ruling house. Notwithstanding its country cousin pedigree, Qin ties to the Zhou suzerain stretched back half a millennium. The Zhou forbears, after all, had arisen in those very western marches that subsequently became the Qin domain; Zhou and Qin were in a sense fellow provincials.

In the eighth century B.C., when barbarian pressure forced the Zhou court to permanently relocate eastward, Qin warriors covered this retreat. Only thereafter did Qin coalesce as a state and receive belated, reluctant acceptance into the Zhou polity.[13] Qin was a living reminder of the royal court's virile bygone days. Like Zhou in its time, Qin grew at first by consolidating lands along the Wei River, during the process taking over the region abandoned by Zhou along with the dynasty's sacred tombs. In a country of ancestor worship, wherein political legitimacy derived from veneration of departed spirits, the practical advantage accruing to Qin by its possession of these tombs should not be underestimated.

At royal request Qin dukes served as sacred acolytes to the Zhou kings, carrying out their ancestral sacrifices by proxy. More senior vassals of the Zhou might view Qin as an upstart but an unbreakable nostalgic link had been forged between the Zhou and Qin houses. With its sheen burnished, the link could again bind politically. Just as the Zhou ancestors buried in Qin soil required propitiation, so too did the living Zhou dynasts need support.

Four hundred years after first receiving vital succor from Qin, the Zhou dynasty again faced threat. By then Zhou holdings had shriveled to city-state proportions on a modest but desirable parcel of ground near the Yellow River. Potent neighbors might conceivably covet this land. Apart from their royal enclave, the Zhou held only the title of king (*wang*), the exclusive right to exercise sovereign ceremonial functions, and the physical regalia of sovereignty. Among these latter tangibles was a revered set of nine cauldrons, symbolic of the nine divisions of the realm believed to have been decreed by Yu the Great some two millennia previous.

Despite the cynicism of the age, the sovereign position of the king, his prerogatives, and the royal relics still counted. These were becoming subject to impingement, beginning with the envied royal title. Hitherto, nearly all the state rulers had borne ranks lower than king; for example, *gong*, or duke. Only the rulers of Chu had been so bold as to style themselves by the royal honorific. But Chu had never been entirely subordinate to the Zhou anyway and was as much a part of the foreign southland as a member of the Zhou system.

Then in 378 B.C. a usurper on the Qi throne also arrogated to himself the title king, trespassing on protocol reserved to Zhou. By so doing Qi had in effect challenged Zhou and all comers who might object to another king on the scene. The Qi move set a precedent among the Zhou's other formal vassals.[14] The Wei (Jin) lord would later follow his Qi counterpart, eventually declaring himself also a king.[15]

For the time being the Zhou monarch's ritual functions were not transgressed nor did the new self-proclaimed kings yet declare an end to the Zhou dynasty; no one state wished to risk the others' combined enmity by doing so. Even the Zhou enclave also continued to serve some purpose as the warring states' mutually convenient meeting ground. But multiple competing kings implicitly cheapened the laurel of kingship, and their existence as much as heralded an end to the Zhou house's era of temporal authority.

Zhou turned to Qin, its protector in olden days. Each saw benefits from reviving the memory of Qin as heroic guardian. In 374 B.C. a high Zhou functionary recalled the ancient bilateral tie during an audience with the then Qin duke. Looking to the future he foresaw a role for Qin as the designated Zhou royal champion, or hegemon.[16]

This formal title of hegemon (*ba*) could be conferred by the Zhou king upon a noble ruler, recognizing him as primus inter pares, sanctioned to bring the other vassal states to order on the king's behalf. If hegemony were entrusted to Qin it would recycle time honored sentiment in an updated guise to serve the diplomatic needs of middle fourth century realpolitik. The Zhou king might count on Qin armies at the Hangu pass and so retain some political leeway and hopes for survival. A hegemon possessed stature, with the royal imprimatur ennobling his own parochial agenda. The lord of Qin, all too long derided as an outsider, stood to earn respect from his peers and a commanding position in the scramble for land.

As proposed, in 364 B.C. the king named Duke Xian of Qin to be hegemon. For the Zhou king a Qin hegemon might restrain bogus kings and save the dynasty. For Qin, hegemony meant an enhanced and legitimized role in multilateral affairs around the main political locus.[17] But the Qin duke also undertook a binding commitment, necessarily relegating other concerns, such as Sichuan, to lower priority.

The Qin Metamorphosis

The institution of hegemony was customarily conferred by the Zhou king upon the person of a duke, not upon the duchy he ruled. That was appropriate, because acceptance of the hegemon's role involved burdens and commitment; it was not an empty accolade. For one reason or another a duke might be unable or unwilling to meet the task. In 361 B.C., a new duke, but twenty years of age, acceded to the throne in Qin.[18] He was called Xiao. Because the office of hegemon was not automatically heritable, the Zhou king held off from bestowing it on Duke Xiao.

Duke Xiao heralded his reign with an edict invoking the past glories of predecessor dukes.[19] He emphasized Qin prestige among the lords of states on the loess lands and central plains, and asserted the old Qin irredentist claim on Hexi, still held by Wei (Jin) west of the Yellow River.[20] This tossed down a gauntlet in challenge. Externally, there was also the Qin steppe frontier, vulnerable to barbarian tribes if left unguarded. So Duke Xiao's priorities would be fighting traditional enemies on the central plains and patrolling the steppes. Sichuan and the south received no mention in this edict.

Qin's foreign policy as enunciated by Duke Xiao continued that of the late Duke Xian. Xiao soon backed his words with deeds, provocatively besieging a Wei (Jin) border town in Hexi, an act that ushered in a generation of sporadic war on that front. At first the

Zhou king held off bestowing hegemon status on this young Qin lord, but in 360 B.C. he did concede one tentative gesture, by sending to Qin certain sacrificial offerings for presentation at the Zhou ancestral tombs.[21] That confirmed the special Zhou-Qin tie in principle. A close relationship with the dynastic sovereign, which was to characterize Qin policy under Duke Xiao, had begun.

Duke Xiao's primary orientation toward Zhou and the central plains effectively channelled Qin concerns away from the south; that is, away from Sichuan. To oppose the populous, well-developed, and militarily potent countries to the east meant unremitting effort. Was the state of Qin equal to the burdens its new duke imposed? Maneuvering against the great powers would sorely try the ordinary people, the tillers, toilers, and soldiers of Qin. Whether or not they could fulfill their duke's ambitions constituted a test of his managerial ability. He had to extract every bit of strength from within the state while expanding its resource base to provide still more deployable strength. To succeed Duke Xiao needed professional assistance.

Strengthening Qin meant rationalizing and centralizing authority, a goal shared with rival states. Their quest for workable forms of government to fit the changing times encouraged active minds. It was the golden age of ancient philosophy. Duke Xiao in particular had a keen sense of urgency and hence an eager willingness to embrace drastic ideas for overcoming Qin's relative retardation. Reforms could not begin without first ensuring that his government exercised maximum control within the duchy's borders. Autonomous subfiefdoms would only hinder progress and weaken the state in its ability to survive, and win, against enemy powers.

As in Qin, other state rulers also struggled to limit the role of vassals in running the government. One widespread means to guarantee the disinterested service of officials on behalf of the state was to recruit them from abroad. An outsider working on contract would receive a salary or at most the income of a modest estate. For a ruler this was preferable to leaving central state functions in the hands of aristocrats enjoying their own landed bases within the state's frontiers.

A retinue of hired scholars and experts may be understood as a kind of think tank to consult, evaluate, and recommend policy options. Seasoned advisors of proven worth might then be entrusted with actually executing policy. An outsider, like a modern consultant (or Mafia *consigliere*, the principal advisor of a family), never came from the family in power. He remained expendable in principle and might be removed if need be without triggering a familial blood feud.

So Duke Xiao issued an open summons for talented, daring, sophisticated experts from other states to join his service and assist in making Qin mighty.

Many, if not most of the political thinkers throughout the warring states consisted of such men, outsiders offering allegiances for hire. This geographically mobile official class facilitated the spread of ideas among the states, as well as what in modern terms could be fairly described as political and military intelligence. Fourth century B.C. practitioners included those whose writings have come down as classical works of political philosophy: Mencius, Sun Zi, Shen Buhai, and Wu Qi. All had been employed as managers, specialists, and consultants. All too were originally men of the central plains states. No known philosophes hailed from rustic, remote Qin.

Wei (Jin), Qin's hostile neighbor to the east, had taken on the innovative Shang Yang. He might have spent a lifetime career there but the ruler who hired him died prematurely.[22] The succeeding Wei (Jin) lord terminated his service and had even been urged to have Shang Yang assassinated. Compelled to leave, Shang Yang next went on to Qin where Duke Xiao was seeking to fill a vacancy. As an expert on Wei (Jin) bearing some fresh animus against that state, Shang Yang could offer much to Qin as a foreign affairs advisor. More important, he also carried a well-thought out blueprint for domestic reform.

The doctrine of Shang Yang emphasized laws (*fa*), legal guidelines backed by force. His formula appealed to rulers eager for an ideology to effectively cope with unprecedented challenges; but culturally, it went against the grain. Codified law until then had remained relatively undeveloped in East Asia, its spread hampered by an older set of values promoting harmony in political relationships. According to this harmonious notion, coercion or threats by a ruler against his subjects were abhorrent. Because law always was backed by a system of punishments, the prejudice against force extended to a distaste for rule via statute.

Confucius and later disciples acting in his name particularly exemplified the antilegalistic predisposition. Instead they promoted moral suasion for ordering relations among states and between rulers and subjects within states. Persuasion presupposed a ruling class imbued in the virtuous principles of an idealized past golden age. Subjects would then emulate the ethical example of upright rulers and make society run smoothly. What counted was a shared moral ethos. Any explicit legal codex, it was felt, could only encourage the clever search for loopholes, to the detriment of behavior founded on deeply held conviction. Proponents of this school, following Confucius, drew upon the centuries-old texts *Shang shu* (history), *Shi jing* (songs, poetry), and *Chun qiu* (chronicles) for documentary inspiration, imagery, and example.

This noble ethical formula was well suited to smaller states hemmed in at the core of the central plains area, those that could not hope to prevail in the big power sweepstakes, states with a hallowed past to perpetuate. But such a doctrine could not satisfy the contemporary expedient needs of large states bent on molding the shape of the future. The times they were a'changing. Furthermore, the old ethical system required rulers who felt secure on their thrones and who were inculcated by a sense of noblesse oblige and a committment to balance among states and within states.

It was this very security, and balance, that had now been jeopardized. The ideals of concord and benevolence seemed plainly inadequate to rulers demanding quick results. Social engineering by decree, the school of *fa*, was an idea whose time had arrived. This term *fa* can mean "law," and consequently the ideology is often known as *Legalism*. Yet *fa* also connotes "method." Shang Yang's program unashamedly promoted practical methods founded on law and backed by force.

The Legalism of Shang Yang offered not merely opportune methods but a coherent methodology as well. It is evident from the writings attributed to him that consistent notions of economics, social classes, human psychology, politics, interstate relations, and a view of the past underlay his actions. He was a man offering a system of government and an agenda founded on it. The measures and methods he advocated issued from his system, but the system itself, as an ideology, never became a counterproductive dogma inimical to achieving practical results. Shang Yang proved to be that rare combination of a man of ideas and a man of actions, melded into one personality.

On arriving in Qin, Shang Yang attended an audience with Duke Xiao at which they sounded out each other. Shang Yang cautiously began to recite a conventional litany of moralistic platitudes, wary at revealing his radicalism. Only when he felt certain of Xiao's readiness to hear something novel did he drop hackneyed pretense to expound the real theory of statecraft he planned to impose on Qin. It envisioned a break with precedent, a thoroughly new direction in the running of society.

Speaking frankly, Shang Yang then revealed proposals amounting to a well-coordinated scheme of central state supremacy enforced through draconian legal sanctions. The doctrine emphasized war and agriculture. Success in war and the achievement of prosperity through assiduous cultivation of the land were to constitute the supreme goals of the state. In its practicality, this doctrine held nothing sacred except the throne of the duke himself. The set of ideas pleased Duke Xiao and won Shang Yang an official government appointment. In due course came a series of promotions, then the state chancery, an income-producing appanage, and the honor of lordship.

During two decades in authority Lord Shang remade the character of his adopted state, building those features that enabled Qin to maximize its human and geographical potential to the very limits set by fourth century B.C. technology. Lord Shang remolded Qin from the ducal palace literally to the grass roots. Borne by arms outside Qin proper, his legacy would shape in turn the Sichuan landscape, then at length all China, in perpetuity. Some mechanisms of social control actively operating in the People's Republic may be traced to antecedents from the Qin chancery of Lord Shang.

Shang Yang radically accelerated a trend already underway in Qin toward strengthening ducal power over the common people, cutting out the middle nobility.[23] State centralization was to make society fully and unquestionably responsive to commands from the palace. One necessary and effective step toward that goal entailed refinements in the local control apparatus, tightening an existing household registration system holding each group of families mutually liable for the conduct of its members and for any irregularities arising in their neighborhood. Failure to report crime or subversion was itself deemed a capital offense, thus ensuring vigilance.[24] The widely promulgated penal code decreed cruel, exemplary modes of execution.

Qin law consisted of authoritarian decrees, injunctions, and prohibitions imposed on subjects by the ruler. It did not issue from the deliberations of enfranchised assemblies nor did it provide a formula for abstract justice. So the Qin codex cannot be equated with law in republican Rome, the spirit of which aimed at protecting citizens' lives, property, and reputations, and redressing grievances. Shang Yang's goal was entirely pragmatic, geared to implementing a state program. But it was law, nonetheless. It made no explicit social distinctions among members of the community, and although harsh, it was not arbitrary. Furthermore, the laws were openly promulgated for all to know.

Lord Shang also extended his efforts to remaking the Qin military system. Within each five-man squad the troops were made accountable for each other's safety. Merit governed promotion with incentives offered to soldiers who presented enemy heads taken in war.[25] This grisly forerunner of the combat infantryman's badge encouraged martial prowess and small unit morale. Rank and file troops were motivated because combat paid materially. Law and regulation thereby guided ordinary Qin subjects' outlook and behavior while granting them a personal stake in the success of their duke's aggressive wars. Violence was not abhorred, but rather monopolized by the state, for the state.

Economically, Shang Yang balanced incentives for agricultural production with obstacles to private commerce. Family household units formed the basic farming units, the men plowing as their women weaved cloth. Land could be bought and sold. Peasant tillers were also encouraged to open waste lands to cultivation. Such new tracts were subject only to the legal strictures of their state, not the caprice of local barons. Meanwhile, Qin state organs gained experience in the management of agricultural pioneering enterprises.[26] A generation later, after Shang Yang, the experience would be ready to apply on a grand scale in Sichuan.

But neither Lord Shang nor Duke Xiao contemplated advances southward to Sichuan. Indeed, the immediate effect of their policies tended to slight matters Sichuanese. One such move entailed the relocation of the Qin capital away from the town of Yong, eastward 140 kilometers to Xianyang. Yong was situated at a point on the Wei River near where the valley of a tributary stream, the Xie, debouches from the Qinling Mountains. Along with the Bao valley farther south this defile offers a rough but traversible access southward toward Shu. Bodies of troops might move either way, and indeed Shu forces once menaced Yong from the Bao-Xie route.

Establishing a new Qin capital out of reach had a defensive security aspect. At the same time, the transfer to Xianyang placed the Qin court in much greater proximity to the central plains, which dominated the foreign policy priorities of Duke Xiao and his chancellor. Xiao was pledged to regain the Hexi district from Wei (Jin) and needed to cite his headquarters suitably near that front. Shang Yang, moreover, had cause for waging a personal vendetta with the ruling clique of Wei (Jin). Sichuan could wait. A new palace complex was constructed at Xianyang, meeting the need for a suitable headquarters to house the organs of central authority.

Shifting the capital constituted but one project in a second stage series of domestic programs undertaken beginning in 350 B.C. These aimed at making the state's political and economic grip still more taut.

Bureaucratic county government was extended throughout Qin, fixing more areas under firm ducal supervision at the petty nobility's expense.[27] Additional ordinances governed the marketplaces, closely monitoring and taxing commercial transactions through a newly standardized series of weights and measures. These permitted exactitude for consumer, merchant, and revenue collector alike.

Other sweeping changes directly affected individual peasant cultivators' home lives. Men were decreed responsible for establishing their own households and forbidden from dwelling together in extended families.[28] Forced relocation took people away from their previous clan and neighborhood compatriots, thus weakening or obliterating outright many traditional ties. Then the principle of collective responsibility, convincingly backed by force, would operate to create a new community out of an amorphous social mass. Its loyalties would be to the state alone. The decree stimulating formation of new households also aimed at expanding population and increasing the extent of land under tillage.

Agriculture formed the basis of wealth and, therefore, state revenue. For this reason Shang Yang devoted great attention to fostering this vital sector. He is personally credited with setting the standard dimensions for a field of arable land.[29] In 350 B.C. he also ordered embankments erected between plots, marking one field from another. This facilitated not only farming operation but also accounting and accurate tax assessment.[30] Two years later a further measure standardized the liability of each household for labor duties and military service.[31]

The state treasury profited from these measures regularizing farm plots, supervising cultivation, and standardizing the weights and measures used in assessing taxes. Revenues rose, in part from levies on grain, but with additional sources tapped, such as profits on the salt and iron industries, also promoted by Lord Shang.[32] He established the state office of iron commissioner (*tie guan*), an important position later featured in Han dynasty administration. The state monopoly over iron production represented not only a source of income but also a means of centrally controlling supplies of useful implements. Set up by Lord Shang before the conquest of Sichuan, this system in due course was transplanted to that large iron-bearing area.

State parceling of land among peasant farmers did not imply outright abolition of all large noble holdings. Estates in fact still were granted to the service nobility of officials as a form of remuneration. Shang Yang himself received such an appanage at a place called Shang, from whence derived the name and title Lord Shang. Noble landholding at this time constituted a form of private income; it is less clear just how much, if any, legal autonomy the aristocrats exercised on their estates. In Qin, central government writ probably reached down to embrace lands held in fief. Still, the aristocrats as a group had not been wholly eliminated, and they continued to play a role. Conflict between powerful, titled magnates and the central organs of state would become an issue during the early period of Qin rule in Sichuan.

Stringent internal security procedures kept the whole web of Lord Shang's system functioning in Qin. Limitations were imposed on personal movement around the country, making it more difficult for subjects to evade taxes or conscription. One effective requirement stipulated that innkeepers refuse lodgings to itinerants lacking properly authorized travel documents. Draft dodgers, dissidents, criminals, or spies attempting to enter Qin would find their mobility severely handicapped through denial of accommodations and by the vigilant local watch organs reporting any suspicious characters.[33]

All this had ramifications for neighboring states outside the Qin boundaries. Because Shu in Sichuan lay beyond Qin, close control over mobility within Qin necessarily limited Shu access to the central plains and enhanced Qin's potential role as a player in Sichuanese affairs. A journey via Qin to Shu, like that recorded in 361 B.C. by someone from Wei (Jin), would be impossible without official permission once Lord Shang had imposed these travel curbs. Thereafter Qin authorities could closely monitor such transit, effectively limiting or sealing off access to foreigners. Regulation on movement through Qin likely accounts for the paucity of references to Sichuan in historical source materials dated to the period of Shang Yang's stewardship.

Qin external policy under Duke Xiao and Lord Shang also progressed. Wei (Jin)'s lord, in 344 B.C., ambitiously had begun to adopt the title of king. Lord Shang led field operations that kept Wei (Jin) in check and enhanced Qin prestige within the polity of states. He annexed some territories and pursued economic warfare by enticing Jin peasants to migrate and resettle on open lands in Qin to strengthen Qin and weaken their home state.[34]

Qin also undertook demarches in multilateral affairs, convening summit conferences that brought together heads of the belligerent Zhou vassals. Duke Xiao's stance combined assertiveness toward other states with deference to the reigning Zhou dynasty. In 343 B.C. Duke Xiao was appointed hegemon by the Zhou king, and in 342 B.C. he received congratulations from all the lords. That same year, with a Qin army nearby, the lords assembled at a place located deep in the eastern portion of Wei (Jin). There all the dukes and even the so-called kings paid homage to the Zhou king as sole Son of Heaven (*tian zi*), acknowledged communicant between humankind and the cosmos.[35]

Qin was manifestly the prop on which the Zhou dynasty rested for this reverential status. The royal house of Zhou persisted as recognized ceremonial sovereign because the duke at Xianyang still desired it to be so. As for the self-declared "king" of Wei (Jin), he had been kept in rein. Faced with a growing Qin threat the Wei (Jin) court subsequently relocated eastward, away from its exposed position too near the Qin border. The retreat implicitly confirmed Qin preeminence as an accomplished fact.[36] Having firmed up its position on the central plains, Qin also put Chu on notice by attacking that state in 340 B.C. The brief bout of hostility punctuated their long mutual peace but secured the southeastern Qin front before quiescence returned.[37]

Through an eventful reign of two decades Duke Xiao had remade his state and humbled its enemy, Wei (Jin), a goal enunciated in his inaugural edict. No one in Qin yet proposed actually supplanting the Zhou king. Leadership as hegemon, not omnipotence, was what had been sought and attained. Qin strove hard to fulfill the role of royal protector and was loath to jettison age-old tradition. Ironically this state balanced radical internal reforms with a conservatism in interstate relations, the outward preservation of the formal status quo.

By its perpetuation of the proper ritual observances, the Zhou dynasty exercised a residual moral sway over the warring states. Such political cohesion as did exist among the states stemmed from their common identity as Zhou vassals. The states were effectively autonomous but not, in theory, sovereign; that is, political legitimacy still derived solely from within the Zhou framework. Thus the renown Qin gained as champion of the Zhou cause did carry some enhancing value. But it also carried a cost, riveting Qin attention eastward to the detriment of other possible strategies, other fields of conquest. Guaranteeing the territory of the Zhou enclave and the dynasty's honor from other would-be hegemons all demanded significant attention and material outlays.

Transferring the Qin capital from Yong to Xianyang had underscored involvement in central plains affairs, as did the maintenance of the forward garrison at Hangu pass. The existence of that outpost virtually provoked armed clashes since it stood in chronic danger of envelopment by Wei (Jin) forces fortified on nearby loess lands to the north. Keeping open a corridor of supply to Hangu must necessarily have demanded constant vigilance and heavy expenses. Nonetheless, despite the looming Wei (Jin) threat to its flank, Qin used the Hangu salient for waging both offensive and defensive war. Politically it served as a visible symbol of Qin commitment to uphold Zhou and intervene at will on the central plains while also providing an early warning tripwire lest rival states contemplate marching against Qin. Enemy armies might be contained near Hangu or delayed until Qin brought up reinforcements.

Giving up the Hangu pass voluntarily would be tantamount to renouncing all that had been gained in terms of prestige and practical gain over past decades. Yet holding Hangu meant inflexibly fixating Qin strategy, in effect pinning Qin down. Determined to maintain this gateway to the central plains, it is unlikely Duke Xiao or Shang Yang had any inclination for pursuing a different course. Their geographic scope of policy options was thus self-limiting even at the peak of success. Although Lord Shang understood and practiced concepts of economic warfare, he apparently never made the mental leap, over the southern horizon to Sichuan, as a field for extending his doctrine of agriculture and war.

The consistency of Qin external policy throughout the administration of Duke Xiao and his chancellor, 361–338 B.C., may explain a long truce prevailing then between Qin and Chu, a truce interrupted just once, in 340 B.C. Had Qin and Chu come into conflict, the Han valley would have been the most probable area of dispute. No actions are recorded there, however, for the two decades when Qin remade itself and established a reputation as hegemon and defender of Zhou. Qin and Chu scarcely clashed because their principal objectives did not yet cross. From the Hangu Pass, hegemonic Qin tended to Zhou and the central plains, while Chu freely expanded along the Yangtze.[38] By and by Qin would reassess its loyalty to Zhou and consider alternative plans; for example, expansion into Chu's southern preserve. But during the 350s and 340s B.C., such a redirection remained beyond the ken of Duke Xiao and his chief advisor.

Notwithstanding all that he had achieved for Qin both domestically and in foreign policy, Lord Shang had his share of enemies at the Xianyang palace. Competing courtier factions sought to discredit and unseat him using whatever excuse seemed effective. Shi ji records a critical diatribe attacking Lord Shang on several counts and comparing him unfavorably with a renowned forerunner as Qin chancellor some centuries previous. The earlier official, a legendary paragon of virtue, was said to have attracted reverence and tribute even from Ba, in Sichuan. Shang Yang had not been so honored.

Although the main point against Shang Yang was his supposed lack of virtue, the criticism incidentally reveals how he had ignored Sichuanese matters, a valid frontier concern for a Qin chancellor.[39]

Shang Yang's career ended in disgrace just half a year after this rebuke. Duke Xiao died in 338 B.C., leaving him exposed to vengeful machinations by palace enemies. Together, duke and chancellor had overseen an iconoclastic but essentially pragmatic reformation from above. Another duke might have shrunk from the implications of such a rigorous program, as indeed the state of Wei (Jin) had originally foregone the chance to retain Shang Yang, forcing him to turn to Qin two decades earlier. There Duke Xiao boldly entrusted his patrimony to Shang Yang, making him Lord Shang, in return for which Lord Shang remade Qin. And in the remade Qin, its duke ruled supreme over all subjects, including top-ranking bureaucrats.

Shorn of his ducal protector, the *consigliere* proved expendable. What followed Xiao's passing amounted to a palace coup d'etat as the retinue of courtiers around the ducal heir apparent, Hui-wen, ousted Shang Yang. Personal and jealous motives guided the chancellor's enemies. An attempted escape proved futile; he was killed and mutilated in accordance with Qin law, the universally applicable law he himself had instituted. The statutes Shang Yang had singlemindedly enforced then remained Qin law, surviving his own ignominious demise. Indeed, the work of Shang Yang could continue precisely because it was depersonalized, and codified.

The downfall of Shang Yang sent his disciples scurrying abroad, including one reportedly to Shu.[40] Perhaps he briefed the Shu court on the momentous events in Qin. This refugee's arrival there heralded things to come, for Shang Yang had transformed Qin into a potential juggernaut that the succeeding generation of leaders would steer southward toward Sichuan. Shang Yang's imprint left Qin unparalleled, indeed notorious, within the Zhou community of states. His methods aroused revulsion tinged by the grudging awareness of Qin power, a power that neither the Sichuanese nor other neighbors could afford to ignore. When Shang Yang left the scene in 338 B.C., no state could match Qin in militancy or the rigor of its internal regimentation. No rival state had dared adopt so avowedly harsh, or so effective, a program as Qin. Qin was unique.

On acceding to the throne, crown prince Hui-wen made Shang Yang's name anathema yet kept his power machinery intact and running.[41] The Qin that Shang Yang left to Hui-wen remained a land of strict but not arbitrary rule. Law, not whim, exacted obedience.

Qin law ensured land to the tiller, who thus had something to fight for. That tiller of the soil doubled as watchman on his land, keeping a keen eye out for wrongdoers, spies, or strangers. As a soldier, he might actually profit by taking enemy heads on the battlefield for the greater glory of his state as it fought to amass still more land.

In Qin, incentives, methods, and laws were all at basis practical. Qin praxis had no use for the high-sounding principles of Confucius exalting decorum and an idealized ethical governance. What the Qin ruling elite lacked in ritualized grace or cultural veneer it made up for in will and skill. As practiced in Qin, Legalist doctrine refined a power at once meticulous and muscular, a power of martial prowess and agrarian toil, of toughness, discipline, and fear. The doctrine worked. A generation hence it would work to carry Qin power over the Qinling Mountains into a very different land, the Sichuan basin.

The Kingdom of Qin

A comparison of conditions when Hui-wen ascended the Qin throne in 338 B.C. with those nearly a quarter-century before when Duke Xiao took over will show how much the state gained in strength and assurance.[42] Duke Xiao had begun his reign by vowing to recover lost ground. Hui-wen, in contrast, took command of a power able to strike boldly on the central plains.[43]

Much diplomatic activity marked Hui-wen's first reigning year, featuring congratulatory visits at Xianyang by delegations from Chu, Han (Jin), and Zhao (Jin). The bitter enemy state of Wei (Jin) as yet dispatched no representative to Qin. But from Sichuan, a Shu marquis (hou) did arrive to pay respects, establishing a cordial relationship between the two ruling houses on opposite sides of the Qinling range.[44]

In addition to hosting ambassadors from neighboring realms, Hui-wen interviewed politicians eager to replace Lord Shang as the top advisor. The applicants outlined plans and prospects for Qin. One aspirant stressed Qin's dual advantage of a natural defensive position and strong offensive power. In his view the state already had reached potential superiority over any combination of foes and so should seize the moment to burst forth, eliminate the opposition, and achieve universal mastery. He proposed that Hui-wen become emperor (di). This daringly implied that Zhou times already were superseded by a new epoch wherein different rules pertained. But the new Qin lord modestly backed away from rash schemes at this incipient stage in his reign. Moreover, having just dispensed with Lord Shang, he was chary of taking on a king maker entertaining such lofty ambitions.[45]

Declaring imperial status for Qin would have amounted to a complete break with hoary tradition, including the time-honored loyalty to Zhou. As Hui-wen did not yet act to depose Zhou, he must have felt the move would be either unfilial or premature. The Zhou king, apparently assured of the new Qin lord's nominal subordination as vassal, conveyed formal regards in 336 B.C. Two years hence he sent some sacrificial viands for presentation to the spirits of the Zhou founder kings at their gravesite shrines in Qin.[46] This act confirmed Hui-wen as guardian of the royal tombs.

Relations between Zhou overlord and Qin vassal proceeded in accordance with precedent. Should the tests of statecraft find Hui-wen to be an auspicious, competent, and successful ruler, he might look forward to attaining the title of hegemon some few years later on. For the time being, however, no hegemon was appointed per se. None would be ever again.

Ominously, the hereditary enemy state of Wei (Jin) withheld envoys and delayed any summit conference with Qin. Wei (Jin) itself was undergoing a leadership succession, followed closely by conclusion of a nonaggression pact with its neighbor Qi, in 336–335 B.C.[47] The two states' rulers soon recognized each other's status as fellow kings (*wang*) and ceased mutual hostilities.[48] Allying with Qi freed the Wei (Jin) eastern flank, permitting a greater concentration of effort against Qin in the west.[49] Wei (Jin) had recovered and was back in action. A broad anti-Qin coalition was forming. It lacked only Chu, which at this time became involved in reducing, annexing, and pacifying the southeastern coastal state of Yue.[50]

Taking advantage of its freer hand, Wei (Jin) renewed fighting along the Qin frontier, where a series of attacks and fragile truces lasted until 329 B.C.[51] Qin energy in these early years of Hui-wen's rule concentrated on containing Wei (Jin) probes and delivering counterthrusts.[52] Eventually, in 329–328 B.C., Qin achieved a stunning victory that ousted Wei (Jin) from long-contended Hexi and other loess lands west of the Yellow River. The area north of Hexi was annexed to Qin as Shangjun, a state-administered commandery (*jun*).[53] This success further aroused the self-protective instincts of other states, Zhao (Jin), Qi, and even Chu. With all the important powers ranging against Qin it is hardly surprising that the title of hegemon was not offered to Hui-wen.

Wary of Qin, the states would not anyway have obeyed a Qin

hegemon's dictates. The pact by Wei (Jin) and Qi acknowledging each other's "royalty" flouted Qin as much as the hapless Zhou monarch, as these supernumerary kings were unwilling to render deference to any hegemon standing lower in protocol terms. So the very institution of hegemony became defunct and irrelevant, ironically a casualty of Qin's alarming advances on the central plains and the reaction they triggered. Statesmen were already starting to look beyond to what dispensation might replace a weak Zhou monarch propped up by Qin.

Bereft of Qin support, the Zhou sovereign retained only a shrunken enclave and his cult prerogatives; that is, the practice of sacrifices as the Son of Heaven on behalf of all. He was still the sole recognized mortal arbiter between mankind and the higher cosmic forces, but had neither an army nor much territory to speak of and no political writ. Without a hegemon as enforcer, the Zhou dynasty represented only a sacred cipher. Its role as a temporal mediator among the states terminated.

This spelled further instability. The states were not exactly sovereign, yet neither were they subservient to Zhou or to a hegemon protecting the dynasty. It was an undefined situation, one over which only a preponderant power might impose some new mandate. The main question of the age concerned how Qin, no longer formal hegemon but still the most dynamic state, would act under the new rules. With the usefullness of their Zhou-oriented policy virtually played out, Qin strategists were free to revive the state's momentum by looking in directions other than the central plains. Chu had long been doing precisely that, in the south, building up strength away from the tumult. Qin's own southern options lay in the Han valley and Sichuan.[54]

Any Qin moves toward the south would have to compete with ongoing exigencies arising from the wars with Wei (Jin). Once Qin had beaten Wei (Jin) in 329 B.C., Hui-wen took on a new advisor, Zhang Yi. A Metternich of his time, Zhang Yi was a consummate tactician in central plains balance of power geopolitics. Whereas his predecessor Shang Yang played the role of both ideologue and administrator, Zhang Yi served as pure practitioner, capable of handling varied assignments. Also unlike Shang Yang, Zhang Yi rose in Qin as just one member of an official collegium without a single dominant figure. It was Zhang Yi who urged that the Qin lord match his enemies in stature and announce himself a king. At last, in 325 B.C., Hui-wen did so. The newly proclaimed kingdom of Qin faced several hostile states in array, now nearly all ruled by a proliferation of self-styled royalty.[55]

Previously, as recognized hegemon, the Qin duke upheld a confederation of members professing fealty to the monarch. A king, by contrast, possessed something more closely approximating sovereignty. Qin's own declaration of a kingdom crossed a political Rubicon. The Zhou community then ceased to exist as a theoretically united and perpetual entity that, ideally, might be reinvigorated at some future date. Instead Qin now acknowledged openly that the Zhou dynasty's days were numbered.

In laying the groundwork for kingly status, Qin sought bestowal from Zhou of the tangible regalia signifying supremacy. This royal treasure consisted of nine ancient ritual cauldrons, corresponding to the nine provinces or regions into which the legendary ruler Yu the Great had divided his realm. The vessels had supposedly been handed down in turn from the Xia to the Shang dynasty, and from Shang to Zhou. In 326 B.C. the Zhou king prepared to convey the nine cauldrons to Qin, either for safekeeping or as an overt sign of abdication. Qin may have had some quasi-legal claim to receive these treasures as the former hegemonic protecting power, and as current custodian of the Zhou house's own holy shrines far to the west. However, while being transported from the Zhou capital to Qin the cauldrons were lost in a river.[56]

Notwithstanding the cauldrons' suspicious disappearance, this incident presaged a formal surrender of sovereignty. Thus the Qin lord's elevation to royal status followed only after careful diplomatic preparation and so differed qualitatively from the pretentions of other state rulers. Henceforth called King Hui of Qin, Hui-wen would advance his own line as the approved aspirant successor to the Zhou dynasty. He further marked the ideological turnabout by promulgating a revised annual calendar for Qin, with 324 B.C. as a new Year One, a second beginning of his reign (see Appendix).

Unlike a hegemon, a king of Qin owed no obligation to Zhou but might still derive some residual propaganda benefit from possession of the Zhou patriarchical holy ground with its royal tombs.[57] When handing over custody of the nine sacred cauldrons, the Zhou court had as much as conceded succession at such time when Qin seemed reasonably well positioned to make good on the claim. Independent in every sense after 325 B.C., Qin could set out to vanquish its rivals through whatever means seemed most effective.

Effective results for Qin still seemingly could be obtained against traditional enemies. After further blows against Wei (Jin) in 324 B.C., Hui-wen detailed Zhang Yi to the defeated state for a time as a resident Qin commissioner. The imposition amounted to a kind of temporary clientage without quite liquidating Wei (Jin) as a separate entity. Zhang Yi earned renown as a power broker and again would figure later as one of the main participants in the eventual Qin advance into Sichuan.

The short-term dispatching of Zhang Yi to Wei (Jin) and the further humbling of that state marked a new Qin apogee, but the bloc to stop Qin revived in response. Countries as well as Wei (Jin) were becoming Qin targets, the latest being Han (Jin) in 322 and again in 319 B.C. Adherents to the anti-Qin *cordon sanitaire* included the Jin states, Qi, Yan, some barbarian entities, and possibly Chu.[58] Sooner or later their grand alliance, they hoped, would bring Qin momentum on the central plains to a halt. It might have, had not King Hui of Qin been simultaneously pursuing an alternative strategy. The move south, to Sichuan, was being readied.

Qin Turns South

During the decade of the 320s B.C. Qin had scored great gains but opposition on the central plains was hardening. Success earned King Hui a relative lull, a chance to broaden the state's geographic horizon of concern. Doing so had become a necessity since the limited resources of Qin in the Wei River valley, even as rationalized by Shang Yang, could not match the combined strength of all its united and determined opponents.

So prospects southward toward Sichuan were assessed. Sichuanese awareness of Qin power had been clear since 337 B.C. when a Shu delegation headed by a marquis (*hou*) had been among those groups of statesmen present to congratulate Hui-wen upon his accession. The visit heralded a revival of lapsed Qin-Shu contacts. This blossoming of an active Qin interest in Sichuan developed in tandem with the cessation of the Zhou-Qin alliance, the pretention to "kingship" by all Zhou vassal states including Qin itself, Qin's avowed intention to succeed Zhou, and the rival states' sharpening resolve to block Qin on the central plains.

Chronological uncertainties deter linking these multifaceted trends in any detailed, strictly causal relationships, but they did unfold by and large simultaneously in the lead-up to Qin's conquest of Shu. Under the old rules Qin had accomplished what it could on the central plains, politically and militarily. The willingness shown by King Hui to cast about in other directions was timely, perhaps even overdue, in light of the political mood, the Qin diplomatic position, and the feasible strategic choices.

Mountains lay in the path of Qin access to Sichuan, making travel difficult yet hardly impossible. Sufficient will to traverse the divide could plant a Qin presence in Sichuan. As Qin power accrued, the Sichuanese for their part had reason to welcome contact with their northern neighbor. Qin might offset Chu, already entrenched in the eastern part of the Sichuan basin, and play off either Ba or Shu against the other. Perhaps a deal could be done by some combination of parties. Later accounts, laced with legend, related the emerging relationship between Qin and Shu largely in terms of their kings' personal contacts. Significant geopolitical content must be extracted from a skein of romance.[59]

King Hui supposedly approached Shu by pandering to the avarice and carnal lust of his royal counterpart, Kaiming XII. He granted several concubines as gifts to Kaiming, whom the sources depict as a hedonist. Kaiming then sent an embassy to express gratitude.[60] However, he did not submit to Qin.[61] Far from rendering fealty, Kaiming indeed displayed a certain playful impudence toward King Hui, an attitude depicted in an incident set in the hilly borderlands between their two states.

Leading several thousand followers on a royal hunting expedition, Kaiming appeared in the Han valley's tributary Bao valley that leads toward Qin.[62] The hunting party's presence could be not be ignored. Hostile Shu forces in the past had approached via the Bao valley route to menace the then Qin capital at Yong, and in 387 B.C. Qin and Shu had contested for Nanzheng, in the Han valley.[63] Whether friendly or not, a Shu force in the buffer zone demanded wary vigilance.

The Qin king accordingly came south to parlay with Kaiming and as a goodwill gift presented a golden box to the Shu monarch. Kaiming reciprocated with some sort of precious bauble, but when Hui received it the object turned into soil.[64] Whether practical joke, sleight of hand, or pointed insult, this gesture angered the Qin king. His aides consoled him, though, by suggesting that the soil augured well because it signified that Qin stood to gain the land of Shu. Each lord returned to his domain. King Hui then contrived a ruse to lull Kaiming while preparing the means to invade Shu. His scheme bears resemblance to the Greek story of the Trojan horse and may be as widely known among the Chinese as that earlier tale is in the West.

At King Hui's behest Qin craftsmen wrought five statues of cattle from stone. Lumps of gold were then placed beneath their tails to lend an impression that the beasts excreted precious metal. The "celestial cattle" (*tian niu*) as they came to be called were put on display along with the golden coprolites. Some credulous people from Shu were led to view the exhibit, and on returning to Sichuan they duly reported on the statues' potentially lucrative excretory functions. Envious to obtain the cattle, Kaiming sent an embassy to Qin with a request for their delivery.[65]

King Hui assented, whereupon the Shu king dispatched five strong men (*wu ding*) to escort the bovine sculptures back to Shu. To facilitate their passage across the difficult terrain, Hui ordered construction of a broad highway about 500 kilometers in length, all the way to Chengdu where the statues were duly hauled. They of course failed to produce any gold, so Kaiming returned them to Qin. There his chagrined envoys derided the Qin people as mere herdsmen. But pleased by the successful hoax, the stolid men of Qin retorted that such herding would gain them the prize of Shu itself.[66]

Perhaps there were stone cattle sculptures; perhaps not. But a thoroughfare indeed was constructed from Qin to Shu, and like the contemporary Appian Way of the Roman consul Appius Claudius, this Stone Cattle Road (*shi niu dao*) must be considered one of the great ancient road-building feats. Necessitating a major outlay of talent and resources, it could hardly have been conceived or undertaken on a whim. King Hui had some purpose in mind, to exploit Sichuan by either trade or conquest. Without the road there are only narrow footpaths; goods carts or the wagons of a military transport column simply cannot penetrate from north to south.

In many places the route followed a trail through hills too steep to accommodate a conventional roadbed. So instead, holes were dug or bored into the rocky cliffs and sturdy horizontal supporting beams set in. A surface of wooden planks was then laid atop these beams to make a corduroy road (*jian dao*). Wherever feasible, vertical columns driven into the slope below provided additional weight bearing support for the corduroy surface. An ancient source says the Stone Cattle Road measured ten meters in width but this seems a bit much, especially for the more mountainous sections.[67]

Traces of several roughly parallel ancient roads through the Qinling Mountains are known archaeologically and have been mapped. The path identified with King Hui led, from Qin, first through the Xie defile. It then skirted the white capped Mt. Taibai to link with the Bao valley where Kings Hui and Kaiming had exchanged gifts and greetings.[68] After fording the Han River just west of Hanzhong the route next had to cross the Daba Mountain range. According to a general concurrence it followed Wu Ding Pass, named for Kaiming's five lieutenants, and debouched at the Jianmen ("Sword Gate") Pass.

Once in Sichuan the road continued southward along a path to the east of the present Baoji-Chengdu railway line and approximately converged with that line at Mianyang. The segment in Sichuan south of the Daba heights is properly called the Stone Cattle Road, although this designation is often loosely applied to the entire route.[69]

These episodes of the royal gift exchange and the Stone Cattle Road take place in a literary gray area set somewhere between history and legend. The legendary elements are readily apparent; for example, a trinket transforming into soil, the five strong men, and the naivete of a king capable of believing gross absurdities about stone figures excreting gold. Kaiming's cupidity indeed conforms to stereotypical Chinese moralizing about the final ruler in a doomed dynasty.[70] His personality to some extent mirrors those of the last Xia and Shang dynasty monarchs, minus some of their cruelties. But where they were fiendish evil doers, Kaiming is more of a lecherous and pathetic buffoon.

More important to the historical outcome than the vices of kings are their enduring deeds. Here the sources offer enough information to reveal a major departure in Qin activity on its Sichuan frontier. Sichuan, or specifically Shu, had become a factor in state policy as calculated at Xianyang. King Hui was instrumental in asserting a Qin presence southward. By building a transmontane road to Chengdu he ensured that Qin-Shu relations would proceed on a permanent, ongoing basis. If the road was sturdy enough to handle stone cattle, real or imagined, then surely it could accommodate the passage of merchants' carts—or swiftly marching troops with their supply wagons.

The erection of such a thoroughfare set atop wooden scaffolding necessarily implied as well a committment for its upkeep. Even under optimal conditions the Bao-Xie and Stone Cattle Roads were doubtless rickety constructions. But timbers rot in moist environments, and the climate of the southern Shaanxi and northern Sichuan highlands is quite damp. Maintaining the highway in passable condition must have meant keeping engineers, loggers, carpenters, labor crews, and security personnel near at hand. That in turn would require a chain of supply depots. The road thus established a physical Qin presence in the Han valley and maybe also inside Sichuan for some time before the actual Qin invasion.

Whether or not the stone cattle part of the story is taken literally, Qin strategists doubtlessly foresaw probable gain in Shu, otherwise it is hard to imagine the road being conceived, constructed, and maintained. Sichuan held exploitable resources but the principal gain envisioned there amounted to territory, the land itself. This is the message behind the metaphor of a gift bauble from the Shu monarch crumbling into soil when received by King Hui. The story conveys the notion that Qin valued land, whereas Kaiming XII cherished trifles and so could justifiably be induced to squander away his patrimony.

A strain of condescending cultural chauvinism toward barbarians, peoples beyond the pale, may also be at work in the sources' caricature of Kaiming. The Shu king does not realize the true value of the realm he possesses and instead is taken in by carnal pleasures. He thus is tragically fated to fail, the victim of his own unrestrained passions. *Shu wang ben ji* offers several more illustrative episodes, telling of a man from a place to the north called Wudu, who moved to Shu with his wife and daughter. They could not adjust to Shu, however, and wished to return home. But Kaiming had become love struck with the daughter. He detained her and tried amusing her by performing a repertoire of bird imitations.

Whether Kaiming's performance constituted an exotic ritual or simply a bizarre personal eccentricity, its inclusion in *Shu wang ben ji* buttresses the case against his sense of royal decorum. Even more damning is the story of another concubine of sorts from Wudu. It seems a man from that locale was transformed into a woman of great beauty, to whom the Shu king took a fancy.[71] But the transsexual could not adapt to Shu and became mortally ill. After this catamite died the king mobilized his forces to transport earth from Wudu to Chengdu and construct a suitably impressive burial mound. Kaiming, in mourning, uttered odd lamentations.[72] The historical source spares no effort to show this Shu king as distracted and so undeserving of the mandate to rule.

Legendary material in the source goes on portraying how Kaiming's lovesickness and depravity made him easy prey to further machinations by King Hui. From Qin, Hui sent five (female) beauties on their way to Shu, as a gift for its oversexed ruler. Kaiming ordered his five strong-man servants to escort the women back to Shu. On the journey they reached a place called Zitong where they noticed a large snake enter a burrow in a mountain.[73] The strong men pulled on the snake but in doing so brought down the mountain and entombed themselves. Thereupon the five beauties turned to stone. Kaiming meanwhile had ascended a high tower in watchful anticipation of their coming. When they failed to arrive, he fell into a deep melancholy.[74]

These fables need not be taken as literal truth. Their value is in recounting how later generations believed Qin had pursued a pur-

poseful design to beguile the Shu king. A more down-to-earth historical passage from *Shi ji* lends corroboration of that aspect. Its setting is
a conference between the king of Chu and a diplomat trying to enlist
his support against Qin. The Chu monarch voices concern about Qin
aggressiveness, saying, "Qin aims to gain Ba and Shu, and annex the
central Han valley."[75] The statement is doubly significant. It offers
some backing in a respected historical source about supposed Qin
intentions and suggests that Qin's rivals, including Chu, were not
unaware of the burgeoning Qin interest in Sichuan.

Chu already had established a sphere of influence in Sichuan
and by the 330s B.C. had turned to advance elsewhere. Preoccupation
on other fronts may explain Chu quiescence regarding the Qin inroads toward Shu.[76] A protracted truce apparently persisted between
Qin and Chu.[77] Under Duke Xiao and Lord Shang, Qin foreign policy
had focused exclusively on the Yellow River states, and the frontier
with Chu in the Han valley remained inactive. But once King Hui
shifted Qin sights to also include Sichuan and the Han valley, the
implications for Chu were clear. Further Chu inactivity could result in
deterioration on the western flank. To avert that danger Chu might be
persuaded to cancel its de facto armistice with Qin and join the other
monarchs' anti-Qin front while an opportunity still existed.[78]

The Qin Conquest of Sichuan

Building the Stone Cattle Road made a practical Sichuan policy
more realistic for Qin. But before King Hui could act decisively in that
direction a flare-up occurred in relations with the central plains states.
By 318 B.C. their broad anti-Qin bloc had become ready for action. It
pressured Qin to abandon stewardship over Wei (Jin) and to with-
draw Zhang Yi, the imposed Qin high commissioner. Zhang Yi com-
plied. In ridding itself of Qin's proxy and returning to the anti-Qin
fold, Wei (Jin) added its troops and the advantage of a close-in position for offensive campaigning.[79]

Qin might have faced disaster had the coalition proved cohesive, but it foundered. Only the three Jin states actually supplied sizeable armed contingents, and these suffered heavy casualties.[80] So Qin
survived immediate peril in 317 B.C. Some enemy forces remained
available for renewed action the next year when forces from Han (Jin)
mobilized for another try against Qin, although the bloc as such
seems to have disbanded. That is where matters stood in 316 B.C.[81]

Meanwhile in Sichuan, dissension had broken out within the
Shu royal household itself, between King Kaiming XII and a younger

brother known as the marquis of Zu. This noble held a fief including part of the central Han valley, the area over which Qin and Shu had fought in 387 B.C., and near where King Hui had exchanged gifts with Kaiming. From the central Han, the marquis of Zu's lands stretched southward, including tracts on both sides of the Daba hills. He thus sat between Shu, Qin, and the truncated but still significant kingdom of Ba. The marquis' town of Jiameng was set near the route from Qin to Shu; that is, the recently built Stone Cattle Road.[82] His strategic vantage point might enable the marquis to interdict communications between Qin and Kaiming's capital at Chengdu.

Probably the construction of the road itself and the Qin presence it brought were destabilizing factors in this previously neglected area. According to classical sources, the occasion of some Ba hostility to Shu lured the marquis of Zu into fraternal disloyalty. When the latter supported Ba, Kaiming XII marched against his brother, causing him to flee first to Ba and thence to Qin. There the marquis appealed for Qin intervention. King Kaiming's envoys also approached Qin.[83] At stake in the matter was the Stone Cattle Road, centerpiece of Qin strategic designs on Sichuan. Taking on the marquis of Zu as a client would protect the road but involve Qin in Shu dynastic politics. Acquiesence in the Shu king's advance against Zu could endanger Qin control over portions of the road.

As seen, Qin just then had been hard pressed to fend off its combined central plains foes. A hostile Han (Jin) army was still in the field. Chu, colossus of the south, meanwhile watched developments from its vantage point in the Han valley. So the Qin monarch faced a fateful decision. He had cleverly sought opportunities in Shu, but unfinished business remained on the central plains, familiar ground. Two roads diverged. If King Hui took the one less traveled it could make all the difference.[84]

In this urgent moment the king of Qin summoned his aides to a council of war, requesting options proposals on where the state might best commit its strength. Zhang Yi responded as did another advisor, Sima Cuo. For Zhang Yi, an expert on central plains matters and lately Qin legate at Wei (Jin), the issue was clear-cut. First Han (Jin) would have to be confronted. To neutralize Han (Jin), Zhang Yi suggested again allying with Wei (Jin) while seeking the goodwill of Chu.

All this amounted to yet another juggle in traditional balance of power politics, but Zhang Yi felt that the time was ripe for a clear-cut result. Bolstered by allies, Qin would then thrust aside Han (Jin) and bear down on Zhou itself, whose jejune royal court already had conceded Qin succession in principle. Then Qin could finally grasp the mandate to rule at the political center. Zhang Yi emphasized the psychological decisiveness of the moment. A majestic display of force at the geographic pivot of affairs, the central plains, had the potential to shatter enemy morale and elevate King Hui to supremacy. Gains on the periphery would duly follow.

To Zhang Yi the notion of a Sichuan campaign was a dubious diversion, the material spoils there a mirage. An expedition against barbarous sorts was beneath King Hui's dignity, he counseled, whereas persistence on the central plains could at last yield a signal victory. This would bring to fruition the efforts begun under Duke Xiao. It sounded enticing. Yet Zhang Yi left unmentioned those previous instances when Qin had attained near mastery, only to be thrust back again by alignments of rival states.

Sima Cuo's counter proposal urged a departure based on the more recent outreach to Shu. The central plains could wait. Sima Cuo advised King Hui that Qin first needed to amass material reserves. He doubted the chances for success of a central plains expedition to abrogate the Zhou monarchy, even if that institution already had declined to little more than a symbol. An attempted knock-out blow at Han (Jin) and seizure of the Zhou court might succeed only in arousing the community of states to reunite against Qin. Instead of prestige, Qin would then reap renewed enmity. Sima Cuo therefore argued in favor of seizing the chance presented by disruption in Sichuan to strike southward. There lay exploitable lands, latent wealth, and stocks of grain. He foresaw a quick, easy campaign, "like a wolf on the fold."[85]

King Hui opted for the Sichuan plan. The king chose a long-term but unprecedented strategic solution over an operational blow against well-known foes. Conveniently, Han (Jin) soon receded as a threat, freeing Qin for the march south to Shu. It was a calculated risk, a step into a land where Qin armies never before had fought. And there remained the factor of Chu, as Sima Cuo's Sichuan plans would have serious repercussions on that neighbor.

Consideration for Chu interests perhaps constrained Qin from striking south in years past, but Chu alignment with the Jin coalition ended a long spell of Chu-Qin mutual nonaggression. Once that coalition faltered Chu even sounded out Han (Jin) on continuing a bilateral anti-Qin entente. This alliance failed as well. Zhang Yi saw here an opportunity to drive in a wedge, a chance for Qin to line up with Chu against Han (Jin). However, it no doubt would demand a quid pro quo, keeping Qin hands off Chu interests in Sichuan in exchange for renewed Chu-Qin rapprochement. When King Hui instead approved the Sima Cuo strategy for a Sichuan campaign he knew full well Chu might be provoked.

King Hui's decision amounted to a historical watershed. To effect the plan, Qin troops still had to cross a geographic watershed, the Qinling and Daba Mountains. They of course would take the Stone Cattle Road. Sima Cuo and surprisingly Zhang Yi as well were entrusted with the cooperative task of carrying out the expedition.[86] It is unfortunate that no ancient sources elaborate on the paradox of Zhang Yi, who had opposed the Sichuan move, being jointly assigned to implement it. Perhaps King Hui used this device to mollify him. Or it may be that the Qin army traveled south in two contingents, one under each commander either from logistical considerations or to balance their ambitions. In any case the inclusion of Zhang Yi as cocommander exemplifies Qin bureaucratic control. Once a policy was decided the state closed ranks.[87]

So in the tenth month of 316 B.C. a Qin force set out over the Stone Cattle Road, crossing the Qinling and Daba ranges to Jiameng.[88] There, near Shaohua in present-day northern Sichuan, Kaiming XII resisted the Qin invaders but suffered a series of reverses. Retreating to Wuyang, Kaiming gave battle again, only to be captured and killed.[89] The Shu chancellor and crown prince fled to nearby Mt. Bailu ("White Deer Mountain") where the Qin army annihilated their forces. Thus in its twelfth generation the Kaiming dynasty lost sovereignty over Shu. Ba also had joined Qin in the attack. However, once having crossed the mountains Qin whetted its appetite for Sichuanese lands. Cynically turning on their allies, Sima Cuo and Zhang Yi went on to seize Zu and Ba, taking the Ba king captive.[90] More of the Han valley as well shortly came under Qin occupation, including the territory of Yong.[91]

Parts of eastern Sichuan still remained under Chu control. But in taking Shu, the upper Han valley, and the Ba area of central and northern Sichuan, Qin had come into a real estate windfall. During the incessant fighting over many centuries, from the Western Zhou period through Spring and Autumn to Warring States times, never had so large a portion of land and population been shifted from one political overlord to another. Never, that is, since the early Zhou, when King Wu sallied out of his base and, together with Sichuanese allies, overthrew the Shang dynasty. That had been some 700 or 800 years previous. Now in 316 B.C. Qin's King Hui emerged from the Zhou's old western base to annex much of Sichuan. Whether by accident or design, this move recreated a historic strategic combination of the Wei and Han valleys together with the western Sichuan basin.

Qin had begun the fourth century B.C. as just one, a relatively weaker one, among the seven seriously contending states under the Zhou sovereign. By 316 B.C. it was the main contender against which the others tried to erect defenses. Thereafter resistance to Qin became ever more a doomed holding action. The Qin power machine that so quickly overwhelmed Shu and Ba had been honed for decades by a ruthlessly pragmatic, totalitarian doctrine. Within Qin's borders the central authority tolerated no rivals and governed supreme, through laws. The goal of this harsh but legalistic rule was total mobilization for agrarian production and war.

At first the wars aimed toward recovering old irredenta along the Yellow River and asserting power at the geopolitical heart, around the Zhou capital. Lord Shang as chancellor had pursued Qin interests there unswervingly. The prestige and might attained by Qin during the reign of Duke Xiao served as a necessary preliminary to the ensuing reign of King Hui. Advised by Sima Cuo, King Hui came to realize that his state's restricted homeland base in the Wei valley simply could not offer up sufficient resources to effect universal conquest. To knock out all comers, Qin needed expanded resources: more farmers, soldiers, horses, livestock, salt, ores, swords, crossbows, arrows, shoes, bucklers, armored corsets, transport carts, and grain; above all grain and grain bearing lands. For these Qin required an expanded base, but its leaders first had to literally expand their horizons.

Qin southern policy entailed a visionary reorientation of thinking, away from the central plains that so long had monopolized concern. King Hui's sights proved equal to the task. Through royal diplomacy he literally paved the way to Chengdu. His actual decision to invade Sichuan combined political and economic considerations. In its political dimension the move to annex Sichuan was set squarely against a new tableau, on which all the major warring states had declared kingship, the right to universal rule. All contended to succeed the Zhou house as sovereign. Economically, King Hui agreed with the assessment that his state could not make good its own bid for succession without enlarging its material assets and productivity.

To all appearances, preparations were well laid for some kind of Qin participation in the Han valley and the Sichuan basin. The proximate motivation behind the armed incursion into Sichuan, however, owed something to fortuitous opportunity, but this too was an opportunity actually created by Qin's having pushed through a road into the region. When the two Sichuanese parties invited Qin intervention, King Hui had to be persuaded, against a competing plan, to risk marching southward. Launching the *coup de main* just then took nerve, because it meant opening a second front while unfinished business still remained on the central plains. King Hui calculated carefully, then moved.

In the Warring States deadlock, no one contender held any significant technological advantages to guarantee dominance over the others. But of all the states, Qin somehow prevailed, adoping organizational and procedural means to transcend the limits imposed by fourth century B.C. technology. The state that annexed Sichuan was still Qin as it had been made over by Lord Shang, rationally and strictly organized from top to bottom. It was governed according to a doctrine, implemented via statute, over a mass of peasant cultivators. Statutes reached down to regulate the cultivator's life in the villages and fields, on the drilling grounds where he served as a soldier, and inside his very cottage. The state was the first and final arbiter of all life's aspects.

Lord Shang's Legalist doctrine as applied in Qin coherently combined an economic dimension and a security dimension. Had Qin remained bottled up in the Wei River valley, Legalism applied within its confines might have caused it to become a kind of ingrown Sparta of east Asia, no more than a curious anomaly, doomed to vanish. But the internal logic of Legalism, and of Qin ambitions, demanded conquest. And by expanding to Sichuan, Qin power and Legalist praxis both matured in the new environment and came to outgrow the conceptions of Lord Shang.

Qin, this prototypical totalitarian state, now imposed itself upon an economically less developed country, over ethnically different people, in a climatically contrasting environment, Sichuan. Legalist doctrine, the Legalist social experiment, was exported there by force of arms. Only flexibility, patience, and compromise could make it work. Applied in Sichuan, Shang Yang's program underwent its first extensive field test beyond the confines of the original Qin metropolitan area. This would be the premier transformation on the Qin model of an alien society, the trial run of sinification. The conquest of Sichuan was to strengthen and position Qin for its drive to empire, the creation of imperial China in 221 B.C.[92] For Sichuan, 316 B.C. signified a prelude, the outset of a century-long sinification process.

5

Sichuan's Century
under Qin

Sinification is an adaptive cultural process ancillary to the political unification of a region with China. Conquest may bring a land within the frontiers of China, but sinification makes its people Chinese. The course may be fairly intense, even peremptory, or drawn out and relatively painless. Each variant path toward absorption within China will leave a historical imprint affecting subsequent patterns; yet sinification, whether swift or slow, throughout history has provided the durable sinew for a united Chinese empire. And in times of political disunion it has always kept alive the aspiration toward restoring unity.

Like the very name *China*, the coined term *sinification* derives from Qin, the former interloper that coerced an empire into being.[1] Indeed, the crowning Qin achievement of Chinese unity is scarcely conceivable without its concomitant process, sinification. Sinification in Sichuan followed on the heels of Sichuan's annexation to Qin and continued for very nearly a full century before the Qin imperium was born.

Of all regions unified by Qin, Shu underwent the longest and most sustained transformation. Pragmatically, Qin tailored a variant model of sinification to fit local needs and realities in Ba. In either region it was an untried, experimental course, and an interactive course as well. Qin soldiers, colonists, bureaucrats, businessmen and engineers integrated Sichuan with their state and were themselves transformed in the Sichuanese environment. The vast colony thus exerted counterplay on the colonial power. All the while Qin exploited Sichuan's resources and geographic position to pressure opposing states. One by one they fell until the last had surrendered by 221 B.C., so inaugurating Year One of imperial China's ensuing two millennia. The sinification of Sichuan and its union with Qin thus

MAP 6

Qin and its possessions in Sichuan

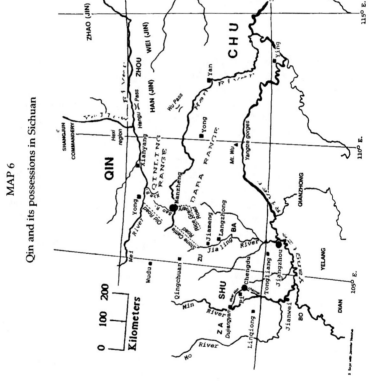

represent signal events in world history. They served as precondi-
tion, preparation, and paradigm for the uniting and sinifying of
China itself.

Qin Neutralizes Chu

By crossing the Qinling Mountains into Sichuan and subduing
Shu, the Han valley, and then Ba, Qin strategists had performed one
of the great military feats of antiquity. However, their achievement
did not confer on Qin any immediately realizable advantage against
rival kingdoms. The annexation of Sichuan supplemented Qin efforts
on the central plains but was no substitute for those operations. Only
with time could the latent Sichuanese potential be actively brought to
bear on other fronts. Meanwhile, heavy involvement continued to pit
Qin against Qi, Chu, and the three Jin states even as Qin's big bite in
Sichuan was being digested.

Digesting Sichuan occasioned pains, even ulcers. In 316 B.C. the
victorious Qin troops in Sichuan faced all the vulnerabilities of over-
extension on strange ground, far from home and outnumbered by
local inhabitants. Qin had risked the state's strategic future on the
security of the Stone Cattle Road, a rickety ribbon of planks and scaf-
folds threading along hillsides not too far from areas still held by Chu.
And sooner or later, Chu would inevitably react to the Qin incursion
into its sphere of influence.

For Qin it was imperative to consolidate the gains in Sichuan
without delay. Practically that meant safeguarding the fragile line of
communication to Shu, constructing parallel alternative routes, and
securing Sichuanese loyalty while neutralizing the external Chu
threat. All this had to be accomplished somehow without draining
excessive resources from the Qin homeland itself, a demanding trek
away across the highlands. Sichuan as a Qin asset could bring final
Qin triumph and secure Chinese unity. A Sichuan in the debit column might imperil Qin itself. So setting up a self-sustaining base,
without delay, was mandatory.

The Chu factor affected Qin moves in Sichuan from the outset.
Chu encroachment had weakened Ba even as Chu culture permeated
the Ba territories. Qin forces then entered Sichuan to strike at Shu,
whose ruling class seems to have enjoyed close relations with Chu.
Yet once having disposed of the last Kaiming king, Qin then extended its writ over Ba as well. Such a move went beyond the limited
pretext of ostensibly responding to a Ba client's plea for help. The

stroke against Ba placed a Qin salient into an area long regarded as a Chu preserve.

Some military steps were consequently taken that straightened out the lines. A Qin campaign in the central Han valley, commanded by generals Wei Zhang and Gan Mao, provided added linkage in the center between Ba and Qin while further intimidating Chu.[2] Qin obviously meant to stay in Sichuan. There the aggressive Legalist state posed an implicit threat to greater Chu and eventually to the Chu homeland itself. Given the gravity of this challenge, it is legitimate to ask why Chu failed to launch an immediate riposte to Qin's *coup de main* of 316 B.C.

Overcommittment and distraction on other fronts may help explain the sluggish Chu response. Just as Qin opted for Sichuan conquest, Chu was engrossed in a similar expansionist project much farther east, near the mouth of the Yangtze. According to *Shi ji*, Chu invaded the sizeable state of Yue (present Zhejiang province) in 333 B.C.[3] A recently discovered bronze inscription shows that Chu operations there continued at least as late as 313 B.C.[4] Pacifying Yue must have tied down considerable military resources. So Chu by no means had written off Sichuan, but happened to be heavily engaged elsewhere at the moment Qin struck.

When Chu finally subdued Yue after 313 B.C., a greatly magnified Qin had materialized on its western flank. The following year Qin and Chu clashed in the Han valley, resulting in a bloody Chu defeat.[5] Stung but aroused, Chu contemplated a new anti-Qin alliance with the mighty eastern coastal state of Qi. Their combined strength might contain or even roll back Qin on the battlefield.

At this stage Qin used diplomacy to weaken Chu resolve, to deflect Chu attention away from the still unstable Qin position in Sichuan, and to drive a wedge between Chu and Qi. Zhang Yi, the same Qin adviser who had counseled against undertaking the invasion of Sichuan, urged trading land for peace. He suggested to King Hui that holding onto the entire Han valley courted disaster, and advised divesting some districts there to Chu in return for an accord.[6] To gain Chu receptivity he would first rely on a bit of browbeating.

In conversations with the Chu king, Zhang Yi detailed how Qin might exploit its newly acquired Sichuan possessions.[7] In just ten days a Qin flotilla could cover 3,000 *li* (roughly 1,600 kilometers) down the Min and Yangtze Rivers, to penetrate Chu proper. Each craft had the capacity to carry fifty troops as well as their rations for three months. Travel by boat would conserve the army's energy and keep it in fit shape for campaigning. Qin forces in any case were accustomed to amphibious operations, having gained experience along the Yellow, Luo, and Wei Rivers in the north while battling Wei (Jin) for the disputed Hexi region.[8]

Ten days' transit across Sichuan remains respectable even by modern criteria for a major surface troop movement. In its own time such speed was tantamount to blitzkrieg. Once Qin armies entered Chu, Zhang Yi added, they could overwhelm Chu in a campaign lasting just three months. He estimated that it would take over half a year for Chu's allies among the other states to put a relieving force in the field, too slowly to do any good. Qin stood to gain the Chu towns east of Gan pass, the Qianzhong region (around the modern Sichuan-Hubei-Guizhou frontier point), and Chu's Wu commandery (straddling the Sichuan-Hubei border).

Zhang Yi also warned that Qin troops could concentrate along a separate, converging vector to achieve a wide but coordinated pincer operation. While the Yangtze-borne amphibious task force menaced Chu, Qin heavy infantry would emerge from the Wu Pass (at the present Shaanxi-Henan-Hubei frontier point) to march southward into Hubei. Floating supplies down the Han River was an easy solution to the troops' logistical problems.[9] The plan's extensive scale incidentally rivals any contemporary campaign by Alexander of Macedonia, his Hellenistic successors, or the Roman republican armies.[10]

Zhang Yi softened the harsh invasion threat by dangling an offer of lands near the Han valley.[11] Some Qin concubines to gratify the Chu king would sweeten the deal. Fearful of renewed hostilities but mesmerized by the conciliatory offer, Chu aborted the budding alliance with Qi. Qin wedge driving had succeeded. As for the territorial concession, Qin subsequently reneged, retaining those districts promised to Chu. Through such bluff Qin earned a respite to digest its gargantuan bite in Sichuan.

Expediency decreed separate strategies in Shu and Ba. The advance against Chu threatened by Zhang Yi was to be staged and supplied from Shu, merely traversing Ba. Although formally a Qin commandery, Ba in military terms could be considered simply an intermediate zone to be transited on the way to the front. To be sure, the river banks through Ba had to be in friendly hands and the Yangtze and tributary waters free of hostile traffic to guarantee Qin flotillas unobstructed passage. But Zhang Yi's apparently credible ultimatum made no mention of Ba as a base or staging ground for offensive operations. The Qin lodgement there had not yet been made firm enough and identifiably indigenous forces continued to exist in Ba well after the annexation of 316 B.C. according to accounts of later developments.

The Qin presence in Ba at first remained relatively unobtrusive and worked to the benefit of Ba against Chu. Ba accordingly accepted Qin suzerainty without attempting revolt. All told, Qin exercised a lighter hand there than in Shu, where a maximization of power was more rapidly achieved. Qin designs envisioned Shu as a sustaining, productive base. The takeover of Ba and the thrust in the Han valley had more imminent operational consequences, providing a broad buffer zone shielding the Shu base and advance posts for moves farther afield. Zhang Yi's adroit negotiations helped keep Chu at bay from both Ba and Shu, and this proved crucial as Shu heaved to toss off the Qin yoke.

The Pacification of Shu

Although Qin's conquest of 316 B.C. had deposed the Kaiming king, the conquerers faced new problems in exercising actual control. Qin for some time maintained but a precarious hold. The occupiers needed food, shelter, and labor auxiliaries. The Shu nobles wished to minimize losses and retain some power; indeed at least one, the marquis of Zu, had allied with Qin before the actual invasion. Given their complementary problems, occupiers and occupied shared a common desire to restore normalcy and keep everyday affairs running smoothly. As in many such situations in ancient or modern history, the result was self-interested mutual collaboration—for a time.

So to facilitate Qin rule and legitimize the occupation, as well as for mundane practical concerns, the local Kaiming dynasty was preserved despite the loss of its last monarch. King Hui set up a hybrid government for Shu with a Kaiming marquis (*hou*), plus a Qin military governor (*shou*) and a minister (*xiang*) on hand to guide and implement. But thousands of emigrant families from Qin meanwhile also were sent to settle in Shu.[12]

By downgrading the Shu ruler from king to marquis, King Hui signaled the subordination of the Shu throne to his own.[13] Like Ba and the central Han valley, Shu was designated a *jun* or frontier commandery. It became the testing ground for successive Qin notions of how a commandery ought to function. In 314 B.C. the Qin king invested the vanquished Kaiming king's son, Yaotong, as marquis of Shu.[14] This relationship contained a personalized feudal element of vassal to lord. Supplementing it was a bureaucratic arrangement under which a Qin officical named Chen Zhuang held the Shu ministerial post and Zhang Ruo became governor.[15]

Three years later, in 311 B.C., King Hui died and King Wu ascended the Qin throne. The Sichuan venture until then had been largely a personal initiative of King Hui. After his death Qin faced the test of seeing this royal project perpetuated as a lasting state concern, one viable enough to survive the tenure of a given ruler or set of officials. If Qin control was to take permanent root throughout the huge Sichuan acquisition, a regularized system of administration and succession there eventually would be required.

Qin precedent for the establishment of commanderies in conquered possessions had only begun in 328 B.C. with the annexation of Shangjun, a tract corresponding to present-day northern Shaanxi province. Shangjun commandery comprised fifteen counties (*xian*), a total apart from the forty-one existing counties of the old Qin area in central Shaanxi. Shangjun lay near Qin home ground, north of the recently regained territory of Hexi. Geographically and culturally familiar, it presented no special problems of remoteness or ethnic dissimilarity. Assimilation into the Qin state structure might proceed with relative ease. Shu, on the other hand, was both distant and exotic and could hardly duplicate the earlier Shangjun style of commandery administration.

Because little established guidance existed for what a commandery was supposed to be, several options could be tried. A commandery might be run by bureaucratic appointees, enfeoffed nobles, or on a condominium basis. The cultural gulf between Qin occupiers and the Shu people argued strongly for entrusting native leaders with some authority. And after all, Qin had entered Shu at the invitation of a local noble. Appointing a Kaiming prince as Shu marquis, subject to the court at Xianyang, implicitly recognized the residual authority of the indigenous elite despite its military defeat by Qin. The compromise was in effect an experiment, a system in evolution.

Qin thereby faced the contradictory tasks of trying to mollify the Kaiming dynasty and its followers in Shu while concurrently extending Xianyang's power at their expense. Success depended on the loyalty of the Kaiming marquis to an alien liege lord and his viceregal representatives. The Kaiming dynasty was thereby resurrected as the indigenous agent of Qin. This amounted to an intrinsically unstable mixed structure, with built-in weaknesses and conflicting interests. Qin central prerogatives would be felt only at a great overland remove. Even regular Qin officials in Sichuan, so distant from the capital, might succumb to local blandishment. The Xianyang court could not entirely trust anyone, least of all surviving Shu nobles from the house of Kaiming.

The system faced crisis in 311 B.C., the same year when diplomacy only narrowly averted a Chu-Qi alliance, and incidentally when Qin's King Hui died. In Shu, the government minister Chen Zhuang revolted, usurped the marquis Yaotong, and killed him.[16] Chen Zhuang might have drawn on discontented elements among the Qin military personnel or settlers present in Shu. Ambitious Qin careerists or freebooters may have been responding to a perceived opportunity created by King Hui's passing. A vacuum or power shuffle at Xianyang perhaps tempted some into subversion, and Shu natives conceivably could have united for convenience with Qin malcontents.

Whatever its cause, the mutiny came to nought. Forces from Qin under Sima Cuo, Zhang Yi, and Gan Mao set out on a second conquest of Shu, quelled the uprising, and executed Chen Zhuang.[17] King Wu, successor to King Hui on the Qin throne, renewed the state's commitment to its Sichuan enterprise by designating a second Shu marquis.[18] Marquis Hui (a different character *hui* from that of King Hui) was to reign over Shu for an eventful decade. During this time Qin planted itself there too firmly to be dislodged from within or without.

Consolidation required establishing a firm center of operations in Shu. To meet this essential requirement, the old Kaiming settlement at Chengdu was accorded county status and improved into a proper administrative headquarters along the lines of the Qin capital itself. Zhang Ruo, who had apparently remained loyal through the revolt of Chen Zhuang, undertook the refounding of the Shu commandery seat in 311 B.C.[19] It would function as an impregnable bastion to ensure the unchallenged say of Qin on the surrounding plains and beyond.

A bastion first of all requires a solid wall. Prior to the Qin invasion Chengdu lacked proper fortifications, being protected at best by a wooden palisade.[20] Zhang Yi and Zhang Ruo organized the building of a real city wall like those ringing towns on the central plains, a defensive necessity in view of Sichuan's continuing unsettled conditions. The Shu towns of Pi and Linqiong were also surrounded by sturdy defensive ramparts. After the construction of the alpine road linking Sichuan to Qin, these walls constituted the first of several great Qin public works projects within Sichuan itself. Carrying them out involved the massive mobilization of regional labor resources, but local precedent for that went back to pre-Qin times in Shu.[21]

When completed, the Chengdu wall's perimeter measured 12 *li* (about 6.4 kilometers), and was roughly square, or 1.6 kilometers on each side. It is a respectable dimension by the standards of ancient cities in China and other parts of the world.[22] The earthen rampart stood an impressive 7 *zhang* in height, or 23.3 meters.[23] Lookout towers and shooting parapets topped the structure, beneath which dugouts housed stored grain. Such a construction represented major outlays in human and material resources. It was hardly put up as a tourism gimmick, but rather to meet a real need and impose a stronghold of stability. The Chengdu wall demonstrated the seriousness with which Qin was committed to defending its stake in Shu.

A tradition asserts the wall required nine years of labor to complete.[24] Nearby, the town of Pi was surrounded by a seven *li* enciente standing six *zhang* high, and that erected around Linqiong was slightly smaller, six *li* and five *zhang*. By investing labor and materials in defenses throughout the Chengdu plain, Qin prudently braced to thwart either uprising or invasion. Whoever might imperil Chengdu and neighboring settlements would confront sturdy bulwarks constructed along the lines of central plains cities. At great cost Shu had become part of the Warring States landscape.

Whatever their cost, Qin defense outlays did offer some compensation in the form of productive economic spinoffs. Building the city wall had required the excavation of an enormous cubic volume of soil from as far as 10 *li* (5.3 kilometers) away. Ingeniously, the large pits formed were filled with water and made into fishponds. Qin city planning thereby combined agriculture, or in this case specifically pisciculture, with a military project. Such a tandem project accorded neatly with the *fa*, or "Legalist," methods espoused by Shang Yang and his pragmatic successors. Mass mobilization, for food production and warfare, had come to Sichuan. The fish farms were called Wansui ("Ten Millennia") Pond and Qianqiu ("Thousand Autumns") Pond, both east of Chengdu, and Liu ("Willow") Pond west of the city, all names conveying a notion of permanence. North of the capital there was also Longba, or "Dragon Levee."[25]

Hua yang guo zhi described the Shu capital's layout as adhering on a reduced scale to that of Xianyang, the Qin royal center. Within Chengdu, a barricade as high as the city wall itself partitioned the town into two districts of unequal size.[26] Government offices occupying the smaller, western compound were thereby separated from dwellings of the general populace in the larger, eastern ward. A gate controlled access to a regulated market containing many shops. According to later tradition, the official district stood on the vanquished Kaiming dynasty's former palace grounds.[27] Apart from the marquis, minister, and governor, officials included a deputy (*chang cheng*) and superintendents of salt and iron. There were also lower functionaries bearing the titles *chen*, *lang zhong*, and *ling*, as well as the Chengdu garrison that was barracked in the official, western ward of the city.[28]

Ensconced in fortress Chengdu, Shu viceregal authority next found itself contending not with the surrounding countryside or some outside invader, but the Xianyang royal court itself. A new king, Zhao, had succeeded to the Qin throne but only after a succession crisis involving disloyalties, intrigues, and defections. Authority at the palace was unstable for a time. In this atmosphere, Shu's marquis Hui, the vassal appointee of King Wu, confronted Qin in 301 B.C. The personal bond of loyalty thus had been broken, as during the previous Shu rebellion a decade earlier when a Qin regal succession coincided with an uprising in Shu. This time, though, Marquis Hui appears to have been the victim of a family intrigue aimed at fomenting discord between him and the king of Qin.[29]

As the story goes, Marquis Hui performed filial sacrifices at mountains and streams and sent a ceremonial offering of the sacrificial meat to his lord the Qin king. Clearly, he was acting in a manner to show fealty. But the marquis had a hostile stepmother residing at the Qin court, and she used this occasion to do him harm. Intercepting the parcel of food, she poisoned it. Then as the king was about to sample items from the parcel, she bid him observe prudence. Because the offering had come from as far as 2,000 *li* away, the marquis' stepmother prudently suggested having it tasted first. The king thereupon offered a portion to a courtier, who ate the tainted dish and died. Enraged, the king ordered Sima Cuo to deliver a sword to Marquis Hui, along with orders to commit suicide. The vile plot had succeeded in setting the stage for the downfall of another marquis of Shu.[30]

So for the third time in just fifteen years a Qin expedition under Sima Cuo crossed over the mountains to subject Shu. Marquis Hui faced him alone. He bore the title of governor in addition to his noble rank, which indicates that Zhang Ruo, the former Shu governor, was not supporting the marquis.[31] The office of governor, however, was a Qin institution. By assuming this role the marquis might be seen as having recognized Qin authority in principle. But such niceties aside, Sima Cuo's force was approaching, intent on ousting him anyway. Bereft and isolated, the marquis panicked and, along with the marquess, committed suicide. Sima Cuo thereupon put to death twenty-seven of their followers. The people of Shu buried the marquis outside the Chengdu city walls, a choice of site implying his disgrace and repudiation.

Once again Qin had exerted costly efforts to reimpose mastery over Shu. It was imperative to rationalize Qin authority there and so ensure a permanent climate of trust between capital and commandery. If unstable, Shu could not realize its strategic potential. Yet despite the preceding troubles, the Qin court made another try to achieve Shu loyalty through the local marquisate dynasty. Enfeoffment of still one more noble to oversee Chengdu in the wake of the unpleasant Hui affair suggests that the marquis' family remained solidly implanted on the local scene, and that Qin had not outgrown the need for either a native facade or practical collaborators to run the commandery. Wan, a son of the unfortunate Hui, was named the new marquis of Shu in 300 B.C.

Only through these uncertain fits and starts did Qin evolve its system of regional government. The commandery, that quintessential institution whereby all the autonomous central plains states were later welded into the Chinese empire, was not born in a day. No single prescription existed at the outset regarding what shape commandery government was supposed to assume. Precedent, continuity, and lessons gained through experience guided Qin in setting up and then modifying political structures for administering newly won territories. Necessary compromises accommodated local political realities, like placing a Shu marquis over lands won at the command of the Qin king and in the interests of the Qin state. Even in the wake of three violent internecine suppressions in Shu, Qin again chose to rule through a Kaiming marquis.

Marquis Wan's sole known achievement was to exonerate his woefully wronged father, two years after he succeeded to the title. Conceding the injustice done to Marquis Hui, the Qin court granted permission for a funeral cortege to convey his body across the mountains for reburial with honor at Xianyang. But even these belated obsequies were ill fated. First a three-month dry spell delayed the procession, followed by seven months of continuous rain. The hearse, mired in mud, sank into the ground at the north gate of Chengdu. That portal henceforth came to be called Xianyang Gate, and the memory of Marquis Hui was honored on the spot. Tradition came to credit Hui's spirit with controlling clouds and rain; so he was supplicated in times of either drought or deluge.[32] The superstition incidentally shows continuing popular support for the house of Kaiming.

Thirteen years after the abortive funeral for Hui, Marquis Wan himself pursued what had become a Shu marquisate tradition, by attempting to shake off the Qin yoke. Again, like his predecessors, he was deposed and killed on the Qin king's orders. Zhang Ruo acted as governor to suppress the rebellion this time. Commanding the Qin army in Shu, he not only subdued Kaiming recalcitrance, but then availed of the occasion to enlarge Qin territory on the Shu frontiers.[33] Zhang Ruo added Za, a Shu frontier district in the foothills of the Chengdu plain, and some areas across the Min River farther south. The extra campaigning there suggests the marquis may have had allies from beyond the zone of Qin control.

Revolt is never undertaken lightly, given the dire consequences of failure. Shu resistance may have stemmed from the misperception that Qin could be driven out of Sichuan, or that the Kaimings might enjoy some real autonomy within the Qin framework. Alternatively, the revolts could have simply been tragic acts of desperation. The laconic sources do not elaborate. Marquis Wan was, finally, the last Shu marquis named in these texts, the last Kaiming. Following Wan's demise the centrally appointed civil and military officials ruled without recourse to a figurehead of dubious loyalty. Through the third century B.C. Shu commandery evolved to resemble a Chinese province–type administrative unit more recognizably antecedent to those of subsequent, imperial ages.

Somehow, during the hundred or so years between Qin's conquest of Sichuan and its unification of China, a set of procedures emerged out of practical experience and ad hoc political tinkering. Shu served as a political laboratory in which the commandery as an institution achieved working form in a southern environment. In the meantime changes took place there in landholding and agricultural management, conducive to rationally ordered government through legal decree as against rule by indigenous chiefs. Inexorably less of a practical role remained for the house of Kaiming. The Shu marquisate became a dispensible anachronism, as confirmed by its futile attempts to subvert Qin control.

The Transformation of Shu

Qin had come to stay. Even before the full suppression of real or imagined revolt, the durability of Qin power in Shu was visibly evident. High walls around fortress Chengdu and other Qin garrison towns reconfigured the horizon. The Stone Cattle Road was supplemented by additional routes, wending over the Daba and Qinling ranges to bring Sichuan grain northward and knit the region ever more tightly to Qin.[34] And below, the Qin presence planted itself firmly, and literally, at the grass roots. By this is meant a thorough-going redistribution of the land, the very sod nurturing those literal roots.

Land reform, simply stated, involves redrawing field boundaries and assigning plots to the tillers. But because basic sustenance is at issue, a land reform can fundamentally redraw as well the social, economic, and political lines in a country. As a tool of rational agricultural exploitation, land reform inevitably would foster the cultural process of sinification too. This of course was the Qin purpose. In 350 B.C. Shang Yang's land reform had restructured metropolitan Qin, invigorating the state just as turning over the sods awakens new life in the soil before a spring planting. Now his political heirs commenced refurrowing the fields of Shu. Land reform was promulgated just a few years after Qin armies first marched over the mountains into Sichuan. The fully transformed Shu never again would be the private preserve of any local dynastic house of chiefs or aristocrats.

Documentary testimony derives from a contemporary textual record found in a Qin tomb in present-day Qingchuan county, northern Sichuan.[35] The burial was excavated during 1979, yielding the corpse of an unidentified man with a mix of central plains and Ba-Shu grave goods. Judging from various furnishings buried with the deceased, he had likely been a Qin figure of some importance, perhaps one of the wave of official personnel and settlers dispatched to Shu just after the conquest.

Among the many vessels, artifacts, and coins inside the grave was a wooden slip bearing 154 characters of Qin writing. The document gives specific details of a land redistribution plan supervised by Gan Mao and other Qin officials. This inscription dates the decree to the second year of a Qin king, either King Wu, in 309 B.C., or King Zhao in 305 B.C.[36]

The text states that a Qin government minister, Gan Mao, and a secretary (nei shi) named Yan were charged with carrying out a land redistribution (geng xiu wei tian lu). According to its provisions the plots were to be rectangularly shaped, of uniform size, and arranged on an orderly grid system. The document stipulates the size of each tract, taking into account even the narrow pathways between neighboring plots. Subdivisions at the lowest level were set to measure eight paces (bu) wide by thirty paces long, forming one working field unit split into two segments by a longitudinal path one pace in width.

In conformity with the plan, raised foot paths of three paces width should crisscross the fields, separating rows of working plots.

Ten rows of ten working plots, a hundred in all, would be grouped together under this system. Not only the width but also the height of the footpaths was prescribed. These passages thus also served as embankments, permitting methodical plot-by-plot irrigation. They channeled cultivators' access to the crops, and through their orderly arrangement also facilitated revenue assessment and close management of the fields.[37]

Nothing about the redistribution plan was haphazard. The document goes on to schedule seasonal maintenance tasks. During the autumn, in the eighth month, the embankments were to be shored up and any grasses growing on them mown, presumably for hay. The following month was reserved for clearing roadways, while the year's tenth month was to be spent working on ponds and bridges. Again, grasses would be cut at this time.

Such meticulous supervision once more shows how seriously Qin had devised a workable and profitable mechanism of control over Shu. Central authority and standard procedure were made to count down at these grass roots. Regularization in agriculture provided the necessary basis, the firm underpinnings of Qin power. Here was the school of *fa*, the methods of Legalism in action. The land apportionment made superfluous any role for a nobility in the countryside. Indeed, the implementation of land reform may have been a key factor in exacerbating relations between the Qin colonial masters and their Shu marquisate collaborators, giving the latter cause to rebel.

No direct information exists on how rapid a timetable Qin followed in actually implementing the cadastral plan throughout Shu. It of course was but an ideal blueprint. Undulations in the lay of the land, the natural course of waterways, plus forests, marshes, barren ground, and the presence of dwellings would all make any geometrically perfect gridiron hard to achieve. The requirements of different crops probably also counted; some areas grew rice, others taro.[38] Practical necessity no doubt tolerated local accommodations in keeping with the larger, overall interest of land redistribution and crop raising. Qin officialdom anyway was motivated more toward results than by perfectionist ideals.

Then there is the question of just who worked the fields under this new system. Were the farmers Shu people, Qin homesteaders, or people of both groups? A native Shu peasantry already was in place when Qin first occupied Sichuan in 316 B.C. Nothing really is known about the land tenure relations prevailing before that date. Shortly therafter, though, waves of immigrants were sent in under Qin sponsorship. Those assigned to farming would doubtless have received plots under the land plan.[39]

FIGURE 14

Qin land reform document on wooden slips, unearthed at Qingchuan, Sichuan. (*Wen wu*, no. 1, 1982, p. 11)

Colonists sent to reside in Shu numbered in the tens of thousands, perhaps hundreds of thousands during the century of Qin control. The statistic is comparable to, and may exceed, the contemporary Hellenization of Egypt and the Persian lands in the wake of Alexander's conquests. Not all Shu-bound migrants came from metropolitan Qin. As Qin armies campaigned on the central plains, broad districts were seized and incorporated along with their entire populations. Many such new Qin subjects were dispatched to the south.[40] Recruiting efforts lured still more peasants.

Qin officials conducted the mass relocations in an orderly, closely supervised fashion, as another recently discovered document discloses.[41] This remarkable piece of textual evidence contains regulations for conveying columns of settlers over the mountain road to Shu. Their long trek proceded along a defined route, from a specified jump-off point at Feiqiu, a Qin county in present Shaanxi. Immigrants were enjoined to remain together in their assigned groups and not to go astray while on the march. The Qin system of organized surveillance thus began even before arrival in the new land.[42] Regulations also prescribed the issuance of their rations. Designated march wardens kept order until the columns reached Chengdu, where the settlers would be remanded over to the Shu governor. On arrival, some of the more well-to-do migrants occasionally were able to influence or bribe officials regarding the location of their resettlement.[43]

Sources often describe the settlers with the term *tu*, often used to denote prisoners and implying that a degree of coercion lay behind their move. In understanding the migrants' status, the translation "exiles" is probably most appropriate for this term. Many settlers in fact were convicts, or amnestied convicts, sentenced to Sichuan banishment.[44] Many others were pioneers, Qin style. Apart from the mass of displaced peasants, prisoners of war, and criminals, these pioneers included also a few aristocrats and merchants.[45] To many, perhaps most, the migration was compulsory. Some men sent to Shu were forced to leave their families behind.[46] Others may have been induced to move by the promise of land or wealth to be gained from commerce and industry in Sichuan.

A few settlers' descendants prospered conspicuously there several generations later, and not all newcomers remained in the agricultural sector. People from the central plains became involved in salt extraction, iron smelting, and the mining of cinnabar for dyes and medicinal purposes. One wealthy widow whose family operated a lucrative cinnabar mine after settling in Sichuan was singled out for honor by the First Qin Emperor.

This and other success stories show that the status of forced migrant carried no indelible opprobrium. Rather, Sichuan under Qin offered chances for economic gain and social mobility.[47] For all these migrants, uprooted from distant homes and set down again amidst an unfamiliar surrounding, the move meant breaking old attachments. Qin law and organization provided new ties and also required new loyalties. Shu commandery under the Qin developed as a land of opportunity, where homesteaders could make a fresh start in life and the enterprising might even amass wealth.

The introduction of Qin metal coinage as a medium of exchange lubricated this vibrant Shu economy and reinforced its specific tie to Qin. Prior to the Qin conquest, bridge-shaped bronze tokens were placed in Ba-Shu boat-coffin tombs but there is no definite proof that these represented money. If market transactions in Ba-Shu Sichuan actually relied on specie, then this system was still in an incipient stage. After 316 B.C. the spread of coins took place rapidly, as it would seem from the archaeological evidence. Graves in Qingchuan and Guangyuan, both in northern Shu, have yielded numismatic finds. At Qingchuan, bronze half-tael (ban liang) coins were recovered from the same tomb containing the land reform document cited earlier. That is not surprising, as it was the burial of a Qin personage who happened to die while on assignment in Shu.

Of even greater significance are similar coins documented from post-conquest Ba-Shu culture boat-coffin–style graves at Guangyuan. Bridge-shaped bronze tokens are found in some of the same burials. The inclusion of half-tael coins in this context indicates how the Qin money economy was imposed upon the indigenous Sichuanese and apparently accepted by them in short order. As the ample accompanying goods attest, these graves were of important persons although their names and positions remain unknown. Those who launched the deceased off to the hereafter via boat coffin had become sufficiently accustomed to using cash that they felt it appropriate to provide a travel advance.[48]

Along with other factors like the redrawing of field boundaries, the thronging in of northerners, the consolidation of Qin bureaucracy, and the establishment of fortified towns with Qin garrisons, the adoption of Qin coinage worked to steadily weaken whatever grip on power was still retained by Shu aristocrats. Unless they too joined in the expanding commercial economy, they could hardly compete with the rising, dynamic class of merchants now avidly tapping and developing the resources of Shu. The rapid spread of specie indeed generated a regional demand for coins on a scale large enough that at least one Qin mint was apparently established in Shu. A coin mold, found in 1980 at Gaoxian, Sichuan, strongly suggests local minting. The mold was designed for casting twenty-eight bronze half-tael coins at a time, in four rows of seven coins each.[49]

Archaeological work in western Sichuan has not yet investigated settlement patterns for the Qin period. Little therefore is understood about how northern colonist communities lived in relation to the indigenous Shu colonial population and the process by which the latter were displaced or absorbed. Excavation results published so far have been limited to findings from the opening of a few tombs such as the one at Qingchuan just cited. In addition to the documents and coins it contained, the burial itself is of some interest. It clearly conforms to central plains mortuary styles, and most of the ceramic and bronze vessel offerings included as grave goods were of central plains types. Just a few Ba-Shu style luxury items, principally lacquerware, figured as part of the Qingchuan man's possessions for the afterlife.

The limited evidence suggests that northern immigrants valued Shu luxury goods, at least for inclusion in burial troves. But this amounts to a merely superficial level of interaction and exchange and should not be taken to indicate cultural assimilation. It is evident from the known burials that Qin colonists and Shu colonials coexisted in Shu for decades following the initial Qin conquest.[50] Western Sichuan graves from the Qin century are readily identifiable as those of either indigenous people or transplanted northerners.

A tomb in Dayi county west of Chengdu is typically that of a local warrior of some means, buried with spears, halberds, long and short Ba-Shu–style swords bearing tiger markings, a crossbow, and a conical helmet. An axe head, one of the swords, and a scyth were of iron but all the other arms had been cast in bronze. Present as well were bronze cauldrons, a half-tael cash, and two signature seals. Here the coin principally differentiates this grave from other Ba-Shu interments dating to before the conquest of 316 B.C.[51] Nonetheless, the iron implements show that this metal was gradually coming into wider use during the Qin century.

The Shu people were not extirpated during the early decades of Qin rule in Sichuan, nor did their aristocracy lose its position at once. Accommodations were made. All the same, Qin culture increasingly dominated the local scene, bit-by-bit displacing that which came before. The natives held on to many aspects of a separate Ba-Shu identity although their numerical proportion decreased relative to the flood of migrants. Shu commandery and many of its inhabitants were becoming Chinese.

Qin Power in Ba

Simultaneously with the transformation of Shu, Qin managed to wage an ongoing struggle against its perennial enemies: Chu, Qi, and the three former Jin states of Han, Wei, and Zhao. The program undertaken by Qin in Shu fit neatly into its strategic blueprint for winning that military and diplomatic struggle. Shu was nurtured as a protected, productive rear-base area materially supporting the war effort. In Ba, the other half of the Sichuan basin, politics and geographic facts dictated a somewhat different course of development. In 316 B.C. Qin had only partially wrested Ba from Chu, which retained outposts and influence near the Yangtze gorges, inside Sichuan. With this potent foe still present, the Qin conquerers were loath to risk alienating their Ba adherents. Caution was taken to avert rebellions like those that plagued Shu. Adapting to the situation in Ba, the Qin rulers again carried out a practical, successful, yet distinct policy.

Formally the legal status of the Han valley, Ba, and Shu were equivalent, as Qin commanderies. What that term meant in actual practice, however, could vary greatly. Little is known of internal governing procedures in the Han valley. In the case of Shu, the commandery, as seen, was first shared with an enfeoffed native marquis in hopes of gaining his collaboration. This did not work out. Only after much blood had been shed, well into the reign of Qin King Zhao and almost four decades after the conquest, did Shu administrators fully supplant the marquisate. Power then came to be exercised by careerist officials bearing ranks in the Qin service system, functionaries owing all to the king as opposed to nobles possessing an autonomous territorial power base.

But Ba, in contrast to Shu, lay on the Qin confrontation line with Chu. Ba-Qin ties in fact long predated the Qin incursion into Sichuan, going back as far as the eighth century B.C. when Ba rulers, pressed by Chu in the Han valley, proffered tribute to Qin. By the fourth century B.C. Chu had pushed the Ba court back to Langzhong on the upper Jialing River, still closer to Qin. The Qin pretext as an ally of a Ba client, the marquis of Zu, had provided some rationale for crossing the Qinling range. These factors, the frontline position of Ba and its longstanding relationship with Qin, granted Ba a de facto status within the Qin state rather unlike that of Shu. Both Ba and Shu at first were treated as protectorates, or clients, but heavy colonization made Shu more rapidly into an integral part of Qin.[52]

On entering Ba in 316 B.C. a Qin force took its king into custody. He is absent from extant sources thereafter, when Ba was declared a

Qin commandery.[53] Nevertheless, for some time after the conquest commentators occasionally omitted Ba from mention of those lands actually ruled by Qin.[54] Qin's King Hui moreover continued, for awhile, to recognize the preeminence of the Ba core group, or clan (*ba shi*), among the broad confederation of native southern peoples (*man yi*) grouped together in Ba territory. They received gifts of women from Qin, so strengthening blood ties to Xianyang. Local aristocrats retained their titles, provided they did not commit any offenses. Annual and triennial monetary tributes of a few thousand cash were imposed upon the Ba, payable through their own chief (*jun chang*). Commoner households were liable for payments in native cloth and in fowl.[55]

No Qin functionary is named by any surviving document as head of Ba commandery. *Hua yang guo zhi* says only that Zhang Yi fortified the settlement of Jiangzhou, near the present Chongqing. However, the text lacks any account to match its rich description of how Chengdu was built. Ba commandery included a number of counties, or *xian*.[56] A Qin logistical access called the "Granary Road" (*mi cang dao*) was built over the Daba range connecting Ba to the Han valley, but in just which decade is not known.[57] From Hanzhong the road linked with the Bao-Xie route across the Qinling range to Qin proper.

By reaching Jiangzhou, Qin power had thrust into the Chu sphere of influence and concern. Further conflict with Chu was bound to follow, and Qin would require strong local support if it were to maintain the advanced position. This probably is the reason for the initially less obtrusive Qin presence in Ba than in Shu. Jiangzhou likely served as the seat of Qin administration, but all evidence suggests that substantive Qin control remained lighter in Ba than in Shu. For one thing, Qin relied heavily in Ba on the willing cooperation of indigenous people, who were not supplanted by any great influx of outside colonists as in Shu. Neither are there accounts of uprisings by Ba feudatories.

Instead of the revolts that troubled Shu during the first three decades of Qin rule, the literary accounts offer a revealing if somewhat metaphoric tale concerning, of all things, a wild tiger. It relates that during the reign of Qin's King Zhao, an albino tiger rampaged through Ba, Shu, and Hanzhong commanderies, attacking people. Other maneating tigers soon joined in, claiming some 1,200 victims in all. The king called on experienced hunters to track the beast and advertised a substantial bounty. This would consist of a cash sum plus a fief with 10,000 families to provide income for the successful killer. At the former Ba capital of Langzhong a member of the Yi people took up the offer.[58] He fashioned a crossbow of bamboo, kept watch for the tiger from a tower, and shot it.

Despite the bounty terms, King Zhao reneged on his offer to enfeoff the Yi brave. In its place he proclaimed a substitute award that was engraved for posterity on a stone tablet. It exempted the Yi from land taxes and payment of bridal fees up to ten wives. Qin law was to be waived in certain legal cases. Disputes involving bodily injury would be arbitrated, whereas homicide cases could be expiated on a cash payment of blood money. Furthermore, under the terms of a mutual pledge, the Qin and the Yi committed themselves to payment of ritual fines if their agreements were broken. Were the Yi to betray Qin, they would be assessed a kind of yellow serpent (*huang long*), and Qin would be liable for a measure (*zhong*) of alcoholic spirit in compensatory damages for betraying the Yi. According to later versions, the Yi were placated by this agreement.[59]

Setting aside the tiger tale's folkloric ingredients, features of genuine historical value remain. The white tiger in Ba myth represented the spirit of the founder hero Linjun who had united five clans under the Ba clan's leadership.[60] The killing of the tiger stands for the elimination of Ba clan overlordship. However, the legend also shows that Qin lacked a monopoly of force as it proceeded to divide the various Ba peoples. Culturally autonomous native entities were treated as auxiliaries with whom Qin signed negotiated compacts. And the terms of the tiger agreement betray a certain ritualistic quality seemingly more in keeping with native custom than rational Qin statute. Power in Ba commandery was apparently shared for a longer time, in contrast to Shu where Qin fought recurring bloody battles to quell unrest and assert authority.

Qin did manipulate the balance of power in Ba at its fulcrum and could influence the tilt provided judicious care was exercised. For example, the Qin king withdrew the promise of a fief to the Yi tiger hunter, but he made sure to offer a satisfactory substitute allowance. If temporary compromise meant waiving laws and making concessions, Xianyang was so willing to maintain authority from a distance. Qin avoided jeopardizing its position in Ba by paying cautious regard to costs and consequences.

The result meant a slower pace toward cultural absorption and outright political domination. Because Qin apparently refrained from sending waves of homesteaders to Ba, the ethnic composition there did not dramatically shift as happened in Shu. Textual references to the migrations make this clear by negative implication; for example,

"Qin's migrants all (*jie*) settled in Shu."[61] That is, northerners did not generally settle in Ba, which remained peopled by its groups of indigenous inhabitants. Qin power had to be erected on preexisting social foundations, unlike in Shu where masses of outsiders new to Sichuan were entirely dependent on the Qin state for rations, assignment to their new homes, and security. Because the populations and arrangements in Ba remained more intact than in Shu, it is hard to imagine a successful implementation of the Qin land redistribution plan, if indeed it was attempted there at all.

Qin policies may have been modified significantly to meet prevailing circumstances, but what impact Qin did have in Ba must not be minimized. A cash economy quickly began to supplement such trade, presumably barter, that hitherto had operated. Finds of Qin bronze coins at several Ba locations confirm the textual evidence of this commercial development.[62] Apart from the native bronze bridge-shaped tokens, no coins of any other state besides Qin have been reported from Sichuan. Acceptance of Qin cash as a means of exchange weakened the institution of enfeoffed landholding in Ba commandery. The deal whereby a Yi brave was persuaded to accept coin and legal exemptions in lieu of a landed appanage exemplifies this passing away of the older value system. These economic changes proved a harbinger to the eventual cultural sinification of Ba. The Qin commercial penetration of Ba took place even though outright political control was still shared, for the sake of expediency.

Artifacts from Ba lands during the Qin century indicate a high degree of cultural continuity with the preceding Ba-Shu period. Tomb excavations confirm this, and some thirty boat graves from two areas of Ba are well documented. One cemetery, at Baolunyuan in present-day Zhaohua county, lay at the northern apex of Ba near the Qin route to Chengdu. Another set of graves was uncovered at Dongxunba, in Ba county some sixty kilometers west of Chongqing city.[63] Despite the distance separating the two groups of interments there is a broad conformity in burial styles and grave goods. Each cemetery contains boat-shaped coffins as well as more conventional rectangular coffins not adhering to the boat design. The presence of Qin half-tael (*ban liang*) copper cash dates certain graves to the Qin century. There also are graves from the same culture dating to Han times at both sites.

These burials reveal that Qin supremacy in Ba did not eradicate the cult that had practiced boat-coffin burials. Neither did Qin rule leave much impact on weaponry and everyday implements. Ceramics, lacquerware, bamboo, and wooden artifacts are like those of the pre-Qin era. Metal objects were cast mainly of bronze as previously, with some axes, knives, and spear points of iron. Most of the weapons were bronze swords and halberd blades in patterns indistinguishable from Ba-Shu types predating the Qin conquest. Many bear the Ba tiger-totem marking. Bronze signature seals at both sites include some examples with Ba-Shu characters. In general, the material from Baolunyuan and Dongxunba seems to show that apart from the momentous adoption of copper cash, cultural life in Ba commandery continued much as before, in the days of the Ba kingdom.

Culture may have evolved at only a modest pace during the Qin century, but politics at higher levels underwent a shift. Eastern Sichuan had always been populated by a plurality of ethnic groups over which the actual Ba ruling lineage had held greater or lesser sway at various times. As noted, in 316 B.C. King Hui recognized the Ba core group as leader among the various peoples in eastern Sichuan. Later on his successors were able to cut separate deals with Ba subgroups, such as the Yi. That incident was reported in the textual sources without specific reference to any so-called Ba group. And by the end of the Qin century in Sichuan all textual allusions to the Ba as a people had ceased, leaving *Ba* no more than a geographic expression. When the natives are mentioned in extant sources it is by their primary ethnic, clan, or local affiliation, like the Yi, the Zong, the Banxunman, and others.[64] Something had happened to the Ba.

Apart from the white tiger parable involving Qin power in Ba, there are indications that Chu delivered its own coup de grace of sorts to the erstwhile Ba ruling clan. A surviving fragment in a late source reports that King Xiang of Chu eliminated the viscount (zi) of Ba and enfeoffed a Chu prince south of the Pu River, with the title marquis of Tongliang.[65] The geography and dates of this information both seem plausible. Tongliang is some sixty kilometers northwest of Chongqing. King Xiang of Chu reigned from 298–263 B.C., after the Qin had extinguished the Ba kingdom as such. That could account for the Ba noble's being referred to by the inferior title of viscount.

The breakup and dispersal of the preeminent Ba lineage is noted elsewhere as well. A Tang dynasty geography recalls that after Chu obliterated Ba, the Ba viscount and his brothers drifted eastward toward Qianzhong from whence, according to legend, the archaic Ba had emerged many centuries earlier. There were five Ba brothers in all according to this source, a figure reminiscent of the original five clans under the Ba. By the Han dynasty each of the five lines ruled over separate river valleys in easternmost Sichuan, southwestern Hubei, or northwestern Hunan provinces.[66]

Although the overt parallelism of this account casts suspicion on matters of detail, it is apparent that the Ba, per se, gradually ceased to be a commanding factor during the Qin century. Later philological and toponymic studies trace some Ba descendants to the Tujia people in northwestern Hunan, which at any rate removes them from the power equation of third century B.C. Sichuan.[67]

Qin may have undercut the Ba clan and established a presence along the Jialing River in central Sichuan but Chu meanwhile managed to maintain a foothold, eastward yet still within the Sichuan basin, at least until 277 B.C. The Qin elimination of that vestigial Chu presence would wait upon events unfolding to the north and south, respectively in the Han valley and on the Guizhou-Yunnan plateau.

The Defeat of Chu

Contemporary observers in the late fourth century sensed an approaching denouement in the protracted multistate struggle. Experts of the age had accorded only two states realistic chances for total victory, these being Qin and Chu. As Zhang Yi was quoted to say, "Of all the powers, it has to be either Qin or Chu. Both cannot prevail."[68] This summary view came from the coarchitect of Qin rule over Sichuan, a veteran of service in Chu as well, an equally astute practitioner of war and of diplomacy. Diplomacy still played a role in relations among states in the erstwhile Zhou community but it no longer worked to maintain equilibrium. The balance of power had begun an inexorable tilt, favoring Qin.

Chu desperately needed allies, preferably for long-term cooperation if Qin was to be stopped. Chu diplomacy aimed at bringing about multistate cooperation on a longitudinal axis (*he cong*) to resist the methodical Qin juggernaut. Yet given the mutual jealousies and a tradition of mistrust by state rulers toward each other, durable coalitions proved impossible to construct. Qin too sought alliance partners, although only as a spoiler. For Qin it would be enough to flirt with other states in temporary latitudinal (*lian heng*) alliances to disrupt Chu hopes.[69] Time was on the side of Qin, which held the upper hand strategically, operationally, and as it turned out, tactically as well.

A decade-long truce between Qin and Chu had ensued upon the Zhang Yi negotiations of 311 B.C. When hostilities resumed at the outset of the third century, most major armed actions took place on the central plains. A Qin general called Bai Qi won renown in these battles, inflicting frightful losses on Chu and other states.[70] Further south, the vital Han valley commandery of Hanzhong was made secure for Qin, under a governor appointed in 294 B.C.[71] Inside the Sichuan basin Qin worked its transformation of Shu while cautiously courting the peoples of Ba with a view to preparing further blows against Chu. Meanwhile, Chu prepared a riposte in the deep south to offset its losses incurred in the Han valley and on the central plains. Fearful of the looming danger posed by Qin in Sichuan, Chu resorted to one more endeavor aimed at reducing risk from that quarter. The goal was to hold on to its remaining enclave in the eastern Sichuan basin and to explore strategic possibilities on the basin's southern rim.

South of Ba lay the territories of Qianzhong, Yelang, and Dian. Qianzhong included parts of southern Sichuan, western Hunan, and northern Guizhou.[72] Yelang comprised much of central Guizhou, whereas Dian occupied part of present Yunnan. If successfully established, a Chu base there would outflank, counterbalance, and thereby neutralize Qin's Shu stronghold. Success for Chu depended on keeping open a line of communication between its home ground in Hubei and these far-flung southwestern lands. Cutting the Chu line likewise became an imperative for Qin. That made confrontation in eastern Sichuan unavoidable, with far more than local issues at stake.[73] What happened on this extreme flank of Chu and Qin inevitably would affect their contest for mastery over the more familiar, traditional marching grounds of the central plains.

The name associated with Chu's southwestern ambitions is Zhuang Qiao, a general related to the Chu royal house. He formerly had staged a rebellion against the king, but then consented to rejoin the state as a top commander. Near contemporaries respected Zhuang Qiao's military skills even before he acquiesced again to Chu royal authority.[74] His southwestern expedition was carried out on the Chu king's orders.[75] That might indicate its importance to Chu grand strategy, although perhaps the move offered incidental means whereby Chu could conveniently dispose of a freebooter. According to *Shi ji*, Zhuang Qiao and his men followed the Yangtze upstream, plundering Ba and Shu before proceeding to Qianzhong and eventually to Dian. The geography varies in other accounts. *Hua yang guo zhi* has Zhuang Qiao entering Qianzhong, that is, western Hunan and northern Guizhou, via the Yuan River without touching on the Yangtze, Ba, or Shu.[76]

Despite disparities of detail, the sources do agree that Zhuang Qiao penetrated some distance into territory south of Sichuan. His presence there provoked Qin to respond. A hostile garrison or colony south of Ba and Shu could be only a thorn, or worse, in the side of the Qin position. Some of the peoples of Ba commandery had cultural affinities to the natives of Guizhou.[77] If ensconced in the region Zhuang Qiao would pose a subversive threat, as a political alternative to Qin. Qin had not yet secured full domination over Ba, and Ba nobles still treated with Chu and accepted Chu titles and fiefs. Meanwhile still farther south on the Yunnan plateau the Dian state had remained literally aloof from the quarrels of Qin, Chu, and Sichuan. Should Chu manage to inveigle Dian into its affairs as an ally or proxy, it would endanger Qin in both Shu and Ba commanderies. The challenge was serious—but ephemeral.

In response, a Qin counterstroke against Zhuang Qiao came in 281 B.C. The Qin general Sima Cuo once again led an army in Sichuan, this time seizing Qianzhong, which became a Qin commandery.[78] Not only did this timely Qin move cordon off the remaining Chu positions in Sichuan, it also intersected Zhuang Qiao's line of retreat. His expedition thus was permanently cut off from its Chu base. Eventually the Chu commander declared himself an independent king in Guizhou and Yunnan where his troops melded into the aboriginal population.[79] Their settling down there constitutes a significant episode in the gradual process of southern cultural assimilation, but they failed to weaken Qin. The rustication in Guizhou of the Chu force under Zhuang Qiao removed an impediment to the Qin advance against Chu. Zhuang Qiao was neutralized, and with him Chu hopes of containing Qin in the south faded.

Once Zhuang Qiao's attempt at encirclement of Sichuan from the south had failed, third century B.C. statesmen referred to the whole Chu enterprise in Sichuan as a debacle.[80] Henceforth Chu found itself permanently on the defensive there. Rebellion had ceased in Shu, leaving that commandery secure to realize its promise as a base for Qin offensive operations. Settlers from the central plains were turning the land into a giant granary. Workshops forged Shu ores into tools and weapons for Qin farmers and soldiers. New roads improved lateral communications between Shu and Qin proper. In Ba commandery the former Ba ruling group had been effectively superseded as a factor, caught between Chu and Qin and worn away as these two giants abraded against each other. Native peoples formerly subordinate to the Ba remained in place, but represented no challenge to Qin. From Ba, Qin strategists by 280 B.C. could realistically contemplate an advance into Chu itself.

Although production and population statistics are not available, a generation of land reform, northern settlement, and robust economic growth in Shu no doubt left the commandery self-sustaining, with ample resources to spare. Adequate labor was available to Qin in both Shu and Ba. Offensives aimed at Chu from Sichuan would not overly tap resources needed by Qin on battlefronts north of the Qinling Mountains. So although steadily pressuring Chu, Qin could simultaneously skirmish on the central plains. Attrition would wear down its enemies, exhausting their human and material capital while Qin nurtured its strength in the Sichuan basin. Surplus production from Sichuan enabled Qin to conduct sustained campaigning in the third century B.C., replacing the stop and go, episodic seasonal fighting of previous times. This qualitatively altered the calculus of ancient Chinese warfare.

Qin strategy benefited from an enhanced operational position. Via the Stone Cattle Road and other parallel routes through the mountains to Sichuan, Qin commanders were able to shift troops on interior lines. They thereby possessed more choices regarding where and when to attack than did their foes. Several land and water passages naturally channeled movement out of Qin-controlled territory toward Chu. These were Wu pass in the north, the Han valley in the center, and the Yangtze farther south out of Ba and Shu. On the Yangtze itself only the precipitous Wu gorge between Sichuan and Hubei separated Ba commandery from Chu proper.[81] When Qin obtained Qianzhong, yet another possible vantage point against Chu was added. Like the Yangtze, the eastward flowing rivers of Qianzhong facilitate an invader's progress along the current into the Chu heartland.

Rivers had become central to Qin military planning. As early as 311 B.C. when Qin authority in Shu seemed shaky, Zhang Yi had averted Chu intervention by raising the specter of an armada poised to strike down the Yangtze. It may have been part bluff, but the mere vision of a Qin landing on the riverbanks of his capital proved sufficient then to deter the Chu king. Whether or not a real force backed Zhang Yi's convincing bluster three decades before, by 280 B.C. effective amphibious units had indeed been created. Qin success in deploying flotillas of river craft to meet military needs is again evidence of the state's practical adaptability. Conceivably the native boatmen of Ba lent their navigational skills to the Qin authorities in preparing operations against Chu.

Complementing the strategic and operational advantages of Qin was a tactical finesse in directing troops. As with the Romans, this is particularly evident in the versatile engineering arm, and in the synchronous employment of task forces separated by great distances. General Bai Qi, a veteran of fighting on the central plains, took charge of an assault by heavy infantry pushing southward down the Han River. Meanwhile still more Qin heavy infantry units assembled in Shu to proceed along the Min and Yangtze Rivers.[82] Their methodical, coordinated pincer advance aimed at breaking through Chu's outer defenses into the Chu heartland itself. It took several years of uninterrupted maneuver. Qin progress can be followed with the aid of a recently discovered chronicle kept on bamboo slips.[83] The data therein confirms other textual accounts and also provides some supplementary information.

First the Han River town of Deng was taken. Deng sits astride a natural crossroad and had been the object of a joint attack by Ba and Chu over four centuries earlier.[84] The episode then facilitated Chu's subsequent expansion up the Han valley. Now in 280 B.C. the tides of power had reversed. General Bai Qi's northern pincer seized Deng and the following year he descended the Han to besiege Yan, applying engineering techniques to the investment of this city. He had a vast ditch dug, diverting the river and drowning Yan's inhabitants en masse.[85]

Once Deng and Yan were secured, amnestied convicts from Qin were dispatched to settle and hold the area indefinitely, following the precedent set in Shu.[86] Qin also proceeded to occupy ground containing the tombs of former Chu rulers and prepared to march against the Chu capital, Ying. Ying is on the Yangtze, deep in Hubei province. Its fall in 278 B.C. amounted to a devastating psychological blow, heralding the ultimate demise of Chu. Bai Qi at once set up a new Qin commandery on the spot. Here again, Qin meant to stay.[87] Domination of the upper Han and of Sichuan on the upper Yangtze had enabled Qin to become a central Yangtze power.[88]

The outcome of this war put Chu permanently on the defensive. Loss of the Chu dynasty's royal tombs undercut political legitimacy and morale, and abandonment of the capital city raised doubts about the state's ultimate viability. From the operational standpoint as it affected Sichuan, the capture of Ying cut off Chu's western bulwark at the Yangtze Gorges. Qin forces from Shu under Zhang Ruo stormed Wu Gorge and Wu Mountain in 277 B.C.[89] With the fall of this principal river gateway between Sichuan and Hubei, Chu had finally been evicted from its last Sichuan toehold. The forward Qin line now bisected Hubei, well beyond the Sichuan basin, which now was completely secure.

Sichuan in the Qin Empire

Chu had suffered a debacle. The Qin stroke of 316 B.C., occupying Sichuan, had been the prerequisite condition for driving Chu successively out of the Sichuan basin, the southern plateau, and then its own capital region, the central Yangtze. These advances hastened the end of Chu and so made possible the ultimate unification of China under Qin. But after 277 B.C. over five decades were to elapse before the final Qin victory. If Sichuan's annexation by Qin is deemed the decisive, strategic turning point in achieving Chinese unification, what accounted for the long delay?[90]

Geography explains why Qin could not immediately press home its advantage and why so many more campaigns and battles had to be fought between 277 B.C. and the date of unification, 221 B.C. The key factor in the Qin campaign against Chu had been the Han River, which together with Qin possession of the upper Yangtze had permitted General Bai Qi's two pronged amphibious advance. East of where the Han meets the Yangtze, there no longer are any convenient north-south waterways. The hammer and anvil effect could not be repeated; victory ironically had deprived Qin of operational maneuverability. Greater difficulties now complicated the tasks of moving armies, their assembly, reinforcement, supply, command, and control while away on long service in hostile territory.

Henceforth the contest of Qin against all would be one of slow attrition, essentially fought on two fronts. In the south Qin faced what remained of Chu, which had relocated its base to the productive lower Yangtze. Marshy ground inhibits the movement of troops in much of this area, making grand flank marches impractical. Northward, on the central plains, Qin armies confronted various coalitions of their old enemies, the three Jin states, intermittently backed by Yan and Qi.

Qin could prevail on the central plains provided enough grain and other resources were brought to bear. However, south to north access from Qin's base areas in Shu and the upper Han valley was limited to dry land routes, the Stone Cattle Road, and similar log and plank constructions appropriately called granary roads through the Qinling Mountains.[91] Overland haulage is tremendously consumptive of resources, involving much wastage and a large "tail-to-tooth" ratio of support personnel to frontline combatants. Qin needed to find some way to step up base-area production to such a high level that en route losses could be compensated, no matter what the cost.

The cost was great. Yet when mandated, Qin planners were

willing to take considerable pains, even to defy nature in making agriculture and war mutually serve the state. This had been demonstrated in building the Stone Cattle Road and again in erecting the walls of Chengdu. The next labor-intensive earth-moving Qin venture in Shu was designed to transform the very shape of the land. In so doing the project would channel water, in regulated volume, to all those fields so carefully parceled out under the land reform program. From the fields would come bigger harvests to feed more troops, a military manpower reserve to wear down the forces of all opposing states.

The project conceived by Qin planners was the massive Dujiangyan water diversion.[92] Dujiangyan translates as "Capital River Dam." It is located in modern Guan county, where the southward flowing Min River debouches from outlying foothills onto the plain. Thereafter the Min's natural course continues due south. However, the river does not pass through the Shu capital or even bisect the Chengdu plain, where it is most needed, but rather inconveniently adheres to foothills near the plain's western edge. This would have to be corrected.

Work on Dujiangyan may have followed upon Kaiming efforts begun prior to Qin rule.[93] More immediately there was the Qin wartime precedent of channeling a river to flood the besieged Chu city of Yan. But the state sponsored development of Chengdu and the plains around it was conceived for permanent results, as a water management installation on a hitherto unseen scale. The Dujiangyan project was to support the Qin land apportioning system in turning the Shu plain into a green mosaic of productivity, rectangle after tiny rectangle.

This mammoth task fell to the successor generation of Qin administrators, those who had taken over from Sima Cuo, Zhang Yi, and Zhang Ruo. The Kaiming marquisate's failed rebellions were finally over. Zhang Ruo's annexation of the hilly region west of Chengdu around the year 285 B.C. provided local security, a prerequisite before the Dujiangyan work could commence. The expulsion of Chu from the Han valley, the Yunnan-Guizhou plateau, and eastern Sichuan further guaranteed that the earth-moving labors in Shu would proceed undisturbed. An undertaking on such a grand scale as the Min River diversion would have hardly been feasible against a background of political instability or external threat.

Placed in charge of Dujiangyan was Li Bing, governor in Shu after Zhang Ruo. Li Bing took over Shu commandery about 277 B.C.[94] Chu had been driven from Sichuan, the Shu marquises' revolts were over, and the long, stable reign of Qin King Zhao had begun.[95]. With the marquisate abrogated and with no incumbent minister (*xiang*) in Shu, Li Bing exercised undisputed control. It is significant that the giant engineering task about to begin was entrusted to an official holding the military title of governor (*shou*). Since the days of Lord Shang, Qin habitually combined endeavors in war and agriculture. The enterprise at Dujiangyan amounted to a multifaceted infrastructure project with both military and economic applications. It alleviated a chronic flood danger, provided a new inland waterway for commercial and riverine naval boat traffic, and irrigated rice crops over a vast area.[96]

Projects like Dujiangyan require time in their conception and execution, and still more time before the material benefits they will provide eventually become available. Qin, like Rome, was hardly built in a day. The time during which massive resources were diverted to build Dujiangyan may partially account for the slower pace of Qin advances against enemy kingdoms in the middle third century B.C., despite heavy fighting. Manpower, grain, and commodities earmarked for earth-moving work in Shu meant less on the central plains battlefronts in the short run. But in due course, the investment would pay dividends. The colossal labors invested in Dujiangyan, after all, had been allocated not for mere subsistence but to warrant success for the state in its scheme to unite China.

Dujiangyan in fact was the largest, most carefully planned public works project yet seen anywhere on the eastern half of the Eurasian continent. To redirect part of the southward flowing Min on a more easterly course, it was first necessary to split the river into two channels. An artificial island made of piled up stone therefore was constructed, carefully streamlined and tapering to a feature known as the "fish's bite" (*yu ju*), so called for the actual stone sculpture of a fish around which the stream parted.

The portion of flow left to continue its natural course in the original Min riverbed was called the outer river, whereas the term inner river referred to the new branch diverted toward Chengdu. A channel had to be cut through the high overlooking bluffs, which entailed removing a huge cubic volume of earth. Beyond the bluffs the diverted flow was provided with a radiating set of subsidiary channels to direct water over a wide area of the Chengdu plain.[97]

A careful hydraulic engineering study doubtless preceded the actual start of work. Prior Qin experience in irrigation had been limited to the relatively arid lands north of the Qinling Mountains, but in Sichuan, wet paddy rice farming benefitted from the water diversion. Li Bing and his staff were undaunted by the markedly contrastive environmental conditions. The feasibility of Dujiangyan bespeaks Qin success in functionally combining features of northern and southern know-how to mutual benefit.

Adequate attention necessarily was paid as well to the logistic, managerial, and public relations aspects of the endeavor. Unlike the later Great Wall and Grand Canal, no horror stories of mass privation and death are associated with the building of Dujiangyan. Here the Qin imprint seems relatively benign and progressive. Li Bing is also credited with erecting seven bridges over streams in the areas around Chengdu.[98] He earned the lasting accolade of history for his care and foresight, even attaining semidivine status in the eyes of local people. The manner in which he came to be so revered is seen in a parable of the sinification process underway in Shu.

This bit of folklore illustrates Li Bing the politician in action, winning confidence in Shu while conquering the Min River. Animist Shu religion had regarded the Min as a deity. The governor coopted this indigenous belief and made it a Qin state cult by building a temple to the god.[99] Prior to his governorship, a local custom had prevailed whereby two maidens were purchased annually, by popular subscription, to provide sacrifice victims for the river spirit. The sacrificial ceremony had proceeded in the manner of a wedding. Superstition had it that unless propitiated each year with a pair of new brides, the Min might overflow.

Li Bing ended the practice by a combination of tact and showmanship. He first offered two daughters of his own in betrothal to the Min god and arranged a nuptial banquet by the riverside. The Li girls were dressed in bridal finery, and an empty throne was set up for their riparian fiance. While crowds looked on, the governor then invited the ethereal bridegroom to drink a toast to the occasion. He drained his own cup but the cup set before the empty throne of course remained full.

As if taking offense at the god's refusal to drink, Li Bing drew a sword, challenged his would-be divine son-in-law to a duel and prudently left the scene. Just then two bulls appeared on the riverbank. They locked horns and began fighting, which was taken to be a duel by proxy for the combat between the governor and the Min River god. After awhile Li Bing returned, sweating profusely as would a swordsman in the heat of action. He commanded his lieutenants to aid him, claiming the bull facing south represented himself, and the other one, facing north, his foe. When an assistant slew the northward facing bull, this symbolic act subdued the river spirit as well. Through the medium of the bull, Li Bing had won.[100] Whether read literally or metaphorically, the tale demonstrates the changes in belief systems underway in Shu society. The old, capricious god was vanquished. In its place, an enduring memorial cult grew around Li Bing. His putative son and successor on the Dujiangyan project, Li Erlang, was also later worshipped.[101] Their mighty efforts seemed to parallel myths of the great hydraulic engineer Yu the Great and his own son Qi performed in a bygone age. Elements of the Yu tradition became attached to localities in Shu where a north Chinese regime and northern settlers were themselves carving out a customized landscape as had the fabled Yu.[102] Native Shu labor probably also helped to build Dujiangyan, but it was the outsiders who prevailed.[103] Sichuan made up a large fraction, probably more than half, of the total Qin land area after 316 B.C. Likewise, the share of Qin subjects residing in Sichuan can be assumed to have leapt upward in the course of the mass migrations to Shu. The proportion of Qin territory and population south of the Qinling range increased as Chu abandoned the Han valley, eastern Sichuan, and the central Yangtze to Qin. Economically and demographically, the Qin center of gravity was shifting south of the Qinling Mountains, although overall political dictates issued from Xianyang. Across the divide, the Sichuanese obeyed.

In Sichuan, these changes involved an ethnic dimension as Qin methodically developed southern resources to direct against its enemies on the central plains. The tale of Li Bing defying the formerly revered river deity shows how indigenous Shu culture endured continuing pressure. Perhaps some native Shu accepted assimilation to the new order. But others chose to abandon their homeland. The Bo people, who had lived near the confluence of the Min River with the Yangtze, were forced out by northern immigrants. Around the iron-producing town of Linqiong south of Chengdu, the native Qiong people were displaced by settlers from Shangjun sent there on the orders of the First Emperor.[104]

Other Shu natives left as an armed band. An account in Chinese and Vietnamese texts tells of how a Shu noble called King Anyang (Vietnamese: An Duong) led some 30,000 troops southward out of Sichuan to the Guangxi-Annam area near the end of the third century. This move occurred in the wake of the Qin conquests of present Guangdong and Guangxi provinces, and northern Vietnam.[105] Anyang bore the surname Shu and the personal name Pan (Vietnamese:

Thuc Phan), and was supposedly a prince of the deposed Shu ruling house.

Some late Shu interments excavated at Jianwei county, in southern Sichuan, have been cited in support of this presumed Shu move southward. The graves contained bronze swords in the typically Ba-Shu willow-leaf pattern, including one marked with the widespread tiger emblem. There were also Ba-Shu axes, vessels, and bronze signature seals in a Ba-Shu script.[106] King Anyang's departure is the last word in the sources regarding the indigenous Shu people. By the end of the Qin century the cultural sinification of Shu was nearly accomplished.

As work on Dujiangyan approached completion and as Shu became wholly Chinese, Qin undertook the concluding stages in its drive to empire. The main scene of action had shifted to the central plains. Methodical siege warfare was conducted city by city. Patience and prudence also characterized Qin diplomacy and for half of the third century B.C. Qin tolerated the enfeebled Zhou dynasty's continued existence.

Qin forbearance continued for awhile even after the Zhou split into two fractious houses and forfeited all shreds of moral authority. Deferential pretense at last was dropped, but again in slow, deliberate stages. No new Zhou monarch was named after 256 B.C., and the lapsed dynasty's estates were finally taken over by Qin. Zhou went out more with a whimper than a bang. Even then Qin waited for a decent, decade-long interval until formally moving to declare a sovereign dynasty in place of the defunct Zhou. This completed the process begun seven decades earlier when Hui-wen of Qin took the title king.

In 246 B.C. a descendent of Hui-wen succeeded to the Qin throne, commanding a realm far larger than that of any rival state monarch. Still, a quarter-century more of sieges and battles had to be fought before he could bring about unification. Qin soldiers slashed their way to victory, armed in part with blades stamped "made in Shu."[107] Among the troops were a unit of specially selected tall warriors from Ba commandery.[108] Grain from harvests on the Chengdu plain fed the Qin armies, north and south. The Qin investment in Sichuan had borne fruit. Finally, all hopeless resistance ceased and the surrenders ensued: the three Jin states (Han, Zhao, and Wei) respectively in 230, 228, and 225 B.C.; Chu, which had never really recovered from losing its capital, capitulated in 223 B.C., followed by Yan and Qi over the next two years.

The now unchallenged king's ambitious minister, Lu Buwei,

therefore convinced his lord to assume a more exalted, epoch-making title. Henceforth and for all time he would be not king, but First Emperor (*qin shi huang*), avowed unifier of all lands into the Qin empire. Ideologically, the accolade transcended anything from the Zhou period. Multiple kings might coexist, but there could be only one emperor. The title was carefully conceived to incorporate majestic powers associated with the last of the three divine Primeval Emperors in mythologized antiquity.[109]

Imperial China was thus born one century after a Qin duke had declared himself king. This time span coincided with the hundred years of Qin rule in Sichuan. Annexation of Sichuan had constituted the initial Qin territorial gain as a kingdom; from Sichuan Qin then commenced its long drive to empire. The Qin experience at governing ethnically diverse peoples in a southern clime had first been gained in Sichuan. In Sichuan, doctrine and practice were joined to beget the working institutions of imperial government. Qin imposed these institutions over all China when at last the enemy holdout states bowed to the inevitable. Like Shu and Ba before them, submitting kingdoms became enrolled into Qin as commanderies, subject to rule from Xianyang. Qin officials displaced noble dynasties that in some cases had governed for a millennium or more.[110] The Qin century of rule over Sichuan, a long morning twilight, merged into the dawn of a new age.

As it happened, the First Emperor governed the whole of China for scarcely more than a decade, ten years spent in a drastic, colossal overhaul of the entire country. The plan entailed massive population transfers, roadway improvements, work on the Great Wall, and military campaigns to invade, pacify, and then colonize the deep south. In Guangxi the Lingqu Canal was dug, connecting the southern river systems to streams tributary to the Yangtze. These projects each had long-term utility. But they were all conducted at once, severely disrupting normal economic life in the newly enrolled commanderies.

The frenetic activity recalls that undertaken following the Qin conquest of Shu, but the First Emperor demanded results at an even swifter pace. To provide on-the-spot guidance he embarked on a series of six grand inspection tours around the transforming empire. Significantly, the commanderies of Ba, Shu, and Hanzhong did not figure on his itinerary. The emperor had no need to visit what were by then long secure, old Qin territories functioning smoothly in accordance with Qin laws.

Shu in particular was a paradigm of security. That is probably the reason underlying its choice by Qin as a venue for internal exile, a practice dating back to the period immediately following the Qin incursion into Sichuan. The First Emperor continued the policy. After an abortive palace coup, he demoted 4,000 nobly titled families and resettled them at Fangling, in Shu.[111] When minister Lu Buwei was ousted following this intrigue, he too was sentenced to exile in Shu, although he preferred suicide to the disgrace and loss of power.[112]

After Chu surrendered, its ruling family may also have been sent to Yandao, on the western frontiers of Shu southwest of Chengdu.[113] Linqiong, where other exiles were sent, was an iron-producing center important in Qin development schemes. Removal to Sichuan locales like these provided some means for safely exploiting the talents of defeated enemies. Depositing them alive and well in Shu offered economic advantages, yet kept down resentment by minimizing the wholesale slaughter that had attended some victories of pre-imperial Qin.

The geography of Sichuan conveniently channeled ingress and egress through a very few easily monitored natural choke points. Travelers had to transit over guarded Qinling Mountain routes or take passage on a Yangtze River boat. Having entered Sichuan it would be difficult to leave unobserved. Qin surveillance agents could closely watch enemies of the state. Tucked away in Shu, deposed aristocrats and subversives would have no chance to interfere in the Qin transformation of China. And lucrative opportunities awaited in Sichuan to absorb their energy.

The demographic characteristics of Shu combined with geography to make it particularly suitable as a place of internal exile. Within a short space Shu had received masses of immigrants all deriving originally from diverse locales, strangers thrown together by the Qin authorities to whom they owed their livelihood. Population displacement ensured state institutions a near monopoly of control, probably more than in any other region where local traditions and non-governmental social structures had better chances of enduring and offering alternatives to the state. In the social environment of Shu commandery the Qin system of local surveillance reached perhaps its optimum efficiency.

Ba, by contrast, had retained some vestiges of native leadership beneath the commandery level. Qin government institutions there coexisted with the surviving political framework of aboriginal peoples remaining in situ. State supervision presumably would have been more lax compared to Shu, making Ba less suitable for relocating untrustworthy elements. As a consequence, no exiles to Ba are recorded in the source material. Some are known to have been confined in the

Han commandery, where political and social conditions more closely approximated those in Shu to provide a secure venue for exile. This factor of security, not harsh physical conditions, is what made Shu ideal for suspected or potential troublemakers. Ironically enough, as a stronghold of Qin power, Shu came to survive the fall of Qin itself.

Ample time had secured Sichuan for Qin, but then only after much trial and error. The rebellions marring the first four Qin decades in Shu were perhaps a necessary concomitant of the transformation process when vigorously applied within a short span. Similar outbreaks had been averted in Ba, but Ba was spared the more intensive regime of sinification via mass immigration as applied in Shu. Qin officials did undercut the Ba rulers as they had the Kaiming dynasts of Shu by courting formerly subordinate ethnic groups and lineages. Both Qin models for assimilating conquered lands and peoples were workable ones, if applied judiciously, in stages. When the First Emperor united China and began remolding it in the Qin image, he failed to adequately account for the time needed, for the short-term economic dislocations and for the likelihood of strong resistance over a wide area.

Things fall apart. Had the First Emperor lived longer there might have been enough time under a strong guiding hand for the transformation to run its course. Then the process could mature, mellow, and pay dividends over all China as it had in Sichuan. But unexpectedly, he died while making his sixth imperial circuit tour of newly acquired commanderies. That sudden loss left the empire bereft of direction at a particularly crucial juncture. The emperor's dynastic successor proved too weak to maintain control as turmoil and revolt erupted and spread seemingly everywhere. Everywhere, that is, except in Sichuan. Ba, Shu, and the Han valley stayed loyal to Qin.

Viewed against prior Qin experience in Sichuan, the fault of the First Emperor after 221 b.c. appears one of miscalculation, of attempting too much too soon. Once he forcibly united the states, he tried to apply almost universally something resembling an accelerated Shu model of sinification, but proceeded incautiously. The result was cataclysmic. If due heed were taken or more of the temperate Ba model adopted in some areas, the final outcome could well have been different. New commanderies earmarked for rapid transformation like Shu might have been interspersed among those undergoing the slower, Ba type of treatment, so to maintain equilibrium. With a balanced approach, local resistance to Qin authority should have been more easily contained and quelled.

But the First Qin Emperor created an imbalance, by impatiently charging ahead in an approach uncharacteristic of Qin practice to date. The fall of Qin owed to impetuous decisions applied on a sub-continental scale, decisions made without due regard for precedent, without regard to likely consequences. As seems evident the First Emperor suffered from an excess of hubris. That does not, however, make the whole of Qin history a drama somehow preordained by fate to a tragic end. South of the Qinling range the Qin social legacy survived uninterrupted. Had Qin power in Shu and Ba been limited to merely superficial control, or were it merely a phenomenon enforced by sheer terror, then surely the edifice would have tottered when pandemonium swept away Qin itself. The Qin order's survival in Sichuan bespeaks the success of sinification there, the living identi-fication of Sichuan's people with the system emplaced by Qin.

Overall, Chinese historiography for 2,000 years has consistently looked back at Qin with fear and loathing.[114] The greatest villain is the First Emperor himself. From him, prejudice extends to tarnish the whole Qin achievement, creating a popular view of China under the lash. Few Qin functionaries have escaped this condemnation.

Li Bing, governor of Shu and architect of Dujiangyan, is one rare exception. Civil engineers even now memorize homilies attributed to him concerning the proper management of dams, channels, and levees. A temple honors Li Bing and his son. Dujiangyan continues in living use today, while the Qin Great Wall has crumbled to total ruin.[115] It is perhaps historical justice that the largest physically tangi-ble trace of Qin, more imposing even than the First Emperor's tumu-lus, is an indispensibly useful and productive irrigation work in Sichuan.

6

Han Sichuan

Over centuries, the word *Han* expanded to encompass ever wider connotations. Han was originally the name of a river valley separating Sichuan from the central plains of north China. Qin annexed this area along with Sichuan in 316 B.C. When the Qin empire tottered a century later, an upstart warlord "king of Han" took refuge in the Han valley. Southward in Sichuan he also controlled Ba and Shu commanderies.

Resources from Sichuan and the Han region served this king of Han well, as they had the preceding kings of Qin. He augmented his own forces with Sichuanese troops, fed them on Sichuan grain, then seized the imperial capital and at length put the empire back together. Thereafter he held on to Sichuan as an imperial domain even while parceling out much of China to reward vassals. The recuperated Han empire advanced China to its maximum extent.

Not surprisingly, since that great era most Chinese have referred to themselves with pride as the Han people. Their sense of unity is axiomatic, an unquestioned cultural patrimony transcending dialect divisions and geographic barriers. From the frigid north to the tropical south, from the Yellow Sea shore to the western deserts, all these "men of Han," by their name, acknowledge a geopolitical debt.

Sichuan and the Restoration of China

The First Qin Emperor died in 210 B.C., a most inopportune moment with the new order still incomplete. Much of the empire remained in flux except for pacified and integrated zones like Sichuan. Northern and eastern China was painfully undergoing the initial traumatic phases of Qin transformation. The social matrix was disrupted over broad, recently incorporated areas where the Qin regime had not fully taken root. Vast masses were displaced from their homes, either permanently relocated or serving as corvee labor on public works and military endeavors like the Great Wall, the Lingqu Canal, road improvements, an invasion of the far south, and other projects.[1] Many of these common folk stood to prosper had the transformation run its course, but with the process cut short they endured hardships to no evident advantage.

Qin transformation also created a class of onetime influential persons whose lives and fortunes were tied up with states vanquished by the First Emperor. Understandably, they longed to recover their property and power. The dispossessed, the stranded, and the formerly well-to-do each nursed their own grievances, their own motives to revolt should the Qin grip seem to slacken. Revolt likewise had followed upon the passing of Qin monarchs during the absorption of Shu a century earlier. Violent outbreaks perhaps were an unavoidable concomitant of the sinification process if applied ineptly and with undue haste. The particularly unlucky circumstance of the First Emperor's demise now again complicated matters.

The precise timing of his departure and its occurrence away from the capital belong to the category of biological happenstance, those accidents that occasionally grab the helm and steer history on an uncharted course.[2] Coming unexpectedly, the death upset imperial succession arrangements. Questions were raised regarding the heir's legitimacy. A suitably decisive prince taking over at such a critical juncture might have saved Qin, but the claimant who emerged lacked appealing charismatic qualities.

Without charisma, that flair for persuading, cajoling, attracting, and commanding support, the new dynast remained passive. He simply failed to project an imperial will beyond the pacified old Qin areas and over the immense, chaotic, newly acquired possessions. Caught at a susceptible moment amidst the tumult of transformation, his palace operatives vacillated. Self-interested courtiers plotted to control the weak imperial successor, then murdered him. A gaping void at the apex of power could not be concealed.

So through want of a firm, guiding personality to replace the strong First Emperor, Qin faltered as smoldering discontent flared into rebellion. The places where insurrection began all lay in eastern China. These districts belonged to former states that had capitulated to Qin no more than two decades before, where memories still vividly recalled the pre-Qin world order. Conditions there were in ferment and Qin rule, albeit demanding, did not yet impress everyone as being necessarily permanent. After all, the long Warring States period had seen reversals of fortune enabling seemingly defeated

MAP 7

Han Sichuan and adjacent areas

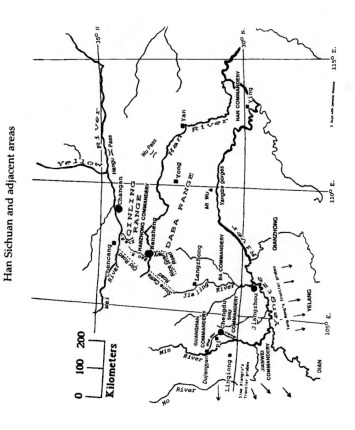

states to recover. A similar turnaround could happen again. Persons with status or property to regain might make common cause with those having little to lose and together toss off the alien yoke once Qin indecision at Xianyang became apparent.

The stringency of Qin transformation caused strains and cracks where rebellion might foment. Breaking up is hard to do, but state demands had become harshly intolerant of normal human failings, of the unavoidable friction arising when large numbers of people are uprooted and shifted about. Extreme penalties were invoked for moderate lapses. Qin courted mortal crisis by attempting too much at once, thereby forfeiting the adaptability displayed decades before in Sichuan. State power, stable while the First Emperor lived, proved brittle once mortality removed him. Stretched taut, rigid, and lacking slack to cope with the unexpected, the Qin sinews of control began to snap.

In the power vacuum, spiraling concatenations of events thrust humble sorts of people to the fore as major figures. Low-ranking functionaries and even ordinary laborers fell into fugitive status as the regimented Qin order went topsy turvy. Normally docile, obedient subjects became deserters. Bereft of sustenance, deserters of need would turn bandit. Successful bandit chiefs proceeded to capture towns, adopt some popular slogan, and shortly be transformed into warlord contestants for kingdoms or even for the imperial throne.

Typically, the scenario unfolded as follows. Quotas for work accomplished might not be met; for example, when corvee detachments failed to report to duty on time, or at full strength, or at all. For failures like this, Qin law condemned the responsible authorities to death. Such unbending discipline drove fair numbers of the regime's own petty officials into hiding, thereby creating a dissident, subversive alternative leadership pool. Around them gathered others fearing reprisal, including many who had decamped from conscript labor brigades. A failing system thus turned ordinary folk into desperados.

As sufficient malfunctions accumulated in the system a critical turning point was reached and general order started to disintegrate. The splendid Qin road net thronged with displaced, hungry persons, prey to the ambitious leader who could provide a meal and promise a way home. Corvee columns in this manner were especially prone to turning overnight into mutinous mobs. Mobs coalesced into rebel armies as still more vagabonds joined. Demagogues arose from among the rabble to impose the rudiments of discipline. Weaponry could be had by plundering Qin armories. Several anti-Qin forces gathered strength in parts of what is now Shandong, Jiangsu, Anhui, and

Henan provinces. Starting from this nucleus in 210 B.C., disorder
spread northward and westward.

Chen She, a peasant who had been placed in charge of a corvee
detachment, was the first to rise. His detachment snowballed into a
horde, successfully seizing many towns and districts in areas that had
once been part of Chu state. Local authorities were either liquidated,
or as happened on occasion, they chose to repudiate Qin and cast
their lot with the revolt. Other bands proliferated throughout the central plains, shrugging off the remnants of Qin authority.

Some leaders resurrected the memory of former states obliterated by Qin, calling themselves kings of Chu, Qi, Zhao, and Yan.
Like their namesakes of Warring States times, these self-styled kings
pursued internecine quarrels as much as they fought against Qin.
Among them Chen She still retained the serious ambition of over-
throwing Qin rule. He even promised fiefdoms among the rich Qin
lands to attract allies. In one such empty gesture Chen She bestowed
the title "Lord of Chengdu" (*cheng du jun*) upon the son of a confeder-
ate, anticipating the conquest of distant Shu commandery.[3]

It was not to be. Rivals murdered Chen She before he could
march on the Qin capital, let alone reach anywhere near Shu.[4]
Xianyang fell instead to Liu Bang, a rebel whose background closely
resembled that of Chen She. Liu Bang too started out as a mere
peasant, becoming a village level Qin functionary in east China while
the First Emperor still reigned. Like Chen She he had led a corvee
column. When some of his charges absconded Liu Bang knew he
risked execution for failing to deliver the requisite number, so he persuaded the remaining laborers to desert with him.

This outlaw band became the core of an insurrectionary army
when Qin power started crumbling and emerged from the central
plains melee to close in on Xianyang.[5] Nearing that city toward the
end of 207 B.C., Liu Bang received delegates offering peaceful capi-
tulation. He accepted the dynastic seals. The dynasty and the state of
Qin thus came to a formal end.

But it must be remembered that Liu Bang had started his career
as a Qin official. In taking over the capital he succeeded to the leadership of an existing structure, one he had no interest in extirpating.
His men took possession of the governmental treasures and archives,
these latter documents affording practical advantage in continuing
the tidy administration and taxing of such Qin lands as had escaped
ravishment and revolt. Liu Bang confirmed most Qin officials in
office, eschewed vindictiveness, and thus won elite support. Some
hitherto enclosed fields and pastures reserved for the imperial house-

hold were opened to cultivation, a measure popular with the peasantry. To the people of metropolitan Qin he announced a conciliatory policy and the repeal of harsh legal measures. Such magnanimity earned the new administration gratitude in an area that so far had been spared the depredations suffered on the central plains when Qin control lapsed.

Unfortunately, this era of good feeling lasted but ephemerally. A large, competing rebel force drew close to the capital, eager for spoils. It included many Chu men who had earlier served under Chen She, calling themselves the army of Chu. Xiang Yu, who had taken over these Chu troops, was a scion of the old Chu nobility and so a hereditary foe of Qin. He possessed a rash, truculent, treacherous nature and backed it by a host outnumbering that under Liu Bang, even after the latter had levied Qin conscripts from around Xianyang. Reluctantly, Liu Bang ceded the city. Xianyang endured a second, crueler occupation, by a general of very different temperament. The two commanders' policies toward defeated Qin could hardly have contrasted more. Where Liu Bang conciliated, Xiang Yu plundered, burned, and massacred, wreaking gratuitous devastation on one of the ancient world's greatest urban centers.

These two mutually suspicious warlords could not coexist and support their forces in the ruined confines of Xianyang, so they agreed to divide the empire between them and go their separate ways. Commanding a stronger contingent, Xiang Yu dictated terms. He compelled Liu Bang to accept a subordinate post as "king of Han," with authority over the central Han valley, Ba, and Shu. This was an unprecedented title.[6] There never previously existed any state of Han per se. The region had always been a borderland divided between Qin, Shu, Ba, and Chu before becoming a Qin commandery. In this sense the birth of a Han kingdom marked a new departure, although it consisted of those very Qin territories that had fortuitously escaped the ravages of rebellion when the dynasty collapsed.

Altogether the Han, Ba, and Shu lands left to Liu Bang comprised forty-one counties, an adequate domain but somewhat tucked away. The seat of this new Han kingdom would be at Nanzheng town, headquarters of Hanzhong commandery. Nearby, a north-south access route to Sichuan bisected the eastward flowing Han River. Liu Bang did not rejoice over this appointment. The fief took him and his army off center stage, amounting to a kind of banishment.[7] When Liu Bang later accused Xiang Yu of a series of ten "crimes" (*zui*), this forced move to Shu and Han topped the list.[8] Xiang Yu for safety's sake enfeoffed three generals in metropolitan Qin to blockade the king of Han in his remote transmontane possessions.[9] Thus sealed off, he was expected to languish impotently in the south.

Instead of dying on the vine, however, Liu Bang defied expectations by plotting a successful return. The date of his virtual exile, 206 B.C., is reckoned Year One in the chronicles of the Han dynasty, of which Liu Bang came to be styled Exalted Progenitor (*gao zu*).[10] His comeback is testimony to the latent potential of the Han and Sichuan commanderies. But although productive, these lands were removed from the seat of imperial power and even farther from many soldiers' native districts in east China.

As might have been expected, desertions during the southward evacuation over the Qinling Mountains partly depleted the army.[11] Even those remaining with Liu Bang longed to return home. For survival's sake he had to act quickly and judiciously, gathering resources from the Han and Sichuan commanderies without antagonizing local opinion. He needed to retain as many of his veteran cadres as possible, reinforce them with locally recruited troops, and then reenter contention on the central plains while his battle-seasoned loyalists still retained their fighting edge.

Again practicing conciliation, the king of Han managed to do a deal with the Shu, Ba, and Han valley people. Liu Bang required a base adequate for equipping, feeding, outfitting, and replenishing his forces. The three commanderies for their part would welcome a protector to shield them against the fate suffered by Xianyang after Xiang Yu took it over. So mutual need gave rise to an odd but complementary marriage of convenience. It paired refugees from the turmoil of Qin collapse, now a hardened rebel force, with the prosperous subjects of three model Qin commanderies, still intact and functioning.

The Sichuanese actually possessed no real option but to accept Liu Bang and in any event were not disposed to troublemaking. Fourth century B.C. Shu defiance of Qin predated living memory. The Ba, Shu, and Han peoples had long acquiesced to dictates from the north. Their acknowledging Liu Bang was natural, because he had been the one to accept Qin's surrender and thus represented legitimate succession. Making common cause with the king of Han guaranteed political continuity and social order.

Liu Bang had already shown a willingness to compromise. Based on the precedent set in his occupation of Xianyang, there is every reason to believe he confirmed most of Sichuan's official incumbents. Here and there a given ordinance might be amended, but the overall Qin structure stayed intact. Although the Han king's need to support a fighting army imposed burdens on his three commanderies, for the inhabitants this was a small premium for escaping the kind of wreckage other districts had suffered. Present in Shu as well was a portion of the previous central plains nobility, separated from their estates and exiled to Sichuan by the First Qin Emperor. These families too would have nothing to lose by aiding Liu Bang and might hope to regain their former wealth or position.

Top lieutenants to Liu Bang counseled him to accept appointment as king of Han and adopt a temporarily complacent pose toward Xiang Yu. Meanwhile they set about turning Han, Shu, and Ba commanderies into a safe haven. On arrival the Han forces deliberately demolished the main corduroy mountain road over the Qinling range to deceptively suggest they held no intention of leaving the Han valley and Sichuan. At the same time as he took this drastic step, Liu Bang placed a trusted subordinate, Xiao He, in charge of collecting revenues from Ba and Shu to provision the army. The plan was to prepare a support base with substantial Sichuanese assistance, then recross the mountains northward to retake what had been the Qin home counties.[12]

Sichuan provided some troop reinforcements in addition to supplies. In the Ba town of Langzhong a subject named Fan Mu calculated that Liu Bang would win and advised him to recruit soldiers locally from among seven clans of the local Zong people. He did so, these clansmen reinforcing the original core of the army and those from Qin who had also joined.[13] By helping Liu Bang the Sichuanese warriors actually protected their homeland as they kept the fighting at a distance.

Having destroyed the road by which he first entered the Han valley, Liu Bang required another route for the return to Qin. He found such an alternative path, the so-called old road (*gu dao*), northwest of and parallel to the Bao-Xie corduroy road by which Qin invaded Shu 110 years before.[14] Over it he led what was left of his original core of followers augmented by the Zong contingent and other Sichuanese and Han reinforcements. Without warning they appeared north of the Qinling Mountains. The political pretext for their invasion was the murder by Xiang Yu of a powerless puppet emperor who had been installed on the throne.[15] This surprise turnabout move routed the three generals whom Xiang Yu had positioned to corral Liu Bang in the south. Xianyang quickly fell to him a second time, but the king of Han now faced a war to the finish with Xiang Yu, now styled king of Chu.

The strategic equation closely resembled that of a century before, when Qin, with its Han valley and Sichuan possessions, con-

fronted Chu and the central plains states. Some of the means duplicated those of the earlier conflict, such as sending supply boats down
the Han river to support the troops' advance against Chu.[16] On
this occasion Liu Bang entrusted the logistics to his lieutenant Xiao
He. As before, the final battles of the war of 206–202 B.C. took place
on the central plains. Getting Shu and Han supplies to that front was
harder because it required conveying grain over the Qinling range.
Again it was done.

Sichuan coolies made the winning contribution in these feats.
Their sweat kept the fighting battlefields, the blood and tears, away
from Shu and Ba. Some Sichuanese, those of the Zong auxiliary force,
opted out of Han service once the combat receded from Sichuan. For
these men of Ba, it was no longer their war. But the Sichuan supplies
kept coming. The acknowledged contribution of Sichuan in Liu
Bang's epoch-making victory owed to the grain it furnished. Food-
stuffs from Shu and the Han valley had sustained his fugitive band at
its bleakest moment, when the weakened king of Han first entered
the area.[17] That was just the beginning.

Sichuan grain continued to be crucial to the Han army even
when the war moved far away from Sichuan to concentrate along the
Yellow River and passes debouching onto the central plains. There
the disputing armies locked horns to decide the issue of empire. Maneuvering marches and swift raids along the major communication
lines alternated with long, grinding periods of siegelike attrition conducted from dug-in positions. During these static episodes, supply
lines counted for everything as living off the land would be impossible; foraging armies will rapidly strip bare a stretch of countryside. By
205 B.C. the civilian population of the passes area was starving, so Liu
Bang ordered the people to go to Shu and the Han commandery to be
fed.[18] These regions thus supported not only the Han armies, but a
mass of refugees as well.

Shu and Han grain supplies enabled the king of Han's men to
maintain their central plains strongholds in the face of protracted Chu
attacks.[19] Han forces depended on a lifeline of extreme length by
ancient standards. Part of the ration transport used boats along the
Wei and Yellow Rivers.[20] Before reaching the Wei, however, these
cargoes still had to be carried overland, that is, across the mountains,
from the growing regions in the Han valley and Shu. Behind the
frontline areas on the central plains approaches porters again were
required to bring sustenance to the fighting troops.

This triumph of logistics proved just feasible as a short-term
measure under desperate conditions despite the huge amount of

rations necessarily consumed en route. The transport feat itself is testimony to the enormous productive capacity of Sichuan. Moving tons of grain required mobilization of a prodigous auxiliary labor corps of porters and carters working to exhaustion, as well as a capable command system. Only the disciplined Qin peacetime apparatus that Liu Bang found intact when he took over the area offered such an organizational structure.

Contemporaries recognized the decisive function of the Han-Shu base in making a comeback possible for Liu Bang when it seemed that Xiang Yu had attained virtual hegemony. As one put it, "The king of Han aroused Ba and Shu, whipped the world, plundered the lords, chased down Xiang Yu, and annihilated him."[21] Their clash of arms, a crescendo prelude for 2,000 years of imperial China, was more than just a dynastic contest. In the Chinese mind it later took on paradigmatic value as the quintessence of war itself. Chinese chessboards, for example, are customarily still captioned to pit the forces of Han against those of Chu.[22] The vendetta of Liu Bang versus Xiang Yu is thus played out in apotheosis probably millions of times each day.

If any political basis had existed for Sichuan separatism it should have manifested itself during these struggles taking place between the Qin collapse and the rise of Han. From 205 to 202 B.C. Liu Bang was preoccupied with battles and politics on the central plains. He entrusted Sichuan to a few officials set down among the mass of natives and settlers making up its populace. Under Xiao He's management, the Sichuan support base stayed in line notwithstanding the enormous military logistical burden.[23]

Shu thereby played an appreciable and duly appreciated role, first by providing a safe redoubt, then by growing, yielding up, and transporting the grain on which Han victory fed. Loyalty had become a political habit, inculcated in Shu during Qin rule following some disastrous initial experiences with rebellion. Decades of ensuing peace then set a pattern of workable government, depending for its direction upon the imperial political center. Liu Bang trusted the Sichuanese. As emperor in 196 B.C., he included crack troops from Ba and Shu among those used to consolidate his power against restive former subordinates on the central plains.[24]

Whether the qualities engendered by Qin in Shu be considered docility, caution, perseverance, or keen and realistic judgement, Liu Bang utilized them to his best advantage. Classical sources duly noted the significance of Shu and the Han valley in furnishing the basis for Han power.[25] A Han dynastic debt to Shu was recalled in many enduring ways. For example, scholars at the imperial court later worked out a cosmological scheme by which phenomena like earthquakes, avalanches, comets, and the like carried portentious significance regarding imperial fate. This belief reflected widely held contemporary beliefs assuming a mutual interaction between nature and human affairs. In its Han state variant, geological disturbances occurring in Shu were viewed with particular concern throughout the life of the dynasty, because of the historical connection of Shu to the dynastic founder.[26]

At a practical level the special meaning of Shu for the Han regime was also shown in its concern for veterans who had accompanied Liu Bang there. These men received generous dispensations and awards, sometimes including income-bearing estates. However, none of the appanages were located in Shu itself, and only one, at Pingzhou, is recorded in Ba.[27] People from Shu and the Han valley, because of the heavy exactions they had endured on behalf of Liu Bang, enjoyed a two-year exemption from taxes and remittances in kind.[28] And even though the Zong warriors from Ba could not be persuaded to fight beyond just one campaign and freely returned to Sichuan, they too nevertheless were excused from taxation. The man who had helped recruit the Zong, Fan Mu, was rewarded by enfeoffment as a marquis.[29]

The Han dynasty's Exalted Progenitor does not seem to have exerted the same degree of control in Ba as in Shu. Ba participated in the saga of founding the Han regime, but on more of its own terms than Shu. Ba resources in the form of rations are mentioned in ancient sources less often than the large grain contribution from Shu. Various groups in Ba maintained their separate identities, having been less affected than Shu by the Qin process of sinification. Subsequent events as Qin gave way to the Han period favored a lingering sense of cultural and ethnic separateness among several peoples in Ba commandery, a sort of autonomy albeit within the framework of Han imperial overlordship.

The victory of Liu Bang over Xiang Yu broadly replayed the unification of China under Qin. Years of warfare devastated northern and eastern China but the combined territories of Ba, Shu, and the Han valley came through whole. Liu Bang, king of Han, made good his claim to be the first Han emperor. The very dynastic name, Han, recalls the crucial role of what had once been a marginal region in determining events affecting the entire empire. Because Shu and the

Han valley had remained unscathed throughout the years of chaos and plunder, these territories insulated a strand of continuity from Warring States and Qin times into the new era.

Shu and Han commanderies stayed under bureaucratic administration as did the metropolitan counties along the Wei River and around Changan, the new supreme capital across the Wei from Xianyang. Most of the empire's remaining area, some half of its territory, was enfeoffed by Liu Bang to vassal kings in return for having served him. Formal unity thus was reestablished over the imperium but real Han authority remained geographically limited.

Several generations of political wrangling and sometimes outright civil war were required by succeeding Han emperors to reclaim the fiefs from the heirs of Liu Bang's generals.[30] Meanwhile the Han dynasty made do with what was left: substantially the old Qin area with its despoiled capital, the newly resurrected city of Changan that replaced Xianyang, some war-ravaged areas on the central plains, the upper Han valley, and Sichuan. Of these parts, Sichuan was the major portion in extent and population. Given its size and the unbroken continuity of direct imperial rule in Sichuan, what transpired there politically during the early Han period retained lasting significance in shaping Chinese governmental norms and practice.

Ba and Shu Under the Han

Different cultural characteristics had distinguished the societies of eastern and western Sichuan since before the Qin conquest. Qin policy subsequently took these separate identities into consideration when first annexing and then governing Sichuan as the commanderies of Ba and Shu. Their diversity persisted into the Han. Sichuan altogether formed a larger regional entity called *Yi zhou*, but this *zhou* or province level of organization was seemingly of lesser practical significance in the early Han dynasty. Sources ignore it beyond mere mention.[31]

Of Ba and Shu, Shu was the more populous, with 268,279 registered households comprising 1,245,929 persons in the year A.D. 1 when a census figure is available.[32] A portion of Shu had been split off administratively by Liu Bang in 201 B.C. and governed as Guanghan commandery.[33] This was located north of Chengdu, on the main route out of Sichuan. Culturally it remained part of Shu, and the term *Shu* should still be understood to embrace Guanghan in all but the most formal administrative usage.[34] Guanghan commandery's population figures greatly increase the overall Shu total, by 662,249 persons living in 167,499 households. Ba commandery by comparison recorded just 158,643 households and 708,148 persons.[35]

Under Shu commandery proper were fifteen counties including its administrative seat of Chengdu. Guanghan commandery had thirteen counties, and Ba eleven counties, centered at Jiangzhou. Shu thus far outnumbered Ba in persons duly registered with the authorities. Some people in either Shu or Ba may have escaped inclusion in these statistics, which were tax registration rolls but not necessarily reliable as all-inclusive head counts. Omissions from the official figure more likely would be expected in Ba where Han governmental organs shared power with surviving indigenous authority, such as clans.

Artifacts from Han times support the impression of cultural dissimilarity in Shu and Ba. Tombs in Shu tend to be nearly indistinguishible from those of northern China in the manner of interment and accompanying grave goods. Signet seals in the "Ba-Shu" style are the only noticeably native Sichuanese item usually found in such burials.[36] In Ba, on the other hand, burials in the uniquely local boat-shaped coffins continued into Han times. These too have yielded Ba-Shu signet seals as well as weapons designed in the Ba manner.[37] Whether taken from boat coffins or from conventional sarcophagi, Han grave goods in Ba retain their typical resemblance to the older Ba and Chu styles.[38]

Qin policy toward eastern Sichuan had left native ethnic groups in situ, not entirely absorbed or culturally sinified. Even in late Han times there are references to distinct ethnic groups in Ba commandery, such as the Banxunman.[39] Ba was spared massive resettling by northern colonists as in Shu. The Han government built on that legacy and allowed local culture to flourish. During the war against Xiang Yu, Liu Bang had turned to good account the famed martial temperament among various peoples of Ba. Continuing tradition, his Han imperial successors also relied on eastern Sichuanese auxiliaries. Soldiers from around Peiling (a.k.a. Fuling) on the Yangtze customarily were inducted into a special Han elite force. Clad in red armor, it made a unique impression. In 169 A.D. this unit repelled a raid into the Han valley by Qiang marauders from the northwestern frontier. Some Ba troops were permanently resettled in the Han valley as a resident garrison, where they maintained their own customs as late as the fourth century A.D.[40]

Ba craftsmen continued making *chun yu* drums in Han times.[41] Native Ba customs even found their way into the Han dynasty imperial court ritual. By a formal decree, the composition of the palace musical ensemble included thirty-six drummers from Ba and Yu (near Chongqing), pounding out the beat to which they had marched and fought alongside Liu Bang during the dynasty's founding saga.[42] With other culturally diverse peoples of the Han empire, they added a vividly exciting touch to courtly life and a nostalgic reminder of the dynastic debt to Ba valor. Spirited Ba performers found favor as well at the mansions of nobles and magnates, powerful men who ostentatiously flaunted their wealth to the consternation of more soberminded Han court officials.[43]

Men from Ba served as privileged armed auxiliaries of the Han dynasty and trusted defenders of its namesake Han valley. As exemplified by the exotic music and dancing, with all their loyalty the Ba people had not yet become integrally Han Chinese in the full cultural sense. However, some adoption of Chinese ways surely did occur. Imperial officials maintained a presence in the main centers. The town of Langzhong seems to have been a Han focus of control in Ba, judging from the biographical notices of eminent persons appended to the local history *Hua yang guo zhi*.[44]

Perhaps the most notable Ba resident to emerge was Luo Xiahong, a mathematician and astronomer born in Langzhong.[45] He served in the court of Emperor Wu around the turn of the first century B.C. Significantly, Langzhong was situated in a portion of Ba close to Shu and to routes leading northward out of Sichuan itself. It thereby lay more open to Han cultural influences than interior sections of Ba persistently pursuing native ways. So it is not surprising that allusions to Ba and its people are rare in historical records of the former Han dynasty, records where achievement is measured according to sinified values. Individuals like Luo Xiahong existed to be sure, but they remained exceptional. Even after Han times an awareness of pre-Han ethnic identity survived in Ba and was still noted in official biographies of some persons from the Ba commandery.[46]

Shu, in contrast to Ba, did achieve a more nearly full absorption into the Han polity. Just as Han recognition of limited Ba autonomy grew out of established Qin policy, so too did Han policy in Shu stem from Qin precedent. Continuities are thus apparent in both Ba and Shu from the Qin period to the Han. Qin had left Shu tightly secure, a rigor that had its uses. Following Qin practice, the Han government designated Shu as a place of banishment for political offenders. Many of those so exiled were actually vassals whose fiefs the central authority moved to repossess.

In one such case the king of Huainan was sent to the districts of

Yandao and Qiongdu, on the hilly southwestern Shu frontier facing unassimilated barbarians.[47] The punishment was mandated by Emperor Wen as a commuted sentence for this noble's insubordination and for having conducted suspicious, unauthorized dealings with tribes beyond the Han frontiers. Apparently the emperor had no fear of the king of Huainan again attempting subversion on the Shu frontier.

This basic security is not to imply that conditions in Shu were always serenely idyllic. At the basis of Shu security lay the old Qin surveillance and control system as carried over into Han times. Officials in charge of such a system could abuse it if unchecked. An entire chapter of the *Historical Records* is devoted to censuring bad bureaucrats and includes passing mention of two such offenders in Shu. One was a governor, Feng Dang, whom the historian labeled a tyrannical oppressor. The other official, Li Zhen, occupied some post of jurisdiction in the Guanghan commandery of greater Shu. There he transgressed proper procedure by condemning some criminals to physical dismemberment.[48] The occurrence of this particularly fiendish means of execution suggests some lingering resort in Shu to Legalist punishment practices. By the time the historian recorded this incident in the early first century B.C. Han dynasty norms had progressed to a point where jurists considered the sentence abhorrent.

Governmental control in Shu was strong but might deviate from the tenor of overall Han administration, as this censure against Li Zhen and Feng Dang suggests. Secure dynastic bastion though it may have been, special attention was required to coordinate Shu with trends in political philosophy emerging at the capital. A concerted program to accomplish this via literacy and learning began during the energetic reign of Emperor Wu. The administrator in charge on the scene was to be the new Shu governor, Wen Weng.

The stewardship of Wen Weng over Shu amounted to an encompassing educational mandate and should be evaluated against the background of an ideological transformation underway at the Han imperial court. Legalist thought there, which in any case never exercised a complete intellectual monopoly, was giving way to a syncretic type of Confucianism promoted by Dong Zhongshu (179–104 B.C.).[49] Dong Zhongshu's system promoted a gnostic system of commentaries on the *Spring and Autumn Annals* (*Chun qiu*). If political doctrines are associated with the particular regions where they arise or take hold, as they emphatically are in China, then this form of Confucianism is a doctrine of the central plains just as Legalism was the ruling creed in Qin—and in Sichuan. And the acceptance of these tenets at the imperial palace coincided with the governorship of Wen Weng in Shu. Wen Weng had his work cut out.

Yet however "Confucian" an educator Wen Weng may have been, his governance of Shu rested on the firm foundation set there earlier by Legalist theory and Qin practice. Shu remained fundamentally secure, notwithstanding the abuses committed by officials of the Feng Dang and Li Zhen ilk. Of all Qin commanderies Shu perhaps most nearly approached the ideal Legalist society. Its people consisted largely of colonists, uprooted from distant places and fully dependent on the Qin state organs that had set them down among strangers in alien surroundings. For such people rule by statute filled a natural vacuum as they had been displaced from the restraining mores and customs of their natural social matrix. The formula functioned adequately enough to keep Shu loyal to Qin through the life of that state.

In taking over Shu on behalf of Emperor Wu, Wen Weng aimed not at eradicating what had been achieved, but at taking the commandery a step further along the road of Han civilization. The age of frenetic Qin social engineering had passed. Tranquil normalcy in Shu was best served by a creed stressing riteousness, decorum, benevolence, filial piety, and loyalty to the ruler. Wen Weng's educational efforts aimed at instilling the values and political vocabulary of the capital in a far-flung but vital region.

The *Han History* (*Han shu*) treats this transformation of Sichuan during the reign of Emperor Wu as almost a missionary endeavor and Wen Weng as something of a Confucian saint. He too was a newcomer to Sichuan, from Lujiang commandery on the central plains in present Anhui province. Confucian scholarship had some traditional following among the elite in this area. According to his laudatory biography in *Han shu*, the young Wen Weng showed precocious aptitude in studying the *Spring and Autumn Annals*. Duly impressed with the youth, Lujiang civil authorities recruited him into official administrative service, which in turn led to an appointment as governor of Shu in 141 B.C. This was the last year of Emperor Jing, the fifth Han sovereign. The remainder of Wen Weng's tenure in Shu took place under the forceful Emperor Wu, who reigned until 87 B.C.[50]

On taking up his duties Wen Weng found Shu relatively rustic, with some unrefined, remnant "barbarian" customs still prevalent. His mission was to redeem the people via their inculcation in Han doctrine as taught at Changan. The new governor began this cultural and educational assignment by selecting a small cadre of capable local personnel. One of these first disciples, Zhang Shu, is known by name; there were ten or so in all.[51] The students were dispatched to the capital to receive training as scholars or administrators. To defray the costs of the students' upkeep there, consignments of Shu-produced crafts, namely blades and fine cloth, were sent to Changan for sale. Whether intended or not these scholarship arrangements also amounted to a promotion of Sichuan wares.

However, any local pride felt by the students remained subordinate to their identity as Han subjects. The assigned curriculum, the canonical *Spring and Autumn Annals* (*Chun qiu*) with its sanctioned commentaries, recounted events of war and politics set geographically around the central plains during the years 722–481 B.C. As historical and moral paradigm it constituted the main reference work, guidance by past example for would-be officials. History that mattered was simply Zhou history and that of the central plains states. *Chun qiu* made up the prism of precedent through which regional problems and issues such as those facing Sichuan would have to be scrutinized.

This meant that the historical background of Sichuan itself was of only marginal relevance, doctrinally, to the encompassing needs of imperial administration. The mere fact that the canonical texts were set on the central plains gave that region an implicit primacy in prestige and in historiography. Han Confucian doctrine, like Legalist doctrine before it, took the unity of the empire for granted, as a given. By their selection and training, Shu students schooled at Changan were shaped to act as agents of the imperial power.

In a few years the students had been graduated and were welcomed back to Shu where they received appointments to responsible official positions. Their further promotion to higher bureaucratic ranks would be through the rudiments of an examination system. A scholars' hostel also was set up at Chengdu. Young men from surrounding counties studied there before performing as administrative interns. The original core of official trainees thus multiplied and graduates were sent as teachers to various localities in Shu. Financial donations by wealthy persons helped support the educational endeavors. By these means the standards of classical learning in Shu rose until they rivaled Qi and Lu, old intellectual centers in eastern China where such scholarship had enjoyed a long tradition.[52]

A shrine to Wen Weng honored his memory, preserving his reputation as the one credited with bringing higher culture to Shu. His biography in *Han shu* concludes, "Down to the present Ba and Shu have esteemed higher culture, due to their transformation by Wen Weng."[53] That incidentally is the only mention of Ba in connection with Wen Weng, who is known to have held an official post formally responsible only for Shu, with his seat at Chengdu. Nevertheless, the recognized cultural preeminence of Shu lent its top official a degree of leadership over the rest of Sichuan as well. No equivalent figure of Confucian enlightenment is recorded in Ba during the former Han dynasty. The statement on Wen Weng points up a dependence by Ba upon Shu, a cultural role reversal from Warring States times.

It is doubtful whether Wen Weng could have attained such successful results had he not been building on the social and political strata laid by Qin. He had no cause to dismantle that foundation as it supported a stable commandery, one producing ample wealth to provide for local well-being and then some.[54] His governorship functioned as heir to that of Li Bing a century before. Besides Wen Weng's accomplishments in the capacity of educator, he furthered the work advanced by Li Bing as a hydraulic engineer and is credited with an irrigation project based on the Qian River, a stream about 100 kilometers northeast of Chengdu in an area astride the route to Changan.[55]

Qin rule had inculcated habits of obedience to authority while at the same time offering opportunities to those possessing talent. Wen Weng subsequently refined, rather than reformed, an already workable system. The refinements were possible because Sichuan was a prosperous place. Refinement in turn was desireable for keeping it peaceful and prosperous. Economic facts and philosophic niceties could be mutually reinforcing.

So social order and a sound productive basis underlay the strengthening bond of Sichuan to China proper during the Han centuries. A rich, tranquil society paid off in further material dividends. The promise of measurable gain served as concrete rationale for the Changan regime's program of attuning Shu still more closely with the capital. Classical learning provided the doctrinal basis for that integration, but it was no airy, idle pursuit. The curriculum's ideology aimed at tutoring local Shu functionaries to serve the Han government in practical ways. On returning to their home region, they would serve by placing its wealth at imperial disposal.

The Sichuan Cornucopia

In Sichuan, natural bounty first of all meant grain. The highest-priority tasks of officials entailed gathering, concentrating, and warehousing Sichuan's grain surplus, then consigning and transporting it to fill the stomachs of people in other regions. Imperial control over grain in Sichuan thus would guarantee imperial control elsewhere in the empire. That, for the dynasty, was the payoff from indoctrinating scholar officials. Men of culture like Wen Weng added some veneer, but at basis their pupils were made into compliant servitors of an imperial will with a vision transcending home regional concerns.

The Han authorities at Changan remembered how supplies moved from Shu had sustained Liu Bang's army during the crucial early struggles. In peacetime as well this agricultural surplus could serve as a mainstay reserve. Over it the Han regime would be the sole broker. This was a legacy from Qin times, going back to the Legalism of Shang Yang. Where staple sustenance was concerned, private merchants could be permitted but a limited role. Officials steeped in classical learning would be better trusted to selflessly serve the dynasty.

Exacting Sichuan's cereal surplus and yielding it to imperial government control proved to be the easy part. A less tractable problem lay in getting the cargo to flow out of Sichuan toward the areas of greatest need. The alpine passage between Sichuan and the north posed tremendous difficulties. Avenues like the old Stone Cattle Road could bear only restricted traffic volumes, although alternative corduroy roads existed. One was the Granary Road (*mi cang dao*) across the Daba range, parallel to and east of the Stone Cattle Road. It probably had been put in by Qin. This route was better situated for access to and from northern Ba, freeing the Stone Cattle Road for exploiting Shu and the Chengdu plain.[56] However, once across the Daba range, the Qinling Mountains remained to be traversed before the north was reached. Moving Ba and Shu grain through the Qinling placed still heavier burdens on the Bao-Xie corduroy road.

Even with multiple highways, overland transit by any route proved prohibitively expensive for moving a bulk commodity like grain, especially over hilly terrain. A waterborne alternative was desired, if some feasible route could be identified and a suitable course engineered. During the First Qin Emperor's time such a waterway had been dug in the south, the Lingqu Canal connecting the Yangtze drainage system with rivers flowing into the South China Sea. The dividend then amounted to no less than Qin consolidation of what is now Guangdong province and northern Vietnam. An even greater bonanza in peacetime gains would accrue if that feat could be matched in the north.

The imperial grand secretary (*yu shi dai fu*), Zhang Tang, proposed developing a navigable channel next to part of the existing Bao-Xie corduroy road. His plan required improving the streams. The Bao amounted to a narrow but convenient tributary of the Han River, partially cutting through the Qinling range, and the Xie rose near the crest of the Qinling and descended northward, to the Wei River. This was historic ground, the Qin invasion route to Sichuan in 316 B.C. Infrastructure facilities already were in place along its length. Dredging the Bao and the Xie to accomodate grain barges, it was hoped, would accelerate shipments while alleviating the strain of constant loads on the parallel road.

Provided grain was first carried over the Daba range, Zhang Tang believed barges could then bring it down the Mian River, a branch of the Han. From there he intended to direct the boats up the Bao. A mountain pathway between the respective headwaters of the Bao and the small Xie River had to be widened and improved. Then a land portage by cart of about a hundred *li*, approximately fifty kilometers, was supposed to link up with the Xie, feeding into the Wei River. It seemed reasonable. Zhang Tang's scheme envisioned continuous water transport once the Xie was reached, via the Xie to the Wei and on downstream to the Yellow River. Although not entirely on water the improvements would in theory reduce hauling expenses over the Qinling obstacle.[57]

The government acted. Zhang Tang's son Zhang Ang was appointed governor of the Hanzhong commandery, scene of the project. A labor force numbering several tens of thousands tried to dredge the streams sufficiently to handle bulk cargoes, but to no avail. Rapids along the mountain rivulets made the project unworkable, so the Bao-Xie project was abandoned.[58] However, visions of diverting Sichuan's abundant staples out of Sichuan still enticed officials who recalled how Shu and Han grain once fed the armies of the Han Exalted Progenitor. Peacetime economics ruled against the exhausting and expensive alpine logistic task. The problem of cost effective waterborne grain shipment from south to north was to remain unsolved until the Sui dynasty completed the Grand Canal in eastern China, some 800 years later.

One other obvious alternative remained: the broad Yangtze. In 115 B.C. the Han government sent grain stocks down the river out of Sichuan to alleviate a famine. Disastrous Yellow River flooding over successive bad years had brought about crop failures in a broad swath of northern and eastern China, where conditions worsened until desperate people resorted to cannibalism. Emperor Wu bid the starving refugees move south into an area between the Huai and Yangtze Rivers and there await rations. Officially organized relief grain supplies from Ba and Shu were dispatched to meet the victims.[59]

Given the limitations of the Bao-Xie-Wei-Yellow River route, Yangtze boats had to handle the shipments this time. Feeding an entire malnourished population presented problems of a different order from provisioning Liu Bang's army; the tonnage surely exceeded available portage capabilities on the corduroy roads.[60] Even if Qinling Mountain porters could carry enough grain down to the Wei and Yellow Rivers, floods along the latter further complicated shipping. The intended relief recipients had anyway abandoned the inundated Yellow River districts, heading toward the Yangtze.

Despite its success on this single occasion the Yangtze route for transfering grain out of Sichuan seems to have been an extraordinary heroic effort but never routine procedure. Bureaucrats shuttled back and forth on special assignment to ensure success. Thereafter, once the famine had eased, no justifiable large-scale need existed downstream for Sichuan grain. The more chronic food deficit areas were located farther north, beyond reach of the Yangtze. Exporting the harvests of Shu in bulk to those places remained a chimera.

So most of Sichuan's grain stayed in Sichuan. There it would feed masses of laborers emancipated from subsistence agriculture, making possible an economic efflorescence during Han times. Although the land routes proved impractical for routine grain movement, more valuble commodities manufactured or processed in Sichuan were exchanged by merchants plying the highland roads. No single category of goods dominated, but rather a range of higher-priced products enough in demand to make the exchange profitable after shipping and handling charges. Sichuan silk, herbs, and ginger were among the cash crops. Manufactures of stone, bronze, iron, bamboo, and wood also reached northern consumers.

Some items, like tea, later became so quintessentially Chinese that it is difficult to conceive of a China without them. Their wider acceptance outside Sichuan is a measure of the impact this region was coming to exert on the empire at large. Tea came from plantations in both Ba and Shu.[61] It was documented in Sichuan by at least the middle part of the first century B.C.[62] In addition to tea, a range of Sichuanese herbs or mineral potions entered the Han Chinese medicine chest. A red stone found in Ba was the source of highly prized cinnabar on which fortunes were built even during the Qin.[63] It seems to have been valued as an elixir of longevity.[64] Many other tonic preparations are known by name but cannot be surely identified with later equivalents. A pharmacopoeia thought to reflect Han period medical usage lists sixteen drugs indigenous to Shu plus another eight from Ba.[65]

As noted, when Wen Weng governed Shu he had arranged for sales of locally made blades and cloth in Changan to raise scholarship funds on behalf of his scholar and bureaucrat trainees. Either a market already existed at the capital for these items or Wen Weng must be accorded credit as an early chamber of commerce style booster. His limited commercial venture toward support of a worthy state cause illustrates a fundamental aspect of Han economic activity in Sichuan; that is, its dependence on state approval if not outright sponsorship. Fortunes could be and were made in various endeavors but only with state compliance and a strong degree of supervision.

Imperial ideology and bureaucratic control prevented the drift of political power to entrepreneurs, as well as the free reinvestment of profits for further commercial gain. Such reins kept a capitalist industrial revolution from getting underway in Han Sichuan. Yet despite these limitations on business activity the extent of progress made nevertheless remains impressive by ancient standards. Metallurgical enterprises in iron and bronze flourished. Salt, a revenue mainstay for imperial regimes over the next 2,000 years, was extracted from Sichuan brine deposits and widely distributed. Handicraft and textile manufacture were well organized as was the exploitation of products from the hills and forests. Each item will be examined.

Sichuan iron manufacturing during the Han was centered at Linqiong, close to Chengdu. A regime-appointed iron commissioner (*tie guan*) oversaw operations there. Other iron commissioners functioned at Wuyang and at Nanan, Jianwei commandery, east and south of Shu proper in Sichuan.[66] No equivalent officials functioned in Ba. The commissioners exercised some overall regulatory supervision, but private operators actually ran the mines and smelteries. The big works at Linqiong were developed by a certain Zhuo family, experienced iron smelters originally sent to Shu from Zhao (Jin) when that state succumbed to Qin conquest. Relocated in Shu, the first Zhuo settler there requested to be set down at Linqiong to pursue his old occupation. The site abutted an ore-bearing mountain set amid a region more than self-sufficient in food. As mining and smelting activities expanded, this abundance would sustain masses of laborers.

In time the Zhuo enterprise employed a work force numbering in the thousands, some from nearby Shu and others recruited beyond Han borders in Dian, part of present-day Yunnan. As locally powerful tycoons, the Zhuo family eventually amassed a large estate having its own fields, ponds, and hunting preserves. Cheng Zheng was another Linqiong iron magnate tracing family roots to an emigre from eastern China who had at first arrived in Sichuan as an involuntary exile. He built up his fortune by selling iron goods to still unassimilated barbarian peoples.[67] This trade has been ascertained archaeologically, with farming implements fashioned at the Linqiong works uncovered as far afield as Yunnan, but bearing the controller's mark "Chengdu, Shu commandery."[68]

Does this mean that Sichuan iron miners and smiths made bronze obsolete and ushered in the Chinese iron age? Not quite. Iron manufacturing did not yet spell the end of bronze, which still found favor for use in weapons and other items. One reason for this prolongation of the so-called bronze age and its overlapping with the "iron age" in Sichuan is simply that accessible copper ores were still in no danger of depletion. A place called South Mountain (nan shan) near Qiongdu in southwestern Sichuan was famous for its great copper veins. The probable site, located about twenty kilometers from the present city of Xichang, contains minerals and slag among shards of Han period pottery. Iron tools at the site hint at how miners used ferrous implements to exploit deeper veins of copper ore.[69]

It is, so to say, ironic that Sichuan enterprises concurrently promoted both iron and bronze in China for a long time past the bronze heyday elsewhere in antiquity. The copper veins at Qiongdu were part of a subterranean copper belt extending to nearby Yunnan as well. There the Dian people had attained high skill as bronzesmiths. Enough copper and tin were available to make bronze agricultural tools, more of which are found in Yunnan than anywhere else in China.[70]

In Sichuan, at any rate, this was a protracted period of metallurgical transition. The evidence from the ground does not support categorically defined metallic ages, be they bronze or iron. Both were mined and used profitably. Iron was beginning to vie with bronze as the practical metal of choice, but second and first century B.C. graves in Shu have yielded mainly bronze swords, knives, spear points, and arrowheads. A burial at Peiling on the Yangtze, however, did contain a fair number of iron weapons among the goods, including an axe head, a knife, and a sword.[71] The newer, cheaper metal found even more common use cast into agricultural tools or cooking vessels; for example, hoes, hammers, axes, and cauldrons. Iron possessed great, even revolutionary economic utility, but bronze continued to represent value in and of itself, as specie in the form of half-tael coins and larger ingots.

Salt, like iron, had enormous revenue-earning potential, and like iron it too came under imperial regulation. Brine deposits from some primordial sea lay beneath the surface in Sichuan at varying depths, often accessible by sinking well shafts. Enough salt was available to make this commercially feasible on a large scale and so attracted the inevitable government control. Linqiong had a salt commissioner in addition to its iron commissioner. Ba also produced salt, with a salt commissioner in charge at Juren county.[72]

Salt wells and works multiplied throughout Sichuan during the Han, coming to include at least fourteen installations ranging from near the Yangtze gorges to points about the Chengdu plain and due south.[73] Each site might operate multiple well shafts, such as the twenty recorded at Linqiong.[74] Natural gas deposits also were encountered in the course of boring into the earth for salt. Conducted to the surface in pipes, gas provided a convenient source of energy to boil away the brine portion, leaving a relatively pure, marketable product.

In addition to necessities like grain, metals, and the literal salt of the earth, Sichuan enterprises turned out several categories of luxury goods. Ancient writers praised the exquisite brocades from Chengdu.[75] State regulation of the production and marketing of brocade and probably other goods as well was exercised by a bureaucrat called the *gong guan*, or works commissioner.[76] As in the case of brocades, lacquer production centered on Chengdu, the site of the works commissioner's office. Pieces bearing the mark of this official have been excavated outside Sichuan, in Han period tombs at Mawangdui, Hunan province.[77]

Certain other products also came under government supervision. For example in the citrus fruit producing area of Juren, in Ba commandery, a resident orange commissioner (*ju guan*) exercised authority. His presence there implies that the orange crop was raised for marketing away from the immediate growing area.[78] No doubt the commodity realized some profit, enough to warrant the commissioner as tax man. It was even said that possession of a thousand orange trees in either Shu or Han commanderies would provide the owner with an income equal to that of a marquis.[79] Besides fruit, Sichuan-made handicraft products of wood and bamboo were traded to other regions, a proportion going north by road across the Qinling range.[80]

By all accounts Han Sichuan prospered. In another milieu, economic muscle might back an assertive separatism, but not here. On the contrary, the profitable economic relations of Shu and of Ba to China reinforced their firm political connections. State policy as promoted by Qin and subsequently by the Han regime had judiciously taken account of local conditions in each main division of Sichuan.

Dissimilar but appropriate programs were pursued in Shu and Ba. "Yi zhou," the regional or provincial level organ joining them was through most of Han times apparently unimportant as a locus of practical policy implementation.

So the two subregions Shu and Ba were bound separately to China proper by ties more significant than their mutual bonds. The carving out of the additional Guanghan commandery from Shu fostered further administrative fragmentation. Even though united to China, Sichuan could hardly be considered a united entity unto itself. Cultural and territorial division within Sichuan was a fact. First as circumstance, then policy, and then ingrained political habit, this fact retarded the growth of an independent political consciousness in the Sichuan basin. Economically the differential progress of commanderies within Sichuan reinforced the cultural and political split.

Ba had sauntered down a less hurried path toward sinification, its indigenous peoples retaining much of their former, pre-Qin customs and identity far into Han times and beyond. In Shu, Han Chinese were inculcated with an ideology and literary heritage in common with the country of their ancestors to the north. These Sichuanese of Shu amassed wealth in the new land, but their yearning for status and refinement still focused loyalties northward. Chengdu city exercised a cultural preeminence in Sichuan, although its glory reflected that of Changan. No Han governor serving at Chengdu would entertain sovereign ambitions of his own as long as the dynasty demonstrated vigor.

With unity to China taken for granted and without the ideological basis for a pan-Sichuan alternative, Sichuanese separatism seems simply inconceivable in the Han context. Chinese unity amounted to an ascendence of thought and organization, a victory of mind over matter. Topography surely mattered in setting Sichuan apart from the rest of China, but the Sichuanese would stay Chinese for evermore. Philosophy, politics, trade, and tradition combined to keep them so. Whether north or south of the Han valley, all the Chinese were men of Han.

Sima Xiangru and the Limits of Han Sichuan

One of these Han Chinese, from Shu, became the first person born and reared in Sichuan to enter history as a fully rounded, believable human personality. He was Sima Xiangru, poet extraordinaire, frontier diplomat, an officer and a gentleman of the Han. All previously documented figures on the Sichuan scene had been either semilegendary types like the last Kaiming king or else outsiders sent to Sichuan as conquerers and sinifiers. Some of them play cameo roles or bit parts in chapters on other themes, only inadvertently revealing an odd fact of Sichuan history. Sima Xiangru by contrast rated a full-length biographical entry unto himself in the *Historical Records*, compiled and written by Han court annalist Sima Qian. The historian's account may be taken as a measure of this man's importance as a Sichuanese and as a Chinese. It tells a great deal as well about the dynamics of unification and sinification, the continuing processes binding Sichuan to China.[81]

In Sichuan, Han power at last confronted its geographic and political limits. Those limits also are particularly evident in the life and times of Sima Xiangru. As politician and frontiersman, much of his activity would be devoted toward defining the bounds that ultimately enclosed the Han empire at its southwestern extremes. Sima Xiangru's long, varied career played against the alternately shifting backdrops of provincial Shu and imperial Changan. His intrigues, escapades, and even his marriage offer glimpses into life-styles of the rich and famous of Han Sichuan. The story endured, celebrated in literary tradition. Well known to most educated Chinese as romance, in the present context the various episodes of his life and times also illustrate the nature of Sichuanese society and the relationship between this far-flung region and Han central authority.

Sima Xiangru was born to a well-off family in Chengdu, sometime around 179 B.C. His boyhood education consisted of training in literature and swordsmanship, both of which he relished. A rambunctious nature earned him a nickname that can translate as "Young Pup." Households with some means at this time might hope to secure junior palace appointments for their promising youths, a good first rung on the official ladder upward. On payment of a fee Sima Xianyru received a post as a cadet courtier in Changan, during the reign of Emperor Jing.

It should have assured success, but the young Sichuanese soon found himself temperamentally unsuited to courtly banality, preferring creative writing instead. He excelled at the *fu* literary form, a kind of ode in an archaic style yet one that did not accord with the reigning emperor's literary tastes. However, a certain northern Chinese provincial noble did appreciate the budding poet who was persuaded to leave the imperial palace to reside on the estates of this semiautonomous prince. Unfortunately for Sima Xiangru his new patron died soon after, whereupon he returned to Shu.

Back home, Sima Xiangru found himself treated as a celebrity, a local boy made good. Even following an abortive official career the patina of Changan was perceived in Shu as a glorious sheen. Soon an invitation came to him from the prefect (*ling*) of Linqiong, that bustling source of salt and iron where merchants entertained lavishly. Sima Xiangru's residing in Linqiong would add some capital city luster and connections to a provincial boom town. Shortly after the poet had relocated there he received a courtesy call from the prefect.[82]

The significance of such an honor was not lost on the Linqiong social circuit, and there followed a banquet invitation to Sima Xiangru from Zhuo Wangsun, head of the Zhuo family. He was the mogul who had struck it rich in Linqiong by mining and smelting iron ore.[83] It was a case of money seeking to trade on the prestige of an imperial courtier. The manner in which Sima Xiangru dealt with these blandishments showed conclusively that in Shu, by around the turn of the first century B.C., prestige was coming to hold the upper hand. He not only managed to snub his wealthy hosts, but after at length deigning to make a guest appearance at their estate he proceeded to utterly scandalize the Zhuo patriarch.

Zhuo Wangsun had in his household a daughter, Zhuo Wenjun, who had been prematurely widowed but was still quite young. Although prevailing morals prescribed a lifetime of chastity for women who lost their husbands, Zhuo Wenjun and Sima Xiangru felt drawn to each other. Their elopement brought disgrace to Zhuo Wangsun who thereupon disowned the girl. The newlyweds settled in Chengdu but after awhile the bride felt homesick and persuaded Sima Xiangru to accompany her on a return to Linqiong. Her father still adamantly refused to make amends or provide an allowance, so the couple made ends meet by operating a tavern in Linqiong town. Eventually one of Zhuo Wenjun's brothers persuaded their father to provide them a cash stipend and some servants. Thus endowed with an estate more befitting his dignity, Sima Xiangru took his wife once more to live in Chengdu.[84] The grant from Zhuo Wangsun, however, fell short of full reconciliation.

Along with its personal elements this love story discloses something of the balance among elites in Shu. Mining magnates tapped the earth for salt and iron, items of immeasurable strategic import. Industry provided much of the imperial dynasty's tax revenue with enough left over for the mine operators to enjoy luxuries rivaling the splendor of kings. Yet politically these creators of wealth dared not overstep their legal status as common subjects of the empire. Linqiong's most prominent businessman properly respected prefectural authority. Meanwhile the prefect himself took care to cultivate an unemployed man of letters having Changan palace connections.

Even though unemployed, the sometime palace courtier and poet might run off with an iron tycoon's daughter and risk nothing more than a temporary cutoff of patronage. The tycoon would be righteously and paternally wrathful but his vast monetary wealth proved no match for the poet's less tangible yet more persuasive grip on influence. Sima Xiangru held renown by dint of literary panache, a dose of calculated arrogance, and his onetime service at the Han emperor's court. In Shu, that subtly translated into authority.

Objectively, the career of Sima Xiangru took a marked upward turn when Emperor Wu ascended to the throne. The imperial succession brought a shift in literary fashion as well, leading to the Sichuanese writer again becoming a sought-after figure at the imperial palace. An element of chance came into play here. His recall to Changan came after the emperor happened to read one of Sima Xiangru's earlier literary pieces, an ode. He praised the poem in an offhand comment to an attending aide. Apparently never having heard before of Sima Xiangru, Emperor Wu wistfully said he regretted not being a contemporary of the author. The courtier, also a native of Shu, knew of the poet's local reputation there. He accordingly informed the emperor that Sima Xiangru indeed still was a living person.[85]

This exchange of remarks on literature was to lead Sima Xiangru back over the road to Changan, the road to power. Summoned to the capital from his estate near Chengdu, he took the occasion to write a long, didactic ode for special presentation to the Emperor Wu. This effort too earned a positive reception, and so the poet laureate of Shu gained appointment as a scholar official with the rank of *lang guan*. Thanks to an old-boy network of fellow provincials a man of Shu had risen close to the peak. The *Historical Records* later would carry long excerpts from his writings, a mark of Sima Xiangru's merit in contemporary eyes. More important, his position and influence would extend quite beyond poetry to shape history in Sichuan itself. Sima Xiangru found himself in a pivotal role first as a man of Sichuan at the imperial court and subsequently as the representative of the imperial power in Sichuan.

The years when Sima Xiangru served Emperor Wu were a time of energetic Han expansion. Military probes penetrated in several directions along the inner Asian perimeter. In the north, Chinese armies campaigned beyond the frontiers to neutralize threats from the open steppes. Other Han forces advanced toward the South China Sea coast, annexing local chiefdoms in the area of present Guangdong province. For its southern campaigns the dynasty used convicts from Ba and Shu, forcibly impressed as soldiers to serve outside Sichuan.[86]

But Ba and Shu had their own barbarian marches, offering possibilities for winning wealth and glory. The great copper mining works at South Mountain, near Qiongdu, were in the southwestern frontier zone.[87] Sichuan merchants had for some time been doing business with various neighboring hill tribes. And more rapacious adventurers from Ba and Shu had launched predatory raids across the borders, horse thieving, cattle rustling, and even taking slaves.[88] An organized expedition into these parts seemed a promising way to bring land, loot, and subjects into the Han imperium. Ambitious soldiers responded to the call.[89]

One such military expedition began in 135 B.C. under general Tang Meng who set out from Sichuan toward Yelang, in present Guizhou province. The indigenous peoples there were collectively known to the Han as "southern barbarians" (nan yi, occasionally nan man). Some already had limited access to Sichuan goods such as cloth and a kind of pepper used as a condiment. More than a century before the area had been penetrated by Chu forces under Zhuang Qiao and thus was not totally unknown. It now seemed open to more direct Han contact and control. Tang Meng made some slow, limited progress amid the daunting mountain terrain. The new areas he brought under Han control were organized as Jianwei commandery.[90]

Not to be outdone by a rival close to home, Sima Xiangru won approval for a second Sichuan campaign. Commissioned as a general (lang zhong jiang), he based his campaign on Shu and pushed into highland regions west of the Chengdu plain inhabited by the "western barbarians" (xi yi). Here too conditions imposed delays. Roads and bridges had to be built and rations brought up to the front by exhausting labor. Sima Xiangru won laurels by subduing enough territory that ten new counties under a frontier zone commander (du wei) were added to Shu commandery.[91] The task of safeguarding communications in the grueling terrain necessitated creation of a special official position, that of roads and bridges superintendent (dao qiao yuan).[92]

The Han reach was exceeding its grasp along these fringes of the empire. Despite the modest successes of Tang Meng and Sima Xiangru, their efforts exacted a toll not only in finances but also of Sichuanese energy and morale. Damp climate, bivouac living in the field, and native guerrilla resistance claimed many casualties. Competing projects elsewhere also clamored for imperial assets and attention.[93] Because the northern situation held more vital security implications for the capital and all China, Emperor Wu eventually was persuaded to accord it priority over the resource-draining southern campaigns, which he bade suspended in 126 B.C.

Vested career interests were at stake in the competing projects but it seemed that officers serving along the northern marches had won imperial favor. One of them, the explorer Zhang Qian, traveled far into the dry wastes of inland central Asia under orders to stabilize relations with steppe peoples. Zhang Qian stayed abroad for several years before reporting back to Emperor Wu. Among other things learned on his epic journey, the explorer noted having seen products from Shu, namely bamboo and cloth, used by central Asians. He suspected the goods must have been traded there via Shendu, that is, India, along some unknown route leading westward or southwestward from Sichuan.[94]

Ironically, this surmise stimulated renewed interest regarding whatever terra incognita lay beyond the Sichuan frontiers. Acting on the advice of Zhang Qian, in 112 B.C. Emperor Wu issued orders for a resumption of the suspended southern reconnaissance operations. Tang Meng once again directed the push from Sichuan into what is now Guizhou, accompanied by a modest armed escort. Yet the craggy, jungled terrain still posed logistical challenges too difficult to surmount, even though Tang Meng was backed by the wealth of Sichuan.

As previously, roads had to be built, grain rations carried up by porters, and hostile frontier natives fought off amidst an unfamiliar, uncharted landscape. This was not a conventional war among civilized states where a few decisive encounters could determine the outcome. Rather, Tang Meng and his men had set out to challenge mountaineers on their home ground. Nuisance tactics wore down the Han intruders as every step up and down the hillsides took them farther from their base.

Frustrated by the sluggish momentum and setbacks, Tang Meng resorted to supply requisitions and extreme measures while trying to make headway. For the first time, Sichuan resources proved inadequate. This is itself a gauge of how exhausting the effort had become, as hitherto Sichuan had always been known as a land of plenty. After military expenses depleted the regular Ba and Shu tax receipts, additional local grain exactions were sold at the capital to raise war funds.

Conscription press-ganged thousands of Ba and Shu residents to fight or labor in the wake of Tang Meng's army.

On his own initiative the general pursued the steps of a harsh attrition strategy, egregiously exceeding authority. One move reminiscent of earlier Qin practice entailed resettling Sichuan delinquents on land seized from the southern barbarians, with a view to raising crops for the army's needs.[95] Tang Meng even decreed a kind of martial law whereby property might be commandeered for military use. These burdens of supporting an apparently endless war weighed heavily on the Sichuanese. A crisis point was reached when he executed a noncompliant local leader, which led to Sichuanese protest and near mutiny.[96]

Emperor Wu, alarmed by the unexpected turn of events in Sichuan, dispatched Sima Xiangru to restrain Tang Meng and placate the people of Ba and Shu. This could be done only by cutting losses, winding down the frontier bush war, holding on to what had been gained, and reaching some sort of diplomatic arrangement with the aroused hill peoples. As a well-connected Sichuanese noted for his eloquence and enjoying the emperor's confidence, Sima Xiangru probably was the man best suited to reassure his fellow provincials. He prepared a statement for that purpose, outlining Han policy. It offered an implicit political compact between the throne and its Sichuanese subjects. Sima Xiangru began by placing the struggle against the southwestern tribes in the context of overall Han frontier policy.

On the northern, northwestern, and southeastern Chinese frontiers, he said, barbarians had accepted Han supremacy. Tang Meng likewise had been sent to approach the barbarians of southern Sichuan using diplomacy. His original contingent of 500 men was characterized as a mere security guard on an embassy bearing goodwill presents to the barbarian chiefs. However, Sima Xiangru now admitted that events had gotten far out of hand, quite contrary to the emperor's purpose. He thus disclaimed imperial responsibility for all the exactions enforced by Tang Meng and the many fatalities incurred. Fairly or not, blame for the costly conflict was set on the shoulders of that field commander.

Sima Xiangru went on to commend his countrymen of Ba and Shu for their gallantry. In a speech since immortalized by its inclusion in classical anthologies, he praised the Sichuanese for selflessly responding to the signal beacons rousing them to action, then bravely confronting the enemy in battle with swords and crossbows. Acknowledging the claims of heroes and their descendants to deserved reward, he warned disgrace would befall unworthy officials guilty of violating the emperor's precepts and mistreating the common folk. Sima Xiangru thus recognized how imperial power over even the most loyal subjects was ultimately constrained. He then ordered the conciliating message to be repeated far and wide for all in the villages and fields to hear.

Promulgation of the writ throughout the countryside was an extraordinary measure indicating concern, and even alarm, about the depths of discontent in Sichuan. By overreaching itself the Han imperium had triggered a political crisis of confidence in the very region that nurtured the dynasty at its inception a century before. Fully two centuries had elapsed since the Qin conquest of Shu, during which time the offspring of migrants from north China prospered there. Agriculture, mining, crafts, and commerce yielded a good life for most Sichuanese and real fortunes for an enterprising few. Economic gain and workaday political normalcy functioned in tandem. Now the exorbitant expenses of probing arduous terrain around the frontiers threatened to jeopardize it all. Taking heed, the dynasty scaled back its goals in Sichuan.

By frankly admitting to his compatriots that they had suffered abuse, Sima Xiangru restored some measure of trust. Disaffection was contained and widespread disorder averted. The throne expressed pleasure at these positive results but there remained the pressing task of restoring border peace by actually winding down the debilitating, destabilizing expeditionary operations. For this delicate mission, Sima Xiangru was made a plenipotentiary (*zhong lang jiang*). Fulsome deference marked the occasion of his ceremonial arrival in Chengdu bearing the new rank. The Shu governor greeted Sima Xiangru's carriage on the outskirts of Chengdu, and the prefect of Chengdu county personally carried a crossbow as a military guard of honor. To all appearances, local boy Sima Xiangru, as imperial representative, had come to supersede all other powers in his home commandery.

Accompanied by the elders of Linqiong, Sima Xiangru's wealthy father-in-law, Zhuo Wangsun, mounted the city gate in an act of humble obeisance. Zhuo Wangsun offered libations and presented an ox, expressing his regret at not having earlier acquiesced in the marriage of his daughter. As a staged public spectacle this went far beyond private family reconciliation. It must be held indicative of the balance of political forces in Shu.[97] Sima Xiangru, the emperor's plenipotentiary, was commissioned to set affairs right. All were expected set aside objections and acknowledge his mandate. The personal grudge of so powerful a person as Sichuan's leading millionaire would have to be set aside in a show of solidarity. He too needed to follow the duly appointed county and commandery authorities paying homage to a legate of the throne.

Having been thus assured of local compliance by the leaders of government and business, Sima Xiangru could set about making peace on the frontiers. He had prepared by bringing along a retinue of officials to help achieve a settlement.[98] They were to contact the peoples neighboring Shu to the west and southwest of Chengdu and enlist native cooperation in following up leads about a route through the mountains to Shendu. This was the inferred path whereby Sichuan goods had purportedly gone west to India, generating Zhang Qian's earlier account.[99]

Coming on the heels of a long and destructive war, Sima Xiangru's deputies faced a delicate mission. They took along a quantity of silk as goodwill gifts for the western barbarian chiefs and a patent to negotiate. The actual frontier compact worked out by Sima Xiangru and his associates set the course of relations between China and its southwestern neighbors for many centuries to come. Judged in terms of initial Han ambitions it amounted to retrenchment. Real territorial acquisitions were marginal when measured against the risk and unforseen costs incurred. Some of the gains may be considered merely cosmetic, consisting of lands formally annexed by the Han empire as commanderies but left under de facto control by their indigenous chieftains. The arrangement rather resembled the laissez-faire formula employed by Qin in the initial stages of its absorption of Ba, whether consciously conceived as such or an inadvertent parallel.

As for the hopeful attempt to find or pioneer a southwestern route through the mountains to Shendu, it too foundered and subsequently was abandoned. The Han envoy charged with this project advised pursuing a cautious, nonantagonistic policy toward the southern neighbors of Shu.[100] His report on the situation recognized that a certain stasis had been reached. The Han line of demarcation was set somewhere in the vicinity of Xichang, where a salient of southern Sichuan juts into the modern boundaries of Yunnan province.

In the highlands directly west of Chengdu, Sima Xiangru again advocated mollifying the natives in return for their pro forma recognition of Han supremacy. Frontier garrison posts were dismantled and chieftains of the Qiong, Za, Ran, Mang, and Siyu accorded confirmation as imperial officials. New commanderies were set up to honor their formal Han status; for example, Yuexi commandery on the southern approaches to Yunnan and Wenshan northwest of Chengdu.[101] Sima Xiangru proclaimed the Mo and Ruo Rivers as the new western border.[102] Although still firmly under its local rulers, part of the Dian Yue kingdom was similarly granted de jure inclusion in the Han empire.

New commanderies might have been established but hardly could be considered fully sinified to the extent prevailing in Shu. Non-Han leaders retained actual power and aboriginal populations stayed in place. Archaeological remains in the form of grave goods attest to a long coexistence of cultures on the barbarian edge of Shu.[103] Separate administrators oversaw the affairs of Han settlers and barbarian natives in these hilly commanderies west of lowland Shu, an indication that the latter were not expected to rapidly assimilate into the Chinese cultural community.

The pace of sinification slowed to a virtual pause.[104] Han China had to content itself with a mere theoretical suzerainty over the Sichuan border regions. As with Ba and Shu during Qin times, the Han commandery status extended to Sichuan frontier territories masked a spectrum of shadings along a gradual continuum toward full cultural and political sinification.

However, by leaving barely or only partially pacified peoples in place on their home ground, the compact aroused unease in Shu. The thinly disguised setback in particular disappointed local eminences in Shu, those who ran affairs beneath the official commandery establishment. Their sacrifices in the prolonged border combat came to little or naught. Ugly rumors hinted at a sellout, damaging the prestige of Sima Xiangru. Restoring frontier tranquility in a manner to mollify both the barbarians and the Han Chinese peoples of Sichuan had not been an easy or popular task. Nevertheless the treaty held, setting up a recognizable zone on the fringe of Shu beyond which Han society faded and the non-Han upland world held on to its own ways.

Relations with the principal power to the south of Ba, namely Yelang on the Guizhou plateau, still remained in the hands of the rogue commander Tang Meng. Although Sima Xiangru conveyed the displeasure of Emperor Wu over Tang Meng's exceeding authority, the general had not actually been recalled. He seems to have been somewhere near Yelang, where factors of range permitted him greater leeway.[105] Finally Tang Meng halted on the Zangge River in present-day Guizhou, setting up a commandery there, but halting after a foundered attempt to annex Yelang outright. Zealousness had propelled him to an extent approaching insubordination but falling short of outright sedition. The historical record may castigate Tang Meng, but his results on the Ba frontier were accepted as a fait accompli, as were those of Sima Xiangru on the Shu frontier.

The stasis on this southwestern extremity of China lasted for centuries. Aggressive probing resumed only after the latter Han dynasty, during the Three Kingdoms period when general Zhuge Liang pushed south. Even then the Yunnan-Guizhou plateau stayed beyond China's grasp. Outside the belt of autonomous tribal territories nominally annexed to Han China, other lands kept aloof, literally aloof, from higher ground. The long pause allowed markedly different civilizations to take shape, the proto-Thai in Yunnan and the Sanskritized culture of Tibet.

Why, it is reasonable to ask, did the expansionist drive of Tang Meng, Sima Xiangru, and others on the Sichuan margins bog down, when on the central Asian desert steppes an irresistible westward momentum swept Han power to the Pamirs? Han Sichuan silos bulged with grain. The mines and workshops of Shu turned out all the iron and bronze that might be needed. Han soldiers and settlers lacked for nothing in the way of swords and crossbows, hoes and plowshares. Sichuan's saltworks, cash crops, and luxury manufactures earned further wealth. Should not this affluence have sufficed for Han power to burst out of the Sichuan basin? In his Changan palace, Emperor Wu certainly had believed so. What went wrong?

The answer may be simply the lay of the land. Chinese civilization, in essence, is a lowland civilization. To irrigate and cultivate low-lying, level areas demands less effort than terracing and watering hillsides. China hardly lacks mountains, to be sure, but culture and control emanate from the flatter, lower stretches of terrain interspersed between and among the cordilleras. At the edges of Sichuan, though, Han commanders faced a solid and seemingly endless massif. This was the mountaineers' own element. Overwhelming Han power might have persisted in advancing a bit farther, but the mountain men, and the mountains, exacted too steep a price to make winning worthwhile.

Mountain men can be stubborn fighters even when vastly outnumbered: ambushing, sniping, and skirmishing, but reluctant to give decisive battle. For mountain people the hills are an ally, not an obstacle. They can retreat and yet still hold the heights, and there is always another hill to climb. Through the ages those who fought in the Scottish highlands, the Basque country, the Caucasus, Afghanistan, central Vietnam, and many another lumpy land all came to learn this same tough lesson. In mountains a preponderance of men and materiel may not count.

Qin, as seen, had traversed mountains to conquer Sichuan in the first place. But after crossing the Qinling range Qin armies reached the familiar, relatively wide, and easily pacified Han valley.

And once through the Daba range Qin could set up a base in the lush, broad lowlands of the Chengdu plain. By contrast, the advancing Han forces of Sima Xiangru ran out of lowlands west of the narrow Mo and Ruo River valleys. There were no more plains on which to establish a base, a la Shu. The limits of Han Sichuan, and Han China, had been attained.

7

Conclusion

Bronze age proto-civilization in Sichuan begins with Sanxing-dui. A thousand years passed between the splendid early Shu era at Sanxingdui and Sima Xiangru's setting the limits of Han Sichuan, by then the largest and richest region in the empire. When, during that millennium, did Sichuan become part of China?

Take pity on a modern Chinese cartographer preparing historical atlas maps. Cognizant of major new finds, he wants to keep his work up to date without somehow offending tradition. He is patriotically aware of how images of the past can bear upon present perceptions. Yet as a scrupulous scholar he knows that relations between China and the outside world have always been complex. For safety's sake he must remain politically correct, but he desires also to be accurate. In what century should this map maker extend the boundary line of "China" to encompass Sichuan?

The cartographer's dilemma is a problem as well for all who seek China's origins. Ancient myth makers knew no such difficulty. Projecting back to an even earlier age, they included Sichuan within the larger realm and kept its patriarchal rulers all in the family. The myth makers could afford to remain unperturbed by facts. They offered a few simple, reassuring. . . myths.

Like cartographers, historians nowadays are burdened by facts, and must account for them. History in China begins with the Shang kings, rulers who sought to learn the future from oracle bones, magnates whose magnificent bronzes grace our museums. Their oracle writing may (or may not) mention a place called Shu. The bronzes were cast contemporary with those in Shu, at Sanxingdui. Yet the Shang kings' political sway never reached Sichuan. Was Sichuan, then, in China?

From the sumptuous bronze figures and masks of Sanxingdui, it is evident that Sichuanese metallurgists shared a common technical tradition with their professional Shang colleagues far off along the

Yellow River and on the central plains. Artistically the Sanxingdui work has a particularly local look within the larger shared identity. Sanxingdui bronzes at one glance are recognizably Sichuanese. But are they Chinese? Were those who designed and wrought them Chinese? Are the faces of those they depict the faces of Chinese?

These Sichuanese, the Shu of Sanxingdui, marched on the central plains in an armed alliance of many peoples. Shu halberds clashed with those of the Shang. Shang power fell and in its place rose the long-lived, classically formative Zhou dynasty. The Shu thus participated in a founding event, a milestone held nearly sacred by later Chinese. Were the Shu themselves Chinese?

Back in Sichuan, the Shu fashioned their bronze halberds like those of the Zhou. They continued to do so centuries after the old-style weapons became passe on the central plains. The Shu had fallen out of touch. They buttoned their tunics on the left side, in the barbarian manner. Their ruler declared himself divine, his status higher even than the Zhou king. Classical historians ceased to mention the Shu; they disappear from written sources into a dark age. Were they Chinese?

In eastern Sichuan and nearby areas another group of people appeared in the histories. They were fierce warriors from several constituent groups, known collectively as the Ba after the leading clan among them. Their totem was the tiger, whose image marked Ba halberds and crouched atop the bronze Ba war drums. The Ba lived on the fringes of Zhou culture. Ba chiefs intermarried with Zhou royalty and were granted the Zhou house's surname. But Ba inscriptions on bronze were in a system of signs unique to the Ba. Modern Chinese scholars cannot read them. Were the Ba Chinese? How should the cartographer solve these problems of the Ba and the Shu?

On the middle Yangtze and Han Rivers, the nearest neighbor to Ba was Chu. Chu straddled the northern and southern worlds, blending Zhou cultural elements with a rice-based economy and a subtropical temperament. This strong state pushed the Ba back into Sichuan and itself became a Sichuan power. By the fourth century B.C. Ba and Shu were showing signs of a cultural blending under heavy Chu influence. A southern, Yangtze-based variant of East Asian civilization was in the making, including Sichuan. Had all Sichuan succumbed to outright Chu control, history surely would have taken a different course. If so, could the result have been called "China"?

In truth, China is an amalgamation of several regions, each contributing aspects to the whole. That which is southern in China owes much to Chu. The central plains region for its part formed the classical heartland, but was not, unto itself, China. When the Zhou dynasty weakened the central plains lands devolved to vassal retainers and became autonomous states. More often than not the fragments were at odds. It was, after all, the Warring States period.

Chronic division fosters yearnings for peace and harmony, the theme of central plains philosophy that survives in the classical literary corpus. Philosophy, inquiring into the proper role of humans in a strife-torn world, is the lasting contribution of the central plains culture to China. The philosophy called Confucianism glorified a bygone golden age. It promoted benevolence, filial piety, ethical conduct, and ceremonial observance as appropriate means for restoring the idealized past. This philosophy may occupy the very core of Chinese identity but it could not unify the lands we know as China.

Unity derived from Qin, as does the very word *China*. The rulers of Qin did not subscribe to the same visions as central plains philosophers. They followed a pragmatic creed preoccupied with maximizing power according to the social vision of Qin's chancellor, Lord Shang. In Qin the state ruled supreme, remolding society via legal statute and backed by force. The dual goals of the state were abundance in agriculture and victory in war. State power superseded natural community units, the village and the family.

Lord Shang's coldly calculated formula wrought a revolution from above. It reconfigured the bonds of people to their relatives, to their neighbors, and to the land they worked. At all levels Qin interpolated the state, guided by laws, as social arbiter. Community surveillance observed every move in the villages and on the roads. State coercion ensured enforcement of the strict laws, but a system of rewards offered its own positive incentives to the ordinary people of Qin. So the system succeeded as designed, making Qin the most aggressive among constituent states belonging to the Zhou political community. This aggressive Qin, from the northwest, wrested Sichuan out of Chu reach.

Before conquering and unifying all the states of the central plains, Qin paused to transform Sichuan. Qin Sichuan was built on prior foundations, the Ba-Shu culture and the archaic Sanxingdui culture below that. Sichuan had been the scene of an advanced society, a proto-civilization, taken over and given a Legalist superstructure adapted to local peculiarities.

In Ba, Qin respected native tradition and won the cooperation of the area's diverse peoples. Their former allegiance to the Ba ruling clan was transferred to Qin. Shu came in for a more rigorous treatment. By pursuing differential courses toward sinification in Ba and Shu, Qin perpetuated their separateness and the long-existing dichotomy within Sichuan. The twin approaches each proved compatible with local circumstances, working in mutually complementary fashion to secure overall Qin advantage.

Shu was thoroughly remade as an image of Qin, only more so, repopulated with a tide of immigrants from Qin itself and the central plains. The program set in motion thousands of people on a pioneering venture simultaneous with but far outlasting the Hellenization of Persia and Egypt. No haphazard, unguided *Volkerwanderung* traversed the Qinling range to Shu, but instead a closely managed colonization launched to meet specific goals. Many more movements like it would follow in Chinese history. This was the first.

Native folk gave way to the newcomers. Prisoners, exiles, and settlers went to their assigned new homes. Arable land was parceled out according to a standard formula tracing back to Lord Shang. Roads built over the mountains ensured Qin communications and control. Fortified walls protected the Qin towns in Shu. Rivers were rechanneled to flow where the state decreed. Salt wells and iron mines probed the very earth. The practical demands of war and agriculture dictated every move.

Shu was, in a word, sinified. The area served as a social laboratory for what was to come. Administrative structures like the commandery were tried out in Shu and progressed toward maturity there. When enfeoffment to local aristocrats failed, Qin replaced the uncooperative vassals with centrally appointed officials. This constituted an integral chapter in the evolution toward Chinese bureaucratic government. The remaking of Shu was the premier instance in history of sinification itself, the initial such transformation of an area outside the original Qin homeland. Shu became "Chinese" before Qin conquered the central plains, lent the unified entity its name, and so created "China." This is no mere semantic point. Let the cartographer draw his map.

Following policies adjusted to local circumstances in Shu and Ba, Qin pragmatically brought about a synthesis of north and south in Sichuan, on Qin terms. Tied to Qin, Sichuan served as both a material base and a reference base of policy precedent when the state set out to forcibly create imperial China, a much grander synthesis of north and south. Sichuan resources counted heavily toward that unifying result as it gained momentum. The geographic position of Sichuan was utilized to best advantage by Qin strategists. Their humiliation of Chu in a gigantic pincer campaign along the Yangtze and Han Rivers figures among the master strokes of ancient warfare.

Qin brought about the unity of China in 221 B.C., a century after annexing Sichuan. The First Emperor then died and Qin fell. Resilient China reunified, quickly enough, under the Han. Han was a truly pan-Chinese regime. Its founder, a petty official from east China, turned rebel against Qin more due to circumstance than choice. He held no grudge toward the Qin establishment or people. These he protected on accepting the surrender of the Qin state. When a truculent Chu rival forced him to retreat toward Sichuan, he maintained Qin institutions there as "king of Han."

The revival of China as the Han empire followed in broad pattern the Qin unification. This is as close as history will come to staging an instant replay, although unlike games, the fighting wrecked broad areas and a multitude of lives. The central plains were ravaged as was the old Qin capital. Yet Sichuan survived unscathed, a safe rear echelon feeding and supplying the Han armies. At length the king of Han emerged triumphant to reunite what had been the Qin empire, bestowing the name *Han* on his dynasty.

Circumstances compelled the new Han emperor to share power with the host of retainers and allied generals whose assistance had brought him victory. Much of northern, central, and eastern China was thus entrusted to these loyalists as "kingdoms," actually semi-autonomous fiefs. The nascent Han dynasty exercised direct, undisputed control over little more than those lands that had comprised preimperial Qin, the Han valley, and Sichuan. Decades of nurturing dynastic strength there were needed before successive Han sovereigns could gradually whittle away the fiefdoms to assert a tight imperial sway over all China.

Within Sichuan the division between Ba and Shu endured. Ba, ethnically distinct, continued on a leisurely path toward cultural sinification. Meanwhile Shu again served as a testing ground for policy implementation because it remained securely under central guidance while the remainder of China largely was still parceled out to vassal rulers. In Shu civil officials could patiently apply Han governmental principles. Bureaucratic administration, that quintessence of China, thereby was preserved in the Han valley and Sichuan despite its lapse in so many other regions. In Sichuan is to be found an unbroken continuity from late classical to early imperial times.

Han Sichuan prospered, a land of silk and money boasting wealth and productivity. Hardly a better environment existed to apply Confucian teaching, that doctrine of loyalty and social harmony worked out by northern Chinese scholars. In Shu, their message softened some of the harsher practices held over from Qin times while keeping the land firmly within the Chinese fold.

Possession of Sichuan and the Han valley had enabled the king of Han to restore imperial unity after Qin power toppled. Unity, realized by Qin and afterward revived and enshrined as Han doctrine, became the only theoretically acceptable political norm. China under the Han dynasty achieved its maximum territorial expanse and spread a vibrant civilization over east and central Asia.

Three successive dynasties, the Zhou, Qin, and Han, arose from a geopolitical union of the Wei and Han valleys with Sichuan, projecting their combined power onto the Yellow River floodplain. What's in a name? It is no quirk that the world knows as "China" the empire Qin created a century after annexing Sichuan. And surely it cannot be mere chance that the Chinese call themselves men of Han, the name of that valley separating, or linking, Sichuan and China.

Appendix

In What Year Did Qin Conquer Sichuan?

Chinese historians cite two conflicting dates, thirteen years apart, for the Qin conquest of Sichuan, 329 B.C. and 316 B.C.; but each is equivalent to one of two different years, both confusingly called Year Nine in the reign of Qin's King Hui. According to a chronological table in *Historical Records* (*Shi ji*, ch. 15, *liu guo nian biao*) of Sima Qian, the earlier date was actually Hui's ninth year on the Qin throne. In 324 B.C. Hui took the royal title and began a new calendrical sequence, which ended with his death fourteen years later. Year Nine of the second Hui sequence coincides with 316 B.C., at which time the *Shi ji* chronology reports Qin subjugated Shu. The *Shi ji* chapter on Qin state history (ch. 5, *qin ben ji*) is consistent. As the earliest extant source offering a date for this event, *Shi ji* has a strong claim to authority. Nevertheless, the repetitive sequence with two separate years numbered Year Nine invited misunderstanding.

A chronological formula corresponding to 316 B.C. is also employed by *Hua yang guo zhi*, the history of Sichuan and the Han valley compiled by Chang Ju during the fourth century A.D. He gives the date as Year Five of Zhou King Shen. During the Song dynasty Guo Yundao made a compendium of Shu history called *Shu jian* which continued to stick by 316 B.C. This date is the one encountered most often in modern treatments of the Warring States period, and it is the working date used in these pages.

As opposed to 329 B.C., the date 316 B.C. seems to fit better into the total context of interstate relations. In 316 B.C. Qin had just defeated a five-state coalition army ranged against it, thereby gaining some freedom of action. Taking advantage of the leeway thus gained, King Hui accepted an invitation by a dissident Sichuanese aristocrat to intervene against Shu. King Hui's other choice would have been to attempt a conclusive mopping up of the five-state alliance's remnants, notably Han (Jin), and to gain control over the Zhou royal

enclave. Han (Jin) did figure prominently in the diplomatic maneuvering leading up to 316 B.C., details of which were reported separately in the *Shi ji* chapter on that state's history (ch. 45, *han shi jia*).

The alternative date 329 B.C. nevertheless has survived, taking
on a textual life of its own. This owes much to an article by Ma
Peitang published in the journal of historical geography *Yu gong ban
yue kan* 2, no. 2 (1934): 2–6. Ma Peitang based his reasoning on a
study of the *Shi ji* biography of Zhang Yi (ch. 70, *zhang yi lie zhuan*).

The order of events in Zhang Yi's career as recounted in the
biographical chapter does not correspond neatly with information
from the chronology (ch. 15) or the annalistic history of Qin (ch. 5) in
Shi ji. At issue is the date when Zhang Yi joined Qin service. Here
again there are different years over a decade apart, during which time
Zhang Yi spent time abroad on Qin service. The Qin invasion of Shu
occurred shortly after Zhang Yi entered, or reentered, Qin. In the *Shi
ji* biography of Zhang Yi, the record of Zhang Yi and Sima Cuo debat-
ing strategic options is placed just after Zhang Yi joined Qin for the
first time; that is, closer to 329 B.C. Sima Cuo urged the Sichuan plan,
whereas Zhang Yi argued in vain for an attack on Han (Jin). However, the chapter does not give a definite calendar date for either
the debate or the Qin action that followed.

In the *Shi ji* chronological tables, Qin invaded Shu shortly after
Zhang Yi left Wei (Jin) and came back to rejoin King Hui. Either the
chronology is wrong, or the Zhang Yi-Sima Cuo strategy debate in
the Zhang Yi biography chapter is simply misplaced, out of timely
sequence. To bring the invasion of Shu in line with the initial period
of Zhang Yi's service to Qin, Ma Peitang assumed the *Shi ji* dates of
the attack given in other chapters to be mistaken. He then further
assumed that the correct date is King Hui Year Nine (first series), even
though no early text actually specifies it as the invasion year.

Despite the weaknesses of the 329 B.C. determination, based as
it is solely on shaky inference, it retained backers for awhile among
modern scholars writing on ancient Sichuan. These notably included
Zheng Dekun, a pioneer researcher in the field, and curator Wang
Jiayou of Sichuan Provincial Museum in Chengdu. As the pace of
research picked up during the 1980s, however, most specialists have
veered toward acceptance of the date specifically given in several
ancient sources; that is, 316 B.C.

No active controversy is underway; partisans of either date have
merely agreed to disagree. The significance of the date is limited
mainly to an understanding of the proximate circumstances preceding King Hui's decision to invade and to annex the Han valley, Ba,

and Shu. Long-term consequences of more lasting import, such as the sinification process, are hardly affected by the issue of precisely in what year Qin armies seized Sichuan.

FIGURE 15

Chronological Chart
(approximating power relations among states and regions,
as recounted in the text)

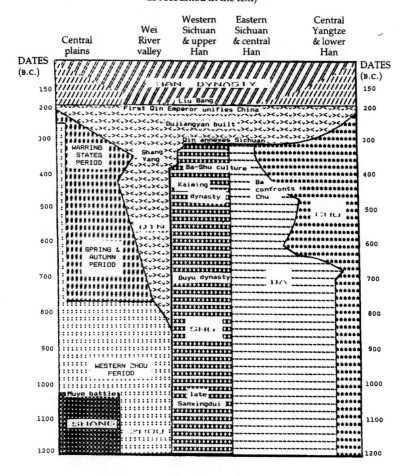

Glossary

Anhui (modern province) 安徽

Anyang (Shang capital, site of oracle bone finds) 安陽

Anyang wang (King Anyang, a Shu noble) 安陽王

Ba (eastern Sichuan and environs) 巴

ba (hegemon) 霸

Ba fang (the country of Ba) 巴方

Ba guo (the country of Ba) 巴國

Ba ji (an herb found in Ba) 巴戟

Ba *ren* (Ba people) 巴人

Bai Qi (a.k.a. Bo Qi, a Qin general) 白起

Baihuatan (a district of Chengdu) 百花潭

Baihuo (early king of Shu) 柏濩

Bailu (mountain in Shu) 白鹿

Ban gui (bronze vessel) 班簋

ban liang (half-tael coin) 半兩

Banxunman (a people in Ba) 板楯蠻

Bao (small river) 褒

bao (to envelop) 包

Baoji (town in Shaanxi) 寶鷄

bi (amulet) 璧

Bieling (Shu king) 鱉靈

bing (character on *Ban gui* bronze) 秉

Bodao (a place south of Ba) 僰道

Bo (a people living in southwestern Sichuan)　僰

Bo Shichang (official assisting Sima Xiangru)　柏始昌

bu (pace: unit of length)　步

can (silkworm)　蠶

Cancong (early Shu king)　蠶叢

Ce (a small state)　夨

cha (agricultural implement)　鍤

chang cheng (deputy)　長丞

Changan (Han dynasty capital)　長安

Changyi (son of Yellow Emperor)　昌意

chao (character on Ban gui bronze)　巢

chen (functionary)　臣

Chen She (anti-Qin rebel)　陳涉

Chen Zhuang (mutinous Qin official in Shu)　陳壯

Cheng Zheng (Shu businessman in Han times)　程鄭

Chengdu (capital of Shu)　成都

Chengdu jun (lord of Chengdu)　成都君

Chenggao (strategic point on the Yellow River)　成皋

Chenggu (archeological site near the Han River)　城固

Chengli (mythical figure)　乘釐

chi (pond)　池

chong (insect)　虫

Chongqing (town in Sichuan, formerly spelled Chungking)　重慶

Chu (a state)　楚

chuan (amulet)　釧

chun yu (a type of Ba drum)　錞于

cong (cylindrical jade object)　琮

Daba Mountains　大巴山

Dan (one of the peoples making up the Ba) 蜑

Daxi (neolithic culture in eastern Sichuan) 大溪

Dayi (archaeological site in Shu) 大邑

Di (a northern barbarian group) 狄

Di Huang (mythical Earthly Emperor) 地皇

Di Ku (mythical figure) 帝嚳

Di Qiang (a branch of the Qiang people) 氐羌

Di Wang (grandiose title assumed by Duyu) 帝王

Dian (kingdom in Yunnan) 滇

Dian Yue (region south of Shu) 滇越

Dianjiang (ancient name for Hechuan, in Sichuan) 墊江

Dong Zhongshu (Han philosopher and official) 董仲舒

Dou Lian (name of a Chu official) 鬭廉

du wei (military official) 都尉

Dujiangyan (irrigation project in Shu) 都江堰

Duyu (king of Shu) 杜宇

Emei (mountain south of Chengdu) 峨眉

Enshi (place in Hubei) 恩施

fan (character on *Ban gui* bronze) 繁

Fan (Ba clan name) 樊

Fan Mu (resident of Langzhong who aided Liu Bang) 范目

Feiqiu (Qin departure point for Shu-bound settlers) 廢丘

Feng Dang (a Han commandant of Shu) 馮當

Fengdu (modern county in Sichuan) 丰都

Fou (ancient place in Shanxi) 缶

fu (axe) 斧

fu (genre of literature) 賦

Fulin (prehistoric culture site in Sichuan) 富林

Glossary

Fuxi (mythical figure)　伏羲

Gan Mao (Qin general)　甘茂

Gan Pass (point on Sichuan-Hubei frontier)　捍関

gang (vat)　缸

Gansu (modern province)　甘肅

gao bing dou (tall-necked goblet)　高柄豆

gao zu ("Exalted Progenitor," a title of Liu Bang)　高祖

ge (halberd)　戈

geng xiu wei tian lu (land redistribution)　更脩為田律

Gong (a people living in Ba)　共

gong (duke)　公

gong guan (works commissioner)　工官

Gongsun Yan　公孫衍

gu dao (old road)　故道

guan (jar)　罐

Guangdong (modern province)　廣東

Guanghan (Han commandery, modern county in Sichuan)　廣漢

Guangxi (modern province)　廣西

gui (type of bronze vessel)　簋

Guizhou (modern province)　貴州

Gun (mythical father of Yu the Great)　鮌

Han (river valley, dynasty, ethnic term)　漢

Han Fu (name of a Ba envoy)　韓服

Han (Jin) (an ancient state)　韓(晉)

Hangu pass (Qin gateway to the central plains)　函谷関

Hanyuan (neolithic site in Shu)　漢源

Hanzhong (commandery on the upper and central Han)　漢中

he (cooking vessel)　盉

he cong lian heng (longitudinal and latitudinal strategies)   合縱联橫

Hechuan (town in central Sichuan)   合川

Hei shui (name of a river, in *Yu gong*)   黑水

Hen Mountain (reputed Ba homeland)   很山

Henan (modern province)   河南

Hexi (disputed region west of the Yellow River)   河西

hou (marquis)   侯

Houzhao (mythical figure)   後照

hu (blade edge of scyth-shaped halberd head)   胡

hu (flask or jar)   壺

Hu Chongguo (official assisting Sima Xiangru)   壺充國

hua hu (conversion of the barbarians)   化胡

Hua Mountain (a peak in Qin, modern Shaanxi)   花山

Huang Di (mythical Yellow Emperor)   黃帝

huang long (yellow serpent)   黃龍

Hua-xia (ethnicity of ancient people near the Yellow River)   華夏

Hubei (modern province)   湖北

Hui; Hui-wen (king of Qin)   惠; 惠文

Hui (marquis of Shu)   惲

Huijindai River (in southern Shu)   會衿帶水

Hunan (modern province)   湖南

Ji (Zhou royal surname)   姬

Jialing River (Yangtze tributary in Sichuan)   嘉陵江

Jiameng (town in Shu)   葭萌

jia sha tao (coarse-textured pottery)   夾砂陶

jian (sword)   劍

jian dao (corduroy road)   棧道

Jian (mountain)   湔(山)

Jiangsu (modern province)　江蘇

Jiangzhou (near Chongqing)　江州

Jianmen Pass (gateway to northern Sichuan)　劍門関

Jianwei (commandery in Sichuan)　犍為

jie (all, entire)　皆

Jing (alternate name for Chu)　荆

jiu you (nine partitions)　九囿

ju guan (orange commissioner)　橘官

jun (commandery, an administrative unit)　郡

jun chang (chief)　郡長

Kaiming (line of kings in Shu)　開明

Ku (mythical figure)　嚳

Kuaiji (place where Yu convened a conference)　會稽

Kui (statelet at the Yangze gorges)　夔

kui long (decorative dragon pattern in bronze)　夔龍

lang zhong (functionary)　郎中

lang zhong jiang (military rank)　郎中將

lang guan (courtier rank)　郎官

Langzhong (town on Jialing River, the last Ba capital)　閬中

lei (type of bronze vessel)　罍

li (unit of distance; neighborhood control unit)　里

Li (consort of Duyu)　利

Li Bing (Qin commandant of Shu)　李冰

Li Bo (Tang dynasty poet)　李白

Li Erlang (son of Li Bing)　李二郎

Li Zhen (Han official in Guanghan)　李貞

Li gui (bronze vessel)　利簋

Liang Mountain (a peak in the Qinling range)　梁山

Liang zhou (name for Shu in *Yu gong*) 梁州

Lijiacun (neolithic culture site) 李家村

Lingqiu Canal (Qin project) 靈渠

ling (official functionary) 令

Linqiong (town southwest of Chengdu) 臨邛

Linjun (Ba culture hero) 廩君

Liu Bang (founder of the Han dynasty) 劉邦

liu ye (willow leaf) 柳葉

Liyuqiao (prehistoric culture site in Sichuan) 鯉魚橋

Longba (a levee near Chengdu) 龍壩

Longshan (neolithic culture type site) 龍山

Lu (ally of Zhou at the Muye battle) 盧

Lu (statelet mentioned in conjunction with Shu) 呂

Lu (state noted for classical learning) 魯

Lu Di (Kaiming king in Shu) 盧帝

Lu Yueren (official assisting Sima Xiangru) 呂越人

Lujiang thome town of Wen Weng) 廬江

Luo River (flows in Shaanxi) 洛水

Luo shu (Book of the Luo, a mythical classic) 洛書

Luo Xiahong, a.k.a. Luo Changgong (Han astronomer) 落下閎

Lushan (site of a Shu town) 蘆山

man yi (southern barbarians) 蠻夷

Manzi (Ba general) 蔓子

Mao (ally of Zhou at the Muye battle) 髳

mi cang dao (the Rice Granary Road) 米倉道

mi li (rice-grain pattern) 米粒

Mian River (Han River tributary) 沔

Mianzhu (archaeological site in Shu) 綿竹

Min (name of a river and mountain in Shu)　岷

Mo River (west of Shu)　沫水

Mo zi (itinerant fourth century B.C. *condottiere*)　墨子

Muye (battle site in Henan province)　牧野

Nachu (place in Chu)　那處

nan man (southern barbarians)　南蠻

nan shan (South Mountain)　南山

nan yi (southern barbarians)　南夷

Nanan (place in Jianwei commandery)　南安

Nanzheng (town on upper Han river)　南鄭

nei jiang (inner channel at Dujiangyan)　內江

nei shi (secretary, Qin official post)　內史

ni dun tao (slipware)　泥質陶

Nu Rang (name of a people in Ba)　奴獽

Peiling (town on Yangtze river)　涪陵

Peng (ally of Zhou at Muye; county near Chengdu)　彭

Peng Zu (mythical longevity figure)　彭祖

Pi (town in Shu)　郫

pi (pike)　鈹

Pingdu (place in Ba)　平都

Pu (ally of Zhou at Muye; constituent group of the Ba)　濮

Qi (state)　齊

qi (battleaxe)　戚

Qian (name of a river)　黔

Qiang (a frontier barbarian people)　羌

Qianqiu (name of a pond outside Chengdu)　千秋

Qianzhong (region in northern Guizhou, southern Sichuan)　黔中

qiao xing bi (bridge-shaped coin)　橋形幣

Qin (state that unified China)　秦

Qin Shi Huang Di (First Qin Emperor)　秦始皇帝

Qing River (in Hubei)　清水

Qingchuan (town in northern Sichuan)　青川

Qingyi River (in southern Shu)　青衣水

Qinling Mountains (between Qin and the Han valley)　秦岭

Qiong (a group on the Shu frontier)　邛

Qiongdu (district in Shu)　邛都

quan zu dou (pedestal bowl)　圈足豆

Qujialing (neolithic culture site)　屈家岭

Ran (a group on the Shu frontier)　毨

Rang (a people living in Ba)　獽

Ren Bi (Qin commandant of Hanzhong)　任鄙

Ren Huang (mythical Human Emperor)　人皇

Rong (a northern barbarian people)　戎

Ruo River (west of Shu)　渃水

San Pass (a gap through the Qinling range in Shaanxi)　散関

Sanxingdui (archaeological site north of Chengdu)　三星堆

Shaanxi (modern province)　陝西

Shandong (modern province)　山東

Shang (dynasty)　商

Shang Qushang (Confucian pupil from Shu)　商瞿上

Shang Yang (Qin reformer, Lord Shang)　商鞅

Shangjun (Qin commandery in Shaanxi)　上郡

Shanxi (modern province)　山西

Shaohao (son of the Yellow Emperor)　少皞

Shaohua (place in northern Sichuan)　昭化

Shen (place in Chu)　申

Shen Buhai (Warring States politician)　申不害

shi (clan)　氏

shi (envoy)　史

shi er qiao jie (Bridge No. 12 Street, in Chengdu)　十二橋街

shi niu dao (Stone Cattle Road)　石牛道

Shi Zi (disciple of Shang Yang)　尸子

Shiniu (reputed Sichuan birthplace of Yu the Great)　石紐

shou (Qin military governor of a commandandery)　守

Shu (area of western Sichuan)　蜀

Shu Pan (name of King Anyang)　蜀泮

Shuiguanyin (archaeological site north of Chengdu)　水觀音

Shun (mythical figure)　舜

Shushanshi (mythical figure)　蜀山氏

si fang (four quarters)　四方

Sichuan　四川

Sima Cuo (Qin statesman)　司馬錯

Sima Xiangru (a Han-period Sichuanese)　司馬相如

Song (mountain)　嵩

Sou (a people identified with the Shu)　叟

Suiren (mythical figure)　燧人

Sun Zi (Warring States general)　孫子

Tai Huang (Sovereign Emperor, a.k.a. Ren Huang)　天皇

Taibai (mountain in the Qinling range)　太白

Taihao (mythical figure)　太暤

Tan (clan name on a bronze vessel)　覃

Tang Meng (Han general)　唐蒙

Tian Huang (mythical Celestial Emperor)　天皇

tian niu (celestial cattle)　天牛

tian zi (Son of Heaven, an imperial title)　天子

tie guan (iron commissioner)　鉄官

tong gu (bronze drums)　銅鼓

Tongliang (site near Chongqing)　銅梁

tu (forced laborer; convict)　徒

Tujia (a people in Hunan)　土家

Tuo River (Yangtze tributary in Sichuuan)　沱江

wai jiang (outer channel at Dujiangyan)　外江

Wan (Shu marquis)　綰

wang (king)　王

wang di (title assumed by Duyu of Shu)　望帝

Wang Ranyu (official assisting Sima Xiangru)　王然于

Wansui (name of a pond near Chengdu)　萬歲

Wei (ally of Zhou at Muye battle)　微

Wei (Jin) (ancient state)　魏(晉)

Wei River (runs through Qin)　渭河

Wei Zhang (Qin general)　魏章

Wen (Han emperor)　文

Wen Weng (Han official in Shu)　文翁

Wenshan (Han commandery on the Shu frontier)　汶山

Wu (Zhou king; Han emperor)　武

Wu (name of gorge, a mountain, and a Chu commandery)　巫

wu di (five emperors)　五帝

Wu Ding (Shang king)　武丁

wu hu (triangular, Shu-style halberd blade)　無胡

Wu Pass　武関

Wu Qi (Warring States general)　吳起

Wu River (another name for Peiling River)　烏江

Glossary

Wudu (place to the north of Shu) 武都

Wuluozhongli Mountain (legendary Ba homeland) 武落鐘離山

Wuxiang (Ba clansman) 務相

Wuyang (last stand of Kaiming XII, king of Shu) 武陽

xi yi (barbarians west of Shu) 西夷

Xia (dynasty founded by Yu the Great) 夏

Xia-li (a Ba district in Ying, the Chu capital) 下里

xian (county) 縣

xiang (minister of state) 相

Xiang (king of Chu) 襄

Xiang (Ba clan name) 相

Xiang Yu (opponent of Liu Bang) 項羽

Xianyang (capital of Qin) 咸陽

Xiao (duke of Qin) 孝

Xiao He (responsible for Shu and Han under Liu Bang) 蕭何

Xie (small river) 斜

Xindu (place near Chengdu) 新都

Xinfan (county north of Chengdu) 新繁

xing (surname, or clan) 姓

Xionger (place south of Chengdu) 熊耳

xun (reading for oracle-bone character) 罘

Yaan (place in southwestern Sichuan) 雅安

Yan (place near Chu) 鄢

Yan (state) 燕

yan guan (salt commissioner) 鹽官

Yandao (district in Shu) 嚴道

Yangshao (neolithic culture) 仰韶

Yanyang (a place in Ba legend) 鹽陽

Yangzishan (site of mound in Chengdu) 羊子山

Yao (mythical figure) 堯

Yaotong (marquis of Shu) 要通

Yelang (kingdom in Guizhou) 夜郎

Yi (tribesmen in Ba) 夷

Yi zhou (Han territorial unit embracing Sichuan) 益州

Yibin (Sichuan town on the Yangtze) 宜賓

Yichang (town on the Yangtze in Hubei) 宜昌

Yicheng (a place in Ba legend) 夷城

Ying (capital of Chu) 郢

Yong (town in Qin) 雍

Yong (small state in Han valley) 庸

Yu (legendary founder of the Xia dynasty; Yu the Great) 禹

Yu (place near Chu) 鄙

Yue (a state conquered by Chu) 越

Yueliangwan (Shu site near Guanghan) 月亮灣

Yufu (a place in eastern Ba) 魚復

Yufu (Shu king) 魚鳧

yu ju ("fish-bite" feature at Dujiangyan) 魚咀

yu shi dai fu (imperial secretary) 御史大夫

Yue (ancient state east of Chu) 越

Yuexi (commandery on the Shu frontier) 越巂

yun lei (thundercloud, whorl pattern) 雲雷

Yunnan (modern province) 雲南

Za (region on the Shu frontier) 筰

Zangge (river, limit of Han expansion in Guizhou) 牂柯

zhang (scepter) 璋

zhang (unit of length) 丈

Zhang Ang (Han commandant of Hanzhong)　張卬

Zhang Qian (Han official and explorer)　張遷

Zhang Ruo (Qin official)　張若

Zhang Shu (Shu student in Changhan)　張叔

Zhang Tang (Han imperial secretary)　張湯

Zhang Yi (Qin official)　張儀

Zhao (king of Qin)　昭

Zhao (Jin) (ancient state)　趙(晉)

Zheng (Ba clan name)　鄭

zheng (resonant gong)　錚

Zhi (town in Ba)　枳

zhong (measure of volume)　鍾

zhong (bell)　鐘

Zhongguo (the central country, i.e., China)　中國

zhongyuan (central plains)　中原

Zhou (dynasty)　周

zhou (province)　州

Zhouyuan (site of oracle-bone find in Shaanxi)　周原

zhu hou (lordly peers)　諸侯

Zhuang Qiao (Chu general)　莊蹻

Zhuanxu (mythical emperor)　顓頊

Zhuo Wangsun (Han businessman in Sichuan)　卓王孫

Zhuo Wenjun (wife of Sima Xiangru)　卓文君

Zhuti (place mentioned in *Hua Yang quo zhi*)　朱提

Zhuwajie (archaeological site)　竹瓦街

zi (viscount)　子

Zifang (a point in Chu attacked by Shu)　茲方

Zitong (a place along the road to Shu)　資通

Ziyang (prehistoric site)   資陽

Zong (a people living around Langzhong in Ba)   賨

zong mu zhi ren (vertical-eyed man)   縱目之人

Zu (a Shu marquisate)   且

zui (crime, wrong doing)   罪

Notes

Chapter One

1. The Li Bo poem was evaluated against its geographic setting by Qu Shouyuan, "'Shu dao nan' suo yu." *Si chuan shi yuan xue bao*, no. 1 (1980): 55–58. The quotation from Theodore H. White may be found in his memoirs, *In Search of History* (New York: Harper and Row, 1978), p. 100.

2. Zhao Dianzeng, "Si chuan shi nian kao gu shou huo," *Si chuan wen wu*, no. 5 (1989): 8–16.

3. The four are sometimes taken to include the Min, Jinsha, Tuo, and Jialing Rivers, although of course, many more streams besides these flow in Sichuan. See Zhang Zhitao, "'Si chuan' di ming cheng you lai he ke qu yan bian," *She hui ke xue yan jiu*, no. 5 (1979): 35.

4. The term *central plains* as used later is a translation of the Chinese term *zhong yuan* and should be understood, like *zhong yuan*, as referring to the entire area of present Henan province, the western part of Shandong, southern Hebei and Shanxi, and northern Hubei, Anhui, and Jiangsu provinces. Some of this ground includes parts of the loess plateau. Not all of the encompassed territory is perfectly flat. But to avoid cumbersome locutions, *central plains* provides the most convenient shorthand phraseology.

Chapter Two

1. In the following narrative, *Shu* without a definite article refers to the region centered around Chengdu, whereas *the Shu* indicates the Shu people. From archaeological inferences the Shu will be treated here as a recognizable ethnic, cultural entity, not merely as inhabitants who happened to live in the land called *Shu* (Song Zhimin, "Zao qi shu wen hua fen qi di zai tan tao," *Kao gu*, no. 5 [1990]: 441).

2. Modern treatments of the Yellow River and central plains zone as the nucleus of preimperial Chinese civilization include Ho Ping-ti's *The Cradle of the East* (Chicago: University of Chicago Press, 1975); and David N. Keightley, ed., *The Origins of Chinese Civilization* (Berkeley: University of California Press, 1983).

3. For example, as in Qian Mu, *Huang di* (Taibei: Dong da tu shu gong si, 1978), and K. C. Wu, *The Chinese Heritage* (New York: Crown, 1982), to cite two recent retellings of tradition. Sarah Allen, *The Shape of the Turtle: Myth, Art, and Cosmos in Early China* (Albany: State University of New York Press, 1991) rigorously dissects the traditions. The appearance of central plains mythological figures in Sichuan is traced by Gu Jiegang in *Lun ba shu yu zhong yuan di guan xi* (Chengdu: Si chuan ren min chu ban she, 1981). See also Kano Naosada, "Kodai ha shoku shi no sai kosei," *Toyoshi Kenkyu* 33, no. 4 (1975): 579–603.

4. This material still sometimes is offered uncritically by Chinese scholars; e.g., by Du Naisong of the Gugong Imperial Palace Museum at Beijing, in "Lun ba shu qing tong qi," *Jiang han kao gu*, no. 3 (1985): 62.

5. The source takes its title from Mt. Hua, westernmost of the five sacred peaks of China, and refers to Sichuan as the country on the south or sunny (*yang*) side of the mountain. Because Sichuan lies outside the perimeter bounded by these sacred peaks, it was the task of *Hua yang guo zhi* to supply the region with a respectable history connecting it to those lands within the perimeter. On *Hua yang guo zhi*, see the following: S. H. Fong, "Hua Yang Kuo Chih," *Journal of the West China Border Research Society*, 12, series A (1940); Huang Fanguang, "Cong fang zhi xue kan hua yang guo zhi," *Zhong guo li shi xue hui shi xue ji kan*, no. 9 (1977): 47–57; Liu Lin, "'Hua yang guo zhi' jian lun," *Si chuan da xue xue bao*, no. 2 (1979): 82–87; and Ren Naiqiang, "'Hua yang guo zhi' jian jie", *Li shi zhi shi*, no. 2 (1980). The most recent edition of *Hua yang guo zhi* is completely annotated by Liu Lin as *Hua yang guo zhi xiao zhu* (Chengdu: Ba shu shu she, 1984). Although this version has been consulted, the page numbers cited here are those of an earlier edition, put out by Shang wu yin shu guan (Shanghai: 1938, reprinted in Taibei, 1974).

6. The opening sentence of ch. 3, *shu zhi*, p. 27. This sentence also is included as a note (*zheng yi*) to the postscript of ch. 13, the table of royal generations, in Sima Qian's *Shi ji* (Beijing: Zhong hua shu ju, 1972), p. 507. It is attributed to an unidentified genealogy.

7. Presumably the Human Emperor set his siblings in charge of the eight outer divisions, although the text does not state so specifically. Chang Ju attributes the Human Emperor story to the *Book of the Luo* (*Luo shu*), a mystical chart supposedly borne on the shell of a turtle that emerged from the Luo River and presented itself before Yu, founder of the Xia dynasty. See *Hua yang guo zhi*, ch. 1, *ba zhi*, p. 1.

8. *Shu wang ben ji* also contains some probably interpolated propaganda from a later age, including an appearance of the sage Lao Zi in Sichuan. The incident smacks of Daoist *hua hu* ("conversion of the barbarians") tracts, aimed at undermining Buddhism by claiming its teachings began with a sojourn Lao Zi made to India. Chengdu could have figured as a way station on

such a fictional trip. The point here is that textual accounts of early Sichuan show evidence of corruption for polemical purposes.

9. See Gu Jiegang, *Lun ba shu yu zhong yuan di guan xi*, pp. 32–33.

10. A very tenuous argument also attempts to locate offspring of the founder of agriculture, Shennong, in southern Shu. However, the reasoning seems forced even by the standards of myth logic, and in any case relies on the unacceptably late evidence of a Song dynasty text, *Lu shi*. See Gu Jiegang, ibid., p. 17.

11. *Shi ji*, ch. 13, *san dai shi biao*, p. 506, postscript to the genealogical tables. Unlike *Hua yang guo zhi*, this is hardly a partisan Sichuanese source.

12. *Shi ji*, ch. 1, *wu di ben ji*.

13. Li Daoyuan, *Shui jing zhu* (Taibei: Shi jie shu ju, 1974), ch. 36, *ruo shui*, p. 441 (quoting *Shan hai jing*) notes the Yellow Emperor's son Changyi as marrying Shushanshi and staying by the Ruo River. The text unequivocally places the Ruo in Shu, i.e., in Sichuan. *Lu shi, qian ji, 4*, locates Shushan in Shu (quoted in Gu Jiegang, *Lun ba shu yu zhong yuan di guan xi*, p. 11). But the "Shu" of Shushanshi elsewhere appears written differently, throwing reasonable doubt on its identification with the Shu of Sichuan. The Ruo River also gives rise to quibbles, presented in detail by Yang Kuan in *Gu shi bian* (Gu Jiegang, Lu Simian, and Tong Shuye, eds., Shanghai: Kai ming shu dian, 1926–1941), vol. 7, part 1a, p. 222; and Lu Simian, also in *Gu shi bian*, vol. 7, part 2b, pp. 376–378.

14. *Shi ji*, ch. 1, *wu di ben ji*, p. 10.

15. *Hua yang guo zhi*, ch. 3, *shu zhi*, p. 27, gives a variant parentage for Emperor Ku, making him the son of Zhuanxu. As for the descendant Shu kings, the text says they emerged sometime during the Zhou dynasty; i.e., during the first millennium B.C.

16. Mt. Song (variant form Mt. Zong) is the central of China's five sacred mountains. *Guo yu* (Shanghai: Shang hai gu ji chu ban she, 1978), ch. 3, *zhou yu* (xia), p. 103, names Yu's father Gun as lord of the mountain. *Yi zhou shu* (Zhu Youzeng, ed., *Yi zhou shu ji xun jiao shi* [Taibei: Shi jie shu ju, 1980]), ch. 4. 37, *shi fu*, p. 96 gives the mountain as birthplace of Yu. *Zhu shu ji nian bu deng*, ch. 1, p. 9 reports Yu established his capital at Yangcheng, in modern north central Henan province. Still other texts place Yangcheng and subsequent Yu capitals within the borders of present day Shanxi province, also in northern China and well removed from Sichuan or its approaches.

17. *Shi ji*, ch. 15, *liu guo nian biao*, p. 686, prologue to the chronological tables. The philosopher Xunzi, writing before Sima Qian, says Yu studied with Xi Wang Guo, whom some commentators take to have been a worthy of the western Qiang. *Xun zi* (Xiong Gongzhe, ed., *Xun zi jin zhu jin yi* [Taibei:

Shang wu yin shu guan, 1975]), ch. 27, *da lue bian*, p. 533. See also Yang Mingzhao, "Si chuan zhi shui shen hua zhong di xia yu," *Si chuan da xue xue bao*,
no. 4 (1959): 4. Accounting for Yu's presence among the Qiang presents a
problem to traditionalists. Qian Mu (*Huang di*, p. 47) ventures only that the
Qiang were much impressed by Yu.

18. *Xin yu, shu shi bian*, and *Hou han shu, dai liang chuan* repeat the *Shi ji*
material quoted previously. *Wu yue chun qiu, yue wang wu yu wai juan*, and *Di
wang ben ji* name Shiniu as Yu's home among the western Qiang. Mencius
mentioned Yu's birth at Shiniu, in a passage not present in the extant text of
his discourses (*Meng zi*) but quoted in commentary on *Shi ji* in ch. 15, *liu guo
nian biao*, p. 686. Yang Xiong, *Shu wang ben ji*, p. 3, also puts the Yu nativity at
Shiniu. Chen Shou, *San guo zhi*, ch. 38, *shu shu, qin mi zhuan*, p. 975, locates
Shiniu at Minchuan, on the upper Min River. See Chen Zhiliang, "Yu sheng
shi niu kao," *Yu gong ban yue kan* 6, no. 6 (1936): 39–48; and Wei Juxian, "Shi
niu tan fang ji," *Shuo wen yue kan* 3, no. 9 (1943):13–20. For Kuaerping and its
nearby "Yu cave," there is the Yuan period geography, *Yuan ho zun xian zhi*,
quoted by Sun Hanqing in "Shen yu gu li," *Si chuan wen wu*, no. 1 (1988):
31–33.

19. The identification of Liang *zhou* with northwestern Sichuan and the
Han valley is undisputed. See Wang Hui, *Yu gong shi di* (Taibei: Shang wu yin
shu guan, 1971), pp. 60–69; and Li Changfu, "Yu gong" *shi di* (ed. Chen
Daiguang, Zhengzhou: Zhong zhou shu hua she, 1982), pp. 76–77. However, the term *Liang* has never been satisfactorily explained, although unsupported conjecture links it with inhabitants who are supposed to have preceded the Shu. Yu Quanyu, "Er lang qin long di shen hua yu kai ming zao
ping kou di shi shi," *Si chuan wen wu*, no. 3 (1988): 44.

20. *Yu gong's* disproportionate attention to northwestern Sichuan and
environs is gauged by the number of place names listed relative to those in
other regions. See Chen Zhiliang, "Yu gong yu si chuan di guan xi," in *Shuo
wen yue kan* 3, no. 9, (1943): 39–41. On possible dates for the composition of
Yu gong, see Xu Daoling, "Cong xia yu zhi shui shuo zhi bu ke xin tan dao yu
gong zhi zhu zuo shi dai ji qi mu di," *Yu gong ban yue kan* 1, no. 4 (1934):
106–108; Qu Wanli, "Lun yu gong zhu cheng di shi dai," in *Zhong yang yan jiu
yuan li shi yu yan yan jiu suo ji kan* (Taibei: Zhong yang yan jiu yuan, 1963), vol.
35, pp. 53–86; and Shi Nianhai, "Lun 'yu gong' di zhu zuo nian dai," *He shan
ji* (Beijing: San lian shu dian, 1981), pp. 391–415.

21. For example, Luo Xianglin, "Xia min zu fa xiang yu min jiang liu yu
shuo," in *Shuo wen yue kan* 3, no. 9 (1943):43–64; also Chen Zhiliang, "Yu yu
si chuan di guan xi," pp. 33–42; and Jiang Yungang, "Zhi shui ji qi ren wu,"
pp. 65–68 in the same journal. Yang Mingzhao, "Si chuan zhi shui shen hua
zhong di xia yu," *Si chuan da xue xue bao*, no. 4 (1959): 1–15, wrote in a similar
vein.

22. *Hua yang guo zhi*, ch. 1, *ba zhi*, pp. 1–2; also *Shi ji*, ch. 2, *xia ben ji*, p. 83, and *Zhu shu ji nian bu deng*, ch. 1, p. 9.

23. Gu Jiegang (*Lun ba shu yu zhong yuan di guan xi*, p. 43); also *Shuo wen yue kan* 3, no. 9 (1943), in particular articles by Cheng Yangzhi, "Gu shu di hong shui shen hua yu zhong yuan di hong shui shen," pp. 25–32; Huang Zhigang, "Da yu yu li bing zhi shui di guan xi," pp. 69–76; and Lin Mingjun, "Si chuan zhi shui zhe yu shen hua," pp. 77–86.

24. Shi Xipeng, a Peng county local antiquarian, interprets the relevant portions of *Shi ben* and *Hua yang guo zhi*, cited along with later gazetteers in "Peng zu qin ren qi mu chu tan," *Si chuan wen wu*, no. 3 (1988): 71–72.

25. On Ziyang Man, see Pei Wenzhong et al., *Zi yang ren* (Beijing: Wen wu chu ban she, 1957). The upper pleistocene date is an educated guess. Attempts at obtaining a carbon-14 determination were foiled when careless handling resulted in contamination of the sample, according to Wu Xinzhi of the Institute of Vertebrate Paleontology and Paleo-anthropology, Academia Sinica (interview with author, Beijing, February 18, 1983). Tong Enzheng of the Sichuan University History Department once ventured Ziyang Man as evidence for hominid evolution in southwestern China, in "Ren lei ke neng di fa yuan di: zhong guo di xi nan di qu," *Si chuan da xue xue bao: zhe xue she hui ke xue ban*, no. 3 (1983): 3–14.

26. Lu Zune et al., "Si chuan zi yang li yu qiao jiu shi qi di dian fa jue bao gao," *Kao gu xue bao*, no. 3 (1983): 331–334; also Fan Guijie and Hu Changyu, "Si chuan zi yang deng xian shi qi shi dai wen hua," *Kao gu*, no. 6 (1983): 481–483.

27. Wei Jingwu, "Han jiang shang yu xin si qi shi dai wen hua chu tan," *Zhong guo kao gu xue hui di er ce nian hui lun wen ji* (1980): 107–115.

28. Some earlier literature on Sanxingdui referred to the place as Zhongxing commune. In addition to the items on Sanxingdui cited here, a 1989 special issue of *Si chuan wen wu, San xing dui yi chi yan jiu zhuan ji*, was devoted exclusively to the site, with contributions by Zhao Dianzeng, Chen Xiandan, Lin Xiang, Luo Kaiyu, Huo Wei, Yang Rongxin, Xu Xueshu, Ba Jiayun, Fan Xiaoping, Sun Zhibin, Zhang Shanxi, and Xiao Kun.

29. Zhong guo she hui ke xue yuan kao gu yan jiu suo shi jian shi, "Fang she xing tan su ce ding nian dai bao gao (shi si)," *Kao gu*, no. 7 (1987), quoted by Song Zhimin, "Zao qi shu wen hua fen qi di cai tan tao," *Kao gu*, no. 5 (1990): 448. The dates given for Sanxingdui strata are those by Song Zhimin, who also draws upon Zhao Dianzeng, "Ba shu wen hua ji ge wen ti di tan tao," *Wen wu*, no. 10 (1987). See also Zhao Dianzeng, "Ba shu wen hua di kao gu xue fen qi," *Zhong guo kao gu xue hui di si ci nian hui hun wen ji* (Beijing: Wen wu chu ban she, 1983), pp. 214–224.

30. Wang Youpeng et al., "Guang han san xing dui yi chi," *Kao gu xue bao*, no. 2 (1987): 227–254, was the site report summarizing work done at Sanxingdui in 1980–81. The presence of ash pits and disrupted stratigraphy greatly complicated efforts at achieving a plausible ceramic sequence. Huang Jiaxiang severly criticized this report's inadequacies in "'Guang han san xing dui yi chi' di chu bu fen xi," *Kao gu*, no. 11 (1990): 1030–1036. The close review of past reports and the continuing meticulous work toward reconstructing ceramic typologies both underscore the profound importance of Sanxingdui.

31. Song Zhimin, "Zao qi shu wen hua fen qi di zai tan tao," *Kao gu*, no. 5 (1990): 441–442. Song Zhimin noncommitally refers to this first stage as a "predecessor" (*qian shen*) of the Shu culture, which he considers in some measure derivative.

32. Huang Jianhua, "Lun guang han san xing dui yi chi di xing zhi," *Si chuan wen wu*, no. 4 (1988): 9–11, 8. The wall thickness of thirty meters as given in this source seems excessive, unless the wall itself once supported structures to serve as a sort of citadel.

33. Chang Kwang-chih, "Urbanism and the King in Ancient China," and "Towns and Cities in Ancient China," in *Early Chinese Civilization: Anthropological Perspectives* (Cambridge, Mass.: Harvard University Press, 1976), pp. 47–71.

34. *Shu wang ben ji* (traditionally attributed to Yang Xiong), p. 1; and *Hua yang guo zhi*, ch. 3, *shu zhi*, p. 27.

35. Chen Wenhua, "Zhong guo dao zuo di qi yuan he dong chuan ri ben di lu xian," *Wen wu*, no. 10 (1989): 24–31 includes a summary of all early rice remains in China; there are none from Sichuan.

36. *Shu wang ben ji* [*Basic Annals of the Shu Kings*] exists in recovered fragments. Although well over a thousand years separate the compilation of this account from the Sanxingdui artifacts, *Shu wang ben ji* probably transmits material from preceding centuries; its observation concerning Shu robes is uncannily accurate. The text was traditionally attributed to the poet Yang Xiong (53 B.C.–18 A.D.), but doubts about his authorship have been expressed on stylistic grounds. See Zhu Xizu, "Shu wang ben ji kao," *Shuo wen yue kan* 3, no. 7 (1942): 117–120; and Xu Zhongshu, "Lun 'shu wang ben ji' cheng shu nian dai ji qi zuo zhe," *She hui ke xue yan jiu* (1979): 99–103.

37. The figure has been cited to challenge a preconception among some art historians that standing statuary did not appear in China until the arrival of Buddhism. See Fan Xiaoping, "Guang han san xing dui qing tong ren xiang zai mei shu shi shang di di wei," *Si chuan wen wu*, no. 6 (1988): 45–47.

38. Chen Xiandan speculates that the "toothed" scepters were used to propitiate the spirit of mountains, as opposed to *Zhou li*, which prescribes a

military use, like a marshal's ceremonial baton. See "'Ya zhang' chu lun," *Si chuan wen wu*, no. 1 (1989): 12–17.

39. Chen Xiandan, "Guang han san xing dui yi, er hao keng liang ge wen ti di tan tao," and "Guang han san xing dui yi chi er hao ji si keng fa jue jian bao," both in *Wen wu*, no. 5 (1989): 1–20 and 36–38. Details for Pits #1 and #2 are in Chen Dean et al., "Guang han san xing dui yi chi yi hao ji si keng fa jue jian bao"; Shen Zhongchang, "San xing dui er hao ji si keng qing tong li ren xiang chu ji"; and Sichuan Provincial Relics Commission et al., "Guang han san xing dui yi chi er hao ji si keng fa jue jian bao," all in *Wen wu*, no. 10 (1987).

40. Zhao Dianzeng, "Si chuan xi chang li zhou xin shi qi shi dai yi chi," *Kao gu xue bao*, no. 4 (1980): 443–456.

41. *Hua yang guo zhi*, ch. 2, *han zhong zhi*, p. 15; Zhang Yachu, "Lun shang zhou wang chao yu gu shu guo di guan xi," *Wen bo*, no. 4 (1988): 32; and Li Boqian, "Cheng gu tong qi qun yu zao qi shu wen hua," *Kao gu yu wen wu*, no. 2 (1983): 66–70. But from Sanxingdui and other sites in Sichuan, it is evident that the Han valley should not be considered an area out of which the Shu culture spread to Sichuan, a point made by Song Zhimin in "Zao qi shu wen hua fen qi di zai tan tao," *Kao gu*, no. 5 (1990): 450.

42. Lin Chun, "Yi chang di qu chang jiang yan an xia shang shi qi di yi zhi xin wen hua lei xing," *Jiang han kao gu*, no. 2 (1984): 29–38. Zhao Dianzeng in "Ba shu wen hua ji ge wen ti di tan tao," *Wen wu*, no. 10 (1987): 20 considers Yichang as marking the eastern extent of the culture in the late neolithic. Sun Hua in "Ba shu wen wu za zhi," *Wen wu*, no. 5 (1989): 39–46, postulated an eastern origin for the Shu people, citing the ladle handles as partial evidence. But Song Zhimin expresses reservations in "Zao qi shu wen hua fen qi di zai tan tao," pp. 450–451, citing evident contrasts as well as similarities among the whole range of ceramic types found at Yichang and in western Sichuan.

43. Song Zhimin, "Zao qi shu wen hua fen qi di zai tan tao," pp. 443, 447.

44. *Chengdu* in Chinese simply means "the capital established," but in the Shu language it has been speculatively suggested to mean "settlement of the high plateau people," referring to Di-Qiang migrants' upland origins. See Wen Shaofeng and Ren Naiqiang, "Shi wei 'cheng du' de ming jin yi jie," *She hui ke xue yan jiu*, no. 1 (1981): 37–44, 77. As the Shu language is unknown, this type of conjecture need not be taken too seriously.

45. Wang Jiayou and Wang Yourun, "Cheng du yang zi shan tu tai yi chi qing li bao gao," *Kao gu xue bao*, no. 4 (1957): 17–31; Tong Enzheng, *Gu dai di ba shu* (Chengdu: Si chuan ren min chu ban she, 1979), pp. 65–67. Yangzishan, like the Chengdu city wall, suffered obliteration during the frenzied socialist reconstruction program of the 1950s. Salvage archaeology was

undertaken at the time. Lin Xiang reconsidered the edifice in "Yang zi shan jian zhu yi chi xin kao," *Si chuan wen wu*, no. 5 (1988): 3–13. Song Zhimin fit Yangzishan into a sequence of early Shu cultural remains in "Zao qi shu wen hua fen qi di zai tan tao," pp. 442–444, 448–449.

46. Li Zhaohe et al., "Cheng du shi er qiao shang dai jian ju yi chi di yi qi fa jue jian bao," *Wen wu*, no. 12 (1987): 1–23, 37. Another Chengdu site at Commander Street (*zhi hui jie*) has not been publicly reported due to troubling discrepancies in the associated carbon-14 determinations. See Song Zhimin, "Zao qi shu wen hua fen qi di zai tan tao," p. 449.

47. Dendochronologically adjusted carbon-14 dates have been given as 3700 to 3500 years B.P. for the structure. However, Song Zhimin in "Zao qi shu wen hua fen qi di zai tan tao," *Kao gu*, no. 5 (1990): 448–449 advised circumspection regarding these determinations, which do not neatly synchronize with the ceramic sequence as worked out at Sanxingdui. Song Zhimin believes the No. 12 Bridge Street sequence belongs to the Western Zhou period.

48. Li Fuhua, "Cheng du qing yang gong gu yi chi qing li jian bao," *Wen wu can kao zi liao*, no. 6 (1955): 44–46, reported on a find of oracle bones at Chengdu in 1954. Curiously, nothing further seems to have been published about them.

49. Chang Kwang-chih, "Towns and Cities in Ancient China," in *Early Chinese Civilization: Anthropological Perspectives*, p. 69; and, *Art, Myth, and Ritual: The Path to Political Authority in Ancient China* (Cambridge, Mass.: Harvard University Press, 1983), chs. 2–6.

50. *Shang shu* (Qu Wanli, ed. *Shang shu jin zhu jin yi*), *mu shi*, p. 71.

51. In dictionaries using the Kangxi system of radicals, "insect" is *chong*, radical no. 142.

52. *Er ya*, ch. 7, p. 52.

53. *Fang yan*, compiled by Yang Xiong, himself a Sichuanese from Shu. See entry for *shu* in Qian Tong (1778–1815), ed., *Fang yan jian shu*, ch. 12, p. 22 (Taibei: Wen hai chu ban she, 1967).

54. Xu Shen, *Shuo wen jie zi* with Du commentary (Taibei: Yi wen yiu shu guan, 1974), ch. 13a, p. 45. Bernard Karlgren in *Grammata Serica* (*Bulletin of the Museum of Far Eastern Antiquities* [Stockholm], no. 12 [1940]: 447–448) followed *Shuo wen*.

55. Shi Tuan in "Ji cheng du jiao tong xiang chu tu di yi jian 'can wen' tong ge," *Kao gu yu wen wu*, no. 2 (1980): 28–30. The design, present on just one halberd blade, is not indubitably that of a larva. It seems weak support for a shaky etymology. An equally wistful attempt to buttress the *can* hypoth-

esis is Zhou Shirong, "Can sang wen cun yu wu shi xue xing yue," *Kao gu*, zno. 6 (1979): 563, 566–567. Earlier literature included Zhu Xizu, "Gu shu guo wei can guo shuo," *Shi shi xin bao: xue huan*, no. 44, n.d.

56. Only in a later set of inscribed oracles from Zhouyuan in Shaanxi does *shu* include this radical, as will be described.

57. Sun Cidan, "Du 'gu shu guo wei can guo shuo' di xian yi," *Qi lu xue bao*, no. 1 (1941):153.

58. *Han fei zi, shuo lin (shang)*; also *Huai nan zi, shuo lin xun*, quoted by Tong Enzheng, *Gu dai di ba shu*, p. 55. In the latter text *shu* is written with an extra "insect" radical.

59. Tong Enzheng suggests Shang usage of a character denoting insects may have been intended to derogate the Shu to low status. See ibid., pp. 55–56.

60. Lin Xiang, "Zhou yuan bu ci zhong di 'shu'," *Kao gu yu wen wu*, no. 6 (1985): 67–68. The "vertical-eyed" feature is imaginatively projected by some in the faces on bronzes from Sanxingdui, e.g., by Fan Xiaoping.

61. The third century B.C. poem *Chu ci, da zhao* also makes passing reference to another "vertical-eyed" creature, located in deserts somewhere to the west. See Qu Yuan (Fu Xiren, ed.) *Chu ci du ben* (Taibei: San min shu ju, 1976), p. 171.

62. According to a fragment of *Shu wang ben ji* reproduced in Zhang Qiao's notes to *Shu du fu*, a history of Chengdu, in the anthology *Gu wen yuan*. It is quoted by Deng Tingliang in "Cong min zu diao cha kan mao wen shi guan zang di bai shi sui zang," *Kao gu yu wen wu*, no. 6 (1985): 102.

63. *Hua yang guo zhi*, ch. 3, *shu zhi*, p. 27.

64. Tong Enzheng, "Si chuan xi bei di qu shi guan zang zu shu shi tan," *Si xiang zhan xian*, no. 1 (1978): 72–77; Jiang Xuanzhong, "Si chuan mao wen ying pan shan di shi guan zang," *Kao gu*, no. 5 (1981): 411–421; and Deng Tingliang, "Cong min zu diao cha kan mao wen shi guan zang di bai shi sui zang," pp. 102–104.

65. Attempts to archaeologically link the Shu to the Qiang via the stone coffin graves include Feng Hanji and Tong Enzheng, "Min jiang shang you di shi guan zang," *Kao gu xue bao*, no. 2 (1973): 41–59; Lin Xiang, "Zhou yuan bu ci zhong di 'shu'," *Kao gu yu wen wu*, no. 6 (1985): 66–74; Shen Zhongchang and Li Fuhua, "Shi guan zang wen hua zhong suo jian di han wen hua yin su chu tan," *Kao gu yu wen wu*, no. 4 (1983): 81–84; Song Zhimin, "Chuan xi he dian xi bei di shi guan zang," *Kao gu yu wen wu*, no. 3 (1987): 66–76.

66. Shen Zhongchang and Li Fuhua, "Guan yu 'shi guan zang wen

hua' di ji ge wen ti," *Zhong guo kao gu xue hui di yi ce nian ui lun wen ji* (1979): 249–257.

67. David Keightley, *Sources of Shang History* (Berkeley: University of California Press, 1978) offers a general introduction to the oracle bones.

68. Chen Dean et al., "Guang han san xing dui yi chi yi hao ji si keng fa jue jian bao," *Wen wu*, no. 10 (1987): 14; Miao Wenyuan, "Zhou yuan jia gu suo jian zhu fang guo kao lue," *Si chuan da xue xue bao ji kan*, no. 10 (1982): 66–67.

69. The alternative reading *xun*, a place in Shanxi, was proposed by Chen Mengjia, in *Yin xu bu ci zong shu* (Beijing: Zhong guo ke xue yuan kao gu yan jiu sou, 1956), p. 295. See also Li Xueqin, *Yin dai di li jian lun* (Beijing: Ke xue chu ban she, 1959), pp. 91–93. Chen Mengjia elsewhere treated the character as *shu*, e.g., "Shang dai di li xiao ji, *Yu gong ban yue kan 7*, nos. 6–7 (1937): 105–106. Most authorities on oracle bones consistently read the character as *shu*, e.g., Shima Kunio, *Inkyo bokuji sorui*, p. 106; Dong Zuobin, "Yin dai di qiang yu shu," *Shuo wen yue kan 3*, no. 7 (1941): 104.

70. Li Xueqin, who earlier argued for *xun* has since revised his views to accept the reading *shu* in at least some inscriptions, in "Xi zhou jia gu di ji dian yan jiu," *Wen wu*, no. 9 (1981): 11. Lin Xiang relates the Zhouyuan *shu* to the Anyang inscriptions in "Zhou yuan bu ci zhong di 'shu'," pp. 66–67.

71. Chen Dean et al., "Guang han san xing dui yi chi yi hao ji si keng fa jue jian bao," p. 14.

72. Li Hu, "Yin dai wai jiao zhi du chu tan," *Li shi yan jiu*, no. 5 (1988): 36.

73. Dong Zuobin, "Yin dai di qiang yu shu," p. 114; and Tong En-zheng, *Gu dai di ba shu*, p. 60.

74. Zhang Yachu, "Yin xu du cheng yu shan xi fang guo kao lue," p. 398. Geographers set Fou in Shanxi since several other inscriptions mention the place along with Guifang, which was been set in Shanxi with some confidence. But Tong Enzheng (*Gu dai di ba shu*, p. 61) believes Fou was located in southern Shaanxi, not Shanxi. Facsimile inscriptions appear in Shima Kunio, *Inkyo bokuji sorui*, p. 106. Transcription follows Chen Mengjia, *Yin xu bu ci zong shu*, p. 295, with allowance for Chen's reading *shu* as *xun*.

75. Zhang Yachu, "Lun shang Zhou wang chao yu gu shu guo di guan xi," *Wen bo*, no. 4, 1988, p. 32.

76. On the Zhouyuan oracles, see Gao Ming, "Lue lun zhou yuan jia gu wen di zu shu," *Kao gu yu wen wu*, no. 5 (1984): 76–85; and Wang Yuzhe, "Shan xi zhou yuan suo chu jia gu wen di lai yuan shi tan," *She hui ke xue zhan xian*, no. 1 (1982): 101–105.

Notes

77. Lin Xiang, "Zhou yuan bu ci zhong di 'shu'," pp. 66–68.

78. Classical sources for identifying *shu* with *sou* are the *Wei kong zhuan* (i.e., Kong Anguo) commentary on the *Shang shu*, *mu shi*, and a note to *Hou han shu*, ch. 72, *dong zhuo lie zhuan*. Both are cited by Tong Enzheng in *Gu dai di ba shu*, p. 56, and by Zhang Yachu, "Lun shang zhou wan chao yu gu shu guo di guan xi," p. 32. Kong Anguo's note is also given in *Shi ji*, ch. 4, *zhou ben ji*, p. 123.

79. Zhang Yachu, ibid., pp. 30–31, presents the evidence on *shu* as *sou* but falls short of proving its case.

80. The identification of the Di Qiang with the Sou hangs on a sentence in *Han shu* (Beijing: Zhong hua shu ju, 1975), ch. 6, *wu di ji*, p. 160, and on the Di and Sou being listed together in *Hua yang guo zhi*, ch. 2, *han zhong zhi*. Huang Lie, "You guan di zu lai yuan he xing cheng di yi xie wen ti," *Li shi yan jiu*, no. 2 (1965): 97–114, reconstructed Di Qiang origins.

81. The argument, of Tong Enzheng and others, was in vogue through the mid-1980s.

82. Liu E, *Tie yun cang gui*, inscription no. 105.3.

83. The Qiang theory was accepted by the Soviet R. F. Its, in *Etnicheskaya istoria yuga vostochnoi Azii* (Leningrad: Nauka, 1972), chapter 1. He interpreted the data to show parallel Qiang and Shu migrations southward, with the Shu occupying the Chengdu plain and the Qiang reaching the western highland belt as far as Yunnan. However, reservations concerning a Qiang presence in Yunnan have been expressed by Zhang Zengqi, in "Guan yu 'kun ming' yu 'kun ming wen hua' di ruo gan wen ti," *Kao gu yu wen wu*, no. 2 (1987): 51–59. And Song Zhimin in "Zao qi shu wen hua fen qi di zai tan tao," p. 450, sees the Shu as a people indigenous to western Sichuan, questioning the need for any migration theory tracing them elsewhere.

84. Gao Ming, "Lue lun zhou yuan jia gu wen di zu shu," pp. 76–85.

85. *Shang shu* (Qu Wanli, ed. *Shang shu jin zhu jin yi*), *mu shi*, p. 71.

86. Shima Kunio, *Inkyo bokuji sorui*, pp. 14–19, lists inscriptions with *qiang*. The oracle bone specialists Shirokawa Shizuka, Tang Lan, Yu Xingwu, and Shang Chengzuo also concurred in associating this character with the historical Qiang (as noted by Tong Enzheng in "Tan jia gu wen qiang zi bing lue lun yin dai di ren ji zhi du," *Si chuan da xue xue bao*, no. 3 [1980]: 104; contrary opinions on 98).

87. *Shi jing* (Ma Chiying, ed., *Shi jing jin zhu jin yi*; Taibei: Shang wu yin shu guan, 1982), *shang song, yin wu*, p. 559; *Zhu shu ji nian* (*Zhu shu ji nian bu deng*), ch. 2, pp. 1, 9.

88. The bronze, called the Li *gui*, gives the cyclical day but not the year in which Muye was fought. Various calculations suggest 1122, 1116, 1111, 1075, 1069, 1066, 1029, and 1027 b.c. See Liu Qiyi, "Xi zhou ji nian tong qi yu wu wang zhi li wang di zai wei nian shu," *Wen shi*, no. 13 (1982): 22–23; Chen Changyuan, "Cong 'li gui' tan you guan wu wang fa zhou di ji ge wen ti," *He nan shi fan xue bao*, no. 4 (1980): 30–37; Huang Shengzhang, "Li gui di zuo zhe shen fen, di li yu li shi wen ti," *Li shi di li yu kao gu lun cong* (Jinan, Shandong: 1982), pp. 256–268; Ma Chengyuan, *Zhong guo gu dai qing tong qi* (Shanghai: Shang hai ren min chu ban she, 1982), pp. 70–71; and Huang Baoquan and Chen Huaxin, "Zhou wu wang ke yin nian dai kao," *Zhong guo li shi wen xian yan jiu ji kan*, no. 1 (1980): 125–128.

89. Yi zhou shu ji xun jiao shi, ch. 59, *wang hui*, p. 191.

90. Guan Weiliang, "Gu dai ba shu: zai wu wang fa zhou he ji ci tong yi zhan zheng zhong di zuo yong," *Chong qing shi fan xue yuan xue bao*, no. 4 (1980): 75.

91. Sun Min et al., "Wen chuan fa xian xi zhou shi qi shu wen hua qing tong lei," *Si chuan wen wu*, no. 4 (1989): 44–45.

92. Xu Zhongshu, "Si chuan peng xian meng yang zhen chu tu di yin dai er zhi," *Wen wu*, no. 6 (1962): 15–18, 23; Lu Liancheng and Hu Zhisheng, "Bao ji ru jia zhuang zhu yuan gou mu di chu tu bing qi di chu bu yan jiu," *Kao gu yu wen wu*, no. 5 (1983): 62–63.

93. Song Zhimin, "Guan yu shu wen hua di ji ge wen ti," *Kao gu yu wen wu*, no. 2 (1983): 71–75; and "Zao qi shu wen hua fen qi di zai tan tao," pp. 441–451.

94. Feng Hanji and Tong Enzheng, "Ji guang han chu tu di yu shi qi," *Si chuan da xue xue bao*, no. 1 (1979): 79–85; also in *Wen wu*, no. 2 (1979): 30–37 with illustrations.

95. Song Zhimin, "Zao qi shu wen hua fen qi di zai tan tao," p. 448. The sequence is based on a progression of ceramic types, rejecting several egregious carbon-14 determinations.

96. Li Boqian, "Cheng gu tong qi qun yu zao qi shu wen hua," p. 67; Deng Boqing, "Si chuan xin fan xian shui guan yin yi chi shi jue jian bao," *Kao gu*, no. 8 (1959): 404–410.

97. Huo Wei and Huang Wei, "Shi lun we hu shu shi ge di ji ge wen ti," *Kao gu*, no. 3 (1989): 251–259, summarize decades of research on halberd blades and their importance as an indicator of major trends in Shu history. The halberd typology is based on nearly a hundred specimens and follows the work of the late Feng Hanji.

98. Li Boqian, "Cheng gu tong qi qun yu zao qi shu wen hua," pp.

66–70; also Lu Liancheng and Hu Zhisheng, "Bao ji ru jia zhuang zhu yuan gou mu di chu tu bing qi di chu bu yan jiu," pp. 56–61.

99. Wang Jiayou, "Ji si chuan peng xian ju wa jie chu tu de tong qi," *Wen wu*, no. 11 (1961): 28–30; Feng Hanji, "Si chuan peng xian chu tu di tong qi," *Wen wu*, no. 12 (1980): 38–47; Li Xueqin, "Lun xin du chu tu di shu guo qing tong qi," *Wen wu*, no. 1 (1982): 38–41.

100. Blades without the scythlike curve are called *wu hu* blades in Chinese. Other sources on Shu-style halberds are Lu Liancheng and Hu Zhisheng, "Bao ji ru jia zhuang, ju yuan gou mu di you guan wen ti di tan tao," *Wen wu*, no. 2 (1983): 11, 17–19; idem., "Bao ji ru jia zhuang zhu yuan gou mu di chu tu bing qi di chu bu yan jiu," pp. 50, 55–61; Xu Pengzhang, "Cheng du san dong qiao qing yang xiao qu zhan guo mu," *Wen wu*, no. 5, 1989, p. 31–35.

101. Song Zhimin, "Guan yu shu wen hua di ji ge wen ti," p. 77; Feng zhou, "Kao gu za ji (yi), *Kao gu yu wen wu*, no. 1 (1983): 102–104; Lu Liancheng and Hu Zhisheng, "Bao ji ru jia zhuang zhu yuan gou mu di chu tu bing qi di chu bu yan jiu," pp. 61– 62, and "Bao ji ru jia zhuang, ju yuan gou mu di you guan wen ti di tan tao," pp. 17–18.

102. Sun Min et al., "Wen chuan fa xian xi zhou shi qi shu wen hua qing tong lei," pp. 44–45.

103. *Shi ben ba zhong* (Shanghai: Shang wu yin shu guan, 1957), p. 16.

104. *Shu wang ben ji*, p. 1, and *Hua yang guo zhi*, ch. 3, *shu zhi*, p. 27. In keeping with the mythlike quality characterizing much of this material, *Shu wang ben ji* reports the reigns from Cancong through Bai Huo to the succeeding king, Kaiming, as lasting 34,000 years. It ain't necessarily so. Still, some believe that these various kings were real persons. Yu Fu's name was perpetuated in several toponyms, as noted by Deng Shaoqin, *Ba shu shi yi tan suo* (Chengdu: Si chuan ren min chu ban she, 1983), p. 139.

105. Ch. 4.27 *shi fu*, plus commentary by Zhu Youzeng, *Yi zhou shu ji xun jiao shi*, p. 56. See also Zhang Yachu, "Lun shang zhou wang chao yu gu shu guo di guan xi," p. 32.

106. *Zho zhuan* commentary to *Chun qiu*. See under *xuan gong*, year 18, and *cheng gong*, year 2, respecitvely on pp. 615 and 636–637 of vol. 2, in Li Zongtong, ed., *Chun qiu zuo zhuan jin zhu jin yi* (Taibei: Shang wu yin shu guan, 1976). Classical annotators have not entertained the notion of *shu* here possibly meaning people, rather than a place; i.e., the Shu soldiers who had accompanied the Zhou but had not yet retired westward to the Han valley and Sichuan.

107. The character *shu* as written in the Zhouyuan inscriptions is virtually identical to its rendition on the Ban *gui* inscription, the only extant

bronze mention of *shu*. The word *gui* simply refers to the shape of the vessel. Bronze specialists have disputed this vessel's date. Various arguments are given by Guo Moruo, "'Ban gui' di cai fa xian," *Wen wu*, no. 9 (1972): 2–13; Li Xueqin, "Xi zhou jia gu di ji dian yan jiu," p. 11; Ma Chengyuan, *Zhong guo gu dai qing tong qi*, p. 85; and Huang Shengzhang, "Ban gui di nian dai, di li yu li shi wen ti," *Kao gu yu wen wu*, no. 1 (1981): 75–82. The Ban *gui* was lost for generations, but supposedly resurfaced in a collection of derelict antiques found in 1972.

108. Guo Moruo, ibid., pp. 2–13, located Bing in northern Jiangsu, Fan in Hebei, and Chao in southern Anhui.

109. Ma Chengyuan, *Zhong guo gu dai qing tong qi*, p. 85, and Huang Shengzhang, "Ban gui di nian dai, di li yu li shi wen ti," pp. 75–82. W. A. C. H. Dobson gave this reading in *Early Archaic Chinese* (Toronto: University of Toronto Press, 1962), pp. 179–184.

110. *Zhu shu ji nian bu deng*, ch. 3, p. 15. An unpublished study outline on Shu history prepared by the Sichuan Provincial Museum staff under direction of Wang Jiayou presents this textual passage as a genuine reference to the Shu of Sichuan. Other authorities demur.

111. *Zhong guo di ming da ci dian*, p. 373.

112. Doubts about these sources have not deterred several Chinese historians of Sichuan from citing them, but usually as an afterthought; e.g., Tong Enzheng in "Wo guo xi nan di qu qing tong jian di yan jiu," *Yun nan qing tong qi lun cong* (Beijing: Wen wu chu ban she, 1981), p. 174, n. 4.

113. *Hua yang guo zhi*, ch. 3, *shu zhi*, p. 27, notes Shu nonparticipation in so many words. It should be remembered, though, that *Chun qiu, Zuo zhuan*, and *Guo yu* represented an eastern geographic vantage point such as in Shandong or Henan, and so were less likely to be concerned with remote southwestern affairs.

114. Song Zhimin, "Zao qi shu wen hua fen qi di zai tan tao," pp. 442–447.

115. Tong Enzheng in *Gu dai di ba shu*, pp. 62–67, posits a house of Duyu lasting several generations.

116. *Shu wang ben ji*, p. 1, and *Hua yang guo zhi*, ch. 3, *shu zhi*, pp. 27–28. The latter text states that Duyu also had a personal name, Pubei. All the following information on Duyu derives from these two sources.

117. *Shu wang ben ji*, p. 1 and *Hua yang guo zhi*, ch. 3, *shu zhi*, p. 27.

118. *Hua yang guo zhi*, ch. 3, *shu zhi*, p. 28. The identification of Xionger with Qingshen is from Gu Zuyu, *Du shi fang yu ji yao* (Taibei: Le tian chu ban

she, 1973), ch. 71. Tong Enzheng, *Gu dai di ba shu*, pp. 62–67, believes *Hua yang guo zhi* may exaggerate the extent of Duyu's control.

119. Tong Enzheng, "Wo guo xi nan di qu qing tong ge di yan jiu," *Kao gu xue bao*, no. 4 (1979): 452–453; Huo Wei and Huang Wei, "Shi lun wu hu shu shi ge di ji ge wen ti," pp. 256–258; Wang Dadao, "Yun nan qing tong wen hua ji qi yu yue nan dong shan wen hua, tai guo ban qing wen hua di guan xi," *Kao gu*, no. 6 (1990): 531–543, 553.

120. A series of inscriptions on stone drums from the state of Qin includes one instance of the character *shu*, but it apparently denotes some type of game animal. See *Shi gu*, drum no. 6, cited by Lin Jianming in *Qin shi gao* (Shanghai: Shang hai ren min chu ban she, 1981), p. 106.

121. In addition to the appearance of Qin, a statelet called Ce arose along upper reaches of the Wei River, around Baoji near the northern terminus of a route through the Qinling range to Shu. See Huang Shengzhang, "Tong qi ming wen yi, yu, ce di di wang ji qi yu wu guo di guan xi," *Kao gu xue bao*, no. 3 (1983): 295–305. Ce at some time must have been absorbed by Qin, the comer, of which great things would by and by be heard.

122. *Shu wang ben ji*, p. 1, refers to Chu here by its alternate name, Jing. The story was also in *Shu lun*, the source for a version of Bieling quoted in *Shui jing zhu*, ch. 33, *jiang shui*, p. 417.

123. The date is from *Lu shi, yu lun*, according to which Duyu's successors ruled for 350 years, i.e., until 316 B.C. See Fan Guijie and Hu Changyu, "Si chuan peng xian xi zhou jiao cang tong qi," *Kao gu*, no. 6 (1981): 496–499, 555.

124. *Shui jing zhu*, ch. 33, *jiang shui*, p. 417, also has Bieling channelling the waters through the Wushan gorge at the eastern frontier of Sichuan where the Yangtze flows into Hubei province.

125. Bieling actually may be identical to Gun, in the view of Wen Yiduo. Sun Hua cites this theory and provides some roundabout arguments supporting it, "Bie ling ming yi kao," *Si chuan wen wu*, no. 5 (1989): 17–24.

126. *Shui jing zhu*, ch. 33, *jiang shui*, p. 417, says Kaiming first stayed along the Qingyi and Huijindai rivers, old names for streams that lead to Yueshan, east of Emei, and a confluence with the Min River. See also Fan Guijie and Hu Changyu, "Si chuan peng xian xi zhou jiao cang tong qi," pp. 496–499, 555; they speculate that the Zhuwajie cache of halberds and bronzes could have been stashed away at this moment of dynastic transition.

127. *Hua yang guo zhi*, ch. 3, *shu zhi*, p. 28, mentions this assertion of Shu as a power, but without supplying dates.

Chapter Three

1. Li Xuanmin and Zhang Senshui, "Tong liang jiu shi qi wen hua zhi yan jiu," *Gu ji tui dong wu ju gu ren lei*, ch. 19, no. 4, 1981, describes the fossil. Lu Zune et al. "Si chuan zi yang li yu qiao jiu shi qi di dian fa jue bao gao," *Kao gu xue bao*, no. 3 (1983): 345, note dissimilarities between the tools and those from near Ziyang.

2. He Jiejun, "Shi lun da xi wen hua," *Zhong guo kao gu xue hui di er ci nian hui lun wen ji*, 1980, pp. 116–123; Zhang Zhiheng, "Shi lun da xi wen hua," *Jiang han kao gu*, no. 1 (1982): 66–71; Li Wenjie. "Da xi wen hua di lei xing he fen qi," *Kao gu xue bao*, no. 2, 1986, pp. 131–151; and Wang Jie, "Dui da xi wen hua zhong ji ge wen ti di tan tao," *Jiang han kao gu*, no. 10 (1984) discuss variant periodizations. Radiocarbon dates from Daxi sites fall in the range 7555–4760 B.P., as summarized by Zhang Zhiheng, n. 13.

3. Li Wenjie, "Shi lun da xi wen hua yu qu jia ling wen hua, yang shao wen hua di guan xi," *Kao gu*, no. 2 (1979): 162. However, there are no early rice finds per se yet noted in Sichuan.

4. Guan Weiliang and Chen Lijing, "Si chuan jia ling jiang zhong xia yu xin shi qi shi dai yi chi diao cha," *Kao gu*, no. 6 (1983): 496–500.

5. Lin Xiang, "Da xi wen hua yu wu shan da xi yi chi," *Zhong guo kao guo xue hui di er ci nian hui lun wen ji*, 1980, pp. 128–130.

6. Wang Jie, "Qu jia ling wen hua yu da xi wen hua guan xi zhong di wen ti tan tao," *Jiang han kao gu*, no. 3 (1985): 34–40.

7. Li Qiliang, "Ba zu yuan yuan tan wei," *Shi xue ji kan*, no. 1 (1985): 55–56.

8. Ma Xingxin, "Chuan dong bei kao gu wen hua fen qi chu lun," *Si chuan wen wu*, no. 6 (1989): 26–30; Wu Jiaan et al., "Si chuan wan xian di qu kao gu diao cha jian bao," *Kao gu*, no. 4 (1990): 314–321.

9. Lin Chun, "Yi chang di qu chang jiang yan an xia shang shi qi di yi zhi xin wen hua lei xing," *Jiang han kao gu*, no. 2 (1984): 37–38; Zhao Dianzeng, "Ba shu wen hua di kao gu xue fen qi," *Zhong guo kao gu xue hui di si ci nian hui lun wun ji* (Beijing: Wen wu chu ban she, 1983), pp. 214–224.

10. In *Shan hai jing* (Guo Pu, comp.; Taibei: Zhong hua shu ju, 1976), *hai nei jing*. Zhao Tiehan considered the evidence in "Xia min zu yu ba shu di guan xi," *Da lu za zhi* 21, nos. 1–2 (1960): 81–82. Decorative motifs associated with a Fuxi cult were identified on a stone sarcophagus of Latter Han dynasty date found near Chongqing, but this may be too late to have bearing. It was reported by Chang Renxia in "Ba xian sha ping ba chu tu zhi shi quan hua xiang yan jiu," *Jin ling xue bao* 8, nos. 1–2 (1938): 1–16.

11. *Hua yang guo zhi*, ch. 1, *ba zhi*, p.1.

12. *Shi jing zhu* (Li Daoyuan, comp.), ch. 37, *ye yu he*, pp. 460–461; Fan ye, *Hou han shu*, ch. 86, *nan man xi nan yi lie zhuan*, p. 2840.

13. Tong Enzheng, *Gu dai di ba shu* (Chengdu: Si chuan ren min chu ban she, 1979), pp. 6–7. Other etymologies interpret *ba* as a type of plant (*Shi ji*, ch. 70, *zhang yi lie zhuan*, p. 2281, notes) or as a serpent able to swallow an elephant (*Shuo wen jie zi*, ch. 14b, p. 22) but neither of these hypotheses directly connect the word to the Ba people.

14. Tong Enzheng, *Gu dai di ba shu*, p. 9; Zhang Xizhou, "Shi lun gu dai ba ren fa yuan yu hu bei chang yang hen shan," *Si chuan da xue xue bao*, no. 1 (1982): 77–79.

15. The title literally translates as "granary master."

16. *Shui jing zhu*, ch. 37, *yi shui*, p. 461. Tong Enzheng in *Gu dai di ba shu*, pp. 9–15, reconstructs the progress of the Ba from Hubei into Sichuan. A variant passage, leading down the Qing River to Yichang in Hubei, has been proposed by Wei Songshan in "Chu gan guan kao," *Jiang han lun tan*, no. 5 (1980): 81–84.

17. Gu Zuyu, *Du shi fang yu ji yao*, ch. 82; also *Chang yang xian zhi*, quoted by Zhang Xizhou, "Shi lun gu dai ba ren fa yuan yu hu bei chang yang hen shan," p. 79.

18. *Hua yang guo zhi*, ch. 1, *ba zhi*, p. 8; and Deng Shaoqin, *Ba shu shi yi tan suo* (Chengdu: Si chuan ren min chu ban she, 1983), pp. 20–21.

19. *Hua yang guo zhi*, ch. 1, *ba zhi*, p. 2.

20. Yang Quanxi, "Tan suo e xi di qu shang zhou wen hua di xian suo," *Jiang han kao gu*, no. 4 (1986): 60–67.

21. Li Qiliang dismisses the Linjun story outright, arguing that it was a product of late sources compiled by northerners unfamiliar with the geography and ethnography of the south. See "Ba zu yuan yuan tan wei," pp. 51–52.

22. Tang Lan first made the reading *ba*, in *Tian rang ge jia gu wen cun kao shi* (Beijing: Fu ren da xue, 1939), p. 54. It was accepted by Luo Kun, "Shang dai ren ji ji xiang guan wen ti," pp. 129, 141; and Han Feng, "Jia gu wen suo jian di shang dai jun zhi shu ce," pp. 416–418, both in Hu Houxuan, ed., *Jia gu tan shi lu* (Beijing: San lian shu ju, 1982). Not all oracle bone compendia acknowledge a *ba fang*, however; it is lacking from Shima Kunio's *Inkyo bokuji sorui*.

Ba adoption of the tiger as a totem also prompted a guess that *hu fang*, or "Tiger Country" in the oracle bone inscriptions, might have some bearing.

See Liu Dunyuan, "Yun meng ze yu shang zhou zhi ji di min zu qian xi," *Jiang han kao gu*, no. 2 (1985): 51–56. This latter approach is probably a non-starter.

23. Zhuang Yanhe, *Gu dai ba shi zhong di ji ge wen ti* (Chongqing: Chongqing chu ban she, 1988), pp. 10–16 proposes the Ba movement down the Han. See also Dong Qixiang, "Gu dai di ba yu yue," *Chong qing shi fan xue yuan xue bao*, no. 4 (1980): 69–70.

24. Tang Jinyu, "Han shui shang yu ba wen hua yu yin zhou guan xi di tan tao," *Wen bo*, no. 1 (1988): 37–39; Wang Shouzhi, "Shan xi cheng gu chu tu di shang dai qing tong qi," *Wen bo*, no . 6 (1988): 3–9. Only the site of this cache may connect it with the Ba; stylistically the pieces are nearly identical to examples from Henan.

25. Sun Bingjun, "Shan xi zu yang bai ma shi ba shu mu fa jue jia bao," *Kao gu yu wen wu*, no. 5 (1987): 17–20, 13; He Xincheng, "Hang zhong shi shi ying sha chang qing li san zuo zhan guo mu," *Wen bo*, no. 6 (1987): 33–36; Zhang Pei, "Shan xi xun yang xian fa xian di ba shu wen hua yi wu," *Si chuan wen wu*, no. 3 (1989): 62–64. Hu Zhiren et al., "Shan xi feng xian liang lu ping xi han mu qing li jian bao," *Wen bo*, no. 3 (1989): 14–16, reports the Fan signet.

26. *Shang shu jin zhu jin yi* (Qu Wanli, ed., Taibei: Shang wu yin shu guan, 1979), *mu shi*, p. 71, lists the Pu among the eight allies of the Zhou at Muye. But *Zuo zhuan* (Lin Zongtong, ed., *Chun qiu zuo zhuan jin zhu jin yi*; Taibei: Shang wu yin shu guan, 1976), *zhao gong* 3, year 9; i.e., 533 B.C., p. 1125, names the Pu and the Ba separately, both as southern affiliates of the Zhou, yet without either Pu or Ba subordinate to each other. *Hua yang guo zhi*, ch. 1, *ba zhi*, p. 2, says the Ba subsumed the Pu. Tong Enzheng treats the Pu as that portion of the Ba occupying central Sichuan along the Jialing River, in *Gu dai di ba shu*, pp. 43–44 and 53, note 19, but the Pu elsewhere are reported living in the Han valley, outside Sichuan.

27. The Zhou's eight allies were the Yong, Shu, Qiang, Mao, Wei, Lu, Peng, and Pu in *Shang shu*, *mu shi*, p. 71. It has been suggested that the Ba were included within the Peng or the Pu. See Tong Enzheng, *Gu dai di ba shu*, pp. 16–17, citing *Shang shu*, *wei kong zhuan*; Deng Shaoqin, *Ba shu shi yi tan suo*, pp. 9–10, citing *Fang yan*; and Wang Ningsheng, "Shi 'wu wang fa zhou qian ge hou wu'," *Li shi yan jiu*, no. 4 (1981): 173–179.

28. Zhu Youzeng, *Yi zhou shu ji xun jiao shi* (Taibei: Shi jie shu ju, 1980), ch. 7. 59, *wang hui*, p. 191; Zhuang Yanhe, *Gu dai ba shi zhong di ji ge wen ti*, p. 5.

29. *Zuo zhuan*, *zhao gong* 3, year 9, i.e., 533 B.C., p. 1125. The passage specifically names Ba, Pu, Chu, and Deng as "our southern lands."

30. *Zuo zhuan* ch. 24 *shao gong* 4, p. 1158; *Hua yang guo zhi*, ch. 1, *ba zhi*, p. 2. Some of the Ba, on the other hand, may have shared the surname Ying with the ducal (later royal and imperial) house of Qin. Another tradition claims King Wu enfeoffed a portion of the defeated Shang royalty among the Ba, giving them the title of viscount, *zi*. See Chen Pan, *Chun qiu da shi biao lie guo jue xing ji cun mie biao zhuan yi* (Taibei: Zhong yang yan jiu yuan li shi yu yan yan jiu suo, 1969), vol. 3, pp. 219–228. This information supplements but does not necessarily contradict the better known continuation of the Shang as the state of Song, in Shandong.

31. Wang Jiayou identifies the white tiger totem with the Hubei Ba, but links the peoples of the upper Han with the dragon totem, in "Xian qin long hu tu an su yuan," *Si chuan wen wu*, no. 4 (1989): 11–15. See also Zhao Dian-zeng, "Ba shu wen hua ji ge wen ti di tan tao," *Wen wu*, no. 10 (1987): 20. The Ba have also been connected with the Di, a group supposedly also kin to the Shu, but this view was criticized by Miao Yue in "'Ba shu wen hua chu lun' shang que," *Si chuan da xue xue bao*, no. 4 (1959): 1–8.

32. *Hua yang guo zhi*, ch. 1, *ba zhi*, p. 2.

33. Wang Jiayou and Wang Zigang, "Pei ling chu tu di ba wen wu yu chuan dong ba guo," *Si chuan da xue xue bao cong kan*, no. 5 (1980): 166–169. Modern archaeology has not yet identified the Ba royal graves reputed to be at Peiling.

34. The Jiangzhou settlement was pinpointed at Dongxunbei, in Ba county, according to Wang Jiayou in "Ji si chuan ba xian dong xun bei chu tu gu yin ji gu huo bi," *Kao gu tong xun*, no. 6 (1955): 48–54. No work subsequently has been published to substantively trace the origins of Chongqing archaeologically. The following materials indicate the inchoate state of research: Zhuang Yanhe and Xian Shuxiu, "Chong qing cheng di you lai he fa zhan," *Si chuan shi yuan xue bao*, no. 2 (1980): 58–62; Ren Naichiang, "Chong qing," *She hui ke xue yan jiu*, no. 3 (1980): 63–67; *Gu cheng cong qing* (Chong-qing: Chong qing chu ban she, 1981); and Dong Qixiang, "Ba shu he shi jian cheng," *Chong qing shi fan xue yuan xue bao*, no. 2 (1988): 23–25.

35. Jian Hong, "Ba yu shu," *Li shi zhi shi*, no. 3 (1980): 13–15.

36. Chen Jinsheng, "'Xia li ba ren' jie," *Wen shi*, no. 13 (1982): 175–83.

37. *Hua yang guo zhi*, ch. 1, *ba zhi*, p. 2, says the Ba had "five grains" and "six domestic animals," but this simply repeats a conventional formula. Ch. 3, *shu zhi*, p. 28 credits King Duyu of Shu with tutoring the Ba in agriculture. The importance of warfare and weapons among the Ba even carried over to the name of one herb, called *ba ji*, or "Ba halberd" (ch. 1, *ba zhi*, p. 2).

38. All of the scientifically excavated, well-documented Ba tombs so far described are of a relatively late date, mostly from the Warring States period.

Descriptions of Ba life before then, i.e., the Spring and Autumn period and earlier, are based on inference. See Wang Jiayou et al., "Pei ling chu tu di ba wen wu yu chuan dong ba guo," pp. 166–169.

39. Li Qiliang, "Ba zu yuan yuan tan wei," pp. 55–56.

40. Li Yantan, "Chun yu shu lue," *Wen wu*, no. 8 (1984): 69–72.

41. Xiong Chuanxin, "Wo guo gu dai chun yu gai lun," *Zhong guo kao gu xue hui di er ci nian hui lun wen ji* (Beijing: Wen wu chu ban she, 1980), pp. 80–89; Sun Kui, "Li chuan xian chu tu yi jian hu niu chun yu," *Jiang han kao gu*, no. 3 (1985): 40; Wang Xiaoning, "Hu bei e xi zi zhi zhou bo wu guan zang qing tong qi," *Wen wu*, no. 3 (1990): 42–51.

42. *Guo yu* (Shanghai: Shang hai gu ji chu ban she, 1978), ch. 11, *jin yu*, p. 402 exemplifies the use of drums on the battlefield. See as well the Zhou ritual text *Zhou li jin zhu jin yi* (Lin Yin, ed.; Taibei: Shang wu yin shu guan, 1979), *di guan* and also the lexicography *Shuo wen jie zi*, both as cited by Xu Zhongshu, "Si chuan pei ling xiao tian xi chu tu di hu niu chun yu," *Wen wu*, no. 5 (1974): 81. Some Ba graves at Peiling have duly yielded drums and gongs together. Si chuan sheng bo wu guan et al., "Si chuan pei ling di qu xiao tian xi zhan guo tu keng mu qing li jian bao," *Wen wu*, no. 5 (1974): 61–80.

43. Xu Zhongshu and Tang Jiahong, "Chun yu he tong gu," in *Gu dai tong gu xue shu tao lun hui lun wen ji* (Beijing: Wen wu chu ban she, 1982), pp. 44–47; Wang Ningsheng, "Lun zhong guo gu dai tong gu," *Yun nan qing tong qi lun cong* (Beijing: Wen wu chu ban she, 1981), p. 149.

44. Most of the twenty six papers in *Gu dai tong gu xue shu tao lun hui lun wen ji* (Beijing: Wen wu chu ban she, 1982) concede a southern origin for the *tong gu* drums, among one or another of the peoples of Yunnan. Li Yantan, "Chun yu shu lue," pp. 69–72, also acknowledges the southern affinities of *chun yu*.

45. Tong Enzheng, "Wo guo xi nan di qu qing tong jian di yan jiu," *Yun nan qing tong qi lun cong* (Beijing: Wen wu chu ban she, 1981), pp. 156–177. A typical example, from Zigui county in Hubei, is reported by Wang Jiade in "Hu bei zi gui you fa xian yi zhi ba shi jian," *Jiang han kao gu*, no. 3 (1985): 78.

46. Feng Zhou, "Kao gu za ji (1)," *Kao gu yu wen wu*, no. 1 (1983): 102–104; Wang Xueli, "Chang pi chun qiu," *Kao gu yu wen wu*, no. 2 (1985): 60–67, 73.

47. Tong Enzheng, "Ji ju tang xia kui jia dong zhong fa xian di ba ren wen wu," *Kao gu*, no. 5 (1962): 253.

48. Yu Weizhao, "'Da wu—bing' tong qi yu ba ren di 'da wu' wu," *Kao*

gu, no. 3 (1963): 153–156; and "'Da wu' wu qi xu ji," *Kao gu*, no. 1 (1964): 54–57. Yu's attribution of this piece to the Ba was disputed by Ma Chengyuan in "Guan yu 'da wu qi' di ming wen ji tu xiang," *Kao gu*, no. 10 (1963). Ma believes it to be of Chu workmanship.

49. An analysis of the alloys used is available in Tian Changxu, "Cong xian dai shi jian pou xi zhong guo gu dai qing tong shou zao di ke xue cheng jiu," *Cheng du ke ji da xue xue bao*, no. 3 (1980), and is based on Ba weapons from Peiling. Tong Enzheng in *Gu dai di ba shu*, pp. 34–35, cited similar data to show that Ba bronze adhered to the technical specifications in the Zhou text *Zhou li*, ch. 10, *kao gong ji*.

50. Lai Youde, "Cheng du nan jia chu tu di tong qi," *Kao gu*, no. 8 (1959): 449–450; Li Xueqin, "Lun xin du chu tu di shu guo qing tong qi," *Wen wu*, no. 1 (1982): 38–41. Although the tiger motif is normally associated with the Ba, some tiger depictions have been found at the Sanxingdui site in Shu. See Chen Dean et al., "Guang han san xing dui yi chi yi hao ji si keng fa jue jian bao," *Wen wu*, no. 10 (1987): 4–5; and Liu Hong, "Ba hu yu kai ming shou," *Si chuan wen wu*, no. 4 (1988): 57–59.

51. Those script examples on *chun yu* are discussed by Xiong Chuanxin in "Wo guo gu dai shun yu gai lun," pp. 84–86.

52. Liu Ying, "Ba shu bing qi ji qi wen shi fu hao" in *Wen wu zi liao cong kan*, no. 7, is the closest thing to a published catalog of the script, but even it is not comprehensive. Additional treatment of the impression seals was provided by Shen Zhongchang and Wang Jiayou, "Ji si chuan ba xian dong xun bei chu tu gu yin ji gu huo bi," *Kao gu tong xun*, no. 6 (1955): 48–56; and more recently Li Xiaoou, "Si chuan ying jing xian lie tai zhan guo tu keng mu qing li jian bao," *Kao gu*, no. 7 (1984): 602–606; and Liu Yuchuan, "Ba shu fu hao yin zhang di chu bu yan jiu," *Wen wu*, no. 10 (1987): 86–93.

53. Xu Zhongshu, *Lun ba shu wen hua* (Chengdu: Si chuan ren min chu ban she, 1981), pp. 40–47; also "Ba shu wen hua fu tu," *Shuo wen yue kan 3*, no. 7 (1942): 11–41; and Sichuan sheng bo wu guan [Sichuan Provincial Museum], *Si chuan chuan guan zang fa jue bao gao* (Beijing: Wen wu chu ban she, 1960), p. 54.

54. Xu Zhongshu, *Lun ba shu wen hua*, p. 42.

55. For recent theoretical views on the role of writing in the development of political and social power in the ancient Near East and Europe, there are contributions by Mogens Trolle Larsen, John Baines, Stephen T. Driscoll, Margaret R. Nieke, and Michael Harbsmeier in John Gledhill, Barbara Bender, and Mogens Trolle Larsen, eds., *State and Society: The Emergence and Development of Social Hierarchy and Political Centralization* (London: Unwin Hyman, 1988).

56. Lin Zongtong, ed., *Chun qiu zuo zhuan jin zhu jin yi*; hereafter cited as *Zuo zhuan*. Tong Shuye at one time expressed doubt that the *Ba* in *Zuo zhuan* actually referred to the entity on the Yangtze in Sichuan. See *Zhong guo gu dai di li kao zheng lun wen ji* (Shanghai: Wen wu chu ban she, 1962), pp. 120–121; also *Chun qiu zuo zhuan yan jiu* (Shanghai: Shang hai ren min chu ban she, 1980), pp. 241–250. A consensus arrived at in the light of archaeological work has since superseded Tong Shuye's reservations. Overviews of Ba-Chu relations are provided by Lin Qi, "Ba chu guan xi chu tan," *Jiang han lun tan*, no. 4 (1980): 87–91; and by Gao Zhixi and Xiong Zhuanxin, "Chu ren zai hu nan di huo dong yi yi gai shu," *Wen wu*, no. 10 (1980): 57–58.

57. On the earliest inscriptional mentions of Chu, see Xu Xitai, "Zhou yuan chu tu di jia gu wen suo jian ren ming, guan ming, fang guo, di ming jian shi," *Gu wen zi yan jiu*, no. 1 (1979): 189; and Wang Guanggao, "Jia wen 'chu' zi bian," *Jiang han kao gu*, no. 2 (1984): 52–63.

58. An archaeological overview of Chu is provided by Heather A. Peters, "The Role of the State of Chu in Eastern Zhou Period China: A Study of Interaction and Exchange in the South" (Ph.D. dissertation, Yale University, 1983).

59. *Zuo zhuan*, ch. 2, *huan gong* year 9, p. 91, records the episode. The location of Deng is from Shi Quan, "Gu deng guo, deng xian kao," *Jiang han lun tan*, no. 3 (1980): 89–96; and from Zhou Yongzhen, "Liang zhou shi qi di ying guo, deng guo tong qi ji di wei zhi," *Kao gu*, no. 1 (1982): 48–53. Atlases marking the position and those of other places mentioned are Zhong guo li shi li tu ji bian ji zu, *Zhong guo li shi di tu ji* (Beijing: Di tu chu ban she, 1975), vol. 1, map 15–16; and Cheng Faren, *Chun qiu zuo shi zhuan di ming tu kao* (Taibei: Guang da shu ju, 1967).

60. *Zuo zhuan*, ch. 4, *zhuang gong* 2, years 18–19, p. 166.

61. *Zuo zhuan*, ch. 7, *xi gong*, (3), year 26, p. 361.

62. *Zuo zhuan*, ch. 10, *wen gong* (2), year 16, p. 501. Xia Mailing and Li Yunsheng interpret this period and what followed in "Deng xian yu shan miao chun yu ji xiang guan we ti," *Kao gu*, no. 10 (1989): 924–926, 951.

63. The tributary relationship was established during the time when Master Wugu (a.k.a. Bai Li Xi) administered the Qin court for Qin Duke Mu, as recalled in *Shi ji*, ch. 68, *shang yang lie zhuan*, p. 2234.

64. Sun Bingjun, "Shan xi zu yang bai ma shi ba shu mu fa jue jian bao," pp. 17–20, 13; He Xincheng, "Han zhong shi shi ying sha chang qing li san zuo zhang guo mu," pp. 33–36; Zhang Pei, "Shan xi xun yang xian fa xian di ba shu wen hua yi wu," pp. 62–64.

65. Although *Shu wang ben ji* (Yang Xiong; Taibei: Yi wen yin shu guan, 1968), p. 1 records Kaiming's origin in Jing, i.e., Chu, Tong Enzheng argues

for a Ba role in the Shu reigning house as of the mid-seventh century. See "Wo guo xi nan di qu qing tong jian di yan jiu," p. 160.

66. *Zuo zhuan*, ch. 31, *ai gong* (2), year 18, p. 1498.

67. Ren Naiqiang, "Chong qing," p. 63.

68. Xu Zhongshu, *Lun ba shu wen hua*, pp. 167–176.

69. Wang Jiayou and Wang Zigang, "Pei ling chu tu di ba wen wu yu chuan dong ba guo," p. 169.

70. *Hua yang guo zhi*, ch. 1, *ba zhi*, p. 2; also *Shi ji*, ch. 40, *chu shi jia*, p. 1709.

71. *Hua yang guo zhi*, ch. 1, *ba zhi*, p. 2, dates the incident no more precisely than "toward the end of the Zhou dynasty."

72. Guan Weiliang somehow calculated the dates 339–329 B.C. for this abandonment of Ba towns to Chu, in "Gu dai chong qing da shi bian nian," *Chong qing shi yuan xue bao*, no. 3 (1989): 65.

73. *Hua yang guo zhi*, ch. 1, *ba zhi*, p. 3; comment by Jian Hong in "Ba yu shu," p. 13; also Xu Zhongshu, *Lun ba shu wen hua*, pp. 99–100. *Shi ji*, ch. 69, *su qin lie zhuan*, p. 2271, notes in passing the fall of Zhi (Peiling) to Chu. *Shi ji*, ch. 5, *qin ben ji*, p. 203, commentary, records Chu in possession of Ba, as does ch. 41, *yue wang ju jian shi jia*, p. 1749, with commentary note no. 17, p. 1750.

74. Zhou Shirong, "Hu nan chu mu chu tu gu wen zi cong kao," *Hu nan kao gu ji kan*, no. 1 (1982): 91 and 93, discusses a typically Shu-style halberd blade with Sichuanese markings found in a Chu grave in Hunan. See also Wu Mingsheng and He Gang, "Gu zhang bai he wan chu mu," *Kao gu xue bao*, no. 3 (1986): 354–357.

75. Yu Weizhao, "Guan yu chu wen hua fa zhan di xin tan suo," *Jiang han kao gu*, no. 1 (1980): 29.

76. *Huai nan zi* (Han Gaoxin, ed., Taibei: Shi jie shu zu, 1974), ch. 15, *bing lue xun*, p. 256; quoted by Xu Zhongshu and Tang Jiahong in "Gu dai chu shu di guan xi," *Wen wu*, no. 6 (1981): 18.

77. *Shi ji*, ch. 5, *qin ben ji*, p. 202.

78. *Hua yang guo zhi*, ch. 1, *ba zhi*, p. 3; and *Shu du fu*, as quoted by Deng Shaoqin, *Ba shu shi yi tan suo*, pp. 74–75; and by Xu Zhongshu, *Lun ba shu wen hua*, pp. 99–100.

79. *Zhan guo ce* (Liu Xiang, comp.; Shanghai: Shang hai gu ji chu ban she, 1978), ch. 3, *qin ce* 1.52, p. 117.

80. *Hua yang guo zhi*, ch. 3, *shu zhi*, p. 28.

81. *Shi ji*, ch. 15, *liu guo nian biao*, p. 688.

82. Cao Gang, "Cheng du chu ti yi pi zhan guo tong qi," *Wen wu*, no. 11 (1990): 68–71.

83. *Hua yang guo zhi*, ch. 3, *shu zhi*; Tong Enzheng, *Gu dai di ba shu*, pp. 86–105; Zhuang Yanhe, *Gu dai ba shi zhong di ji ge wen ti*, pp. 39–45.

84. Fan Yong provides the typology and interpretation suggesting that progress in metallurgical technique proceded from north to south, from the Ba-Shu culture area to the Dian people in Yunnan. An east-west wave of influence brought Ba-Shu bronze technology to the western Sichuan plateau. The routes traverse districts inhabited by the Bo, Qiong, and Za. See "Wo guo xi nan di qu di qing tong fu yue," *Kao gu xue bao*, no. 2 (1989): 161–185.

85. Lin Qi, "Ba chu guan xi chu tan," pp. 88–89.

86. *Huai nan zi*, ch. 2, *shu zhen xun*, p. 33, cited by Tong Enzheng, *Gu dai di ba shu*, p. 117.

87. The following are excavation reports on Ba-Shu boat graves: Liang Wenjun, "Si chuan pi xian fa xian zhan guo chuan guan zang," *Kao gu*, no. 6 (1980): 560–561; Zhao Dianzeng et al., "Si chuan peng xian fa xian chuan guan zang," *Wen wu*, no. 5 (1985): 92–93; idem., "Si chuan da yi wu long zhan guo ba shu mu zang," *Wen wu*, no. 5 (1985): 29–40; Wang Youpeng, "Si chuan mian zhu xian chuan guan mu," *Wen wu*, no. 10 (1987): 22–23.

88. Swords are an exception. Sword blades taken from some of the Ba boat graves vary somewhat in workmanship from the Shu swords associated with other burials, but this would not seem to touch on matters of the beliefs behind boat burial.

89. Li Fuhua et al., "Si chuan xin du zhan go mu guo mu," *Wen wu*, no. 6 (1981): 1–16; Shen Zhongchang, "Xin du zhan guo mu guo mu yu chu wen hua," *Wen wu*, no. 6 (1981): 26–28; Li Xueqin, "Lun xin du chu tu di shu guo qing tong qi," pp. 38–41; Song Zhimin, "Guan yu shu wen hua di ji ge wen ti," *Kao gu yu wen wu*, no. 2 (1983): 75–78; Sun Zhibin, "Xin du zhan guo mu guo mu wen hua yin su pou xi," *Jiang han kao gu*, no. 1 (1986): 58–62; Zhang Xiaoma, "Cheng du jing chuan fan dian zhan guo mu," *Wen wu*, no. 2 (1989): 62–66. Chen Xianshuang, "Si chuan ying jing zeng jia gou 21 hao mu qing li jian bao," *Wen wu*, no. 5 (1989): 21–30; Xu Pengzhang, "Cheng du san dong qiao qing yang xiao qu zhan guo mu," *Wen wu*, no. 5 (1989): 31–35.

90. Ba-Shu lacquer work may recall that of Chu but is not so slavishly imitative as to be indistinguishable. A typology differentiating the two variants in this medium has been worked out by Li Zhaohe, in "'Ba shu' yu 'chu' qi qi chu tan," *Zhong guo kao gu xue hui di er ci nian hui lun wen ji* (Beijing: Wen wu chu ban she, 1980), pp. 93–99. According to Li Zhaohe, it was not until after the Qin conquest of both Sichuan and the Chu heartland, i.e., well

into the third century B.C., that Ba-Shu and Chu lacquer production fully converged in style.

91. Wang Youpeng, "Si chuan mian zhu xian chuan guan mu," pp. 22–33; Chen Liqing, "Si chuan e mei xian chu tu yi pi zhan guo qing tong qi," *Kao gu*, no. 11 (1986): 982–983.

92. Si chuan sheng wen wu guan li wei yuan hui, "Cheng du yang zi shan di 172 hao mu fa jue bao gao," *Kao gu xue bao*, no. 4 (1956): 1–19; Si chuan sheng bo wu guan, "Cheng du bai hua tan zhong xue shi hao mu fa jue ji," *Wen wu*, no. 3 (1976): 40–46; Zhang Caiqun, "Cheng du zhan guo tu keng mu fa jue jian bao," *Wen wu*, no. 1 (1982): 28–29; Cao Gang, "Cheng du chu ti yi pi zhan guo gong qi," pp. 68–71. The latter two graves retain decidedly Shu features within an overall Ba-Shu context.

93. Li Xiaoou et al., "Si chuan ying jing tong xin cun ba shu mu fa jue jian bao," *Kao gu*, no. 1 (1988): 49–54; Wu Yi, "Shi xi ba shu qing tong qi shang di niao, yu, gui, chong [can] wen shi," *Si chuan wen wu*, no. 5 (1989): 25–30.

94. On halberd blades in general and their hafting to staffs, a still useful source is Zhou Wei, *Zhong guo bing qi shi gao* (Taibei: Ming wen shu ju, 1982 reprint), pp. 88–98.

95. Li Xueqin, "Lun xin du chu tu di shu guo qing tong qi," pp. 38–43.

96. Ma Xingxin, "Chuan dong bei kao gu wen hua fen qi chu lun," p. 29.

97. A Lushan example of short sword and scabbard is discussed by Zhong Jian in "Lu shan chu tu qing tong qiao duan jian," *Si chuan wen wu*, no. 1 (1990): 80–81.

98. Tong Enzheng, "Wo guo xi nan di qu qing tong jian di yan jiu," pp. 156–162.

99. Feng Zhou, "Kao gu za ji (1)," p. 103.

100. Tong Enzheng, "Wo guo xi nan di qu qing tong jian di yan jiu," *Yun nan qing tong qi lun cong* (Beijing: Wen wu chu ban she, 1981), pp 156–177. Use of the sword as a missile weapon recalls the legend cited earlier whereby the early Ba clans selected a leader via a sword throwing contest.

101. Feng Zhou, "Kao gu za ji (1)," p. 103.

102. The importance of the crossbow is evident from discoveries of examples on the central plains and ample allusions to the weapon in Warring States military handbooks like *Sun bin bing fa* (excavated from a tomb in 1971) and other contemporary texts.

103. Si chuan sheng wen wu guan li wei yuan hui, "Cheng du yang zi shan di 172 hao mu fa jue bao gao," pp. 5–8.

104. The Chengdu iron item is a triangular frame, from Warring States period grave no. 172 at the Yangzishan site. See ibid.

105. Tong Enzheng in *Gu dai di ba shu*, p. 34.

106. He Tangkun, "Si chuan e mei xian zhan guo qing tong qi di ke xue fen xi," *Kao gu*, no. 11 (1986): 1037–1041, 1050.

107. No reliable texts exist to confirm that the techniques of silk manufacture actually began in Sichuan before other places, despite a widespread popular belief among modern Sichuanese to that effect. Extant textual sources for early sericulture in Shu are admittedly late, but purportedly transmit legendary material. Tong Enzheng (*Gu dai di ba shu*, p. 110) cites *Shu zhong guang ji* ch. 71, and *Si chuan tong zhi*, chs. 44 and 56. *Hua yang guo zhi* (quoted by Tong, p. 111) notes that an official charged with overseeing silk production was appointed by Qin following its annexation of Shu, suggesting that the basis for this industry already existed. Pictorial evidence for gathering mulberry leaves is present on a decorated bronze vessel (see later text).

108. Luo Kaiyu, "Lun gu dai ba, shu wang guo di qiao xing tong bi," *Kao gu yu wen wu*, no. 3 (1990): 77–84.

109. The primary source on the Kaimings' water diversion is *Shui jing zhu*, ch. 33, *jiang shui*, p. 417. Tong Enzheng elucidates the sources in *Gu dai di ba shu*, pp. 107–108. See also Yu Quanyu, "Bao ping kou he tuo jiang shi li bing zhi qian kai zuo di," *Li shi yan jiu*, no. 1 (1978): 95–96.

110. A cache of seals from Lushan, west of Chengdu, is reported by Zhou Rilian in "Si chuan lu shan chu tu ba shu fu hao yin ji zhan guo qin han si yin," *Kao gu*, no. 1 (1990): 32–35. The Xindu signature seals are discussed by Li Xueqin, "Lun xin du chu tu di shu guo qing tong qi," pp. 38–41. Additional treatment of Ba-Shu seals is provided by Li Xiaoou, "Si chuan ying jing xian lie tai zhan guo tu keng mu qing li jian bao," pp. 602–606; and by Liu Yuchuan, "Ba shu fu hao yin zhang di chu bu yan jiu," pp. 86–93. Liu observes that the seals may have influenced later Qin and Han signets.

111. Li Fuhua, "Si chuan pi xian hong guang gong she chu tu zhan guo tong qi," *Wen wu*, no. 10 (1976): 90–93; and Liu Hong, "Ba hu yu kai ming shou," pp. 57–59, both discuss the incidence of Ba tiger-totem markings and characters in Ba-Shu script on items in Shu during the Kaiming, i.e., Ba-Shu culture period.

112. Li Xueqin in "Lun xin du chu tu di shu guo qing tong qi," pp. 41–43, was among the first to propose a phonetic basis for the Ba-Shu script.

113. Qian Yuzhi, "Gu shu di cun zai guo pin yin wen zi zai tan," *Si*

chuan wen wu, no. 6 (1989): 42–49. Qian might also have considered a similar tiger marked, scyth shaped halberd blade illustrated on p. 62 of *Wen wu*, no. 9, 1963, in a report by Shen Zhiyu. Qian calls the script "old Shu" (*gu shu*) although it is from the period of Ba-Shu culture. He connects the script to that of the historical Yi people, a.k.a. the Lolo, or Naxi tribes.

114. Qian Yuzhi, "Gu shu di cun zai guo pin yin wen zi," pp. 3–8. This article adventurously compares the Baihuatan lid to scripts in India and the Middle East. Liu Zhiyi criticized Qian's speculations in "Gu shu wen zi shi 'can si wen zi' ma?" *Si chuan wen wu*, no. 6 (1989): 54–57. See also Wei Xuefeng, "Gu shu di cun zai guo pin yin wen zi zhi yi," *Si chuan wen wu*, no. 6 (1989): 50–53.

115. Peng Jingzhong, "Gu dai ba shu tong qi wen zi shi shi," *Si chuan da xue xue bao cong kan*, no. 5 (1980): 173–175, is a purely conjectural attempt at guessing the meaning of some Ba-Shu characters, but Peng's notions have failed to gain acceptance.

116. Si chuan sheng bo wu guan, "Cheng du bai hua tan zhong xue shi hao mu fa jue ji," *Wen wu*, no. 3 (1976): 46. Jenny F. So believes the *hu* might be a Shaanxi product. See "The Inlaid Bronzes of the Warring States Period," in Wen Fong, ed., *The Great Bronze Age of China* (New York: Alfred A. Knopf, 1980), pp. 316–317.

117. A bronze taken from a boat grave in Mianzhu county bears stylistically close animal embellishments. It is reported by Wang Youpeng, "Si chuan mian zhu xian chuan guan mu," pp. 22–33. Other pieces from the central plains are very similar in spirit. If these Sichuan vessel finds were actually wrought in Sichuan, then artists there had again come under close tutelage from the north.

118. *Shi ji*, ch. 15, *liu guo nian biao*, p. 713.

119. *Yu gong* is included in the first book of *Shang shu jin zhu jin yi*, as pp. 31–46. Regarding the date of the text's composition, see Qu Wanli, "Lun yu gong zhu cheng di shi dai," *Zhong yang yan jiu yuan li shi yu yan yan jiu suo ji kan*, vol. 35, pp. 53–86 (Taibei: 1963); and Shi Nianhai, "Lun 'yu gong' di zhu zuo nian dai," in *He shan ji*, vol. 2, pp. 391–415 (Beijing: San lian shu dian, 1981).

120. *Zhu shu ji nian bu deng* (Taibei: Shi jie shu ju, 1977), ch. 4, p. 17; Wang Hui, *Yu gong shi di* (Taibei: Shang wu yin shu guan, 1971), pp. 60–61; and Shi Nianhai, ibid., 401–402.

121. Li Changfu, *"Yu gong" shi di* (Zhengzhou: Zhong zhou shu hua she, 1982), p. 82.

122. Because in historical times the soil of Sichuan has always been

famed for its fecundity, this rating in *Yu gong* may be taken as evidence for the shallowness of northern knowledge about "Liang province."

123. *Shan hai jing, hai nei xi jing, wu zang shan jing,* and *hai wai jing,* with Meng Wentong, "Lue lun 'shan hai jing' di xie zuo shi dai ji qi chan sheng di yu," *Ba shu gu shi lun shu* (Chengdu: Si chuan ren min chu ban she, 1981), pp. 146–184.

124. *Shan hai jing, hai nei xi jing,* as quoted by Meng Wentong. The allusion to Shu occurs in a separate chapter describing that land's relation to the Yangtze and an otherwise unknown tributary called the Bai shui ("White River"). This geographical tidbit is typical of the tantalizing but not altogether too informative material in *Shan hai jing.*

125. These peoples on the western and southern periphery of Sichuan are known primarily from their mortuary customs. Megalithic tombs are found in southwestern Sichuan, and peoples in the Sichuan-Guizhou area suspended their dead from the sides of cliffs. Still farther south were the Dian and Yelang cultures in Yunnan and Guizhou. Occasional Ba-Shu style artifacts are present in these areas, but textual sources are virtually lacking.

126. It would in any case be futile to impose a model of unilinear progression on Sichuan until more data become available, particularly as regard the extent of urbanization in pre-Qin Ba and Shu. The word *tribe* has been used sparingly here in the light of rethinking about its applicability to China, e.g., Morton Fried's "Tribe to State or State to Tribe in Ancient China?" in David N. Keightley, ed., *The Origins of Chinese Civilization* (Berkeley: University of California Press, 1983), pp. 467–494. And some recent and highly articulate theoretical work questions the very need for locating every early society somewhere on a suprahistorical continuum. See John Gledhill's "Introduction: The Comparative Analysis of Social and Political Transitions" in Gledhill, Bender, and Larsen, eds., *State and Society: The Emergence and Development of Social Hierarchy and Political Centralization,* pp. 1–27. Here particular considerations are seen to outweigh universals.

127. In *Zhan guo ce,* ch. 3, *qin ce* 1.52, p. 117. The speaker was Sima Cuo, promoting a Qin conquest of Shu. His reference to the Di here uses a different character *di* from the Di branch of the Qiang, whom some scholars identify with the early Shu (see Chapter 2).

Chapter Four

1. Hsu Cho-yun, *Ancient China in Transition* (Stanford, Calif.: Stanford University Press, 1965).

2. See David N. Keightley, "Where Have All the Swords Gone? Reflections on the Unification of China," *Early China,* no. 2 (Fall 1976): 31–34.

3. A duke (*gong*) was inferior only to a king in the Chinese system of nobility, but some duchies had vastly outgrown others by the fourth century B.C.

4. Chinese historians often refer to the trio together as the "three Jin". Here, Jin is added in parentheses to recall the states' common origin and to distinguish Han (Jin) and Wei (Jin) from the unrelated states Han and Wei. These latter were not part of the former Jin state and are written with different characters although they share the same romanized spelling.

5. On the importance of the Hangu pass, there is Sima Qian, *Shi ji* (Beijing: Zhong hua shu ju, 1972), ch. 6, *qin shi huang ben ji*, pp. 278–279.

6. Somewhat like the contemporary Macedonian rulers in their relation to urbane Greece, Qin's aristocracy was deemed uncouth. Each outlier state, Qin and Macedonia, was to first subdue its respective cultured neighbors and then go on to create an empire.

7. Zhang Pei, "Shan xi xun yang xian fa xian di ba shu wen hua yi wu," *Si chuan wen wu*, no. 3 (1989): 62–64.

8. See earlier, Chapter 3. The later Chu interest in the Han valley is discussed by Yan Gengwang in "Chu zhi han zhong jun di wang kao lue," *Ze shan ban yue kan* 2, no. 16 (1941): 906–910.

9. This passage from Chang Ju, *Hua yang guo zhi* (Shanghai: Shang wu yin shu guan, 1938), ch. 3, *shu zhi*, p. 28 reveals that Shu on rare occasions had come to exert a force on the outskirts of the warring states, but in the absence of any firm date or stated *casus belli*, further evaluation of the incident cannot be made.

10. *Shi ji*, ch. 15, *liu guo nian biao*, p. 713, chronicles Shu as taking Nanzheng in 387 B.C., whereas ch. 5, *qin ben ji*, p. 199, for the same year reports only that "Qin attacked Shu and captured Nanzheng." The ambiguity leaves unsolved which side had been the aggressor, and which one retained control of Nanzheng and the Han valley. *Hua yang guo zhi*, ch. 3, *shu zhi*, pp. 28–29, relates that during the reign of Zhou King Xian, 368–321 B.C., the king of of Shu possessed the territory of Bao and Han, i.e., the upper Han valley.

11. Chu thereupon strengthened its garrison at Gan pass, a gateway between Chu proper and Sichuan (*Shi ji*, ch. 40, *chu shi jia*, p. 1720). The matter is discussed by Xu Zhongshu and Tang Jiahong in "Gu dai chu shu di guan xi," *Wen wu*, no. 6 (1981): 17–25.

12. *Zhu shu ji nian bu deng* (Taibei: Shi ji shu ju, 1977), ch. 4, p. 17. Specifically, the account says this trip was to the Min and the Qingyi Rivers, both in Shu. For commentary see Lin Mingjun, "Si chuan zhi shui zhe yu shui shen," *Shuo wen yue kan* 3, no. 9 (1943): 79.

13. *Shi ji*, ch. 5, *qin ben ji* recounts early Zhou-Qin relations.

14. Kinship, either fictive or genuine, had doubtless played some part in preserving the Zhou dynasty. The Zhou were the senior branch of their surname lineage, whereas many of the vassal state rulers originally belonged to cadet branches owing the Zhou place of precedence—"It's a family affair." But the Chu ruling house was not of the same surname, and in Qi the Zhou cousins had been overthrown. On kinship, see Chang Kwang-chih, "The Lineage System of the Shang and Chou Chinese and Its Political Implications," *Early Chinese Civilization: Anthropological Perspectives* (Cambridge, Mass.: Harvard University Press, 1976), pp. 72–92.

15. *Shi ji* ch. 5, *liu guo nian biao*, p. 718, lists the Wei (Jin) ruler reigning from 370–335 B.C. as a king (*wang*). However, other passages elsewhere in *Shi ji* give conflicting dates on when the Wei (Jin) lord Hui asserted royal prerogatives. See Liang Yusheng, *Shi ji zhi yi* (Beijing: Zhong hua shu ju, 1981), vol. 1, pp. 141 and 143 on the discrepancies. Mencius in *Meng zi* (Shi Ciyun, ed., *Meng zi jin zhu jin yi*; Taibei: Shang wu yin shu guan, 1974), ch. 1, *liang hui wang*, pp. 1–55, refers to Hui as king. Not until 344 B.C. did the Wei (Jin) and Qi kings recognize each other's ranks.

16. For example, *Shi ji*, ch. 4, *zhou ben ji*, pp. 158–159.

17. *Shi ji*, ch. 5, *qin ben ji*, p. 201, notes the new significance infused into ancient Zhou-Qin ties. On the background of hegemony as an institution, see Sydney Rosen, "Changing Conceptions of the Hegemon in Pre-Ch'in China", in David T. Roy and Tsuen-hsuin Tsien, eds., *Ancient China: Studies in Early Civilization* (Hong Kong: Hong Kong University Press, 1978), pp. 99–114.

18. The date was also that of a rare visit to Shu by a traveler from Wei (Jin), as tersely recorded by *Zhu shu ji nian*, ch. 4, p. 17, without elaboration. The source is an official archive, and so presumably the traveler was an envoy. Could he have been suggesting a Wei (Jin) alliance with Shu, aimed against Qin?

19. *Shi ji*, ch. 5, *qin ben ji*, p. 202.

20. Hexi, like Alsace-Lorraine or Transylvania, was one territorial dispute that would not quit. See Yao Shuangnian, "Qin wei 'he xi' zhi zheng yu dang di di shui lu jiao tong," *Wen bo*, no. 6 (1989): 54–57.

21. *Shi ji*, ch. 15, *liu guo nian biao*, p. 720.

22. Shang Yang at that time still was known as Gongsun (his surname) Yang, or Wei (his native state) Yang. Shang is the name of an estate later awarded to him by Qin. Here the names Shang Yang and Lord Shang are used throughout to avoid confusion. Writings attributed to Shang Yang and his disciples were collected as *Shang jun shu* (Gao Heng, ed., *Shang jun shu zhu*

yi; Beijing: Zhong hua shu ju, 1974). J. J. L. Duyvendak translated the work as *The Book of Lord Shang* (London: Arthur Probsthain, 1928). An introduction discusses Lord Shang's pivotal role in history and his impact as a social reformer. See also Benjamin Schwartz, *The World of Thought in Ancient China* (Cambridge, Mass.: Harvard University Press, 1985), pp. 321–335.

23. For a discussion of Shang Yang's precursors in reforming Qin, see Lin Jianming, *Qin shi gao* (Shanghai: Shang hai ren min chu ban she, 1982), pp. 172–175.

24. *Shi ji*, ch. 68, *shang yang lie zhuan*, p. 2230.

25. *Shang jun shu*, ch. 5, *shuo min*, pp. 52–60.

26. *Shang jun shu*, ch. 2, *ken ling*, ch. 3, *nong zhan*, and ch. 6, *suan di*.

27. *Shi ji*, ch. 5, *qin ben ji*, p. 203, states Lord Shang established forty-one *xian*, whereas ch. 68, *shang jun lie zhuan*, p. 2232, and ch. 15, *liu guo nian biao*, p. 723, report thirty-one *xian*.

28. *Shi ji*, ch. 68, *shang jun lie zhuan*, p. 2230.

29, Xu Shen, *Shuo wen jie zi* (Taibei: Yi wen yin shu guan, 1974), ch. 13b, p. 44; *Shi ji*, ch. 5, *qin ben ji*, p. 203.

30. *Shi ji*, ch. 15, *liu guo nian biao*, p. 723, lists this decree in a chronological table usually reserved for royal and noble successions and for major military events. Its inclusion in that context is an indicator of how important the decree was seen to have been from the vantage point of a Han historian. Four decades after its promulgation a version of the field boundary decree was applied in Shu. See later, Chapter 5.

31. *Shi ji*, ch. 68, *shang jun lie zhuan*, p. 2230.

32. *Yan tie lun* (Huan Kuan, comp., *Yan tie lun xiao zhu*; Taibei: Shi jie shu ju, 1970), ch. 2.7, *fei yang*, p. 50 with note, p. 54. This work was evaluated and partly translated by Esson M. Gale as *Discourses on Salt and Iron* (Taibei: Cheng wen, 1973). Ban Gu, *Han shu* (Beijing: Zhong hua shu ju, 1975), ch. 62, *si ma qian zhuan*, p. 2708, traces the institution of iron commissioners to pre-imperial Qin.

33. *Shi ji*, ch. 68, *shang jun lie zhuan*, p. 2236.

34. Chapter 15 in the book attributed to Lord Shang details the Qin policy to encourage immigration, but its wording is likely that of disciples. Gao Heng, ed., *Shang jun shu*, pp. 116–125.

35. *Shi ji*, ch. 5, *qin ben ji*, p. 203; and ch. 15, *liu guo nian biao*, p. 725.

36. *Shi ji*, ch. 44, *wei shi jia*, p. 1847.

37. *Shi ji*, ch. 40, *chu shi jia*, p. 1720.

38. *Hua yang guo zhi*, ch. 1, *ba zhi*, p. 3, furthermore notes a certain Chu weakness or decrepitude at this time. *Hua yang guo zhi*, ch. 3, *shu zhi*, p. 29, mentions an exchange involving Qin's King Hui and Shu as taking place "during the twenty-second year of Zhou King Xian"; i.e., 347 B.C. However, the Qin ruler at this time was Duke Xiao, not King Hui, so the incident in all likelihood is misdated. Scholars at the Sichuan Provincial Museum believe the date should be understood as 337 B.C., ten years later. That would accord with the redirected Qin foreign policy following the deaths of Lord Shang and Duke Xiao.

39. The speech, in ch. 68, *shang jun lie zhuan*, p. 2234, suffers from anachronisms and should be considered more as literary contrivance than verbatim transcript. What counts in the present context are the ideas embodied within, especially the oblique reference to Ba.

40. An adherent of Shang Yang, Shi Jiao (also known as Shi Zi; i.e., "Master Shi") fled to Shu after Shang Yang's overthrow and death, according to commentary on *Shi ji*, ch. 74, *meng zi xun qing lie zhuan*, p. 2349. See also Jin Dejian, in Gu Jiegang, Lu Simian, and Tong Shuye, eds., *Gu shi bian* (Shanghai: Kai ming shu dian, 1926–1941), vol. 6, pp. 306–313. What impact, if any, Shi Jiao had on Shu cannot be determined from the sparse source material.

41. *Han fei zi* (Chen Qiyou, ed., *Han fei zi ji shi*; Taibei: He luo tu shu chu ban she, 1974), p. 43, *ding fa*, p. 907; Zhang Jinguang, "Qin zi shang yang bian fa hou di du fu yao yi zhi du," *Wen shi zhe*, no. 1 (1983): 18–25.

42. *Shi ji* never uses the term *duke* (*gong*) for Hui-wen, referring to him as lord (*jun*) during the period prior to his becoming king or (*wang*), in 325 B.C. See ch. 5, *qin ben ji*, passim.

43. *Shi ji*, ch. 69, *su qin lie zhuan*, p. 2242.

44. *Shi ji*, ch. 5, *qin ben ji*, p. 205, and ch. 15, *liu guo nian biao*, p. 727. Allowances must be made for a discrepancy in dates. *Hua yang guo zhi*, ch. 3, *shu zhi*, p. 29, says the Shu marquis went to Qin during the twenty-second year of Zhou's King Xian; i.e., 347 B.C., or nine years before Hui-wen ascended the Qin throne. If a calligraphic stroke is added to the number twenty-two, making the date equivalent to 337 B.C., then the embassy coincides with that mentioned in *Shi ji*, ch. 15, *liu guo nian biao*, p. 727. Scholars at the Sichuan Provincial Museum have undertaken just much a correction in the chronological table guiding their work. Even with that correction, however, the *Hua yang guo zhi* story seems out of sequence, related after other substantive contacts between Hui-wen and his Shu neighbors. Tong Enzheng (*Gu dai di ba shu*, p. 139) accepts that the Shu marquis dealt with Hui-wen but does not account for the discrepancy in *Hua yang guo zhi*'s dates or narrative sequence.

45. *Shi ji*, ch. 69, *su qin lie zhuan*, p. 2242.

46. *Shi ji*, ch. 40, *chu shi jia*, p. 1721.

47. *Shi ji*, ch. 15, *liu guo nian biao*, p. 727.

48. *Shi ji*, ch. 46, *tian jing zhong wan shi jia*, p. 1894.

49. The Wei (Jin)-Qi axis also turned against Zhao (Jin), according to *Shi ji*, ch. 15, *liu guo nian biao*, p. 728.

50. *Shi ji*, ch. 41, *yue wang ju qian shi jia*, p. 1751.

51. *Shi ji*, ch. 5 *qin ben ji*, pp. 205–206.

52. *Shi ji*, ch. 15, *liu guo nian biao*, p. 728. The principal Qin advisor of this period was Gongsun Yan, himself a native of Wei (Jin).

53. This was the first instance of Qin creating a commandery, the status that later would be granted in turn to Shu, Ba and the upper Han valley. The term *jun* may have been borrowed by Qin from the administrative practice of other states. See Yan Gengwang, *Zhong guo di fang xing zheng zhi du shi* (Taibei: Zhong yang yan jiu yuan li shi yu yan yan jiu suo, 1974), vol. 1, pp. 1–8; and Yang Kuan, *Zhan guo shi* (Shanghai: Shang hai ren min shu ban she, 1980), Appendices 1 and 2, pp. 534–552.

54. The essay *Guo qin lun* (in *Shi ji*, ch. 6, *qin shi huang ben ji*, p. 279) may be read to infer that King Hui was following the testament of Duke Xiao in turning attention southward to the Han valley and Sichuan. However, as seen, nothing of Xiao's practical actions uphold that inference.

55. *Shi ji*, ch. 15, *liu guo nian biao*, p. 730, records the stampede toward kingship by the remaining state lords, completed by 323 B.C. The chronology of events as recounted here owes much also to Lin Jianming, *Qin shi gao*, pp. 234–246.

56. *Zhu shu ji nian*, ch. 4, p. 22; *Shi ji*, ch. 23, *feng chan shu*, p. 1365.

57. There are no subsequent notices of Qin undertaking the propitiating rites to the spirits of ancient Zhou kings, but the mere fact of their tumuli being within Qin borders ensured an enduring special connection.

58. There are some discrepancies in *Shi ji* regarding the exact composition of the anti-Qin alliance. The chronological table, ch. 15, *liu guo nian biao*, p. 731, lists the three Jin, Yan, and Chu as members, omitting Qi, whereas ch. 5, *qin ben ji*, p. 207, mentions the three Jin, Yan, Qi, and the Xiongnu steppe tribe, omitting Chu. Of greatest interest in the present context is the participation of Chu, which was best situated to focus its power directly against Qin and compete with Qin in Sichuan.

59. *Hua yang guo zhi*, ch. 3, *shu zhi*, pp. 28–29, and Yang Xiong, *Shu*

wang ben ji (Taibei: Yi wen yin shu guan, 1968), pp. 2–3, both offer fragmentary accounts, corroborative in some aspects, complementary in others.

60. *Hua yang guo zhi*, ch. 3, *shu zhi*, p. 29.

61. *Shu wang ben ji*, p. 2, reports the Shu refusal to accept Qin overlordship in the sentence *qin hui wang shi shu wang bu xiang qin*, the inclusion of which could indicate that some form of Shu subordination to Qin had been expected.

62. *Hua yang guo zhi*, ch. 3, *shu zhi*, p. 28, reports the expedition, but out of place in any logical sequence of events. *Shu wang ben ji* numbers Kaiming's retinue at 10,000 whereas the Jin dynasty fragment "Jin niu" (in *Shuo fu*, reprinted as *Wan xiang shan tang ben*; vol. 60, n.p.: 1647) says several thousand.

63. *Hua yang guo zhi*, ch. 3, *shu zhi*, p. 28.

64. *Hua yang guo zhi*, ch. 3, *shu zhi*, p. 28, refers to the item as *zhen wan zhi wu*, a gemstone, whereas *Shu wang ben ji*, p. 2, records simply a gift, *li wu*. Although the occurrence as recorded appears to be a simple myth of transubstantiation, it also is possible to infer a playful if somewhat insolent practical joke by Kaiming. Apart from its obvious metaphoric import, the tale may perhaps rest on a grain of historical truth.

65. According to *Shu wang ben ji*, p. 2, a thousand Shu troops went along to make the request.

66. *Hua yang guo zhi*, ch. 3, *shu zhi*, p. 28, describes the people of Qin as laughing over the affair. *Shu wang ben ji*, pp. 2–3, and the fragment "Jin niu" relate how in due course Qin armies would follow the Stone Cattle Road on their way to conquer Shu.

67. A variant name is the Golden Cattle Road (*jin niu dao*). *Shu wang ben ji*, p. 2, gives the figure three *zhang* for the width of the road, each *zhang* being equal to $3\frac{1}{3}$ meters or some 140 inches. Sources on the construction of the road and its archaeology are Han Wei and Wang Shihe, "Bao xie dao shi men fu jin jian dao yi ji ti ke di diao cha," *Wen wu*, no. 11 (1964): 25–42; and Lan Yong, "Si chuan gu dai jian dao yan jiu," *Si chuan wen wu*, no. 1 (1988): 2–10.

68. In 1979, a Shaanxi provincial team hiked through the hills surveying the positions of 56 holes for horizontal beams bored into the cliff sides and 190 holes for upright supports, in 22 separate locations. See Qin Zhongxing et al., "Bao xie jian dao diao cha ji," *Kao gu yu wen wu*, no. 4 (1980): 42–47; Ren Shoufang, "Qin shu jian dao: gu dao, lian yun dao he bao xie dao gai shu," *Bao ji shi yang xue bao*, no. 4 (1986): 126; Huang Banghong, "Shu dao kao cha shi ling," *Si chuan wen wu*, no. 1 (1988): 11–14; and Guo Rongzhang, "Lun gu bao xie dao shang jian ge di fen bu xing zhi, ji you yi deng jian zhu she shi," *Wen bo*, no. 5 (1988): 39–46. Determining the Qinling portion of the

route was once one of those perennial quibbles, like the attempts to find Hannibal's path through the Alps. An old source is Lin Zhao et al. "Shu dao kao," *Wen shi za zhi* 3, nos. 5–6 (1944): 4–19. Now it appears likely that the Bao-Xie road indeed was the Qinling Mountain link to the Stone Cattle Road. Perhaps because the path's starting point is west of the Qin capital of Xianyang, many ancient sources refer to Shu itself as lying west of Qin.

69. Wang Daisheng, "Jian men shu dao yu jian men shu dao wen wu," *Si chuan wen wu*, no. 1 (1988): pp. 15–35, discusses the Sichuan portion of the Stone Cattle Road.

70. The comparison to "disorders of Jie and Zhou" is made explicit in Liu Xiang, comp., *Zhan guo ce* (Shanghai: Shang hai gu ji chu ban she, 1978), ch. 3, *qin ce* (1), p. 117, alluding respectively to the final Xia and Shang rulers.

71. This story appears in both *Hua yang guo zhi*, ch. 3, *shu zhi*, p. 28 and *Shu wang ben ji*, p. 2. Wudu is on higher ground, within the present frontiers of Gansu province.

72. *Shu wang ben ji*, p. 2, says the king sent troops to bring back the soil, whereas *Hua yang guo zhi*, ch. 3, *shu zhi*, p. 29, identifies the earth movers as the king's five strong men. The tumulus measured seven *zhang* in height and three *mou* in area.

73. Zitong is northeast of Chengdu, halfway between that city and the present Sichuan-Shaanxi frontier.

74. *Hua yang guo zhi*, ch. 3, *shu zhi*, p. 28, emphasizes Kaiming's grief. The source explains the name of a particular hill, "Five Strong-Men Mound" (*wu ding zhong*) in terms of this tale. *Shu wang ben ji*, p. 3, says Kaiming built a spectacular tomb for the avalanche victims, but does not divulge where.

75. *Shi ji*, ch. 69, *su qin lie zhuan*, p. 2261, gives the quote but does not fix the date of the meeting. Tong Enzheng (*Gu dai di ba shu*, p. 140) ventures it as taking place in 332 B.C.; i.e., considerably before the actual Qin conquest of Shu. But the passage seems a bit too convenient; perhaps it is merely an ex post facto interpolation.

76. *Hua yang guo zhi*, ch. 1, *ba zhi*, p. 3, moreover notes an undefined weakness in Chu through the middle fourth century B.C., perhaps an allusion to internal discord at the palace or to the demands of defending so large a territorial expanse.

77. *Shi ji*, ch. 40, *chu shi jia*, p. 1720; and ch. 15, *liu guo nian biao*, pp. 727–731. As noted earlier, only one isolated clash is reported, in 340 B.C., resulting in a Qin victory.

78. *Shi ji*, ch. 69, *su qin lie zhuan*, pp. 2259–2261.

79. The Wei (Jin) prime minister who took Zhang Yi's place was Gong-

sun Yan. He formerly had served Qin and thus had intimate knowledge of
Qin plans and potential. *Shi ji*, ch. 5, *qin ben ji*, p. 207; ch. 15, *liu guo nian biao*,
pp. 731–732; ch. 44, *wei shi jia*, p. 1850.

80. *Shi ji*, ch. 15, *liu guo nian biao*, p. 731.

81. *Shi ji*, ch. 45, *han shi jia*, p. 1870.

82. *Hua yang guo zhi*, ch. 3, *shu zhi*, p. 29.

83. *Shi ji*, ch. 70, *zhang yi lie zhuan*, p. 2281, and *Hua yang guo zhi*, ch. 3,
shu zhi, p. 29, record the diplomatic activity but do not divulge the causes of
disagreement between Shu and Ba or between Kaiming XII and the marquis
of Zu.

84. *Zhan guo ce*, ch. 3, *qin ce* (1), p. 117, and *Shi ji*, ch. 70, *zhang yi lie
zhuan*, p. 2281, recount King Hui's dilemma as a choice between attacking
Han (Jin) or intervening in Shu. But *Hua yang guo chi*, ch. 3, *shu zhi*, p. 29,
inexplicably describes the former option as a Qin attack against Chu instead
of Han (Jin).

85. Sima Cuo's simile anticipated Lord Byron's colorful verses recounting an Assyrian attack in "The Destruction of Sennacherib." Several sources
record this council of war. The account in *Xin xu* (Lu Yuanqun, ed., *Xin xu jin
zhu jin yi*; Taibei: Shang wu yin shu guan, 1975), ch. 9 *shan mou*, pp. 302–305,
closely follows *Zhan guo ce*, ch. 3, *qin ce* (1), p. 117, and *Shi ji*, ch. 70, *zhang yi
lie zhuan*, pp. 2281–2284, in giving the supposed minutes of the conference.
Although the dialog no doubt is contrived, it represents the view of strategic
thinkers living and writing soon after the event and thus retains validity as
historical evidence.

86. In *Shu wang ben ji*, p. 3, *Hua yang guo zhi*, ch. 3, *shu zhi*, p. 29, and
Shui jing zhu, ch. 33, *jiang shui*, p. 420, Zhang Yi is named with Sima Cuo in
charge of the Shu expedition. *Hua yang guo zhi* also lists another officer named
Mo. *Shi ji*, ch. 70, *zhang yi lie zhuan*, the biography of Zhang Yi, omits mention
of his participating but ch. 87, *li si lie zhuan*, p. 2542, says his plan was used.
"Jin niu" credits Zhang Yi. On the other hand, *Shi ji*, ch. 5, *qin ben ji*, p. 210,
says Sima Cuo conquered Shu, whereas *Han shu*, ch. 62, *si ma qian zhuan*, p.
2708, gives his name as both conquerer of Shu and its first Qin commandant.

87. Analogous instances are known in history at similarly critical junc-
tures. Consider the intriguing parallel of Hitler and his panzer commander
Heinz Guderian in the summer of 1941. By August, having smashed Soviet
forces on the central front leading to Moscow, Guderian pleaded for a quick
assault toward the Kremlin while time still allowed and the Red Army remained in disarray. Hitler, thinking in economic terms, chose instead to seize
the Ukraine with its resources. He diverted the panzers south, under Guderian, just as King Hui sent Zhang Yi to Sichuan. The Germans captured the
Ukrainian breadbasket and over 600,000 prisoners, perhaps the largest encir-

clement battle in history. But here the parallel ends, because the failure to gain Moscow is often said to have lost Hitler the war. It is incidentally rather unlikely that the *Fuhrer* or his commanders had ever heard of Qin, King Hui, or Zhang Yi. See John Keegan, *The Second World War* (New York: Viking Books, 1989) pp. 192–196, for a recent retelling.

88. *Hua yang guo zhi*, ch. 3, *shu zhi*, p. 29, and *Shi ji*, ch. 70, *zhang yi lie zhang*, p. 2284, record the event as taking place in the tenth month. Sources are inconsistent regarding the year. The Appendix discusses these discrepancies.

89. Wuyang is in eastern Pengshan county, Sichuan. *Shu wang ben ji*, p. 3 notes Kaiming's capture, whereas *Hua yang guo zhi*, ch. 3, *shu zhi*, p. 29, says he was killed.

90. *Hua yang guo zhi*, ch. 1, *ba zhi*, p. 3, says Zhang Yi coveted the wealth of Zu and Ba, so he took Ba and arrested its king, but ch. 3 *shu zhi*, p. 29, attributes the conquest of Zu and Ba to Sima Cuo and unnamed others.

91. Yong was the Han valley mini-state earlier annihilated by Ba, Qin, and Chu, but which had become part of Shu, according to *Hua yang guo zhi*, ch. 2, *han zhong zhi*, p. 19.

92. *Shi ji*, ch. 6, *qin shi huang ben ji*, pp. 278–279.

Chapter Five

1. The initial consonant in *sinification* reflects pronunciation shifts to an initial sibilant as the name Qin became known in other languages, including Latin and Arabic. The usage of sinification is here restricted to mean social reordering under Qin rule, as distinguished from the cultural impact that other states, e.g., Chu, may have had on their neighbors. As a latecomer to the Zhou polity and an outlying state bordering on the northwestern steppe zone, Qin always had its own peculiarities. And, after the reforms of Shang Yang, Qin had become sufficiently distinctive to warrant this exclusive use of the term sinification.

2. Sima Qian, *Shi ji* (Beijing: Zhong hua shu ju, 1972), ch. 71, *shu li zi gan mao lie zhuan*, p. 2311.

3. *Shi ji*, ch. 40, *chu shi jia*, p. 1721, note 1, referring to year 7 in the reign of Chu King Wei.

4. Ma Chengyuan, *Zhong guo gu dai qing tong qi* (Shanghai: Shang hai ren min chu ban she, 1982), pp. 126–130; and Chen Zhenyu, "Chu mie yue di nian dai wen ti," *Jiang han lun tan*, no. 5 (1980): 84.

5. *Shi ji*, ch. 15, *liu guo nian biao*, p. 733.

6. *Zhan guo ce* (Liu Xiang, comp.; Shanghai: Shang hai gu ji chu ban she, 1978), ch. 3, *qin ce* (2), pp. 135–137, specifies the area of Shangyu as the Qin sop proffered to Chu.

7. *Zhan guo ce*, ch. 14, *chu ce* (1), p. 506; *Shi ji*, ch. 70, *Zhang yi lie zhuan*, p. 2287.

8. Yao Shuangnian, "Qin wei 'he xi' zhi zheng yu dang di di shui lu jiao tong," *Wen bo*, no. 6 (1989): 54–57.

9. Chu vulnerability to a synchronized Qin assault on the two fronts is also stated in *Shi ji*, ch. 69, *su qin lie zhuan*, p. 2260.

10. Arthur Banks, *Atlas of Ancient and Medieval Warfare* (New York: Hippocrene, 1982) pp. 35–57.

11. *Shi ji*, ch. 40, *chu shi jia*, p. 1723.

12. *Hua yang guo zhi*, ch. 3, *shu zhi*, p. 29, says "10,000" (*wan*) Qin families (*jia*) emigrated to Shu, but this is merely a locution signifying a multitude, so the number should not be taken literally.

13. *Shi ji*, ch. 70 *zhang yi lie zhuan*, p. 2284, and *Zhan guo ce*, ch. 3, *qin ce* (1), p. 119, relate in identical wording, "The title of the Shu king was changed to marquis." Neither passage actually names the marquis. On the Qin decision to entrust the marquisate to a surviving scion of the Kaiming house, see Jiang Jiahua, "Qin shu hou fei qin ren kao bian," *Zhong guo li shi wen xian yan jiu ji kan*, no. 2 (1981): 99–104. Tong Enzheng gives a similar interpretation (*Gu dai di ba shu* [Chengdu: Si chuan ren min chu ban she, 1979], pp. 142–143) as does Yang Kuan ("Lun qin han di fen feng zhi," *Zhong hua wen shi lun cong*, no. 1 [1980]).

14. *Shi ji*, ch. 5, *qin ben ji*, pp. 207–208; *Shi ji*, ch. 15, *liu guo nian biao*, p. 733, gives the date as one year later, in 313 B.C. *Hua yang guo zhi*, ch. 3, *shu zhi*, p. 29, records the Shu marquis' name as Tongguo.

15. *Hua yang guo zhi*, ch. 3, *shu zhi*, p. 29, although *Han shu*, ch. 62, *si ma qian zhuan*, p. 2708, says the first governor was Sima Cuo.

16. *Shi ji*, ch. 5, *qin ben ji*, p. 207, and ch. 15, *liu guo nian biao*, p. 733; also *Hua yang guo zhi*, ch. 3, *shu zhi*, p. 29. Tong Enzheng (*Gu dai di ba shu*, p. 148) portrays Yaotong and Chen Zhuang as collaborators in treason until Chen Zhuang betrayed the marquis. This and subsequent revolts against Qin are reviewed by Chen Jin, "Ru he ping jie qin wang chao zai shu jun di san ci zhen ya," *Si chuan shi yuan xue bao*, no.3 (1981): 78–81.

17. *Hua yang guo zhi*, ch.3, *shu zhi*, p. 29; *Shi ji*, ch. 15, *liu guo nian biao*, p. 734. *Shi ji*, ch. 71, *shu li zi gan mao lie zhuan*, p. 2311, is inconsistent, reporting (Chen) Zhuang and Marquis Hou as rising together in rebellion against Qin. Other sources name Marquis Hou as Yaotong's successor after Chen

Zhuang had been executed. Gan Mao later deserted Qin service and defected to Qi. Shi Zhimian compared the sources in "Qin ding shu," *Da lu za zhi* 49, no. 6 (1974): 302.

18. *Hua yang guo zhi*, ch. 3, *shu zhi*, p. 29.

19. Apart from Yang Xiong, *Shu wang ben ji* (Taibei: Wen hai chu ban she, 1967) and *Hua yang guo zhi*, ch. 3, *shu zhi*, sources on the establishment of Chengdu include two classical literary works, both titled *Shu du fu* or "Ode on the capital of Shu." The first was by Yang Xiong of the former Han dynasty, and the latter, by Zuo Si, is a product of Jin times some four centuries thereafter. Although their purely historical value is slight, both odes preserve some of the epic grandeur with which later generations cloaked these early Qin pioneering days in Shu. The dating of the latter piece was discussed by Fu Xuanzong, "Zuo si 'san du fu' xie zuo nian dai zhi yi," *Zhong hua wen shi lun cong*, no. 2 (1979): 319–329.

20. Li Hao, *Chuang zhu yang ma cheng ji*, quoted in Wang Wencai, "Cheng du cheng fang kao" (part 1), *Si chuan shi fan xue bao*, no. 1 (1981): 58.

21. Late legend had Zhang Yi putting up an initially unsuccessful wall that collapsed. A turtle then emerged from the nearby river, crawled to a point east and south of the city and died. Zhang Yi consulted a witch, who advised him to try building again at that spot. It was called *gui hua cheng*, or "Wall of the Transformed Turtle." A version of *Shu wang ben ji* in *Shuo fu*, ch. 7, has the story, which is discussed by Sun Hua in "Bie ling ming yi kao," *Si chuan wen wu*, no. 5 (1989): 20, 23–24. Another case of *deus ex reptilia* with a mutant turtle revealing gnostic secrets to mankind as in the *Book of the Luo* (see Chapter 2).

22. By way of comparison, Chengdu outranked in size the Jerusalem of its day. It was only slightly smaller than Egyptian Alexandria, a near contemporary foundation. Chengdu's fortifications enclosed an area about half that within the walls of republican Rome. See Richard J. A. Talbert, ed., *Atlas of Classical History* (London and Sydney: Croom Helm, 1985), pp. 81, 123, 164.

23. *Hua yang guo zhi*, ch. 3, *shu zhi*, p. 30. The dimensions seem plausible, as the wall remained standing when *Hua yang guo zhi* was written. Of course, the height could have been augmented in the interim. All vestiges of the wall were regrettably razed in urban renewal projects of the early 1950s without any effort at archaeological investigation.

24. Li Hao, *Chuang zhu yang ma cheng ji*, quoted in Wang Wencai, "Cheng du cheng fang kao" (part 1), p. 58.

25. *Hua yang guo zhi*, ch. 3, *shu zhi*, p. 30.

26. *Yi zhou ji*, as quoted in Wang Wencai, "Cheng du cheng fang kao" (part 1), p. 58.

27. *Yi zhou ji*; see also Wang Wencai, "Cheng du cheng fang kao" (part 1), p. 59, quoting *Yi zhou ming hua lu, Hua yang ji*, and Zhao Bian, *Cheng du gu jin ji ji*.

28. Chang Ju, *Hua yang guo zhi* (Shanghai: Shang wu yin shu guan, 1938), ch. 3, *shu zhi*, p. 30. Wang Wencai ("Cheng du cheng fang kao", part 1, p. 59) also claims that superintendents overseeing the production of silk brocade and wagons had offices, respectively, to the west and southwest of the city wall, but it is not clear on what classical or archaeological authority this statement rests.

29. *Hua yang guo zhi*, ch. 3, *shi zhi*, p. 30, offers a fair amount of detail on what preceded the falling out between king and marquis, but the source is marred by one major flaw. It mistakenly names the Qin king as Xiaowen, who did not assume the throne until 250 B.C. according to *Shi ji*, ch. 15, *liu guo nian biao*, p. 749.

30. A later commentator's note to *Shi ji*, ch. 5, *qin ben ji*, p. 221 , obfuscates matters by stating that the *Hua yang guo zhi* story just related does not refer to the same Hui, marquis of Shu. However, the comment ends there without clearing up the issue.

31. *Shi ji*, ch. 15, *liu guo nian biao*, p. 736.

32. *Hua yang guo zhi*, ch. 3, *shu zhi*, p. 30; and *Shu wang ben ji*, p. 3.

33. *Hua yang guo zhi*, ch. 3, *shu zhi*, p. 30.

34. Shi Nianhai, *He shan ji*, vol. I, p. 128, interpreting material in *Zhan guo ce*, ch. 5, *qin ce* (3). In addition to the Stone Cattle Road, at least two other routes date to Qin times. One was the "Old Road" or *gu dao*, sometimes called *chen cang dao*, indicating the presence of a granary. It terminates at Baoji, in Shaanxi, west of the Bao-Xie route. See Huang Banghong, "Shu dao kao cha shi ling," *Si chuan wen wu*, no. 1 (1988): 11–14. Another road, to Ba, was the *mi cang dao* or Rice Granary Road across the Daba Mountains, whence it fed into the Bao-Xie route. See Lan Yong, "Mi cang dao di ta cha yu kao zheng," *Si chuan wen wu*, no. 2 (1989): 12–17.

35. Qingchuan county is located near where Sichuan touches Gansu and Shaanxi provinces, not far west from the Qin road leading to Shu.

36. Calligraphic details and numismatic evidence from the tomb support that chronological finding. See Li Zhaohe et al., "Qing chuan xian chu tu qin geng xiu tian lu mu du"; and Yu Haoliang, "Shi qing chuan qin mu mu du," both in *Wen wu*, no. 1 (1982): 1–27. The case for 305 B.C. is argued by Wang Yun in "Guan yu qing chuan qin du di nian dai," *Si chuan wen wu*, no. 5 (1989): 31–33. The latter date accords better with what is known of the career of Gan Mao, who is mentioned in the text.

37. The following studies interpret the land redistribution document: Lin Jianming, "Qing chuan qin mu mu du nei rong tan tao," *Kao gu yu wen wu*, no. 6 (1982): 62–64, 112; Yang Kuan, "Shi qing chuan qin du di tian mou zhi du," *Wen wu*, no. 7 (1982): 83–85; Li Xueqin, "Qing chuan hao jia ping mu du yan jiu," *Wen wu*, no. 10 (1982): 68–72; and Tian Yizhao et al., "Qin tian lu kao shi," *Kao gu*, no. 6 (1983): 545–548.

38. Evidence for taro as a crop in Qin and Han period Shu is found in *Shi ji*, ch. 129, *huo zhi lie zhuan*, p. 3728, n. 4.

39. Luo Kaiyu argues that the land distribution provided private plots for immigrant homesteaders, in "Qing chuan qin du 'wei tian lu' suo gui ding di 'wei tian' zhi," *Kao gu*, no. 8 (1988): 728–731, 756.

40. For example, *Shi ji*, ch. 129, *huo zhi lie zhuan*, p. 3277, mentions a Zhuo family from the state of Zhao (Jin) as having been sent to Shu.

41. Qin records inscribed on bamboo slips were taken from a grave at Shuihudi, Yunmeng, Hubei province in 1975. They include one piece outlining march procedures for Shu-bound immigrants. The full text is given in Shui hu di qin mu zhu jian zheng li xiao zu, *Shui hu di qin mu zhu jian* (Beijing: Wen wu chu ban she, 1978), pp. 261–262.

42. In this regard the Shuihudi document employs the term *li*, a neighborhood unit of local responsibility and control.

43. *Shi ji*, ch. 129, *huo zhi lie zhuan*, states that Jiameng, near the road to Xianyang and not far from Chengdu, was a preferred resettlement location.

44. *Han shu* (Beijing: Zhong hua shu ju, 1975), ch. 1, *gao di ji*, notes, states specifically that "under Qin law, malfeasors (*zui*) were sent as exiles (*tu*) to Shu and Han."

45. *Shi ji*, ch. 6, *qiu shi huang ben ji*, p.227.

46. The separation of a husband sent to Shu away from his wife is lamented in the Qin silken manuscript *Wu shi er bing fang*, taken from Han period tomb no. 3 at Mawangdui, Hunan. See Chen Yong, "Qin han wen zi zha cong," *Shi xue ji kan*, no. 4 (1986): 72. On the other hand, *Hua yang guo zhi*, ch. 3, *shu zhi*, p. 29, reported 10,000 families emigrating to Shu.

47. *Shi ji*, ch. 129, *huo zhi lie zhuan*, pp. 3260, 3277.

48. Luo Kaiyu, "Lun gu dai ba, shu wang guo di qiao xing tong bi," *Kao gu yu wen wu*, no. 3 (1990): 77–84.

49. Zhu Huo, "Tan ba shu qin ban liang," *Si chuan wen wu*, no. 1 (1990): 31–37. The coin mold is reported here for the first time, a full decade after its discovery, but without details on the circumstances of the find.

50. Song Zhimin, "Lue lun si chuan di qin ren mu," *Kao gu yu wen wu,* no. 2 (1984): 82–90.

51. Huang Jiaxiang, "Si chuan da yi xian wu long xiang tu keng mu qing li jian bao," *Kao gu,* no. 7 (1987): 604–610.

52. Luo Kaiyu has studied in detail the contrast between the Qin administration in Shu and Ba. Relevant articles are "Qin zai ba shu di jing ji guan li zhi du shi xi," *Si chuan shi yuan xue bao,* no. 4 (1982): 78–83; and "Qin zai ba shu di qu di min zu zheng ce shi xi," *Min zu yan jiu,* no. 4 (1982): 27–33.

53. *Hua yang guo zhi,* ch. 1, *ba zhi,* p. 3.

54. A passing reference in *Zhan guo ce,* ch. 5, *qin ce* (3), p. 216, for example, makes mention of Shu and Han without noting Ba as belonging to Qin.

55. Fan Ye, *Hou han shu* (Beijing: Zhong hua shu ju, 1973), ch. 86, *nan man xi nan yi lie zhuan,* p. 2841.

56. The number of eleven *xian* is given, but without classical reference, by Guan Weiliang in "Gu dai chong qing da shi bian nian," *Chong qing shi fan xue yuan xue bao,* no. 3 (1989): 65.

57. Chen Xianyuan, "'Mi cang dao' kao lue," *Wen bo,* no. 1 (1988): 40–43. The road was used in 206 B.C. during the early Han struggles, so it must have been constructed some time earlier.

58. *Yi* in later usage can refer to barbarians in general, but here the term signifies a specific group. See Wang Xiantang, "Ren yu yi," *Zhong hua wen shi lun cong,* no. 1 (1982): 203–226. Meng Mo speculatively traced the subsequent history of the Yi in "Shi lun han dai xi nan min zu zhong di 'yi' yu 'qiang'," *Li shi yan jiu,* no. 1 (1985): 11–32.

59. The stone tablet inscription is not extant, but the incident is recorded in *Hua yang guo zhi,* ch. 1, *ba zhi,* p. 3, and in *Hou han shu,* ch. 86, *nan man xi nan yi lie zhuan,* p. 2840. Tong Enzheng recalled that the tiger was a Ba totem and interpreted the tiger hunt as an instance of class warfare against the surviving Ba slave-owning aristocracy, giving the story a Marxist twist, in *Gu dai di ba shu,* pp. 149–150.

60. See Chapter 3.

61. *Shi ji,* ch. 7, *xiang yu ben ji,* p. 316.

62. Si chuan sheng bo wu guan, *Si chuan chuan guan zang fa jue bao gao,* (Beijing: Wen wu chu ban she, 1960) pp. 62–63, 82–90, and 127–128; also Zhu Huo, "Tan ba shu qin ban liang," pp. 31–37.

63. Si chuan sheng bo wu guan, *Si chuan chuan guan zang fa jue bao gao,* pp. 62–63, 82–90.

64. *Han shu*, ch. 86, *nan man xi nan yi lie zhuan*, p. 2840, names seven additional clan, or surname (*xing*) units active in Ba during the transition between the Qin and Han periods: the Luo, Pu, Du, E, Du, Xi, and Long. These should be distinguished from the five clans (*shi*) that legend has entering Sichuan with the Ba founder hero Linjun.

65. The source is *Yi bu qi jiu zhuan*, excerpted and preserved in *Yu di ji sheng*, ch. 159, and quoted by Tong Enzheng, *Gu dai di ba shu*, pp. 43–44. The Pu River cannot be placed with certainty, but a people called the Pu had been one of the constitutent Ba groups.

66. The river valleys were the Qiu, Chen, Yuan, and two called the Wu but written with different characters, according to *Shi dao zhi*. This Tang period geography is quoted by Deng Shaoqin in *Ba shu shi yi tan suo* (Chengdu: Si chuan ren min chu ban she, 1983), p. 74.

67. For a reconstruction of the later history of the Ba based on philological guesswork, see Pan Guangdan, *Xiang xi bei di 'tu jia' yu gu dai di ba ren* (Beijing: Min zu yan jiu suo, 1955), pp. 1–134.

68. The quotation from *Shi ji*, ch. 70, *zhang yi lie zhuan*, p. 2290, reflects Zhang Yi's estimate shortly before his death in 310 B.C.

69. *Zhan guo ce*, passim, is the source for most information about the longitudinal vs. latitudinal coalition strategies.

70. *Shi ji*, ch. 5, *qin ben ji*; ch. 15, *liu guo nian biao*; and ch. 40, *chu shi jia*, give the dates of sieges and battles. Much of this material has been confirmed by a newly dicovered chronology on bamboo slips, found at Yunmeng, Hubei. See Ma Feibai, "Yun meng qin jian da shi ji ji chuan," *Zhong guo li shi wen xian yan jiu ji kan*, no. 2 (1981): 66–92.

71. *Shi ji*, ch. 5, *qin ben ji*, p. 212, ch. 15, *liu guo nian biao*, p. 738, and ch. 73, *bai qi wan jian lie zhuan*, p. 2331, all give the Hanzhong governor's name as Ren Bi, but no further information is available on this figure. Less is known regarding administrative arrangements in Hanzhong commandery under the Qin than about Shu or Ba commanderies.

72. The location of Qianzhong was determined by Yan Gengwang, in "Chu qin qian zhong jun di wang kao," *Ze shan ban yue kan* 2, no. 19 (1941): 977–984.

73. The basic classical source is *Shi ji*, ch. 116, *xin nan yi lie zhuan*, p. 2993, with additional material in *Han shu*, ch. 95, *xi nan yi liang yue chao xian zhuan*, p. 3838. Thorough secondary treatment on the different versions and ancillary material is offered by Meng Wentong in *Ba shu gu shi lun shu* (Chengdu: Si chuan ren min chu ban she, 1981), pp. 114–145.

74. *Xun zi jin zhu jin yi* (Xiong Gongzhe, ed.; Taibei: Shang wu yin shu guan, 1975), ch. 10, *yi bing bian* (15), pp. 283, 296.

75. Which Chu monarch ordered the venture cannot be unequivocally determined from the textual sources. *Shi ji,* ch. 116, says it was King Wei, who reigned during the decade 339–329 B.C.; i.e., before Qin invaded Sichuan. *Hou han shu* and *Hua yang guo zhi* credit King Xiang (r. 298–262 B.C.), which is more acceptable to modern authorities like Meng Wentong in reconstructing the sequence of events. See *Ba shu gu shi lun shu,* pp. 114–145.

76. *Hua yang guo zhi,* ch. 4, *nan zhong zhi,* p.47, terminates the Zhuang Qiao expedition at Yelang within modern Guizhou, omitting mention of Dian in Yunnan.

77. Evidence is summarized by Zhou Chunyuan, "Lue lun gu ye lang di zu shu wen ti, " in *Ye lang kao* (Guiyang: Gui zhou ren min chu ban she, 1981), pp. 140–151.

78. *Shi ji,* ch. 5, *qin ben ji,* p. 213.

79. *Yan tie lun xiao zhu* (Huan Kuan, comp.; Taibei: Shi jie shu ju, 1970), ch. 10, *lun gong,* 52, p. 327.

80. In *Shi ji,* ch. 69, *su qin lie zhuan,* p. 2271, the foreign policy consultant Su Dai is quoted as telling the king of Yan, "Chu took Zhi [a Ba town on the Yangtze] but then perished."

81. This area had once belonged to the statelet of Kui, which Chu annexed in 634 B.C. before penetrating upstream into Sichuan. See Chapter 3. The Wu of Wu ("military") Pass and the nearly homophonic Wu ("sorceress") Gorge are two separate characters denoting locations hundreds of kilometers distant.

82. *Shi ji,* ch. 69, *su qin lie zhuan,* p. 2272.

83. A year-by-year list of Qin military operations was included among the bamboo slip documents found in 1975 at Shuihudi, Yunmeng, Hubei province. It is referred to as the *Yun meng chronology.* The chronology's correlation with *Shi ji* is considered by Ma Feibai, "Yun meng qin jian da shi ji ji chuan," pp. 66–92; and by Huang Shengzhang, "Yun meng qin jian 'bian nian ji' di li yu li shi wen ti," *Li shi di li yu kao gu lun cong* (Jinan: Qi lu shu she, 1982), pp. 46–88.

84. See Chapter 3 on the pre-Qin history of Ba.

85. *Shui jing zhu* (Li Daoyuan, comp.; Taibei: Shi jie shu ju, 1974), ch. 38, *mian shui zhu,* p. 364. This monstrous atrocity lends some plausibility to the high fatality figures given by *Shi ji* for Warring States period campaigns. Truly massive losses were possible despite the technological limitations of the age.

86. *Yun meng chronology* in Ma Feibai, "Yun meng qin jian da shi ji ji chuan," p. 71. The capture of Yan was recorded in 279 B.C. by *Shi ji,* ch. 5, *qin ben ji,* p. 213, and ch. 15, *liu guo nian biao,* p. 742.

87. *Shi ji*, ch. 5, *qin ben ji*, p. 213, ch. 40, *chu shi jia*, p. 1735, and ch. 15, *liu guo nian biao*, p. 742, report the fall of Ying to Qin in 278 B.C. The new commandery was designated *nan* (south) *jun*.

88. In its broad strategic pattern, this campaign anticipates that of Khubilai Khan's conquest of the Southern Song a millennium and a half later; in both offensives the main push came down the Han, with a subsidiary thrust out of Sichuan down the Yangtze. See Morris Rossabi, *Khubilai Khan* (Berkeley: University of California Press, 1988), pp. 82–89.

89. *Shi ji*, ch. 5, *qin ben ji*, p. 213. The *Yun meng chronology* records an attack on a mountain, but its name is not completely legible. Ma Feibai, "Yun meng qin jian da shi ji ji chuan," pp. 66–92, believes it to be Wu Mountain, although Huang Shengzhang ("Yun meng qin jian 'bian nian ji' di li yu li shi wen ti," p. 77) is less certain.

90. The passage in *Shi ji*, ch. 6, *qin shi huang ben ji*, pp. 278–282 (known as *guo qin lun*, or "On the Faults of Qin"), makes it unambiguonsly clear that in the early Han, statesmen looking back on the Warring States period saw the annexation of Sichuan and the Han valley by Qin as the turning point in the protracted struggle toward unification. Regarding the delay before that took place, an analogy from chess may be pertinent, i.e., Capablanca's adage noting that the hardest task for any player is to win a won game.

91. The *chen cang dao* (Granary Road) and the *mi cang dao* (Rice Granary Road).

92. A recent overview of Dujiangyan is by Deng Zixin and Tian Shang, "Shi lun du jiang yan jing jiu bu shuai di yuan yin," *Zhong guo shi yan jiu*, no. 3 (1986): 101–110.

93. Yang Xiangkui, "Zhong guo gu dai di shui li jia — li bing," *Wen shi zhe*, no. 3 (1961): 27–28; and Yu Quanyu, "Bao ping kou he tuo jiang shi li bing zhi qian kai zuo di," *Li shi yan jiu*, no. 1 (1978): 95–96. The latter scholar has spent half a lifetime reinterpreting folklore to argue that the Kaiming kings inaugurated Dujiangyan as a link between the Min and Tuo Rivers. See also his "Er lang qin long di shen hua yu kai ming zao ping kou di shi shi," *Si chuan wen wu*, no. 2 (1988): 38–44. But the hazy case for a Kaiming antecedent to Li Bing is unsupported archaeologically. A convincing counter to Yu Quanyu is argued by Tian Shang and Deng Zixin in "Tuo jiang, mo shui, li dui kao bian," *Li shi di li*, no. 5 (1987): 70–75.

94. See Yang Xiangkui, "Zhong guo gu dai di shu li jia — li bing," pp. 23–31, 62. Yang attempts to reconcile scraps of information from *Shi ji*, ch. 29, *he qu shu*, p. 1407; *Hua yang guo zhi*, ch. 3, *shu zhi*, p. 303; and a fragment of *Feng su tong yi* (Ying shao, comp; Wang Liqi, ed,; Beijing: Zhong hua shu ju, 1981) preserved in *Shui jing zhu*, ch. 33, *jiang shui*, p. 415.

95. *Feng su tong yi*, pp. 583–584, reported that Li Bing worked at the behest of King Zhao, which was accepted by annotators of *Shi ji*, ch. 29, *he qu shu*, p. 1407. But *Hua yang guo zhi* placed the events later, within the reign of King Xiaowen, i.e., after 250 B.C. See also Xie Zhongliang, "Guan yu du jiang yan li shi di liang ge wen ti," *Si chuan da xue xue bao*, no. 3 (1975): 78–79, 22.

96. *Hua yang guo zhi*, ch. 3, *shu zhi*, p. 31.

97. There are toponymic problems regarding the bluffs at Lidui, and the name of the river that some ancient sources give as the Mo, rather than calling it the Min. Geographic details of just what Li Bing is supposed to have accomplished are straightened out by Zhang Xunliao, "Li bing zuo li dui di wei zhi he bao ping kou xing cheng di nian dai xin tao," *Zhong guo shi yan jiu*, no. 4 (1982); and by Tian Shang and Deng Zixin, "Tuo jiang, mo shui, li dui kao bian," pp. 70–75.

98. *Hua yang guo zhi*, ch. 3, *shi zhi*, p. 33.

99. *Shi ji*, ch. 28, *feng chan shu*, pp. 1372–1373. He also erected a shrine at Du Mountain. Luo Kaiyu extols Li Bing's political acumen in "Lun du jiang yan yu shu wen hua di guan xi," *Si chuan wen wu*, no. 2 (1988): 32–37.

100. The story is transmitted by a fragment of *Feng su tong yi* included in *Shui jing zhu*, ch. 33, *jiang shui*, p. 415. Lest the custom of "marrying" the river be thought of as primitive or exotic, we may recall a medieval Venetian counterpart, Christianity notwithstanding, whereby the Doge would personally take the sea as his bride in a sumptuous annual state ceremony. This went on for centuries, in a city then the commercial capital of the Mediterranean world.

101. Yang Xiangkui explores the notion that Li Erlang may have been an adoptive son of Li Bing, in "Li bing yu er lang shen zi xu," *Ze shan ban yue kan* 1, no. 19 (1940): 426–429. Luo Kaiyu dismisses Erlang as a wholly mythical creation, in "Lun du jiang yan yu shu wen hua di guan xi." p. 34. Yu Quanyu thinks Erlang represents a Kaiming precursor to Li Bing, not his successor, but that later commentators obscured this fact. See "Er lang qin long di shen hua yu kai ming zao ping kou di shi shi," pp. 38–44. The state cult of Li Bing honored him with a statue, used as a water-level marker, and set in the Min River during the Eastern Han dynasty. See Si chuan sheng guan xian wen jiao ju, "Du jiang yan chu tu dong han li bing shi xiang," *Wen wu*, no. 7 (1974): 27–28; and Wang Wencai, "Dong han li bing shi xiang yu du jiang yan 'shui ce'," also in *Wen wu*, no. 7 (1974): 29–33.

102. See Huang Zhigang, "Da yu yu li bing zhi shu di guan xi"; and Lin Mingjun, "Si chuan zhi shui zhe yu shui shen," both in *Shuo wen yue kan* no. 9 (1943).

103. Luo Kaiyu. "Lun du jiang yan yu shu wen hua di guan xi," pp. 32–37.

104. *Hua yang guo zhi*, ch. 3, *shu zhi*, pp. 35, 39.

105. *Guang zhou ji* is the oldest extant text on King Anyang. His story is also recorded in *Shui jing zhu*, ch. 37, *ye yu he*, pp. 458–459; in *Jiao zhou wai yu ji*, and in the Vietnamese history *Da yue shi ji* (Ngo Si Lien, *Dai viet su ky toan thu*). Secondary treatments of this material include Xu Zhongshu, "'Jiao zhou wai yu ji' shu wang zi an yang wang shi yi jian zheng," *Si chuan da xue xue bao cong kan*, no. 5 (1980); and Leonard Aurousseau, "Le Premier Conquete chinoise des pays annamites," *Bulletin de l'Ecole Française d'Extreme-Orient*, no. 23 (1923): pp. 137–264.

106. Wang Youpeng discussed archaeological aspects of the Shu shift southward in "Si chuan jian wei xian ba shu mu fa jue jian bao," *Kao gu yu wen wu*, no. 3 (1984): 18–21; and "Jian wei ba shu mu di fa jue yu shu ren di nan qian," *Kao gu*, no. 12 (1984): 1114–1117. There is also Kuang Yuanying et al., "Si chuan jian wei jin jing xiang ba shu tu keng mu qing li jian bao," *Wen wu*, no. 5 (1990): 68–75.

107. Yu Haoliang, "Si chuan pei ling di qin shi huang er shi liu nian tong ge," *Kao gu*, no. 1 (1976): 21–23, examines the inscription on one such bronze halberd blade. It is dated at the twenty-sixth year of the First Emperor's reign.

108. Xu Guang annotation to *Shi ji*, ch. 6, *qin shi huang ben ji*, p. 233.

109. Here is but a hint of a Sichuan connection. The *huang* came from Tai Huang, an alternative designation for Ren Huang, discussed in Chapter 2 with reference to this figure's special place in the foundation myths of Sichuan. The documentary source is *Shi ji*, ch. 6, *qin shi huang ben ji*, p. 236.

110. Thirty-six is the number of commanderies listed in the Qin empire, but enumerating and identifying each commandery runs into problems. None of the discrepancies directly affects the present inquiry into the Shu, Ba, and Han commanderies. Studies include Zeng Zhaoxuan, "Qin jun kao," *Ling nan xue bao*, no. 2 (1947): 121–140; and Shi Zhimian, "Qin san shi liu jun you nei shi kao," *Da lu za zhi*, no. 11 (1951): 5, 12.

111. This was the plot of Lao Ai and his retainers, in *Shi ji*, ch. 6, *qin shi huang ben ji*, p. 227. The *Hua yang guo zhi*, ch. 3, *shu zhi*, p. 33, describes those sent to Shu by the First Emperor as *hao jia*, a term sometimes translated as "courageous braves" or even "knight errants."

112. *Shi ji*, ch. 85, *lu bu wei lie zhuan*, p. 2512.

113. The source for this is *Tai ping yu lan*, ch. 166, quoting a lost history of Shu, *Shu ji* as in Tong Enzheng, *Gu dai di ba shu*, pp. 158 with notes, p. 169. See also Gu Jiegang, *Lun ba shu yu zhong yuan di guan xi* (Chengdu: Si chuan ren min chu ban she, 1981), pp. 84–90.

114. For example, the essay *Guo qin lun* ("On the Faults of Qin") by Jia Yi (in *Shi ji*, ch. 6, *qin shi huang ben ji*, pp. 278–282), a set piece in literary anthologies and school curricula.

115. The Great Wall on every modern tourist's route near Beijing of course is a product of Ming times, erected in an entirely different location from the Qin barrier. On the recent vicissitudes of Dujiangyan, there is Shen Guozheng, "Du jiang yan di bian qian," *Si chuan da xue xue bao*, no. 4 (1979): 101–106.

Chapter Six

1. At the outset of the Han dynasty, only some 20–30 percent of the registered population remained in their home areas, according to Sima Qian, *Shi ji* (Beijing: Zhong hua shu ju, 1972), ch. 18, *gao zu gong chen ho zhe nian biao*, p. 877.

2. Guo Xingwen, "Qin wang yuan yin xin tan," *Wen bo*, no. 2 (1988), is a thoughtful essay exploring the interaction of inevitable and chance factors in the fall of Qin.

3. *Shi ji*, ch. 89, *zhang er chen yu lie zhuan*, p. 2576; ch. 48, *chen she shi jia*, p. 1955; Xun Yue, *Han ji* (Taibei: Shang wu yin shu guan, 1973), ch. 2, pp. 10–11.

4. *Shi ji*, ch. 48, *chen she shi jia*, pp. 1960–1961.

5. *Shi ji*, ch. 8, *gao zu ben ji*, pp. 341–394, and its counterpart in *Han shu* (ch. 1, *gao di ji*, pp. 1–84) are the sources for most of the following narrative on the rise of Liu Bang, the Han dynasty founder.

6. The title king of Han is specifically derived from the Han River, according to commentary to *Shi ji*, ch. 8, *gao zu ben ji*, pp. 365–366.

7. *Shi ji*, ch. 8, *gao zu ben ji*, p. 365; *Han shu*, ch. 1a, *gao di ji*, p. 28; Chang Ju, *Hua yang guo zhi* (Shanghai: Shang wu yin shu guan, 1938), ch. 2, *han zhong zhi*. The last source gives the size of the king of Han's fief as thirty-one counties (*xian*) in Ba and Shu and goes on to say that Tian Shu, his regional governor at Hanzhong, administered twenty counties.

8. *Han shu*, ch. 1a, *gao di ji*, p. 45.

9. *Shi ji*, ch. 7, *xiang yu ben ji*, p. 316.

10. *Shi ji*, ch. 16, *qin chu zhi ji yue biao*, p. 773.

11. Liu Bang's general Han Xin tried to desert along a Daba Mountain byway called the Granary Road (*mi cang dao*), but he was overtaken and arrested by another aide, Xiao He. See Chen Xianyuan, "'Mi cang dao' kao lue," *Wen bo*, no.1 (1988): 40–43.

12. Liu Bang's aide Han Xin devised the counterattack strategy. The burning of the corduroy road (*jian dao*) was proposed by another advisor. Ban Gu, *Han shu* (Beijing: Zhong hua shu ju, 1975), ch. 1a, *gao di ji*, pp. 29–30, reports the incidents.

13. *Hua yang guo zhi*, ch. 1, *ba zhi*, p. 3.

14. *Han shu*, ch. 1a, *gao di ji*, p. 31, states that Liu Bang's force emerged from the mountains via the old route at Yong and seized Chencang, the name of which implies that stocks of grain were stored there. Yong and Chencang are located near present Baoji, in western Shaanxi. Hisamura Yukari identified the route of the "old road" in "Shin kan jidai no nyu shoku ro ni tsuite," *Toyo Gakuho* 38, no. 3 (1955): 68–106. Making use of inscriptional evidence, Guo Yingzhang concurred in "Bei wei 'shi men ming' kao," *Kao gu yu wen wu*, no. 4 (1983): 104. An on-the-spot authority is Ren Shoufang, writing in "Qin shu jian dao: gu dao, lian yun dao he bao xie dao gai shu," *Bao ji shi yuan xue bao (zhe she)*, no. 4 (1986): 126. Huang Banghong sorts out all the roads to Shu in "Shu dao kao cha shi ling," *Si chuan wen wu*, no. 1 (1988): 11–14.

15. *Shi ji*, ch. 97, *li sheng lu jia lie zhuan*, p. 2695.

16. *Hua yang guo zhi*, ch. 3, *shu zhi*, p. 31.

17. *Han shu*, ch. 24a, *shi huo zhi*, p. 1127.

18. *Han shu*, ch. 1a, *gao di ji*, p. 35.

19. *Shi ji*, ch. 91, *jing bu lie zhuan*, p. 2600.

20. *Shi ji*, ch. 97, *li sheng lu jia lie zhuan*, p. 2695.

21. *Shi ji*, ch. 97, *li sheng lu jia lie zhuan*, p. 2697.

22. Liu Yudong, *Zhong guo xiang qi jiao ke shu* (Beijing: Hua xia chu ban she, 1988), pp. 1–2.

23. *Shi ji*, ch. 52, *xiao xiang guo shi jia*, p. 2014.

24. *Han shu*, ch. 1b, *gao di ji*, p.73.

25. For example, in *Shi ji*, ch. 15, *liu guo nian biao*, p. 686.

26. *Han shu*, ch. 27d, *wu xing zhi*, p. 1457.

27. *Shi ji*, ch. 10, *xiao wen di ji*, p. 421, notes the granting of estate incomes to sixty-eight soldiers who had followed Liu Bang to Shu and the Han region. *Han shu*, ch. 1b, *gao di ji*, p. 73, records the lifetime tax exemption for veterans of Shu and Han service. *Shi ji*, ch. 98, *fu jin kuai cheng lie zhuan*, p. 2711, contains a similar reference. The Pingzhou estate award is noted in *Shi ji*, ch. 18, *gao zu gong chen hou zhe nian biao*, pp. 963–964.

28. Xun Yue, *Han ji*, ch. 2, p. 13; *Han shu*, ch. 1a, *gao di ji*, p.31.

29. *Hua yang guo zhi,* ch. 1, *ba zhi,* p.3.

30. *Shi ji,* ch. 17, *han xing yi lai zhu hou wang biao,* pp. 801–803; *Han shu,* ch. 14, *zhu hou wang biao,* pp. 393–394; Tao Tien-yi, "Vassal Kings and Marquises of the Former Han Dynasty," *Zhong yang yan jiu yuan: li shi yu yan yan jiu suo ji kan 46,* part 1 (1974). Zhou Jiuxiang examines the special role of Sichuan in the early Han, in "Xi han qian qi si chuan di qu gong gu xin xing feng jian zhi di dou zheng," *Si chuan da xue xue bao,* no. 3 (1975): 63–71.

31. *Hua yang guo zhi,* ch.3, *shu zhi,* p. 36.

32. The empirewide total that year was 59,594,978, a total derived from the sum of the figures for all commanderies as listed in *Han shu,* ch. 28, *di li zhi.*

33. *Hua yang guo zhi,* ch. 3, *shu zhi,* p. 31. Guanghan is also the site of the archaic Shu center at Sanxingdui. But did Liu Bang know that?

34. Later still a third Shu commandery, Jianwei, was formed in the south.

35. *Han shu,* ch. 28a, *di li zhi,* pp. 1597, 1603.

36. Examples of early Han interment in Shu are reported by Wang Youpeng, et. al., "Si chuan mian zhu xian xi han mu ban mu fa jue jian bao," *Kao gu,* no. 4 (1983): 296–300; Zhao Dianzeng, "Si chuan mian yang fa xian mu ban mu," *Kao gu,* no. 4 (1983): 372–373; and Hu Changyu, "Cheng du shi yang xi han mu guo mu," *Kao gu yu wen wu,* no.2 (1983): 26–27.

37. On the boat graves, there is Si chuan sheng bo wu guan, *Si chuan chuan guan zang fa jue bao gao* (Beijing: Wen wu chu ban she, 1960), passim. Han graves in both Ba and Shu often include half-tael coins, which have aided the task of dating.

38. Other Han period graves in Ba are reported by Chen Lijing, "Si chuan wu xing kuang jia bei han dai zhuan yao shi jue ji," *Kao gu yu wen wu,* no. 2 (1980): 61–63; Hu bei sheng bo wu guan, "Yi chang qian ping zhan guo liang han mu," *Kao gu xue bao,* no. 2 (1976): 136; Gong Tingwan et al., "Chong qing shi nan an qu di liang zuo xi han tu keng mu," *Kao gu yu wen wu,* no. 7 (1982): 28–29; and Jiang Wanxi, "Pei ling xian yi jia bei xi han mu fa xian jian bao," *Kao gu yu wen wu,* no. 5 (1990): 44–49.

39. *Hou han shu,* ch. 86, *xi nan yi lie zhuan,* p. 2843.

40. *Hua yang guo zhi,* ch. 1, *ba zhi,* p. 11, with commentary by Xu Zhongshu in *Lun ba shu wen hua* (Chengdu: Si chuan ren min chu ban she, 1981), pp. 29–30.

41. One late *chun yu* drum is reported from a rural location in Henan province, by Xia Mailing and Li Yunsheng in "Deng xian yu shan miao chun yu ji xiang guan wen ti," *Kao gu,* no. 10 (1989): 924–926, 951. The authors

consider it to be a Ba product, although showing some Han Chinese characteristics.

42. *Han shu*, ch. 22, *li yue zhi* (2), p. 1074, with commentary.

43. *Yan tie lun xiao zhu* (Huan Kuan, comp.; Taibei: Shu jie shu ju, 1970), ch. 2.9, *ci quan*, p. 65.

44. ch. 12, *xu zhi*, pp. 217–221.

45. He was also known as Luo Changgong and is mentioned in *Shi ji*, ch. 26, *li shu* (4), p. 1260. Lu Zijian, "Ba jun luo xia hong," *Li shi zhi shi*, no. 4 (1980): 22–24, is a reappraisal of Luo from the standpoint of Sichuanese provincial pride.

46. As in the *Jin shu* biography of Li Xiong, a reputed Zong, as cited by Lin Jiyou, in "Cheng du wai nan cheng han mu zhu shi tan," *Si chuan wen wu*, no. 6 (1989): 31–32.

47. Hisamura Yukari discussed the Han practice of banishment to Shu in "Zen kan no sen shoku kei ni tsuite," *Toyo Gakuho* 37, no. 2 (1954), pp. 95–125. The sources for the exile imposed on the king of Huainan are *Shi ji*, ch. 10, *xiao wen ben ji*, p. 426; and ch. 118, *huai nan heng shan lie zhuan*, p. 3079. There is a similar instance of aristocratic banishment mentioned in *Shi ji*, ch. 90, *wei bao peng yue lie zhuan*, p. 2594.

48. *Shi ji*, ch. 122, *ku li lie zhuan*, p. 3154. Unfortunately, no dates are available on when these two officials held office and perpetrated their misdeeds, nor are details supplied on Feng Dang's alleged tyranny.

49. Fung Yu-lan, *A History of Chinese Philosophy* (Princeton, N.J.: Princeton University Press, 1952) vol. 1, pp. 403–406, and vol. 2, pp. 7–87.

50. *Han shu*, ch. 89, *xun li zhuan*, pp. 3625–3627.

51. *Hua yang guo zhi*, ch. 3, *shu zhi*, p. 31, gives the figure of eighteen students.

52. *Hua yang guo zhi*, ch. 3, *shu zhi*, p. 31. By this comparison the text reveals how, in scholarship, the central plains continued to set the standard to which Sichuan aspired. No particularly Sichuanese trends in thought can be identified at this time. However, odd aspects of central plains lore were relocated in Shu. Regarding Confucius's school, a local claim was made to the effect that one of the master's original disciples, a certain Shang Qushang, had been a native of Shu. According to late tradition he was supposedly buried in a county near Chengdu. There is a brief discussion by Shi Zhimian in "Du shi ji hui zhu kao deng zha ji," *Da lu za zhi*, no. 3 (1977): 143.

53. Ch. 89, *xun li lie zhuan*, pp. 3625–3627.

54. Yan Buke pointed out the general continuity of bureaucratic prac-

tice from Qin to Han times in "Qin zheng, han zheng yu wen li, ru sheng," *Li shi yan jiu*, no. 3 (1986): 143–159.

55. *Hua yang guo zhi*, ch. 3, *shu zhi*, p. 31.

56. Chen Xianyuan, "'Mi cang dao' kao lue," pp. 40–43; Lan Yong, "Mi cang dao di ta cha yu kao zheng," *Si chuan wen wu*, no. 2 (1989): 12–17.

57. A detailed survey of the Bao-Xie route was provided by Qin Zhong-xing et al. in "Bao xie jian dao diao cha ji," *Kao gu yu wen wu*, no. 4 (1980): 42–47. This material supplements Lin Zhao et al., "Shu dao kao," *Wen shi za zhi* 3, nos. 5–6 (1944): 4–19. Guo Yingzhang in "Bei wei 'shi men ming' kao," pp. 94–104, presents additional material in the form of later inscriptions along the route.

58. *Shi ji*, ch. 29, *he qu shu*, p. 1411.

59. *Han shu*, ch. 24b, *shi huo zhi*, p. 1172.

60. *Shi ji*, ch. 129, *huo zhi lie zhuan*, p. 3267, notes in the general context of economic relations that the old Chu area of western Hubei was in communication with the Wu gorge region and Ba to the west. Some basis thus existed for activating the Yangtze route on a larger scale.

61. *Hua yang guo zhi*, ch. 1 *ba zhi*, p. 11; and ch. 3, *shu zhi*, p. 37.

62. *Tong yue*, literary fragment quoted by Chen Zugui and Zhu Zizhen, eds., *Zhong guo cha ye li shu zi liao xuan ji* (Beijing: Nong ye chu ban she, 1981), p. 202. See also Chen Zugui, "Zhong guo cha ye shi lue," *Jin ling xue bao* 10, nos. 1–2, (1940): 189–195.

63. *Shi ji*, ch. 129, *huo zhi lie zhuan*, p. 3260.

64. Tang Jiahong, "Ba shi san ti," *Si xiang zhan xian*, no. 2 (1981): 25–27.

65. Wu Jin, comp., *Shen nong ben cao jing* (Beijing: Ren min wei sheng chu ban she, 1983), ch. 1–3, pp. 6–10, 21, 26–27, 44, 75–79, 97–99, 102–105, 114–119, 131–137.

66. *Han shu*, ch. 28a, *di li zhi*, pp. 1598–1599, notes the places where an iron commissioner was resident. The treasury bureau charged with salt and iron control was set up in 119 B.C., according to *Shi ji*, ch. 30, *ping jun shu*, p. 1429.

67. *Shi ji*, ch. 129, *huo zhi lie zhuan*, pp. 3277–3278, reports the fortunes of the Zhuo family and Cheng Zheng. The success of such businessmen engendered opposition at the capital by those reluctant to see private individuals controlling strategic commodities too closely and exploiting the labor of uprooted individuals. *Yan tie lun* records a first century B.C. palace debate by economic advisors on salt and iron monopoly management, an ongoing issue in Han politics.

68. Li Jinghua, "Han dai tie nong qi ming wen shi shi," *Kao gu*, no. 1 (1974): 62–63, illustrates a *cha*, or hoe, bearing this factory mark. There are as yet no archaeological data on the actual mining and smithy sites around Linqiong.

69. *Han shu*, *Hou han shu*, and *Hua yang guo shi* all mention Nanshan at Qiongdu as producing copper or bronze (*tong*). The mine's actual whereabouts have long been a mystery, but a convincing case for its identification has been made by Liu Shixu in "Han 'qiong du nan shan chu tong' di kao," *Si chuan wen wu*, no. 6 (1989): 33–34, and in Liu Shixu and Zhang Zhengning, "Sichuan xi chang shi dong ping cun han dai lian tong yi chi di diao cha," *Kao gu*, no. 12 (1990): 1069–1075.

70. Cai Kui, "Lun gong yuan qian 109 nian yi qian di yun nan qing tong qi zhi zao ye," *Shi xue lun cong*, no. 3 (1988).

71. Fan Guijie, "Si chuan pei ling xi han tu keng mu fa jue jian bao," *Kao gu*, no. 4 (1984): 338–344. Other Han dynasty burials containing bronze and iron objects have been well documented in the following articles: Bao xing xian wen hua guan, "Si chuan bao xing chu tu di xi han tong qi," *Kao gu*, no. 2 (1978): 139–140; Wang Yaoqi, "Si chuan xi chang li zhou fa xian di han mu," *Kao gu*, no. 5 (1980); and Wang Youpeng et al., "Si chuan mian zhu xian xi han mu ban mu fa jue jian bao," pp. 296–300.

72. *Han shu*, ch. 28a, *di li zhi*, p. 1603. A Ba saltworks north of the Yangtze at Wuxi had a natural market in Hubei, a salt-deficit area. Transport would have been along a corduroy road paralleling the Daning River through highland country, suggests Ran Ruiquan in "Da ning he gu jian dao chu tan," *Si chuan wen wu*, no. 2 (1989): 18–19.

73. Tong Enzheng, *Gu dai di ba shu* (Chengdu: Si chuan ren min chu ban she, 1979), p. 161; Wu Tianying "Zhong guo jing yan kai zhan shi er san shi," *Li shi yan jiu*, no. 5 (1986): 123–139.

74. *Hua yang guo zhi*, ch. 3, *shu zhi*, p. 32; also *Shu wang ben ji*, p. 4.

75. For example, in the odes describing Chengdu by Yang Xiong and Zuo Si, each entitled *Shu du fu*.

76. Fang Shiming studied the works commissioner's duties in "Han dai di 'shu jun gong guan' he 'guang han jun gong guan'," *Li shi zhi shi*, no. 5 (1980): 23–26.

77. Yu Weizhao and Li Jiahao, "Ma wang dui yi hao han mu chu tu qi qi zhi di zhu wen ti," *Kao gu*, no. 6 (1975): 344–348.

78. Commentary on *Han shu*, ch. 28a, *di li zhi*, p. 1603.

79. *Shi ji*, ch. 129, *huo zhi lie zhuan*, p. 3272.

80. *Shi ji*, ch. 29, *he qu shu*, p. 1411.

81. *Shi ji*, ch. 117, *si ma xiang ru lie zhuan*.

82. *Shi ji*, ch. 117, *si ma xiang ru lie zhuan*, pp. 2999–3001.

83. *Shi ji*, ch. 129, *huo zhi lie zhuan*, pp. 3277–3278.

84. *Shi ji*, ch. 117, *si ma xiang ru lie zhuan*, p. 3001.

85. *Shi ji*, ch. 117, *si ma xiang ru lie zhuan*, p. 3002.

86. *Shi ji*, ch. 113, *nan yue lie zhuan*, p. 2975.

87. Liu Shixu, "Han 'qiong du nan shan chu tong' di kao," pp. 33–34.

88. *Shi ji*, ch. 116, *xi nan yi lie zhuan*, p. 2993.

89. Recent treatments of the Han push southward are Xiao Fan, "Qin han shi qi zhong guo dui nan fang di jing ying," *Shi yuan*, no. 4 (1973): 17–54; and Lao Gan, "Xiang jun zang ge he ye lang di guan xi," *Lao gan xue shu lun wen ji jia bian* (Taibei: zhong yang yan jiu yuan, 1976), pp. 589–604.

90. *Shi ji*, ch. 116, *xi nan yi lie zhuan*, p. 2994.

91. *Shi ji*, ch. 116, *xi nan yi lie zhuan*, pp. 2996–2997; *Hua yang guo zhi*, ch. 3, *shu zhi*, pp. 32–35. Sima Xiangru's campaigns have been studied by two French scholars: Emile Gaspardone, "Sseu-me Siang-jou chez les Barbares," *Sinologica* [Basel] 6, no. 3 (1960) and 7, no. 1 (1962); and Yves Hervouet in the second chapter of *Sseu-ma Siang-jou* (Paris: Presses universitaires de France, 1964).

92. The post is mentioned in Sichuan inscriptions in the compendium *Li shi*, and interpreted by Huang Liuzhu in "Han bei suo jian 'dao qiao yuan' kao," *Wen bo*, no. 6 (1988): 50–53.

93. *Shi ji*, ch. 112, *ping jing hou zhu fu lie zhuan*, pp. 2949–2950, records a high level remonstrance against the heavy toll of campaigning in the southwest of the empire, with its deleterious effect on the people of Ba and Shu.

94. *Shi ji*, ch. 116, *xi nan yi lie zhuan*, p. 2995.

95. *Shi ji*, ch. 30, *ping jun shu*, p. 1421.

96. Curiously, neither *Shi ji*, ch. 116, *xi nan yi lie zhuan*, ch. 117, *si ma xiang ru lie zhuan*, nor the account in *Han shu*, ch. 95, *xi nan yi liang yue chao xian zhuan*, relate these events specifically to the Shu governance of Wen Weng.

97. Chu T'ung-tsu proposed this view of Zhuo Wangsun's submissive humiliation in *Han Social Structure* (Seattle: University of Washington Press. 1972), pp. 87–88.

98. *Shi ji*, ch. 116, *xi nan yi lie zhuan*, pp. 2995–2996, lists the aides' names as Wang Ranyu, Bo Shichang, and Lu Yueren, but ch. 117, *si ma xiang ru lie zhuan*, pp. 3046–3047, substitutes Hu Chongguo for Bo Shichang. There may have been more than three officials on the staff assisting Sima Xiangru.

99. Geographic particulars of this mission are examined by Wen Jiang, "Dian yue kao — zao qi zhong yin guan xi di tan suo," *Zhong hua wen shi lun cong*, no. 2 (1980): 61–66. The existence of a route has never since been conclusively proven, or disproven, despite long controversy. See Ji Xianlin, "Zhong guo can si yu ru yin du wen ti di chu bu yan jiu," *Li shi yan jiu*, no. 4 (1955): 51–94; Rao Zongyi, "Shu bu yu Chinapatta — lun zao qi zhong, yin mian zhi jiao tong," *Zhong yang yan jiu yuan li shi yu yan yan jiu suo ji kan*, 45 (1972): 561–584; Schuyler van R. Cammann, "Archaeological Evidence for Chinese Contacts with India During the Han Dynasty," *Sinologica* 5, no. 1 (1956): 1–19; Sang Xiuyun, "Shu bu qiong zhu chuan zhi da xia lu jing di li ce," *Zhong yang yan jiu yuan li shi yu yan yan jiu suo ji kan* 41, no. 1 (1969): 67–86; Chen Qian, "Preliminary Research on the Ancient Passage to India from Sichuan via Yunnan and Burma," *Social Sciences in China* [Beijing] 2, no. 2 (1981): 113–148; and Mao Ruifen, "Gu dao mi zong," *Si chuan wen wu*, no. 1 (1988): 23–25, 14.

100. *Shi ji*, ch. 116, *xi nan yi lie zhuan*, pp. 2995–2996.

101. *Han shu*, ch. 28a, *di li zhi*, p. 1600; and *Hua yang guo zhi*, ch. 3, *shu zhi*, p. 38. Burials in the northwestern areas include Han coins, but otherwise follow native, non-Han custom. See Ding Zuchun et al., "Za gu he xia yu xi han yan mu diao cha jian bao," *Si chuan wen wu*, no. 2 (1989): 76–79.

102. *Shi ji*, ch. 117, *si ma xiang ru lie zhuan*, pp. 3047 and 3051, record the frontier. The Mo and Ruo are labeled, respectively, the Dadu and Yalong Rivers on most modern maps. Both flow south, then turn east. Sima Xiangru no doubt meant the southward-flowing portions as marking the western border.

103. Han period graves from hilly areas west and southwest of the Chengdu plain are documented in the following papers: Wang Yaoqi, "Si chuan xi chang li zhou fa xian di han mu," pp. 405–416; Bao xing xian wen hua guan, "Si chuan bao xing chu tu di xi han tong qi," pp. 139–140; *Kao gu*, no. 2 (1978): and Zhao Dianzeng et al., "Si chuan a bei zhou fa xian han mu," *Wen wu*, no. 11 (1976): 90–93.

104. Fan Ye, *Hou Han shu* (Beijing: Zhong hua shu ju, 1973), ch. 86, *nan man xi nan yi lie zhuan*, pp. 2857–2858.

105. *Shi ji*, ch. 117, *si ma xiang ru lie zhuan*, p. 3046.

Bibliography

Transliteration of Chinese names and titles takes the modern standard form, *pinyin*. Alternate forms are given for Chinese authors who have published in languages other than Chinese and whose names are best known by variant spellings. The Japanese language entries are in Hepburn romanization.

Classical Sources

Ban Gu (班固). 漢書 (*Han shu* [*The Book of the Han*]), 5 vols. Beijing: Zhong hua shu ju, 1975.

Chang Ju (常璩). 华陽國志 (*Hua yang guo zhi* [*An Account of the Country South of Mt. Hua*]). Shanghai: Shang wu yin shu guan, 1938.

Chen Qiyou (陳奇猷), ed. 韓非子集釋 (*Han fei zi ji shi* [*The Book of Master Han Fei with Collected Notes*]). Taibei: He luo tu shu chu ban she, 1974.

Chen Shou (陳壽). 三國志 (*San guo zhi* [*Chronicle of the Three States*]). Beijing: Zhong hua shu ju, 1972.

爾雅注疏(*Er ya zhu shu* [*The Annotated Er Ya Dictionary*]), in 十三經注疏 (*Shi san jing zhu shu* [*The Thirteen Classics, Annotated*]), 2 vols. Beijing: Zhong hua shu ju, 1980.

Fan Ye (范曄). 後漢書 (*Hou han shu* [*Book of the Latter Han*]), 6 vols. Beijing: Zhong hua shu ju, 1973.

Gao Heng (高亨), ed. 商君書注譯 (*Sang jun shu zhu yi* [*The Book of Lord Shang, Annotated*]). Beijing: Zhong hua shu ju, 1974.

Gu Zuyu (雇祖禹). 讀史方輿紀要 (*Du shi fang yu ji yao* [*Geographic Notes from a Reading of History*]), 6 vols. Taibei: Le tian chu ban she, 1973.

Guo Pu (郭璞), comp. 山海經 (*Shan hai jing* [*The Classic of Mountains and Seas*]). Taibei: Zhong hua shu ju, 1976.

國語 (*Guo yu* [*Discourses on the States*]). Shanghai: Shang hai gu ji chu ban she, 1978.

Guo Yundao (郭允蹈), comp. 蜀鑑 (*Shu jian* [*A Mirror of Shu*]). Taibei: Shang wu yin shu guan, 1973.

Han Gaoxiu (漢高誘), ed. 淮南子 (*Huai nan zi* [*The Book of Master Huai-nan*]). Taibei: Shi jie shu zu, 1974.

Huan Kuan (桓寬), comp.; Wang Liqi (王利器), ed. 鹽鉄論校注 (*Yan tie lun xiao zhu* [*Discourses of Salt and Iron, Annotated*]). Taibei: Shi jie shu ju, 1970.

Li Daoyuan (麗道元), comp. 水經注 (*Shui jing zhu* [*Notes on the Classic of Waters*]). Taibei: Shi jie shu ju, 1974.

Lin Yin (林尹), ed. 周禮今註今譯 (*Zhou li jin zhu jin yi*, Modern notes on the rites of Zhou). Taibei: Shang wu yin shu guan, 1979.

Lin Zongtong (李宗侗), ed. 春秋左傳今註今譯 (*Chun qiu zuo zhuan jin zhu jin yi* [*The Spring and Autumn Annals with Zuo's Commentary and Modern Annotation*]), 3 vols; cited as *Zuo Zhuan*. Taibei: Shang wu yin shu guan, 1976.

Liu Lin (劉琳), ed.; Chang Ju (常璩), comp. 華陽國志校注 (*Hua yang guo zhi xiao zhu* [*An Annotated Account of the Country South of Mt. Hua*]). Chengdu: Ba shu shu she, 1984.

Liu Xiang (劉向), comp. 戰國策 (*Zhan guo ce* [*Chronicles of the Warring States*]). Shanghai: Shang hai gu ji chu ban she. 1978.

Lu Buwei (呂不偉) (traditional attribution). 呂氏春秋 (*Lu shi chun qiu* [*Lu's Spring and Autumn Annals*]). Taibei: Zhong hua shu ju, 1975.

Lu Yuangqun (盧元夋), ed. 新序今註今譯 (*Xin xu jin zhu jin yi* [*Modern Notes on the New Preface*]). Taibei: Shang wu yin shu guan, 1975.

Luo Bi (羅泌). 路史 (*Lu shi* [*The Path of History*]). Taibei: Zhong hua shu ju, 1975.

Ma Chiying (馬持盈), ed. 詩經今註今譯 (*Shi jing jin zhu jin yi* [*Modern Notes on the Book of Songs*]). Taibei: Shang wu yin shu guan, 1982.

Ngo Si Lien (吳仕連). 大越史記全書 (*Dai Viet su ky toan thu* [*The Complete Historical Records of Vietnam*]). (Toyo Bunko manuscript).

Qu Wanli (屈萬里), ed. 尚書今註今譯 (*Shang shu jin zhu jin yi* [*The Book of Documents with Modern Annotation*]). Taibei: Shang wu yin shu guan, 1979.

Qu Yuan (屈原); Fu Xiren (傅錫壬), ed. 楚辭讀本 (*Chu ci du ben* [*Reader in the Songs of Chu*]). Taibei: San min shu ju, 1976.

Ren Yu (任豫), comp. 金牛 ("Jin niu" ["The Golden Cattle"]). In

說郛宛香山堂本 (*Shuo fu*, reprinted as *Wan xiang shan tang ben*), vol. 60. N.p. 1647.

世本八種 (*Shi ben ba zhong* [*Eight Versions of the Book of Generations*]). Shanghai: Shang wu yu yin shu guan, 1957.

Shi Ceyun (史次耘), ed. 孟子今註今譯 (*Meng zi jin zhu jin yi* [*The Classic of Mencius with Modern Annotation*]). Taibei: Shang wu yin shu guan, 1974.

Sima Qian (司馬遷). 史記 (*Shi ji* [*Historical Records*]), 6 vols. Beijing: Zhong hua shu ju, 1972.

Wu Jin, comp. (吳晉). 神農本草經 (*Shen nong ben cao jing* [*The Herbal Classic of the Deity of Agriculture*]). Beijing: Ren min wei sheng chu ban she, 1983.

Xiong Gongzhe (熊公哲), ed. 荀子今註今譯 (*Xun zi jin zhu jin yi* [*The Classic of Master Xun with Modern Annotation*]). Taibei: Shang wu yin shu guan, 1975.

Xu Shen (許慎). 說文解字 (*Shuo wen jie zi* [*An Explanation of Words*]). Taibei: Yi wen yin shu guan, 1974.

Xun Yue (荀悅). 漢紀 (*Han ji* [*A Record of the Han*]). Taibei: Shang wu yin shu guan, 1973.

Yang Xiong (揚雄) (traditional attribution). 蜀王本紀 (*Shu wang ben ji* [*Basic Annals of the Kings of Shu*]). In 經典集林 (*Jing dian ji lin* [*Collected Forest of Classics*]), vol. 2, no. 5 (Taibei: Yi wen yin shu guan, 1968).

————; Qian Tong (錢侗), ed. 方言箋疏 (*Fang yan jian shu* [*Notes on Dialects*]). Taibei: Wen hai chu ban she, 1967.

————. 蜀都賦 (*Shu du fu* ["Ode on the Capital of Shu"]). Ch. 384 in 欽定四庫全書 (*Qin ding si ku chuan shu*). Taibei: 1972.

Ying Shao (應劭), comp. Wang Liqi (王利器), ed. 風俗通義 (*Feng su tong yi* [*Compendium of Customs*]). Beijing: Zhong hua shu ju, 1981.

竹書紀年補證 (*Zhu shu ji nian bu deng* [*Corrected Text of the Bamboo Annals*]). In 竹書紀年八種 (*Zhu shu ji nian ba zhong* [*Eight Versions of the Bamboo Annals*]). Taibei: Shi jie shu ju, 1977.

Zhu Youzeng (朱右曾), ed. 逸周書集訓校釋 (*Yi zhou shu ji xun jiao shi* [*Collected Annotations on the Lost Book of the Zhou*]). Taibei: Shi jie shu ju, 1980.

Zuo Si (左思). 蜀都賦 (*Shu du fu* ["Ode on the Capital of Shu"]). In Xiao Tong (蕭統), ed. 文選 (*Wen xuan* [*Literary Selections*]). Taibei: Shang wu yin shu guan, 1960.

Zuo zhuan. See Lin Zongtong, ed.

Modern Sources

Frequently Cited Chinese and Japanese Language Serial Publications

重慶師範學院學報 *Chong qing shi fan xue yuan xue bao* [*Journal of the Chongqing Normal Institute*]), Chongqing.

大陸雜誌 (*Da lu za zhi* [*Mainland Magazine*]), Taibei.

江漢考古 (*Jiang han kao gu* [*Yangtze and Han Archaeology*]), Wuhan.

江漢論壇 (*Jiang han lun tan* [*Yangtze and Han Discourse Podium*]).

考古 (*Kao gu* [*Archaeology*]), Beijing.

考古學報 (*Kao gu xue bao* [*Journal of Archaeological Study*]), Beijing.

考古與文物 (*Kao gu yu wen wu* [*Archaeology and Artifacts*]), Xi'an.

歷史地理 (*Li shi di li* [*Historical Geography*]), Shanghai.

歷史研究 (*Li shi yan jiu* [*Historical Research*]), Beijing.

歷史語言研究所集刊 (*Li shi yu yan yan jiu suo ji kan* [*Journal of the Institute of History and Philology, Academia Sinica*]), Taibei.

歷史知識 (*Li shi zhi shi* [*Historical Knowledge*]), Chengdu.

農史研究 (*Nong shi yan jin* [*Agricultural History Research*]), Beijing.

史學集刊 (*Shi zue ji kan* [*Collected Papers in Historical Studies*]), Changchun.

說文月刊 (*Shuo wen yue kan* [*Literary Monthly*]), Chongqing and Chengdu.

四川大學學報 (*Si chuan da xue xue bao* [*Journal of Sichuan University*]), Chengdu.

四川師院學報 (*Si chuan shi yuan xue bao* [*Journal of Sichuan Normal College*]), Chengdu.

四川文物 (*Si chuan wen wu* [*Sichuan artifacts*]), Chengdu.

思想戰綫 (*Si xiang zhan xian* [*Frontline of Thought*]), Kunming.

東洋學報 (*Toyo Gakuho* [*Oriental Studies*]), Tokyo.

文博 (*Wen bo* [*Relics and Museology*]), Xi'an.

文史 (*Wen shi* [*Culture and History*]), Beijing.

文史哲 (*Wen shi zhe* [*Culture, History, and Philosophy*]), Jinan, Shandong.

文物 (*Wen wu* [*Cultural Artifacts*]), Beijing.

禹貢半月刊(*Yu gong ban yue kan* [*Tribute of Yu Bimonthly*]), Beijing.

責善半月刊(*Ze shan ban yue kan* [*Ze shan Bimonthly*]), Chengdu.

中國考古學年會第二次論文集(*Zhong guo kao gu xue hui di er ci nian hui lun wen ji* [*Annual Conference Papers of the Chinese Institute of Archaeology*]), Beijing.

中國歷史文献研究集刊(*Zhong guo li shi wen xian yan jiu ji kan* [*Collected Research on Chinese History and Documents*]), Changsha.

中華文史論叢 (*Zhong hua wen shi lun cong* [*Papers on Chinese Culture and History*]), Shanghai.

中央研究院歷史語言研究所集刊*Zhong yang yan jiu yuan li shi yu yan yan jiu suo* [*Papers of the Academia sinica Institute of History and Philology*]), Taibei.

References

Allan, Sarah. *The Shape of the Turtle: Myth, Art, and Cosmos in Early China.* Albany: State University of New York Press, 1991.

An Zhimin. "Zhong guo shi qian nong ye" ["China's Prehistoric Agriculture"]. *Kao gu xue bao*, no. 4 (1988): 369–381.

Aurousseau, Leonard. "Le Premier Conquete chinoise des pays annamites" ["The First Chinese Conquest of Annam"]. *Bulletin de l'Ecole Francaise d'Extreme-Orient*, no. 23 (1923): 137–264.

Banks, Arthur. *Atlas of Ancient and Medieval Warfare.* New York: Hippocrene, 1982.

"Ba shu wen hua fu tu" ["Appendix of Written Symbols from the Ba-Shu Culture"]. *Shuo wen yue kan* [Chongqing] 3, no. 7 (1942): 11–41.

Bagley, Robert W. "A Shang City in Sichuan Province." *Orientations* 21, 11 (November 1990): 52–67.

———. "Sacrificial Pits of the Shang Period at Sanxingdui in Guanghan county, Sichuan Province". *Arts Asiatique*, 43 (1988): 78–86.

Bao xing xian wen hua guan [Baoxing County Cultural Office]. "Si chuan bao xing chu tu di xi han tong qi" ["Western Han Bronze Implements Unearthed at Baoxing, Sichuan"]. *Kao gu*, no. 2 (1978): 139–140.

Cai Kui. "Lun gong yuan qian 109 nian yi qian di yun nan qing tong qi zhi zao ye" ["A bronze implement dated 109 B.C. from Yunnan"] *Shi xue lun cong* no. 3 (1988).

Cammann, Schuyler van R. "Archaeological Evidence for Chinese Contacts with India During the Han Dynasty." *Sinologica* [Basel] 5, no. 1 (1956).

Cao Gang. "Cheng du chu ti yi pi zhan guo tong qi" ["A Collection of Warring States Period Bronzes Unearthed at Chengdu"]. *Wen wu*, no. 11 (1990): 68–71.

Chang Kwang-chih. *The Archaeology of Ancient China*, 3d ed. New Haven, Conn.: Yale University Press, 1977.

——. *Art, Myth, and Ritual: The Path to Political Authority in Ancient China*. Cambridge, Mass.: Harvard University Press, 1983.

——. *Early Chinese Civilization: Anthropological Perspectives*. Cambridge, Mass.: Harvard University Press, 1976.

Chang Renxia. "Ba xian sha ping ba chu tu zhi shi guan hua xiang yan jiu" ["A Study of the Illustrations on a Stone Coffin Excavated at Shaping Levee, Ba County"]. *Jin ling xue bao* 8, nos. 1–2 (1938): 1–16.

Chen Changyuan. "Cong 'li gui' tan you guan wu wang fa zhou di ji ge wen ti" ["The Li Bronze Vessel and Several Problems Concerning King Wu's Campaign Against Zhou"]. *He nan shi fan xue bao*, no. 4 (1980): pp. 30–37.

Chen Dean et al. "Guang han san xing dui yi chi yi hao ji si keng fa jue jian bao" ["Report on the Excavation of Votary Objects Pit No. 1 at the Sanxingdui, Guanghan Remains"]. *Wen wu*, no. 10 (1987): 1–15.

Chen Jin, "Ru he ping jie qin wang chao zai shu jun di san ci zhen ya" ["How To Explain the Qin Regime's Third Suppression in Shu"]. *Sichuan shi yuan xue bao*, no. 3 (1981): 78–81.

Chen Jinsheng. "'Xia li ba ren' jie" ["An Explanation of the Xiali Ba People"]. *Wen shi*, no. 13 (1982): 175–183.

Chen Lijing. "Si chuan wu xing kuang jia bei han dai zhuan yao shi jue ji" ["Report on a Test Excavation of a Western Han Brick Kiln at Kuangjiabei, Wuxing, Sichuan"]. *Kao gu yu wen wu*, no. 2 (1980): 61–63.

Chen Liqing. "Si chuan e mei xian chu tu yi pi zhan guo qing tong qi" ["A Hoard of Warring States Period Bronze Objects Unearthed at Emei County, Sichuan"]. *Kao gu*, no. 11 (1986): 982–983.

Chen Mengjia. "Shang dai di li xiao ji" ["A Short Note on Shang Period Geography"]. *Yu gong ban yue kan* 7, nos. 6–7 (1937): 101–108.

——. *Yin xu bu ci zong shu* [*Summary of the Oracle Bones from the Yin Ruins*]. Beijing: Zhong guo ke xue yuan kao gu yan jiu suo, 1956.

Chen Mingda. "Bao xie dao shi men ji qi shi ke" ["Shimen on the Bao-Xie Road and Its Stone Inscriptions"]. *Wen wu*, no. 4–5 (1961): 57–61, 30.

Chen Pan. *Chun qiu da shi biao lie guo jue xing ji cun mie biao zhuan yi* [*Compilation of Important Events, Noble Genealogy, and the Fortunes of States During the Spring and Autumn Period*], 7 vols. Taibei: Zhong yang yan jiu yuan li shi yu yan yan jiu suo, 1969.

———. "Chun qiu shu guo" ["The Country of Shu During the Spring and Autumn Period"]. *Da lu za zhi* 32, no. 6 (1966): 167–170.

Chen Qian. "Preliminary Research on the Ancient Passage to India from Sichuan via Yunnan and Burma." *Social Sciences in China* [Beijing] 2, no. 2 (1981): 113–148.

Chen Wenhua. "Zhong guo dao zuo di qi yuan he dong chuan ri ben di lu xian" ["The Origins of Rice Cultivation in China and the Path of Its Spread to Japan"]. *Wen wu*, no. 10 (1989): 24–36.

Chen Xiandan. "Guang han san xing dui yi, er hao keng liang ge wen ti di tan tao" ["A Discussion of Two Problems Regarding Pits No. 1 and 2 at San-xingdui, Guanghan"]. *Wen wu*, no. 5 (1989): 36–38.

———. "Lun guang han san xing dui yi chi di xing zhi" ["On the Nature of the Ruins at Sanxingdui, Guanghan"]. *Si chuan wen wu*, no. 4 (1988): 8–12.

———. "'Ya zhang' chu lun" ["On 'Toothed Scepters'"]. *Si chuan wen wu*, no. 1 (1989): 12–17.

Chen Xiandan et al. "Guang han san xing dui yi chi er hao ji si keng fa jue jian bao" ["A Brief Report on the Excavation of Sacrifice Pit No. 2 at the San-xingdui Ruins, Guanghan"]. *Wen wu*, no. 5 (1989): 1–20 with plates.

Chen Xianshuang. "Cheng du xi xiao zhan guo mu" ["A Warring States Period Grave on the Western Outskirts of Chengdu"], *Kao gu*, no. 7 (1983): 597–600.

———. "Si chuan ying jing zeng jia gou 21 hao mu qing li jian bao" ["An Inventory Report of the Excavation of Tomb No. 21 at Zengjiagou, Ying-jing, Sichuan"]. *Wen wu*, no. 5 (1989): 21–30.

Chen Xianyuan. "'Mi cang dao' kao lue" ["A Study of the 'Granary Road'"]. *Wen bo*, no. 1 (1988): 40–43.

Chen Yong. "Qin han wen ze zha cong" ["Notes on Qin and Han Written Remains"]. *Shi xue ji kan*, no. 4 (1986): 71–75.

Chen Zhenyu. "Chu mie yue di nian dai wen ti" ["Problems of the Date of the Chu Conquest of Yue"]. *Jiang han lun tan*, no. 5 (1980): 84.

Chen Zhiliang. "Yu gong yu si chuan di guan xi" ["The Relationship of the 'Tribute of Yu' to Sichuan"]. *Shuo wen yue kan* 3, no. 9 (1943): 33–42.

———. "Yu sheng shi niu kao" ["Investigation of the Birth of Yu at Shiniu"]. *Yu gong ban yue kan* 6, no. 6 (1936): 39–48.

————. "Yu yu si chuan di guan xi" ["The Relation of Yu to Sichuan"]. *Shuo wen yue kan* 3, no. 9 (1943): 33–42.

Chen Zugui. "Zhong guo cha ye shi lue" ["The History of Tea in China"]. *Jin ling xue bao* 10, nos. 1–2 (1940): 189–195.

Chen Zugui and Zhu Zizhen, eds. *Zhong guo cha ye li shi zi liao xuan ji* [*Collected Historical Material on Tea in China*]. Beijing: Nong ye chu ban she, 1981.

Cheng Faren. *Chun qiu zuo shi zhuan di ming tu kao* [*A Study of Toponyms in the Spring and Autumn Annals with Zuo Commentary*]. Taibei: Guang da shu ju, 1967.

Cheng Xuehua. "Bao xie dao lian yun jian nan duan diao cha jian bao" ["Summary Investigative Report of the Southern Lianyun Spur of the Bao-Xie Road"]. *Wen wu*, no. 11 (1964): 43–45.

Cheng Yangzhi. "Gu shu di hong shui shen hua yu zhong yuan di hong shui shen hua" ["The Flood Myths of Ancient Shu and of the Central Plains"]. *Shuo wen yue kan* 3, no. 9 (1943): 25–32.

Chu T'ung-tsu. *Han Social Structure*. Seattle: University of Washington Press, 1972.

Deng Boqing. "Si chuan xin fan xian shui guan yin yi chi shi jue jian bao" ["A Brief Report on Test Excavations at the Shuiguanyin Site, Xinfan County, Sichuan]. *Kao gu*, no. 8 (1959): 404–410.

Deng Shaoqin. *Ba shu shi yi tao suo* [*An Investigation of Traces of Ba and Shu History*]. Chengdu: Si chuan ren min chu ban she, 1983.

Deng Tingliang. "Cong min zu diao cha kan mao wen shi guan zang di bai shi sui zang" ["The White Stone Grave Goods of the Stone Coffin Burials at Maowen, Seen in the Light of Ethnic Investigations"]. *Kao gu yu wen wu*, no. 6 (1985): 102–104.

Deng Zixin and Tian Shang. "Shi lun du jiang yan jing jiu bu shuai di yuan yin" ["On the Reasons for the Imperishable Endurance of Dujiangyan"]. *Zhong guo shi yan jiu*, no. 3 (1986): 101–110.

Ding Zuchun, et al. "Za gu he xia yu xi han yan mu diao cha jian bao" ["A Summary Report on Investigations of Cliff Graves of Western Han Date Along the Lower Reaches of the Zagu River"]. *Si chuan wen wu*, no. 2 (1989): 76–79.

Dobson, W. A. C. H. *Early Archaic Chinese*. Toronto: University of Toronto Press, 1962.

Dong Qixiang. "Gu dai di ba yu yue" ["Ancient Ba and Yue"]. *Chong qing shi fan xue yuan xue bao*, no. 4 (1980): 69–70.

———. "Ba shu he shi jian cheng" ["When Were Cities Established in Ba and Shu?"]. *Chong qing shi fan xue bao*, no. 2 (1988): 23–25.

Dong Xizhen. "Chang jiang xi ling xia kao gu diao cha yu shi jue" ["Investigation and Test Excavation at Xiling Gorge on the Yangtze"]. *Kao gu,* no. 5 (1961): 231–236.

Dong Zuobin (Tung Tso-pin). "Yin dai di qiang yu shu" ["The Qiang and the Shu of the Yin Period"]. *Shuo wen yue kan* 3, no. 7 (1942): 103–115.

Du Naisong. "Lun ba shu qing tong qi" ["On Ba and Shu Bronze Implements"]. *Jiang han kao gu*, no. 3 (1985).

Duyvendak, J. J. L., trans. *The Book of Lord Shang*. London: Arthur Probsthain, 1928.

Fan Guijie. "Si chuan pei ling xi han tu keng mu fa jue jian bao" ["Brief Report on the Excavation of a Western Han Pit Grave at Peiling, Sichuan"]. *Kao gu*, no. 4 (1984): 338–344.

Fan Guijie and Hu Changyu. "Si chuan peng xian xi zhou jiao cang tong qi" ["A Hoard of Western Zhou Bronzes at Peng County, Sichuan"]. *Kao gu*, no. 6 (1981): 496–499, 555.

———. "Si chuan zi yang deng xian shi qi shi dai wen hua" ["The Stone Age Culture of Ziyang County and Other Counties of Sichuan"]. *Kao gu*, no. 6 (1983): 481–483.

Fan Xiaoping. "Guang han san xing dui qing tong ren xiang zai mei shu shi shang di di wei" ["The Place in Art History of the Bronze Statuettes of People from Sanxingdui, Guanghan"]. *Sichuan wen wu*, no. 6 (1988): 45–47.

Fan Yong. "Wu guo xi nan di qu di qing tong fu yue" ["Bronze Axes of China's Southwestern Region"]. *Kao gu xue bao*, no. 2 (1989): 161–186.

Fang Shiming. "Han dai di 'shu jun gong guan' he 'guang han jun gong guan'" ["The Works Commissioner of Shu Commandery and the Works Commissioner of Guanghan Commandery in Han Times"]. *Li shi zhi shi*, no. 5 (1980): 23–26.

Feng Hanji. "Guan yu 'chu gong—' ge di zhen wei bing lue lun si chuan 'ba shu' shi qi di bing qi" ["The Genuineness of the Chu Ducal Halberd and Sichuan Weapons of the Ba-Shu Period"]. *Wen wu*, no. 11 (1961): 32–34.

———. "Si chuan peng xian chu tu di tong qi" ["Bronze Artifacts Excavated at Peng County, Sichuan"]. *Wen wu*, no. 12 (1980): 38–47.

———. "Xi nan gu nu li wang guo" ["Ancient Slave States of the Southwest"]. *Li shi zhi shi*, no. 4 (1980): 18–22.

Feng Hanji and Tong Enzheng. "Ji guang han chu tu di yu shi qi" ["A Report on Jade Objects Unearthed at Guanghan"]. *Si chuan da xue xue bao*, no. 1 (1979): pp. 79–85; also in *Wen wu*, no. 2 (1979): 30–37.

——. "Min jiang shang you di shi guan zang" ["The Stone Coffin Burials on the Upper Reaches of the Min River"]. *Kao gu xue bao*, no. 2 (1973): 41–59.

Feng Zhou. "Kao gu za ji—1" ["Random Archaeological Notes—No. 1"]. *Kao gu yu wen wu*, no. 1 (1983): 102–104.

Fong, S. H. "Hua Yang Kuo Chih". *Journal of the West China Border Research Society* [Chengdu] 12, series A (1940): 225–233.

Fu Shuyao. "Gu dai shu guo lue shu" ["An Overview of the Ancient Country of Shu"]. *Yu gong ban yue kan* 1, no. 6 (1934): 11–25.

Fu Xuanzong. "Zuo si 'san du fu' xie zuo nian dai zhi yi" ["Questions on the Period of Composition of Zuo Si's Ode on the Three Capitals"]. *Zong hua wen shi lun cong*, no. 2 (1979): 319–329.

Fu Zhenlun. "Shu shou li bing zhi shui shi ji kao lue" ["A Study of the Evidence of Hydraulic Management by Shu Commandant Li Bing"]. *Shuo wen yue kan* 3, no. 9 (1943): 87–94.

Fung Yu-lan. *A History of Chinese Philosophy*. Princeton, N.J.: Princeton University Press, 1952.

Gale, Esson M. *Discourses on Salt and Iron*. Taibei: Cheng wen, 1973.

Gao Ming. "Lue lun zhou yuan jia gu wen di zu shu" ["A Discussion of the Ethnic Affinity of the Zhouyuan Oracle Bones"]. *Kao gu yu wen wu*, no. 5 (1984): 76–85.

Gao Zhixi and Xiong Zhuanxin. "Chu ren zai hu nan di huo dong yi yi gai shu" ["Traces of Chu Activity in Hunan"]. *Wen wu*, no. 10 (1980): 50–60.

Gaspardone, Emile. "Sseu-ma Siang-jou chez les Barbares" ["Sima Xiangru Among the Barbarians"]. *Sinologica* [Basel] 6, no. 3 (1960) and 7, no. 1 (1962)..

Gledhill, J., B. Bender, and M. T. Larsen, eds. *State and Society: The Emergence and Development of Social Hierarchy and Political Centralization*. London: Unwin Hyman Ltd., 1988.

Gong Tingwan et al. "Chong qing shi nan an qu di liang zuo xi han tu keng mu" ["Two Former Han Pit Graves on the South Bank District of Chongqing City"]. *Kao gu yu wen wu*, no. 7 (1982): 28–29.

Gu Jiegang. *Lun ba shu yu zhong yuan di guan xi* [*On the Relations Between Ba and Shu and the Central Plains*]. Chengdu: Si chuan ren min chu ban she, 1981.

Gu Jiegang, Lu Simian, and Tong Shuye, eds. *Gu shi bian* [*Articles on Ancient History*], 7 vols. Shanghai: Kai ming shu dian, 1926–1941.

Guan Weiliang. "Gu dai ba shu: zai wu wang fa zhou he ji ci tong yi zhan zheng zhong di zuo yong" ["The Role of Ancient Ba and Shu in King Wu's Campaign Against Zhou and Several Wars of Unification"]. *Chong qing shi fan xue yuan xue bao*, no. 4 (1980): 75.

———. "Gu dai chong qing da shi bian nian", ["A Chronology of Old Chong-qing"]. *Chong qing shi fan xue yuan xue bao*, no. 3 (1989): 64–72.

Guan Weiliang and Chen Lijing. "Si chuan jia ling jiang zhong xia yu xin shi qi shi dai yi chi diao cha" ["An Investigation of Neolithic Sites Along the Middle Jialing River"]. *Kao gu*, no. 6 (1983): 496–500.

Guo Moruo. "'Ban gui di zai fa xian'" ["The Rediscovery of the Ban *gui* Vessel"]. *Wen wu*, no. 9 (1972): 2–13.

———, ed. *Zhong guo shi gao di tu ji* [*Draft Historical Atlas of China*], vol. 1. Beijing: Di tu chu ban she, 1979.

Guo Rongzhang, "Lun gu bao xie dao shang jian ge di fen bu xing zhi, ji you yi deng jian zhu she ji" ["On the Nature and Construction Design Aspects of the Old Bao Xie Road"]. *Wen bo*, no. 5 (1988) 39–46.

Guo Xingwen, "Qin wang yuan yin xin tan" ["A New Inquiry on Why Qin Fell"]. *Wen bo*, no. 2 (1988).

Guo Yingzhang. "Bei wei 'shi men ming' kao" ["A Study of the Northern Wei Period 'Stone Gate Inscription'"]. *Kao gu yu wen wu*, no. 4 (1983): 99–104.

Han Feng. "Jia gu wen suo jian di shang dai jun zhi shu ce" ["Shang Period Military Strength as Seen in the Oracle Bones"]. In Hu Houxuan, ed., *Jia gu tan shi lu* [*Investigations of Oracle Bones*], pp. 400–449. Beijing: San lian shu ju, 1982.

Han Wei and Wang Shihe. "Bao xie dao shi men fu jin jian dao di yi ji ti ke di diao cha" ["An Investigation of Remains and Inscriptions on the Bao-Xie Road in the Vicinity of Shimen"]. *Wen wu*, no. 11, (1964): 25–42.

He Jiejun. "Shi lun da xi wen hua" ["On the Daxi Culture"]. *Zhong guo kao gu xue hui di er ci nian hui lun wen ji* (1980): 116–123.

He Tangkun. "Si chuan e mei xian zhan guo qing tong qi di ke xue fen xi" ["Scientific Analysis of Warring States Bronze Implements from Emei County, Sichuan"]. *Kao gu*, no. 11 (1986): 1037–1041, 1050.

He Xincheng. "Hang zhong shi shi ying sha chang qing li san zuo zhang guo mu" ["An Inventory of Three Warring States Graves at a Quartzite Plant in Hanzhong City"]. *Wen bo*, no. 6 (1987): 33–36.

He Zhiguo. "Si chuan mian yang chu tu zhan guo tong bing qi" ["Warring States Bronze Weapons Unearthed at Mianyang, Sichuan"]. *Wen wu*, no. 3 (1986): 94–95.

Hervouet, Yves. *Sseu-ma Siang-jou* [*Sima Xiangru*]. Paris: Presses universitaires de France, 1964.

Higham, C. F. W. "Prehistoric Rice Cultivation in Southeast Asia." *Scientific American* 250, no. 4 (1984): 138–146.

Hisamura Yukari. "Shin kan jidai no nyu shoku ro ni tsuite" ["On the Routes to Shu in Qin and Han Times"]. *Toyo Gakuho* 38, no. 3 (1955): 68–106.

———. "Zen kan no sen shoku kei ni tsuite" ["On Banishment to Shu During the Former Han Dynasty"]. *Toyo Gakuho* 37, no. 2 (1954): 95–125.

Ho Ping-ti. *The Cradle of the East*. Chicago: Chicago University Press, 1975.

———. "The Loess and the Origin of Chinese Agriculture." *American Historical Review* 75, no. 1 (October 1969): 1–36.

Hsu Cho-yun. *Ancient China in Transition*. Stanford, Calif.: Stanford University Press, 1965.

Hu bei sheng bo wu guan [Hubei Provincial Museum]. "Yi chang qian ping zhan guo liang han mu" ["Warring States and Han Graves at Qianping, Yichang"]. *Kao gu xue bao*, no. 2 (1976): 115–136.

Hu Changyu. "Cheng du shi yang xi han mu guo mu" ["A Western Han Wooden Coffin Grave at Shiyang, Chengdu"]. *Kao gu yu wen wu*, no. 2 (1983): 26–27.

Hu Zhiren et al. "Shan xi feng xian liang lu ping xi han mu qing li jian bao" ["A Brief Inventory Report of a Western Han Period Grave at Liangluping, Feng County, Shanxi Province"]. *Wen bo*, no. 3 (1989): 14–16.

Huang Banghong. "Shu dao kao cha shi ling" ["Investigating Details About the Road to Shu"]. *Si chuan wen wu*, no. 1, (1988): 11–14.

Huang Baoquan and Chen Huaxin. "Zhou wu wang ke yin nian dai kao" ["A Study of the Date of Zhou King Wu's Conquest of Yin"]. *Zhong guo li shi wen xian yan jiu ji kan*, no. 1 (1980): 125–128.

Huang Fanguang. "Cong fang zhi xue kan hua yang guo zhi" ["An Account of the Country South of Mt. Hua Viewed from the Local History Genre"]. *Zhong guo li shi xue hui shi xue ji kan* [*Collected Historical Studies of the Chinese History Institute*, Taibei], no. 9 (1977): 47–57.

Huang Jianhua. "Lun guang han san xing dui yi chi di xing zhi" ["Aspects of the Sanxingdui site at Guanghan"]. *Si chuan wen wu*, no 4 (1988): 9–11, 8.

Huang Jiaxiang. "'Guang han san xing dui yi chi' di chu bu fen xi" "A Preliminary Analysis of the Sanxingdui Site Report"]. *Kao gu*, no. 11 (1990).

———. "Si chuan da yi xian wu long xiang tu keng mu qing li jian bao" ["An Inventory of a Pit Grave at Wulong Village, Dayi County, Sichuan"]. *Kao gu*, no. 7 (1987): 604–610.

Huang Lie. "You guan di zu lai yuan he xing cheng di yi xie wen ti" ["Several Problems Concerning the Origin and Formation of the Di People"]. *Li shi yan jiu*, no. 2 (1965): 97–114.

Huang Liuzhu. "Han bei suo jian 'dao qiao yuan' kao" ["A Study of the 'Officer for Roads and Bridges' as Seen in Han Period Stone Inscriptions"]. *Wen bo*, no. 6 (1988): 50–53.

Huang Shengzhang. "Ban gui di nian dai, di li yu li shi wen ti" ["Chronological, Geographic, and Historical Problems of the Ban *gui*"]. *Kao gu yu wen wu*, no. 1 (1981): 75–82.

———. "Bao xie dao yu shi men shi ke" ["The Bao-Xie Road and the Inscriptions at Shimen"]. *Wen wu*, no. 2, (1963): 29–33.

———. "Li gui di zuo zhe shen fen, di li yu li shi wen ti" ["Identification, Geographic, and Historical Problems of the Li *gui*"]. In *Li shi di li yu kao gu lun cong* [*Collected Essays on Historical Geography and Archaeology*], pp. 256–268. Jinan, Shandong: 1982.

———. "Qing chuan xin chu qin tian lu mu du ji qi xiang guan wen ti" ["The Qin Wooden Slip Documents Newly Unearthed at Qingchuan and Problems Associated with Them]. *Wen wu*, no. 9: 71–75.

———. "Tong qi ming wen yi, yu, ce di di wang ji qi yu wu guo di guan xi" ["The Location of Yi, Yu, and Ce in Bronze Inscriptions, and their Relation to the State of Wu"]. *Kao gu xue bao*, no. 3 (1983): 295–305.

———. "Yun meng qin jian 'bian nian ji' di li yu li shi wen ti" ["Geographic and Historical Problems of the Qin Chronology on Bamboo Slips from Yunmeng"]. In *Li shi di li yu kao gu lun cong*, pp. 46–88. Jinan: Qi lu shu she, 1982.

Huang Zhigang. "Da yu yu libing zhi shui di guan xi" ["The relationship of Yu the Great to Li Bing in Ordering the Waters"] *Shuo wen yue kan*, 3, no. 9 (1943): 69–76.

Huo Wei and Huang Wei. "Shi lun wu hu shu shi ge di ji ge wen ti" ["On Several Problems Concerning Shu-Style Halberds Without Tapered Blades"]. *Kao gu*, no. 3 (1989): 251–259.

Its, R. F. *Etnicheskaya istoria yuga vostochnoi Azii* [*An Ethnological History of Southeast Asia*]. Leningrad: Nauka, 1972.

Ji Xianlin. "Zhong guo can si yu ru yin du wen ti di chu bu yan jiu" ["Initial Research on the Entry of Chinese Silk into India"]. *Li shi yan jiu*, no. 4 (1955): 51–94.

Jian Hong. "Ba yu shu" ["Ba and Shu"]. *Li shi zhi shi*, no. 3 (1980): 13–15.

―――. "Min jiang shui li yu ba shu fan rong" ["Hydraulic Management on the Min River and the Efflorescence of Ba and Shu"]. *Li shi zhi shi*, no. 5 (1980): 20–26.

Jiang Jiahua. "Qin shu hou fei qin ren kao bian" ["A Determination That the Qin Marquis of Shu Was Not a Man of Qin"]. *Zhong guo li shi wen xian yan jiu ji kan*, no. 2 (1981): 99–104.

Jiang Wanxi, "Pei ling xian yi jia bei xi han mu fa xian jian bao" ["A Brief Report on the Excavation of a Western Han Period Tomb at Yijiabei, Pei-ling County"]. *Kao gu yu wen wu*, no. 5 (1990): 44–49.

Jiang Xuanzhong. "Si chuan mao wen ying pan shan di shi guan zang" ["Stone Coffin Burials at Mt. Yingpan, Maowen County, Sichuan"]. *Kao gu*, no. 5 (1981): 411–421.

Jiang Yungang. "Zhi shui ji qi ren wu" ["Water Management and Its Person-nel"]. *Shuo wen yue kan* 3, no. 9 (1943): 65–68.

Kano Naosada. "Kodai ha shoku shi no sai kosei" ["A Reconstruction of the Ancient History of Ba and Shu"]. *Toyoshi Kenkyu* [*Researches in Oriental History*, Tokyo] 33, no. 4 (1975): 579–603.

Keegan, John. The Second World War. New York: Viking Books, 1989.

Keightley, David N. *Sources of Shang History*. Berkeley: University of Califor-nia Press, 1978.

―――, ed. The Origins of Chinese Civilization. Berkeley: University of Cali-fornia Press, 1983.

Kuang Yuanying. "Cheng du shi chu to di yi pi zhan guo tong bing qi" ["A Trove of Warring States Period Bronze Weapons Unearthed in Chengdu City"]. *Wen wu*, no. 8 (1982): 51–52.

―――, et al. "Si chuan jian wei jin jing xiang ba shu tu keng mu qing li jian bao" ["Report on a Ba-shu Pit Grave from Jinjing, Jianwei, Sichuan"]. *Wen wu*, no. 5 (1990): 68–75.

Lai Youde. "Cheng du nan jia chu tu di tong qi" ["Bronzes Unearthed at Nanjia, Chengdu"]. *Kao gu*, no. 8 (1959): 449–450.

Lan Yong. "Mi cang dao di ta cha yu kao zheng" ["Tracing and Confirming the Path of the Rice Granary Road"]. *Si chuan wen wu*, no. 2 (1989): 12–17.

———. "Si chuan gu dai jian dao yan jiu" ["A Study of the Ancient Corduroy Road to Sichuan"]. *Si chuan wen wu*, no. 1 (1988): 2–10.

Lao Gan. "Xiang jun zang ge he ye lang di guan xi" ["The Relationship of Xiang Commandery, Zangge, and Yelang"]. In *Lao gan xue shu lun wen ji jia bian* [*Collected Scholarly Writings of Lao Gan, First Series*], pp. 589–604. Taibei: Zhong yang yan jiu yuan 1976.

Li Boqian. "Cheng gu tong qi qun yu zao qi shu wen hua" ["The Hoard of Bronze Implements at Chenggu and Early Shu Culture"]. *Kao gu yu wen wu*, no. 2 (1983): 66–70.

Li Changfu. *"Yu gong" shi di* [*An Elucidation of the Lands in the "Tribute of Yu"*]. Zhengzhou: Zhong zhou shu hua she, 1982.

Li Fuhua. "Cheng du qing yang gong gu yi chi qing li jian bao" ["A Brief Inventory Report on the Ancient Ruin at Qingyang Gong, Chengdu"]. *Wen wu can kao zi liao*, no. 6 (1955): 44–46.

———. "Where Have All the Swords Gone? Reflections on the Unification of China." *Early China* no. 2 (Fall 1976): 31–34.

———. "Si chuan pi xian hong guang gong she chu tu zhan guo tong qi" ["Warring States Bronzes Unearthed at Hongguang Commune, Pi County, Sichuan"]. *Wen wu*, no. 10 (1976): 90–93.

———, et al. "Si chuan xin du zhan guo mu guo mu" ["A Warring States Period Wood Paneled Tomb at Xindu, Sichuan"]. *Wen wu*, no. 6 (1981): 1–16.

Li Hu. "Yin dai wai jiao zhi du chu tan" ["A Preliminary Investigation into the Foreign Affairs System in Shang Times"]. *Li shi yan jiu*, no. 5 (1988): 36–47.

Li Jinghua. "Han dai tie nong qi ming wen shi shi" ["Explanation of an Inscription on a Han Period Iron Agricultural Implement"]. *Kao gu*, no. 1 (1974): 62–63.

Li Li. "Si chuan feng jie xian feng xiang sia ya guan zang", A cliff inhumation at Fengxiang gorge, Fengjie county, Sichuan. *Wen wu*, no. 7, 1978, p. 89–90.

Li Qiliang. "Ba zu yuan yuan tan wei" ["An Investigation of Small Clues on the Origin of the Ba People"]. *Shi xue ji kan*, no. 1 (1985): 51–57.

Li Shuicheng. "Cong da xi chu tu shi diao ren mian tan ji ge wen ti" ["Several Problems Discussed in Respect to a Carved Human Face Unearthed at Daxi"]. *Wen wu*, no. 3 (1986): 89–91.

Li Wenjie. "Da xi wen hua di lei xing he fen qi" ["The Form and Periodization of the Daxi Culture"]. *Kao gu xue bao*, no. 2 (1986): 131–151.

———. "Shi lun da xi wen hua yu qu jia ling wen hua, yang shao wen hua di guan xi" ["On the Relations Between the Daxi Culture and the Qujialing and Yangshao Cultures"]. *Kao gu*, no. 2 (1979): 161–164, 185.

Li Xiaoou. "Si chuan ying jing xian lie tai zhan guo tu keng mu qing li jian bao" ["Revised Report on a Warring States Pit Grave at Lietai, Yingjing County, Sichuan"]. *Kao gu*, no. 7 (1984): 602–606.

Li Xiaoou et al. "Si chuan ying jing tong xin cun ba shu mu fa jue jian bao" ["A Brief Excavation Report of a Ba-Shu Grave at Tongxin Village, Yingjing, Sichuan"]. *Kao gu*, no. 1 (1988): 49–54.

Li Xuanmin and Zhang Senshui. "Tong liang jiu shi qi wen hua zhi yan jiu" ["Research on the Paleolithic Culture of Tongliang"]. *Gu ji tui dong wu yu gu ren lei*, Ancient vertebrates and early man, no. 4, 1981.

Li Xueqin. "Lun xin du chu tu di shu guo qing tong qi" ["On Shu Bronze Artifacts Unearthed at Xindu"]. *Wen wu*, no. 1 (1982): 38–41.

———. "Qing chuan hao jia ping mu du yan jiu" ["Research on the Wooden Tablets from Haojiaping, Qingchuan"]. *Wen wu*, no. 10 (1982): 68–72.

———. "Xi zhou jia gu di ji dian yan jiu" ["Research on Several Aspects of the Western Zhou Oracle Bones"]. *Wen wu*, no. 9 (1981): 7–12.

———. *Yin dai di li jian lun* [*A Brief Discourse on Yin Period Geography*]. Beijing: Ke xue chu ban she, 1959.

Li Yantan. "Chun yu shu lue" ["An Overview Review of *chun yu* Drums"]. *Wen wu*, no. 8 (1984): 69–72.

Li Zhaohe. "'Ba shu' yu 'chu' qi qi chu tan" ["A Preliminary Study of Ba-Shu and Chu Lacquerware"]. *Zong guo kao gu xue hui di er ci nian hui lun wen ji*, pp. 93–99. Beijing: New wu chu ban she, 1980.

———. "Qing chuan chu tu mu du wen zi jian kao" ["A Brief Study of the Characters Inscribed on Wooden Tablets Unearthed at Qingchuan"]. *Wen wu*, no. 1 (1982): 24–27.

Li Zhaohe et al. "Cheng du shi er qiao shang dai jian ju yi chi di yi qi fa jue jian bao" ["Initial excavation report on the Shang Period Structure at No. 12 Bridge Street, Chengdu"] *Wen wu*, no. 12 (1987): 1–23, 37.

Li Zhaohe et al. "Qing chuan xian chu tu qin geng xiu tian lu mu du" ["Wooden Tablets Inscribed with the Revised Qin Land Law Unearthed at Qingchuan County"]. *Wen wu*, no. 1 (1982): 1–21.

Liang Wenjun. "Si chuan pi xian fa xian zhan guo chuan guan zang" ["Warring States Period Boat Coffin Burials Discovered at Pi County, Sichuan"]. *Kao gu*, no. 6 (1980): 560–561.

Liang Yusheng. *Shi ji zhi yi* [Notes to the Historical Records] Volume 1. Beijing: Zhong hua shu ju, 1981.

Liao Guanghua. "Peng xian zhi he xiang chu tu zhan guo qing tong qi" ["Warring States Period Bronzes Excavated at Zhiho Village, Peng County"]. *Si chuan wen wu*, no. 1 (1989): 66.

Lin Chun. "Yi chang di qu chang jiang yan an xia shang shi qi di yi zhi xin wen hua lei xing" ["A New Cultural Pattern of the Xia and Shang Period from the Banks of the Yangtze River in the Area of Yichang"]. *Jiang han kao gu*, no. 2 (1984): 29–38.

Lin Jianming. *Qin shi gao* [*Draft History of Qin*]. Shanghai: Shang hai ren min chu ban she, 1981.

———. "Qing chuan qin mu mu du nei rong tan tao" ["A Discussion of the Contents of the Qin Tomb Wooden Tablets from Qingchuan"]. *Kao gu yu wen wu*, no. 6 (1982): 62–64, 112.

Lin Mingjun. "Si chuan zhi shui zhe yu shui shen" ["Hydraulic Engineers and Water Spirits of Sichuan"]. *Shuo wen yue kan* 3, no. 9 (1943): 77–86.

Lin Qi. "Ba chu guan xi chu tan" ["A Preliminary Investigation of Ba-Chu Relations"]. *Jiang han lun tan*, no. 4 (1980): 87–91.

Lin Xiang. "Da xi wen hua yu wu shan da xi yi chi" ["The Daxi Culture and the Daxi Remains at Wu Mountain"] *Zhong guo kao gu xue hui di er ci nian hui lun wen ji* (1980): 128–130.

———. "Yang zi shan jian zhu yi chi xin kao" ["A New Study of the Remains of the Yangzishan Edifice"]. *Si chuan wen wu*, no. 5 (1988): 3–13.

———. "Zhou yuan bu ci zhong di 'shu'" ["'Shu' in the Oracle Bones from Zhouyuan"]. *Kao gu yu wen wu*, no. 6 (1985): 66–74.

Lin Zhao et al. "Shu dao kao" ["A Study of the Road to Shu"]. *Wen shi za shi* [*Magazine of Culture and History*] 3, nos. 5–6 (1944): 4–19.

Liu Dunyuan. "Yun meng ze yu shang zhou zhi ji di min zu qian xi" ["Yunmeng Marsh and Ethnic Migrations of the Shang-Zhou Transition Period"]. *Jiang han kao gu*, no. 2 (1985): 51–56.

Liu Hong. "Ba hu yu kai ming shou" ["Ba Tigers and the Animals of the Kaimings"]. *Si chuan wen wu*, no. 4 (1988): 57–59.

Liu Lin. "'Hua yang guo zhi' jian lun" ["A Brief Statement on 'Account of the Country South of Mt. Hua'"]. *Si chuan da xue xue bao*, no. 2 (1979): 82–87.

Liu Qiyi. "Xi zhou ji nian tong qi yu wu wang zhi li wang di zai wei nian shu" ["Commemorative Bronzes of the Western Zhou and the Calendrical De-

termination of King Wu's Years on the Throne"]. *Wen shi*, no. 13 (1982):
1–24.

Liu Shixu. "Han 'qiong du nan shan chu tong' di kao" ["A Study on the
   Whereabouts of the 'Copper Producing South Mountain at Qiongdu' in
   Han Times"]. *Si chuan wen wu*, no. 6 (1989): 33–34.

———. "Shi lun chuan xi nan da shi mu di qi yuan yu fen qi" ["Tentative
   Discussion of the Origin and Periodization of Megalithic Tombs in Southwestern Sichuan"]. *Kao gu*, no. 6 (1985): 559–567.

Liu Shixu and Zheng Zhongning. "Si chuan xi chang shi dong ping cun han
   dai lian tong yi chi di diao cha" ["An Investigation of Han Period Copper
   Smelting at Dongping Village, Xichang, Sichuan"]. *Kao gu*, no. 12 (1990):
   1069–1075.

Liu Xing et al. "Cheng du shi er qiao shang dai jian zhu yi chi di yi qi fa jue
   jian bao" ["A Brief Report on the First Stage of Excavation of the Shang
   Period Building Ruin at Bridge No. 12, Chengdu"]. *Wen wu*, no. 12
   (1987): 1–23, 37.

Liu Ying. "Ba shu bing qi ji qi wen shi fu hao" ["Record of Ba-Shu Script
   Writings on Bronze"]. *Wen wu zi liao cong kan* [*Collected Papers on Cultural
   Artifact Materials*], no. 7. Beijing: 1983.

Liu Yuchuan. "Ba shu fu hao yin zhang di chu bu yan jiu" ["Preliminary
   Research on Ba-Shu Script Seals"]. *Wen wu*, no. 10 (1987): 86–93.

Liu Yudong. *Zhong yuo xiang qi jiao he shu* [*"A Textbook of Chess"*]. Beijing: Hua
   xia chu ban she, 1988.

Liu Zhiyi. "Gu shu wen zi shi 'can si wen zi' ma?" ["Were the Ancient Shu
   Writings 'Silkworm Characters'?"]. *Si chuan wen wu*, no. 6 (1989): 54–57.

Lu Liancheng and Hu Zhisheng. "Bao ji ru jia zhuang, ju yuan gou mu di you
   guan wen ti di tan tao" ["An Investigation of the Tomb at Zhuyuangou,
   Rujiazhuang, Baoji"]. *Wen wu*, no. 2 (1983): 11, 17–19.

———. "Bao ji ru jia zhuang zhu yuan gou mu di chu tu bing qi di chu bu yan
   jiu" ["Preliminary Research on Weapons Unearthed at Zhuyuangou, Ru-
   jia Village, Baoji"]. *Kao gu yu wen wu*, no. 5 (1983): 50–65.

Lu Zijian. "Ba jun luo xia hong" ["Luo Xiahong of Ba Commandery"]. *Li shi
   zhi shi*, no. 4, (1980): 22–24.

Lu Zune et al. "Si chuan zi yang li yu qiao jiu shi qi di dian fa jue bao gao"
   ["Excavation Report from the Paleolithic Site at Liyu Bridge, Ziyang,
   Sichuan"]. *Kao gu xue bao*, no. 3 (1983): 331–344.

Luo Kaiyu. "Lun du jiang yan yu shu wen hua di guan xi" ["On the Relationship of Dujiangyan to Shu Culture"]. *Si chuan wen wu*, no. 2 (1988): 32–37.

——. "Lun gu dai ba, shu wang guo di qiao xing tong bi" ["On Bridge-Shaped Coins of the Ancient Ba and Shu Kingdoms"]. *Kao gu yu wen wu*, no. 3 (1990): 77–84.

——. "Qin guo fu ji zhi kao bian: lun yun meng qin jian zha ji" ["A Study of the Personal Registration System in the State of Qin: Comments upon Reading the Qin Bamboo Slip Writings from Yunmeng"]. *Zhong guo li shi wen xian yan jiu ji kan*, no. 3 (1982): 211–217.

——. "Qin zai ba shu di jing ji guan li zhi du shi xi" ["An Explanation of Qin Economic Management in Ba and Shu"]. *Si chuan shi fa xue yuan xue bao*, no. 4 (1982): 78–83.

——. "Qin zai ba shu di qu di min zu zheng ce shi xi" ["An Explanation of the Qin Nationalities Policy in Ba and Shu"]. *Min zu yan jiu [Ethnic Studies]*, no. 4 (1982): 27–33.

——. "Qing chuan qin du 'wei tian lu' suo gui ding di 'wei tian' zhi" ["The 'Land Apportionment' System Stipulated by the 'Land Aportionment Law' in the Qin Documents from Qingchuan"]. *Kao gu*, no. 8 (1988): 728–731, 756.

Luo Kun. "Shang dai ren ji ji xiang guan wen ti" ["Human Sacrifice and Associated Problems of the Shang Period"]. In Hu Houxuan, ed., *Jia gu tan shi lu [Investigations of Oracle Bones]*, pp. 112–191. Beijing: San lian shu ju, 1982.

Luo Xianglin. "Xia min zu fa xiang yu min jiang liu yu shuo" ["The Origin of the Xia Race in the Min River Area"]. *Shuo wen yue kan* 3, no. 9 (1943): 43–64.

Ma Chengyuan. "Guan yu 'da wu qi' di ming wen ji tu xiang" ["Regarding the Inscription and Images on the 'Wardance' Halberd"]. *Kao gu*, no. 10 (1963): 562–564.

——. *Zhong guo gu dai qing tong qi [Ancient Chinese Bronzes]*. Shanghai: Shang hai ren min chu ban she, 1982.

Ma Feibai. *Qin ji shi [Collected Material on Qin History]*. Beijing: Zhong hua shu ju, 1982.

——. "Yun meng qin jian da shi ji ji chuan" ["Collected References on the Qin Chronology from Yunmeng"]. *Zhong guo li shi wen xian yan jiu ji kan*, no. 2 (1981): 66–92.

Ma Peitang. "Ba shu gui qin kao" ["The Annexation of Ba and Shu by Qin"]. *Yu gong ban yue kan* 2, no. 2 (1934): 2–6.

Ma Xingxin. "Chuan dong bei kao gu wen hua fen qi chu lun" ["On the Periodization of Archaeological Cultures in Northeastern Sichuan"]. *Si chuan wen wu*, no. 6 (1989): 26–30.

Mao Ruifen. "Gu dao mi zong" ["Ancient Roads Scrutinized"]. *Si chuan wen wu*, no. 1 (1988): 23–25, 14.

Meng Mo. "Shi lun han dai xi nan min zu zhong di 'yi' yu 'qiang'" ["On the Southwestern 'Yi' and 'Qiang' Nations During Western Han Times"]. *Li shi yan jiu*, no. 1 (1985): 11–32.

Meng Wentong. *Ba shu gu shi lun shu* [*Discourses on Ancient Ba and Shu History*]. Chengdu: Si chuan ren min chu ban she, 1981.

Miao Wenyuan. "Zhou yuan jia gu suo jian zhu fang guo kao lue" ["A Study of Place Names Encountered in the Oracle Bones from Zhouyuan"]. *Si chuan da xue xue bao ji kan*, no. 10 (1982): 66–67.

Miao Yue. "'Ba shu wen hua chu lun' shang que" ["A discussion of 'An initial treaties on Ba-Shu culture'"]. *Si chuan da xue xue bao*, no. 4 (1959): 1–8.

Pan Guangdan. *Xiang xi bei di 'tu jia' yu gu dai di ba ren* [*The Tujia People of Northwestern Hunan and the Ancient Ba People*], in the series *Zong guo min zu wen ti yan jiu ji kan* [*Collected Research on Problems of Chinese Nationalities*], no. 4. Beijing: Min zu yan jiu suo, 1955.

Pei Wenzhong et al. *Zi yang ren* [*Ziyang Man*]. Beijing: Wen wu chu ban she, 1957.

Peng Botong. *Gu cheng chong qing* [*The Ancient City of Chongqing*]. Chongqing: Chong qing chu ban she, 1981.

Peng Jingzhong. "Gu dai ba shu tong qi wen zi shi shi" ["An Inquiry into the Script on Ancient Ba-Shu Bronzes"]. *Si chuan da xue xue bao cong kan*, no. 5 (1980): 173–176.

Peters, Heather. "The Role of the State of Chu in Eastern Zhou Period China: A Study of Interaction and Exchange in the South." Ph.D. dissertation, Yale University, 1983.

Qian Mu. *Huang di* [*The Yellow Emperor*]. Taibei: Da tong shu gong si, 1978.

Qian Yuzhi. "Gu dai di cun zai guo pin yin wen zi zai tan" ["A Reinvestigation of Phonetic Writing Remains from Ancient Shu]. *Si chuan wen wu*, no. 6 (1989).

———. "Gu shu di cun zai guo pin yin wen zi" ["Extant Phonetic Writing from Ancient Shu"]. *Sichuan wen wu*, no. 6 (1988): 3–8.

Qin Zhongxing et al. "Bao xie jian dao diao cha ji" ["Investigation Report of the Bao-Xie Route"]. *Kao gu yu wen wu*, no. 4 (1980): 42–47.

Qu Shouyuan. "'Shu dao nan' suo yu" ["Trivial Talk about the Poem 'The Road to Shu is Difficult'"]. *Si chuan shi yuan xue bao*, no. 1 (1980): 55–58.

Qu Wanli. "Lun yu gong zhu cheng di shi dai" ["On the Composition Date of the Tribute of Yu"]. *Zong yang yan jiu yuan li shi yu yan yan jiu suo ji kan*, vol. 35, pp. 53–86. Taibei: Zhong yang yan jiu yuan, 1963.

Ran Ruiquan. "Da ning he gu jian dao chu tan" ["A Preliminary Investigation of the Ancient Corduroy Road Along the Daning River"]. *Si chuan wen wu*, no. 2 (1989): 18–19.

Rao Zongyi. "Shu bu yu Cinapatta—lun zao qi zhong, yin mian zhi jiao tong" ["Shu Cloth and Cinapatta—On Early Chinese, Indian, and Burmese Intercourse"]. *Zhong yang yan jiu yuan li shi yu yan yan jiu suo ji kan* 45 (1972): 561–584.

———. "Xi nan wen hua" ["The Culture of the Southwest"]. *Zhong yang yan jiu yuan: li shi yu yan yan jiu suo ji kan* 45, part 1 (1974): 173–203.

Ren Naiqing. "Chong qing" ["Chongqing"]. *She hui ke xue yan jiu* [*Social Sciences Research*], no. 3 (1980): 63–67.

———. "'Hua yang quo zhi' jian jie" ["A Summary of the Account of the Country South of Mt. Hua"]. *Li shi zhi shi*, no. 2 (1980).

Ren Shoufang. "Qin shu jian dao: gu dao, lian yun dao he bao xie dao gai shu" ["The Qin-shu corduroy road: Old Road, Cloud Road, and Bao-Xie Road in Outline"] *Bao ji shi yuan xue bao* (*Baoji Normal College Journal*) no. 4 (1986): 126.

Rosen, Sydney. "Changing Conceptions of the Hegemon in Pre-Ch'in China." In David T. Roy and Tsuen-hsuin Tsien, eds., *Ancient China: Studies in Early Civilization*, pp. 99–114. Hong Kong: Hong Kong University Press, 1978.

Rossabi, Morris. *Khubilai Khan*. Berkeley: University of California Press, 1988.

Sang Xiuyun. "Shu bu qiong zhu chuan zhi da xia lu jing di li ce" ["Speculation on the Route of Transmission of Shu Cloth and Qiong Bamboo to Daxia"]. *Zhong yang yan jiu yuan li shi yu yan yan jiu suo ji kan* 41, no. 1 (1969): 67–86.

Schwartz, Benjamin. *The World of Thought in Ancient China*. Cambridge, Mass.: Harvard University Press, 1985.

Service, Ellman R. *Origins of the State and Civilization*. New York: Norton, 1975.

———. *Primitive Social Organization*. New York: Random House, 1962.

Shaughnessy, Edward L. "Historical Geography and the Extent of the Earliest Chinese Kingdoms" (unpublished conference paper, 1990).

Shen Guozheng. "Du jiang yan di bian qian" ["Changes at Dujiangyan"]. *Si chuan da xue xue bao*, no. 4 (1979): 101–106.

Shen Zhongchang. "San xing dui er hao ji si keng qing tong li ren xiang chu ji" ["Preliminary Report on a Bronze Image of a Standing Man from Votary Objects Pit No. 2 at Sanxingdui"]. *Wen wu*, no. 10 (1987): 16–17.

———. "Xin du zhan guo mu yu chu wen hua" ["The Warring States Period Wood Paneled Tomb at Xindu and Chu Culture"]. *Wen wu*, no. 6 (1981): 26–28.

———. and Li Fuhua. "Guan yu 'shi guan zang wen hua' di ji ge wen ti" ["Several Problems relating to the 'stone coffin culture'"]. *Zong guo kao gu xue hui di yi ce nian hui lun wen ji* (1979): 249–257.

———. "Shi guan zang wen hua zhong suo jian di han wen hua yin su chu tan" ["Preliminary Investigation of Elements of Han Culture Seen in the Stone Coffin Burial Culture"]. *Kao gu yu wen wu*, no. 4 (1983): 81–84.

Shen Zhongchang and Wang Jiayou. "Ji si chuan ba xian dong xun bei chu tu gu yin ji gu huo bi" ["A Report on Ancient Seals and Cash from Dongxun Levee, Ba County, Sichuan"]. *Kao gu tong xun [Archaeological Bulletin]*, no. 6, (1955): 48–56.

Shi Nianhai. *He shan ji [Collection on Rivers and Mountains]*. 2 volumes. Beijing: San lian shu dian, 1981.

Shi Quan. "Gu deng guo, deng xian kao" ["A Study of the Ancient State of Deng, and Deng County"]. *Jiang han lun tan*, no. 3 (1980): 89–96.

Shi Tuan. "Ji cheng du jiao tong xiang chu tu di yi jian 'can wen' tong ge" ["Report on a Bronze Halberd Decorated with a 'Silkworm Design' Excavated at Traffic Lane, Chengdu"]. *Kao gu yu wen wu*, no. 2 (1980): 28–30.

Shi Xipeng. "Peng zu qin ren qi mu chu tan" ["A Preliminary Investigation of Peng Zu and His Tomb"]. *Si chuan wen wu*, no. 3 (1988): 71–72.

Shi Zhimian. "Du shi ji hui zhu kao deng zha ji" ["Collected Notes on Reading the *Historical Records*"]. *Da lu za zhi* 55, no. 3 (1977): 143.

———. "Qin ding shu" ["The Qin Pacification of Shu"]. *Da lu za zhi* 49, no. 6 (1974): 302.

———. "Qin san shi liu jun you nei shi kao" ["A Study of the Inner History of the Thirty-Six commanderies of Qin. *Da lu za zhi* 2, no. 11 (1951): 5, 12.

Shima Kunio. *Inkyo bokuji sorui [Collected Oracle Writings from the Yin Site]*. Tokyo: Daian Kabushiki Kaisha, 1967.

Shui hu di qin mu zhu jian zheng li xiao zu [Shuihudi Qin Tomb Bamboo Tablet Compilation Group]. *Shui hu di qin mu zhu jian [Qin Bamboo Tablets from Shuihudi]*. Beijing: Wen wu chu ban she, 1978.

Si chuan sheng bo wu guan [Sichuan Provincial Museum]. "Cheng du bai hua tan zhong xue shi hao mu fa jue ji" ["A Report on the Excavation of Tomb No. 10 at Baihuatan Middle School, Chengdu"]. *Wen wu*, no. 3 (1976): 40–46.

————. *Si chuan chuan guan zang fa jue bao gao* [*Excavation Report on the Boat Graves of Sichuan*]. Beijing: Wen wu chu ban she, 1960.

————. "Si chuan wen wu kao gu gong zuo san shi nian" ["Thirty Years of Artifacts and Archaeological Work in Sichuan"]. In *Wen wu kao gu gong zuo san shi nian, 1949–1979* [*Thirty Years of Artifacts and Archaeological Work, 1949–1979*], pp. 349–359. Beijing: Wen wu chu ban she, 1979.

————. "Si chuan pei ling di qu xiao tian xi zhan guo tu keng mu qing li jian bao" ["An Inventory of a Warring States Period Pit Grave at Xiaotian Brook in the Peiling Area of Sichuan"]. *Wen wu*, no. 5 (1974): 61–80.

Si chuan sheng guan xian wen jiao ju [Cultural Propagation Bureau of Guan County, Sichuan Province]. "Du jiang yan chu tu dong han li bing shi xiang" ["A Stone Statue of Li Bing from the Eastern Han Unearthed at Dujiangyan"]. *Wen wu*, no. 7 (1974): 27–28.

Si chuan sheng wen wu guan li wei yuan hui [Sichuan Provincial Relics Commission]. "Cheng du yang zi shan di 172 hao mu fa jue bao gao" ["Excavation Report on Grave No. 172 at Yangzishan, Chengdu"]. *Kao gu xue bao*, no. 4 (1956): 1–19.

————, et al. "Guang han sun xing dui yi chi er hao ji si keng fa jue jian bao" ["A brief report on the excavation of sacrificial pit no. 2 at Sanxingdui, Guanghan"]. *Wen wu*, no. 10 (1987).

So, Jenny F. "The Inlaid Bronzes of the warring States Period," in Wen Fong, ed., *The Great Bronze Age of China*. New York: Alfred A. Knopf, 1980.

Solheim, Wilhelm G. II. "Chinese and Southeast Asian Art Styles and their Relationship". Transcript of lecture presented to the China Society of Singapore, November 24, 1979.

————. "An Earlier Agricultural Revolution." *Scientific American* 226, no. 4 (1972): 34–41.

————. "New Data on Late Southeast Asian Prehistory and Their Interpretation." *Journal of the Hong Kong Archaeological Society* 8 (1979).

Song Zhimin. "Chuan xi he dian xi bei di shi guan zang" ["Stone Coffin Burials of Western Sichuan and Northwestern Yunnan"]. *Kao gu yu wen wu*, no. 3 (1987): 66–76.

————. "Guan yu shu wen hua di ji ge wen ti" ["Concerning Several Problems of Shu Culture"]. *Kao gu yu wen wu*, no. 2 (1983): 71–80.

———. "Lue lun si chuan di qin ren mu" ["On Qin Graves in Sichuan"]. *Kao gu yu wen wu*, no. 2 (1984): 82–90.

———. "Lue lun si chuan zhan guo qin mu zang di fen qi" ["The Periodization of Warring States Period Qin Graves in Sichuan"]. *Zhong guo kao gu xue hui di yi ci nian hui lun wen ji*. Beijing: Wen wu chu ban she, 1979.

———. "Zao qi shu wen hua fen qi di zai tan tao" ["The Periodization of the Early Shu Culture Reexamined"]. *Kao gu*, no. 5 (1990): 441–451.

Sun Bingjun. "Shan xi zu yang bai ma shi ba shu mu fa jue jian bao" ["A Brief Report on a Ba-Shu Grave Excavated at Baimashi, Zuyang, Shannxi"]. *Kao gu yu wen wu*, no. 5 (1987): 17–20, 13.

Sun Cidan. "Du 'gu shu guo wei can guo shuo' di xian yi" ["Doubts on Reading 'The Notion of Ancient Shu as the Country of Silkworms'"] *Qi lu xue bao* [*Qi and Lu Journal*], no. 1 (1941).

Sun Hanqing. "Shen yu gu li" ["The Ancient Abode of Holy Yu"]. *Si chuan wen wu*, no. 1 (1988): 31–33.

Sun Hua. "Ba shu wen wu za shi" ["Notes on Ba-Shu Artifacts"]. *Wen wu*, no. 5 (1989): 39–48.

———. "Bie ling ming yi kao" ["A Study of the Significance of the Name Bieling"]. *Si chuan wen wu*, no. 5 (1989): 17–24.

Sun Kui. "Li chuan xian chu tu yi jian hu niu chun yu" ["A Tiger-Decorated Drum Unearthed at Lichuan County"]. *Jiang han kao gu*, no. 3 (1985): 40.

Sun Min et al. "Wen chuan fa xian xi zhou shi qi shu wen hua qing tong lei" ["A Shu Culture Bronze Jar of the Western Zhou Period Discovered at Wenchuan"]. *Si chuan wen wu*, no. 4 (1989): 44–45.

Sun Zhibin. "Xin du zhan guo mu guo mu wen hua yin su pou xi" ["An Analysis of Cultural Features in the Warring States Wooden Coffin Grave at Xindu"]. *Jiang han kao gu*, no. 1 (1986): 58–62.

Talbert, Richard J. A., ed. *Atlas of Classical History*. London and Sydney: Croom Helm, 1985.

Tang Jiahong. "Ba shi san ti" ["Three Aspects of Ba History"]. *Si xiang zhan xian*, no. 2 (1981): 25–27.

———. "Shi lun si chuan xi nan di qu shi mu di zu shu" ["Suggestions on the Ethnic Identity of the Southwestern Sichuan Stone Tomb Builders"]. *Kao gu*, no. 5 (1979): 455–458.

Tang Jinyu. "Han shui shang yu ba wen hua yu yin zhou guan xi di tan tao" ["A Discussion of the Relationship Between Yin and Zhou and the Ba Culture on the Upper Reaches of the Han River"]. *Wen bo*, no. 1 (1988): 37–39.

Tang Lan. *Tian rang ge jia gu wen cun kao shi* [*A Study of Oracle Bone Remains at the Tianrang Chamber*]. Beijing: Fu ren da xue, 1939.

Tao Tien-yi. "Vassal Kings and Marquises of the Former Han Dynasty." *Zhong yang yan jiu yuan li shi yu yan yan jiu suo ji kan* 46, part 1 (1974): 150–172.

Tian Changxu. "Cong xian dai shi jian pou xi zhong guo gu dai qing tong shou zao di ke xue cheng jiu" ["Ancient Chinese Scientific Accomplishments in Bronze Casting in Light of Modern Experimental Analysis"]. *Cheng du ke ji da xue xue bao* [*Journal of Chengdu University of Science and Technology*], no. 3 (1980).

Tian Shang and Deng Zixin. "Tuo jiang, mo shui, li dui kao bian" ["A Study of the Tuo River, the Mo River, and Lidui"]. *Li shi di li*, no. 5 (1987).

Tian Yizhao et al. "Qin tian lu kao shi" ["A Study of the Qin Land Law"]. *Kao gu*, no. 6 (1983): 545–548.

Tong Enzheng. *Gu dai di ba shu* [*Ancient Ba and Shu*]. Chengdu: Si chuan ren min chu ban she, 1979.

———. "Ji ju tang xia kui jia dong zhong fa xian di ba ren wen wu" ["A Report on Ba Artifacts Discovered at Armor Cave, Jutang Gorge"]. *Kao gu*, no. 5 (1962): 253.

———. "Jin nian lai zhong guo xi nan min zu di qu zhan guo qin han shi dai di kao gu fa xian ji qi yan jiu" ["Recent Discovery and research on the Warring States, Qin, and Han Period Archaeology of the Southwestern Peoples of China"]. *Kao gu xue bao*, no. 4 (1980): 417–442.

———. "Ren lei ke neng di fa yuan di: zhong guo di xi nan di qu" ["A Possible Place of Human Origins: Southwestern China"]. *Si chuan da xue xue bao: zhe xue she hui ke xue ban*, no. 3 (1983): 3–14.

———. "Shi tan gu dai si chuan yu dong nan ya wen ming di guan xi" ["Tentative Inquiry into the Ancient Relations Between Sichuan and Southeast Asian Civilization"]. *Wen wu*, no. 9 (1983): 73–81.

———. "Si chuan xi bei di qu shi guan zang zu shu shi tan" ["Tentative Inquiry into the Ethnic Identity of the Stone Coffin Interments of Northwestern Sichuan"]. *Si xiang zhan xian*, no. 1 (1978): 72–77.

———. "Si chuan xi nan di qu da shi mu zu shu shi tan" ["Tentative Inquiry into the Ethnic Identity of the Southwestern China Megalithic Tomb Builders"]. *Kao gu*, no. 2 (1978): 104–110.

———. "Wo guo xi nan di qu qing tong ge di yan jiu" ["Researches on Bronze Halberds from the Southwest of Our Country"]. *Kao gu xue bao*, no. 4 (1979): 441–457.

————. "Wo guo xi nan di qu qing tong jian di yan jiu" ["Researches on Bronze Swords from the Southwest of Our Country"]. *Yun nan qing tong qi lun cong* [*Collected Theses on Yunnan Bronze Artifacts*], pp. 156–177. Beijing: Wen wu chu ban she, 1981.

————. "Tan jia gu wen qiang zi bing lue lun yin dai di ren ji zhi du" ["A Discussion of the Oracle Bone Character *qiang* and the Human Sacrifice System of the Yin Period"]. *Si chuan da xue xue bao*, no. 3 (1980).

Tong Shuye. *Chun qiu zuo zhuan yan jiu* [*Research on the Zuo Commentary to the Spring and Autumn Annals*]. Shanghai: Shang hai ren min chu ban she, 1980.

————. *Zhong guo gu dai di li kao zheng lun wen ji* [*Collected Critical Theses on the Ancient Geography of China*]. Shanghai: Wen wu chu ban she, 1962.

Treistman, Judith M. "China at 1000 B.C.: A Cultural Mosaic." *Science* 160, (May 24, 1968): 853–856.

————. "The Early Cultures of Szechwan and Yunnan." *Cornell University East Asia Papers*, no. 3 (1974).

Wang Dadao. "Yun nan qing tong wen hua ji qi yu yue nan dong shan wen hua, tai guo ban qing wen hua di guan xi" ["The Relationship of the Bronze Culture of Yunnan to the Dongson Culture of Vietnam and the Ban Chiang Culture of Thailand"]. *Kao gu*, no. 6 (1990): 531–543, 553.

Wang Daisheng. "Jian men shu dao yu jian men shu dao wen wu" ["The Road to Shu at Jianmen and Its Artifacts"]. *Si chuan wen wu*, no. 1 (1988): 15–20, 35.

Wang Guanggao. "Jia wen 'chu' zi bian" ["An Analysis of the Character Chu in Oracle Bones"]. *Jiang han kao gu*, no. 2 (1984): 52–63.

Wang Hui. *Yu gong shi di* [*An Elucidation of the Lands in the "Tribute of Yu"*]. Taibei: Shang wu yin shu guan, 1971.

Wang Jiade. "Hu bei zi gui you fa xian yi ji ba shi jian" ["Another Ba-Style Sword Discovered at Zigui, Hubei Province"]. *Jiang han kao gu*, no. 3 (1985): 78.

Wang Jiayou. "Ji si chuan ba xian dong xun bei chu to gu yin ji gu huo bi" ["Report on Ancient Seals and Coins Excavated at Ba County, Sichuan"]. *Kao gu tong xun*, no. 6 (1955): 48–54.

Wang Jiayou. "Ji si chuan peng xian ju wa jie chu tu de tong qi" ["Report on Bronze Artifacts Excavated at Juwajie, Peng county, Sichuan"]. *Wen wu*, no. 11 (1961): 28–30.

————. "Xian qin long hu tu an su yuan" ["Tracing the Origins of Pre-Qin Totemic Dragons and Tigers"]. *Si chuan wen wu*, no. 4 (1989): 11–15.

Wang Jiayou and Wang yourun. "Cheng du yang zi shan tu tai yi chi qing li bao gao", ["An Inventory of the Altar Mound Ruin at Yangzishan, Chengdu"]. *Kao gu xue bao*, no. 4 (1957): 17–31.

Wang Jiayou and Wangzigang. "Pei ling chu tu di ba wen wu yu chuan dong ba guo" ["Ba Relics Unearthed at Peiling and the Ba Country of Eastern Sichuan"]. *Si chuan da xue xue bao cong kan* [*Collected Papers from the Journal of Sichuan University*], no. 5 (1980): 166–169.

Wang Jie. "Dui da xi wen hua zhong ji ge wen ti di tan tao" ["A Discussion of Several Problems of the Daxi Culture"]. *Jiang han kao gu*, no. 10 (1984): 61–68.

———. "Qu jia ling wen hua yu da xi wen hua guan xi zhong di wen ti tan tao" ["Investigation of Problems in the Relationship Between the Qujia-ling and Daxi Cultures"]. *Jiang han kao gu*, no. 3 (1985): 34–40.

Wang Ningsheng. "Lun zhong guo gu dai tong gu" ["On Ancient Chinese Bronze Drums"]. In *Yun nan qing tong qi lun cong* [*Collected Theses on Yun-nan Bronzes*], pp. 108–143. Beijing: Wen wu chu ban she, 1981.

———. "Shi 'wu wang fa zhou qian ge hou wu'" ["An Explanation of the Singing and Dancing Before and After King Wu's Campaign Against Zhou"]. *Li shi yan jiu*, no. 4 (1981): 173–179.

Wang Shimin. "Ping 'si chuan chuan guan zang fa jue bao gao'" ["A Critique of a Review of the Excavation Report on the Boat Graves of Sichuan"]. *Kao gu*, no. 8 (1961): 464–467.

Wang Shouzhi. "Shan xi cheng gu chu tu di shang dai qing tong qi" ["Bronze Artifacts of Shang Date Unearthed at Chenggu, Shaanxi Province"]. *Wen bo*, no. 6 (1988): 3–9.

Wang Wencai. "Cheng du cheng fang kao: shang" ["A Study of the Ram-parts of Chengdu: Part 1"]. *Si chuan shi fan xue bao*, no. 1 (1981).

———. "Dong han li bing shi xiang yu du jiang yan 'shui ce'" ["The Eastern Han Stone statue of Li Bing and Water Level Measurement at Dujiang-yan"]. *Wen wu*, no. 7 (1974): 29–33.

Wang Xiantang. "Ren yu yi" ["People and Barbarians"]. *Zhong hua wen shi lun cong*, no. 1 (1982): 203–226.

Wang Xiaoning. "Hu bei e xi zi zhi zhou bo wu guan zang qing tong qi" ["The Bronze Collection at the Museum of the Western Hubei Auton-omous District"]. *Wen wu*, no. 3 (1990): 42–51.

Wang Xueli. "Chang pi chun qiu" ["An Account of Long Pikes"]. *Kao gu yu wen wu*, no. 2 (1985): 60–67, 73.

Wang Yaoqi. "Si chuan xi chang li zhou fa xian di han mu" ["Han Graves

Discovered at Li District, Xichang, Sichuan"]. *Kao gu*, no. 5 (1980): 405–416.

Wang Youpeng. "Jian wei ba shu mu di fa jue yu shu ren di nan qian" ["The Excavation of a Ba-Shu Grave at Jianwei and the Southward Shift of the Shu"]. *Kao gu*, no. 12 (1984): 1114–1117.

———. "Si chuan jian wei xian ba shu mu fa jue jian bao" ["Brief Report on the Excavation of a Ba-Shu Grave at Jianwei County, Sichuan"]. *Kao gu yu wen wu*, no. 3 (1984): 18–21.

———. "Si chuan mian zhu xian chuan guan mu" ["A Boat Coffin Grave from Mianzhu County, Sichuan"]. *Wen wu*, no. 10 (1987): 22–33.

———. "Si chuan mian zhu xian xi han mu ban mu fa jue jian bao" ["A Brief Study of the Wood Paneled Western Han Grave Excavated at Mianzhu County, Sichuan"]. *Kao gu*, no. 4 (1983): 296–300.

Wang Youpeng et al. "Guang han san xing dui yi chi" ["Remains at Sanxingdui, Guanghan"]. *Kao gu xue bao*, no. 2 (1987): 227–254.

Wang Yun. "Guan yu qing chuan qin du di nian dai" ["Regarding the Date of the Qin Documents from Qingchuan"]. *Si chuan wen wu*, no. 5 (1989): 31–33.

Wang Yuzhe. "Shan xi zhou yuan suo chu jia gu wen di lai yuan shi tan" ["An Investigation of the Origins of the Oracle Bones Found at Zhouyuan, Shaanxi Province"]. *She hui ke xue zhan xian* [*Frontline of Social Science*], no. 1 (1982): 101–105.

Wei Jingwu. "Han jiang shang yu xin shi qi shi dai wen hua chu tan" ["Preliminary Investigations into the Neolithic Culture of the Upper Han"]. *Zhong guo kao gu xue hui di er ci nian hui lun wen ji*, (1980): 107–115.

Wei Jingwu et al. "Shan xi nan zheng long gang shi fa xian di jiu shi qi" ["Ancient Stone Tools Discovered at Longgang Town, Nanzheng, Shaanxi Province"]. *Kao gu yu wen wu*, no. 6 (1985): 1–12.

Wei Juxian. "Ba shu wen hua" ["The Culture of Ba and Shu"]. *Shuo wen yue kan* 3, no. 7: 41–70.

———. "Shi niu tan fang ji" ["In Search of Shiniu"]. *Shuo wen yue kan* 3, no. 9 (1943): 13–20.

Wei Songshan. "Chu gan guan kao" ["An Investigation of Gan Pass in Chu"]. *Jiang han lun tan*, no. 5 (1980): 81–84.

Wei Xuefeng. "Gu shu di cun zai guo pin yin wen zi zhi yi" ["Doubts Regarding the Phonetic Nature of Ancient Shu Writings"]. *Si chuan wen wu*, no. 6 (1989): 50–53.

Wen Fong, ed. *The Great Bronze Age of China*. New York: Alfred A Knopf, 1980.

Wen Jiang. "Dian yue kao—zao qi zhong yin guan xi di tan suo" ["A Study of Dian Yue—A Clue to Early Sino-Indian Relations"]. *Zhong hua wen shi lun cong*, no. 2 (1980): 61–66.

Wen Jiao. "Ancient Bronze Statues Discovered in Sichuan." *China Reconstructs* (July 1987): 20–23.

Wen Shaofeng and Ren Naiqiang. "Shi wei 'cheng du' de ming jin yi jie" ["A Tentative Explanation of the Name 'Chengdu'"]. *She hui ke xue yan jiu* [*Social Science Research*], no. 1 (1981): 37–44, 77.

White, Theodore. *In Search of History*. New York: Harper and Row, 1978.

Wu Jiaan et al. "Si chuan wan xian di qu kao gu diao cha jian bao" ["A Brief Report of Archaeological Investigations of the Wanxian Region in Sichuan"]. *Kao gu*, no. 4 (1990): 314–321.

Wu, Kuo-Cheng. *The Chinese Heritage*. New York: Crown, 1982.

Wu Mingsheng and He Gang. "Gu zhang bai he wan chu mu" ["The Chu Grave at Baihewan, Guzhang"]. *Kao gu xue bao*, no. 3 (1986): 339–357.

Wu Tianying. "Zhong guo jing yan kai zhan shi er san shi" ["Two or Three Matters Regarding the Development of Salt Wells in China"]. *Li shi yan jiu*, no. 5 (1986): 123–139.

Wu Yi. "Shi xi ba shu qing tong qi shang di niao, yu, guei, chong [can] wen shi" ["A Tentative Analysis of the Bird, Fish, Turtle, and Insect [Silkworm] Decorations on Ba-Shu Bronzes"]. *Si chuan wen wu*, no. 5 (1989): 25–30.

Xia Mailing and Li Yunsheng. "Deng xian yu shan miao chun yu ji xiang guan wen ti" ["The *chun yu* Drums of Yushanmiao, Deng County and Associated Problems"]. *Kao gu*, no. 10 (1989): 924–926, 951.

Xiao Fan. "Qin han shi qi zhong guo dui nan fang di jing ying" ["China's Management of the South During the Qin and Han"]. *Shi yuan* [*Sources of History*], no. 4 (1973): 17–54.

Xie Zhongliang. "Guan yu du jiang yan li shi di liang ge wen ti" ["Regarding Two Problems of the History of Dujiangyan"]. *Si chuan da xue xue bao*, no. 3 (1975): 78–79, 22.

Xiong Chuanxin. "Wo guo gu dai chun yu gai lun" ["An Outline of the Ancient Chinese *chun yu* Drums"]. *Zhong guo kao gu xue hui di er ci nian hui lun wen ji*, (Beijing: Wen wu chu ban she, 1980), pp. 80–89.

Xu Daoling. "Cong xia yu zhi shui shuo zhi bu ke xin tan dao yu gong zhi zhu zuo shi dai ji qi mu di" ["The Composition Date and Purpose of the 'Tribute of Yu' Considered from a Skeptical Standpoint Regarding the Account of Yu of Xia's Ordering the Waters"]. *Yu gong ban yue kan* 1, no. 4 (1934): 106–108.

Xu Pengzhang. "Cheng du san dong qiao qing yang xiao qu zhan guo mu" ["A Warring States Period Grave at Three Caves Bridge, Blue Sheep District, Chengdu"]. *Wen wu*, no. 5 (1989): 31–35.

Xu Xitai. "Zhou yuan chu tu di jia gu wen suo jian ren ming, guan ming, fang guo, di ming jian shi" ["A Brief Account of Names of Persons, Official Ranks, Countries, and Places Encountered in the Oracle Bone Writings Unearthed at Zhouyuan"]. *Gu wen zi yan jiu* [*Research on Ancient Scripts*], no. 1 (1979): 184–202.

Xu Zhongshu. "'Jiao zhou wai yu ji' shu wang zi an yang wang shi yi jian zheng" ["A Study of Historical Traces of the Shu Prince Anyang in the Record of the Outer Regions of Jiaozhou"]. *Si chuan da xue xue bao cong kan*, no. 5, (1980).

———. *Lun ba shu wen hua* [*On the Ba-Shu Culture*]. Chengdu: Si chuan ren min chu ban she, 1981.

———. "Lun 'shu wang ben ji' cheng shu nian dai ji qi zuo zhe" "On the Date of Composition and Authorship of the 'Basic Annals of the Kings of Shu'"]. *She hui ke xue yan jiu* [*Social Science Research*] (1979): 99–103.

———. "Si chuan pei ling xiao tian xi chu tu di hu niu chun yu" ["A Tiger-Decorated *chun yu* Drum Unearthed at Xiaotian Brook, Peiling, Sichuan"]. *Wen wu*, no. 5, 1974, pp. 81–83.

———. "Si chuan peng xian meng yang zhen chu tu di yin dai er zhi" ["Two *zhi* Bronzes of the Yin Period Excavated at Mengyang Town, Peng County, Sichuan"]. *Wen wu*, no. 6 (1962): 15–18, 23.

Xu Zhongshu and Tang Jiahong. "Chun yu he tong gu" ["The *chun yu* and Bronze Drums"]. In *Gu dai tong gu xue shu tao lun hui lun wen ji* [*Collected Papers of the Conference on the Technology of Ancient Bronze Drums*], pp. 44–47. Beijing: Wen wu chu ban she, 1982.

———. "Gu dai chu shu di guan xi" ["Relations Between Chu and Shu in Antiquity"]. *Wen wu*, no. 6 (1981): 17–25.

Xun Shi. "Si chuan chuan guan zang fa jue bao gao" ["A Review of 'Excavation Report on the Boat Graves of Sichuan'"] *Kao gu*, no. 7 (1961): 391–394.

Yan Buke. "Qin zheng, han zheng yu wen li, ru sheng" ["Qin and Han Government Civil Functionaries and Scholar Officials"]. *Li shi yan jiu*, no. 3 (1986): 143–159.

Yan Gengwang. "Chu qin qian zhong jun di wang kao", ["A Study of the Chu and Qin Commandery of Qianzhong"]. *Ze shan ban yue kan*, 2, no. 19 (1941): 977–984.

———. "Chu zhi han zhong jun di wang kao lue" ["A Study of the Location of the Central Han Commandery of Chu"]. *Ze shan ban yue kan* 3, no. 16 (1941): 906–910.

———. *Zhong guo di fang xing zheng zhi du shi* [*History of the Regional and Local Administration of China*]. Taibei: Zhong yang yan jiu yuan li shi yu yan yan jiu suo, 1974.

Yan Jiaqi. "Shan xi han zhong di qu liang shan long gang shou ce fa xian jiu shi qi" ["The First Ancient Stone Tools Discovered at Longgang, Mt. Liang, Hanzhong Region, Shaanxi Province"]. *Kao gu yu wen wu*, no. 4 (1980): 1–5, 99.

Yan Jiaqi et al. "Shan xi liang shan shi qi zhi yan jiu" ["Research on Stone Tools from Mt. Liang, Shaanxi Province"]. *Shi qian yan jiu* [*Prehistoric Research*], no. 1 (1983): 51–56.

Yang Kuan. "Lun qin han di fen feng zhi" ["On the Qin and Han Systems of Enfeoffment"]. *Zhong hua wen shi lun cong*, no. 1 (1980).

———. "Shi qing chuan qin du di tian mou zhi du" ["An Explanation of the Cadastral System on the Qin Wooden Tablets from Qingchuan"]. *Wen wu*, no. 7 (1982): 83–85.

———. *Zhan guo shi* [*History of the Warring States*]. Shanghai: Shang hai ren min chu ban she, 1980.

Yang Mingzhao. "Si chuan zhi shui shen hua zhong di xia yu" ["Aquatic Deities of Sichuan and Yu of the Xia"]. *Si chuan da xue xue bao*, no. 4 (1959): 1–13.

Yang Quanxi. "Tan suo e xi di qu shang zhou wen hua di xian suo" ["Tracing the Strands of Shang and Zhou Culture in the Area of Western Hubei Province"]. *Jiang han kao gu*, no. 4 (1986): 60–67.

Yang Shiting. "Cong kao gu fa xian shi tan wo guo cai pei tao di qi yuan yan bian ji qi chuan bo" ["Archaeological Discoveries Concerning the Origin, Development, and Spread of Paddy Rice in Our Country"]. *Nong shi yan jiu*, no. 2 (1982): 64–77.

Yang Xiangkui. "Li bing yu er lang shen zi xu" ["A Preface to Li Bing and Erlang"]. *Ze shan ban yue kan* 1, no. 19 (1940): 426–429.

———. "Zhong guo gu dai di shui li jia—li bing" ["An Ancient Chinese Hydraulic Engineer—Li Bing"]. *Wen shi zhe*, no. 3 (1961): 27–28.

Yao Shuangnian. "Qin wei 'he xi' zhi zheng yu dang di di shui lu jiao tong" ["The Struggle Between Qin and Wei for the 'Land West of the Yellow River' and Amphibious Transit in This Area"]. *Wen bo*, no. 6 (1989): 54–57.

You Rende. "Shang dai yu niao yu shang dai she hui" ["Jade Birds of the Shang Period and Shang Society"]. *Kao gu yu wen wu*, no. 2 (1986): 51–60.

Yu Haoliang. "Shi qing chuan qin mu mu du" ["Transcription of the Qin Tomb Wooden Tablets from Qingchuan"]. *Wen wu*, no. 1 (1982): 22–27.

———. "Si chuan pei ling di qin shi huang er shi liu nian tong ge" ["A Bronze Halberd Blade from the First Qin Emperor's Twenty-Sixth Year from Pei-ling, Sichuan"]. *Kao gu*, no. 1 (1976): 21–23.

Yu Quanyu. "Bao ping kou he tuo jiang shi li bing zhi qian kai zuo di" ["Baopingkou and the Tuo River Were Channeled Prior to Li Bing"]. *Li shi yan jiu*, no. 1 (1978): 95–96.

———. "Er lang qin long di shen hua yu kai ming zao ping kou di shi shi" ["The Myth of Er-lang Capturing a Dragon and the Historical Fact of Kaiming Channeling Baopingkou"]. *Si chuan wen wu*, no. 2 (1988): 38–44.

Yu Weizhao. "'Da wu—bing' tong qi yu ba ren di 'da wu' wu" ["A Bronze Halberd Blade and the War Dance of the Ba People"]. *Kao gu*, no. 3 (1963): 153–156.

———. "'Da wu' wu qi xu ji" ["The War Dance Halberd Blade, Continued"]. *Kao gu*, no. 1 (1964): 54–57.

———. "Guan yu chu wen hua fa zhan di xin tan suo" ["Delving Anew into the Development of Chu Culture"]. *Jiang han kao gu*, no. 1 (1980): 17–30.

——— and Li Jiahao. "Ma wang dui yi hao han mu chu tu qi qi zhi di zhu wen ti" ["Several Problems on the Provenance of Lacquer Objects Un-earthed at Tomb No. 1, Mawangdui"]. *Kao gu*, no. 6 (1975): 344–348.

Yu Youren. "Ba shu gu wen hua zhi yan jiu" ["Research on the Ancient Ba-Shu Culture"]. *Shuo wen yue kan* 3, no. 7: 3.

Yu Zhong. "Han jin shi qi di xi nan yi" ["The Southwestern Barbarians of Han and Jin Times"]. *Li shi yan jiu*, no. 12 (1957): 13–36.

Yuan Ke. *Zhong guo gu dai shen hua* [*Mythology of Ancient China*]. Beijing: Zhong hua shu ju, 1960.

Yue Runlie. "Si chuan han yuan chu tu shang zhou qing tong qi" ["Shang and Zhou Bronze Objects Unearthed at Hanyuan, Sichuan"]. *Wen wu*, no. 11: 91.

Zeng Zhaoxuan. "Qin jun kao" ["A Study of the Commanderies of Qin"].

Ling nan xue bao [*Lingnan Journal*] 7, no. 2 (1947): 121–140.

Zhang Caiqun. "Cheng du zhan guo tu keng mu fa jue jian bao" ["A Brief Report on the Excavation of a Warring States Pit Grave at Chengdu"]. *Wen wu*, no. 1 (1982): 28–29.

———. "Si chuan pei ling xiao tian xi si zuo zhan guo mu" ["Four Warring States Period Graves from Xiaotian Stream, Peiling, Sichuan"]. *Kao gu*, no. 1 (1985): 14–15, 32.

Zhang Deci. "Zhong guo zao qi tao zuo li shi" ["The Early History of Paddy Rice in China"]. *Nong shi yan jiu*, no. 2 (1982): 83–94.

Zhang Dianwei. "Hu bei chang yang chu tu yi pi qing tong qi" ["A Hoard of Bronze Objects Unearthed at Changyang, Hubei"]. *Kao gu*, no. 4 (1986): 370–371, 374.

Zhang Ji. "Si chuan gu ji di diao cha" ["Investing the Traces of Ancient Sichuan"]. *Shuo wen yue kan* 3, no. 7 5–6.

Zhang Jinguang. "Qin zi shang yang bian fa hou di du fu yao yi zhi du" ["The Qin System of Taxes and Conscription After the Transformation by Shang Yang"]. *Wen shi zhe*, no. 1 (1983): 18–25.

Zhang Pei. "Shan xi xun yang xian fa xian di ba shu wen hua yi wu" ["Ba-Shu Cultural Remains Found at Xunyang County, Shaanxi"]. *Si chuan wen wu*, no. 3 (1989): 62–64.

Zhang Xiaoma. "Cheng du jing chuan fan dian zhan guo mu" ["A Warring States Grave at Jingchuan Hotel, Chengdu"]. *Wen wu*, no. 2 (1989): 62–66.

———. "Cheng du shi jin niu qu fa xian liang zuo zhan guo mu zang" ["Two Warring States Graves Discovered at Jinniu District, Chengdu City"]. *Wen wu*, no. 5 (1985): 41–43.

Zhang Xizhou. "Shi lun gu dai ba ren fa yuan yu hu bei chang yang hen shan" ["On the Origin of the Ancient Ba People at Mt. Hen, Changyang, Hubei Province"]. *Si chuan da xue xue bao*, no. 1 (1982): 7–79.

Zhang Xunliao. "Li bing zuo li dui di wei zhi he bao ping kou xing cheng di nian dai xin tao" ["A New Investigation into the Date of Li Bing's Channeling Through Lidui, Its Place, and the Formation of Baoping-kou"]. *Zhong guo shi yan jiu*, no. 4 (1982).

Zhang Yachu. "Lun shang zhou wang chao yu gu shu guo di guan xi" ["On the Relations of Ancient Shu with the Shang and Zhou Dynasties"]. *Wen bo*, no. 4 (1988): 30–38.

———. "Yin xu du cheng yu shan xi fang guo kao lue" ["A Study of the

Shang Capital City and Countries in Shanxi"]. *Gu wen zi yan jiu*, no. 10 (1985): 397–399.

Zhang Zengqi. "Guan yu 'kun ming' yu 'kun ming wen hua' di ruo gan wen ti" ["Several Problems Relating to Kunming and the Kunming Culture"]. *Kao gu yu wen wu*, no. 2 (1987): 51–59.

Zhang Zhiheng. "Shi lun da xi wen hua" ["On the Daxi Culture"]. *Jiang han kao gu*, no. 1 (1982): 66–71.

Zhang Zhitao. "'Si chuan' di ming cheng you lai he ke qu yan bian" ["The Origin of the name "Sichuan" and Changes in Its Administrative Status"]. *She hui ke xue yan jiu*, no. 5 (1979): 35.

Zhao Dianzeng. "Ba shu wen hua di kao gu xue fen qi" ["The Archaeological Periodization of the Ba-Shu Culture"]. *Zhong guo kao gu xue hui di si ci nian hui lun wun ji*, pp. 214–224. Beijing: Wen wu chu ban she, 1983.

———. "Ba shu wen hua ji ge wen ti di tan tao" ["Discussion of Several Problems in Ba-Shu Culture"]. *Wen wu*, no. 10 (1987): 18–21.

———. "Si chuan mian yang fa xian mu ban mu" ["A Wood Paneled Grave Discovered at Mianyang, Sichuan"]. *Kao gu*, no. 4 (1983): 372–373.

———. "Si chuan shi nian kao gu shou huo" ["The Achievements of Ten Years of Archaeology in Sichuan"]. *Si chuan wen wu*, no. 5 (1989): 8–16.

———. "Si chuan xi chang li zhou xin shi qi shi dai yi chi" ["Neolithic Remains at Lizhou, Xichang, Sichuan"]. *Kao gu xue bao*, no. 4 (1980): 443–456.

Zhao Dianzeng et al. "Si chuan a bei zhou fa xian han mu" ["A Han Grave Discovered at Abei District, Sichuan"]. *Wen wu*, no. 11 (1976): 90–93.

———. "Si chuan da yi wu long zhan guo ba shu mu zang" ["Warring States Period Ba-Shu Graves at Wulong, Dayi, Sichuan"]. *Wen wu*, no. 5 (1985): 29–40.

———. "Si chuan peng xian fa xian chuan guan zang" ["Boat Coffin Burial Discovered at Peng County, Sichuan"]. *Wen wu*, no. 5 (1985): 92–93.

Zhao Tiehan. "Xia min zu yu ba shu di guan xi" ["The Xia Race and Its Relation to Ba and Shu"]. *Da lu za zhi* 21, nos. 1–2 (1960): 82–83.

Zheng Dekun (Cheng Te-k'un). "An Ancient History of Szechwan." *Journal of the West China Border Research Society* 16, series A (1945): 1–15.

———. "Archaeological Chronology in Szechwan." *Antiquity* 21, no. 81 (1947): 46–50.

———. *Archaeological Studies in Szechwan.* Cambridge: Cambridge University Press, 1957.

————. *An Introduction to Szechwan Archaeology*. Chengdu: West China Union University Museum, 1947.

————. *Si chuan gu dai wen hua shi* [*A History of Ancient Sichuan*]. Chengdu: West China Union University, 1944.

————. "The Slate Tomb Culture of Li-fan." *Harvard Journal of Asiatic Studies* 9, no. 2 (1946): 63–80.

Zhong guo di ming da ci dian [*Dictionary of Chinese Toponyms*]. Taibei: Shang wu yin shu guan, 1975.

Zhong guo li shi di tu ji bian ji zu [Editorial Group for the Historical Atlas of China]. *Zhong guo li shi di tu ji* [*Historical Atlas of China*], vol. 1 of 7 vols. Beijing: Di tu chu ban she, 1975.

Zhong Jian. "Lu shan chu tu qing tong qiao duan jian" ["A Bronze Short Sword and Scabbard Unearthed at Lushan"]. *Si chuan wen wu*, no. 1 (1990): 80.

Zhou Chunyuan. "Lue lun gu ye lang di zu shu wen ti" ["On the Problem of the Ethnic Identity of Ancient Yelang"]. In *Ye lang kao* [*Yelang Studies*]. Guiyang: Gui zhou ren min chu ban she, 1981.

Zhou Jiuxiang. "Xi han qian qi si chuan di qu gong gu xin xing feng jian zhi di dou zheng" ["The Struggle to Reassert Feudalism in Sichuan During Early Western Han Times"]. *Si chuan da xue xue bao*, no. 3 (1975): 63–71.

Zhou Rilian. "Si chuan lu shan chu tu ba shu fu hao yin ji zhan guo qin han si yin" ["Ba-Shu Script Seals and Warring States, Qin, and Han Signets Excavated at Lushan, Sichuan"]. *Kao gu*, no. 1 (1990): 32–35.

Zhou Shirong. "Hu nan chu mu chu tu gu wen zi cong kao" ["A Study of Ancient Scripts Unearthed from Chu Graves in Hunan"]. *Hu nan kao gu ji kan* [*Hunan Archaeological Studies*], no. 1 (1982): 87–99, 126.

————. "Can sang wen cun yu wu shi xue xing yue" ["Silkworm and Mulberry Tree Designs on a *cun* Bronze Vessel and a Battle Axe Shaped Like a Warrior's Boot"]. *Kao gu*, no. 6 (1979): 566–567, 563.

Zhou Wei. *Zhong guo bing qi shi gao* [*A Draft History of Chinese Weapons*]. Taibei reprint: Ming wen shu ju, 1982.

Zhou Yongzhen. "Liang zhou shi qi di ying guo, deng guo tong qi ji di li wei zhi" ["Geographic Location and Bronzes of Ying and Deng States During the Period of the Two Zhou"]. *Kao gu*, no. 1 (1982): 48–53.

Zhu Huo. "Tan ba shu qin ban liang" ["A Discussion of Half Tael Denomination Qin Coins in Ba and Shu"]. *Si chuan wen wu*, no. 1 (1990): 31–37.

Zhu Xizu. "Gu shu guo wei can guo shuo" ["The Notion of Ancient Shu as the Country of Silkworms"]. *Shi shi xin bao: xue huan*, no. 44, n.d.

————. "Shu wang ben ji kao" ["A Study of the Basic Annals of the Shu Kings"]. *Shuo wen yue kan* 3, no. 7 (1942): 117–120.

Zhuang Yanhe. *Gu dai ba shi zhong di ji ge wen ti* [*Several Problems in the History of Ancient Ba*]. Chongqing: Chongqing chu ban she, 1988.

———— and Xian Shuxiu. "Chong qing cheng di you lai he fa zhan" ["The Origins and Development of Chongqing"]. *Si chuan shi yuan xue bao*, no. 2 (1980): 58–62.

Index

Made in United States
North Haven, CT
26 December 2024